FAITH IN FAITHLESSNESS

To the memory of
Herman C. Herrlich
(1914–2008)

FAITH in FAITHLESSNESS

An Anthology of Atheism

selected and with Introduction, Epilogue by
Dimitrios Roussopoulos

Montreal/New York/London

Black Rose Books No. LL361

National Library of Canada Cataloguing in Publication Data

Faith in faithlessness : an anthology of atheism / Dimitrios Roussopoulos

Includes bibliographical references.

ISBN 978-1-55164-313-7 (bound) ISBN 978-1-55164-312-0 (pbk.)

1. Atheism. II. Roussopoulos, Dimitrios I., 1936–

BL2747.3.F35 2007   211'.8   C2007-901922-6

Please see page 418 for a list of credits and permissions. Every effort has been made to contact or trace all copyright holders. The publisher will be glad to make good any errors or omissions brought to our attention in future editions.

Preface, Introduction, and Epilogue Copyright © 2008 by Dimitrios Roussopoulos.

BLACK ROSE BOOKS

C.P. 1258	2250 Military Road	99 Wallis Road
Succ. Place du Parc	Tonawanda, NY	London, E9 5LN
Montréal, H2X 4A7	14150	England
Canada	USA	UK

To order books:

In Canada: (phone) 1-800-565-9523 (fax) 1-800-221-9985
email: utpbooks@utpress.utoronto.ca

In the United States: (phone) 1-800-283-3572 (fax) 1-800-351-5073

In the UK & Europe: (phone) 44 (0)20 8986-4854 (fax) 44 (0)20 8533-5821
email: order@centralbooks.com

Our Web Site address: http://www.blackrosebooks.net

Printed in Canada

Contents

Preface viii

Introduction x

FROM THE EARLY CLASSICS

1 Theologico-Political Treatise 3
   Benedict de Spinoza

2 Thoughts on Religion 8
   Denis Diderot

3 The System of Nature 15
   Paul-Henry Thiry, Baron d'Holbach

4 The Natural History of Religion 24
   David Hume

5 The Age of Reason 30
   Thomas Paine

6 A Refutation of Deism. 34
   Percy Bysshe Shelley

7 Immortality 41
   John Stuart Mill

8 Evangelical Teaching 46
   George Eliot

9 The Spirit of Rationalism In Europe 66
   W.E.H. Lecky

10 The Christian Church and Women 72
   Elizabeth Cady Stanton

11 Humanity's Gain from Unbelief. 81
   Charles Bradlaugh

12 Miracle 93
   Anatole France

13 Autobiography. 97
   Charles Darwin

14 The Antichrist. 101
   Friedrich Nietzsche

15 God and the Constitution 109
   Robert G. Ingersoll

16 The Essence of Religion in General 119
   Ludwig Feuerbach

17 God and the State 137
   Michael Bakunin

18 Contribution to the Critique of Hegel's Philosophy of Right 141
   Karl Marx

FROM THE EARLY 20TH CENTURY CLASSICS

19 The Philosophy of Atheism 155
   Emma Goldman

20 On the Scopes Trial 160
   H.L. Mencken

21 The Lord's Day Alliance 166
   Clarence Darrow

22 Why I Am an Unbeliever. 180
   Carl Van Doren

23 Is There a God? 185
   Bertrand Russell

24 The Claims of Theology 192
   A.J. Ayer

25 The Unbelievers and Christians. 201
   Albert Camus

26 Science and Religion 205
   Albert Einstein

FROM THE LATER 20th CENTURY and 21st CENTURY

27 Monotheism and Its Discontents 211
   Gore Vidal

28 How Is Atheism to Be Characterized? 218
   Kai Nielsen

29 Atheism. 239
   Christine Overall

30 The Atheist Manifesto 242
   Sam Harris

31 Why There Almost Certainly Is No God 252
   Richard Dawkins

32 Religion as an Original Sin 291
   Christopher Hitchens

33 In the Service of the Death Fixation 299
   Michel Onfray

34 Thank Goodness! 311
   Daniel C. Dennett

35 For the Love of Reason 316
   Louise M. Anthony

36 If God Is Dead, Is Everything Permitted? 336
   Elizabeth Second Anderson

37 An Atheist Childhood 354
   Tariq Ali

   A Rapper's Song 362
   Greydon Square

38 Humanism and the Territory of Novelists 364
   Salman Rushdie

39 Why My Dog Is Not a Humanist 367
   Kurt Vonnegut

Epilogue: A New Enlightenment: The Second Wave 371
   Dimitrios Roussopoulos

Notes On The Contributors 384

Resource Guide from the Website of Richard Dawkins 395

Credits and Permissions 418

Celebrity Quotes Throughout, Including from George Bernard Shaw, Voltaire, Ralph Waldo Emerson, Aldous Huxley, Tennessee Williams, Charles Bukowski, Jean-Paul Sartre, Noam Chomsky, Sigmund Freud, Ingmar Bergman, Katharine Hepburn, John Malkovich, Robert Altman, Jodie Foster, Bill Gates, Angelina Jolie, Jack Nicholson, Howard Stern, Isaac Asimov, Woody Allen, Richard Leakey, James Watson, Gene Roddenberry, Gloria Steinem

Preface

During August of 2006, my good friend Andrea Levy expressed her concern about the rise of religious fundamentalism on the one hand and the general silence around atheism on the other. There did not appear to be enough of a public debate around such concerns as the juxtaposition of these two different ways of looking at the world and universe. In the course of our discussions she discovered the 'Atheist Manifesto' by Sam Harris [included in this anthology]. The strong line of argument of Harris' text and its lucidity sparked further discussion eventually leading to Andrea Levy's idea of a book project which would include the best texts on atheism. The timeliness of this idea was remarkable as Sam Harris' *The End of Faith* was not only published soon thereafter but became a best seller as were a number of subsequent books such as Richard Dawkins's *The God Delusion*, Daniel Dennett's *Breaking the Spell*, and Christopher Hitchens's *God is Not Great*. At the same time the film by our friend Julian Samuel *Atheism* was publicly viewed and the biting satire of comedian Bill Maher circulated. More books, articles and interviews were on the way. Slowly but surely a debate was beginning.

What is not desirable however is another media fad. Atheism, some in the media mentioned softly, was the flavour of the month. If the timing of this debate supported by a growing body of critical literature is to have an accumulative effect, this book had to be published sooner than later. The title "Faith in Faithlessness" was suggested by Andrea Levy, from a folk song by a beloved legend Peter Seeger titled *Our Generation* which begins with the lyrics,

> Here we are knee deep in garbage shooting rockets at the Moon.
> Our Generation wears sandals like Vietnamese.
> Our Generation wears long hair.
> With our clobbered minds we still wink an eye and say,

we'll meet at the bottom of the stairs.
Our Generation whistlers in the dark, has *faith in faithlessness* and in blue skies
our heroes are either none or everyone..." (my emphasis)

We are grateful to Andrea Levy for her early collaboration in this project although circumstances prevented bringing the original project to fruition. The final version of this book therefore is entirely my responsibility.

I must express my deep gratitude to Emilie Connolly who worked hard in a variety of ways to prepare the content of this book. Also thanks are due to my life partner Lucia whose eagle-eye made sure that the introduction and epilogue were edited with all necessary rigor.

The book is dedicated to the memory of Herman C. Herrlich, an extraordinary human being. He returned to nature recently at the ripe age of 92. During his remarkable lifetime he never waived from his basic philosophy of common sense and decency based on humanism. Educated as a pharmacologist he had a clear grasp of the cool beauty of science; however instead of being confined to a university he freed himself from institutional constrain and he choose instead with his wife Cristina and children Alan and Katherine to live in rural Vermont as an organic farmer. Devoted to a simple life of conservation he nevertheless was very much part of the real world of politics and related social concerns. While some of us were discovering the new atheists and their new books, his living room floor was strewn with the works of Dawkins, Hitchens, Harris, and E.O.Wilson upon publication, and with piles of humanist and atheist magazines and journals. Uncle Billy, as he was known to his family, was a model for many people in many more ways than one.

Dimitrios Roussopoulos

Introduction

Here we are into the 21st Century and we are still obliged to deal with the theme of this book. The obligation has become a renewed political one, as the underlying premise is an admission of failure. It is a failure which recognizes that notwithstanding all the considered arguments of prominent thinkers like those included in this anthology and others like them, and the considerable additional literature that has been written both past and present, monotheistic religion continues to exist especially in North America, and particularly in the USA. Not only does it continue to exist as a belief system but more importantly it continues to exercise considerable political influence shaping public policy in every social nick and cranny it can penetrate. In the face of this threat to reason we have to admit to a wider failure of our education system, of the mass media, and of the avoidance of public personalities to deal with the absurdities of religious belief systems based on a god and which often require despising those who are different and who dissent.

It is only in the last few years that atheism and religion have become subjects of public debate again, thanks to a handful of articulate, knowledgeable and courageous persons. The fact that a public debate is taking place can mean one of two things: either this kind of debate has to take place with every generation, for reasons that are not clear or there has been a failure of a secular and humanist culture that we took for granted with its underpinnings of the separation of Church and State and related resolutions. During this renewed public debate we have to admit that the political Left has been largely absent. Indeed the obligation to deal with this matter is also another failure of the Left which may have erroneously assumed that the issue was settled. The epilogue in this book will deal more substantially with this aspect of our concern.

There is a case to be made that atheism is not a philosophy; it is not even a world view. Rather it should be considered as a vital dimension of a broader philosophical world view which incorporates a concern for freedom, human rights and civil liberties, social justice, world peace, economic and political democracy. As such, making of atheism an exclusive position in and of itself is in the end, perhaps self-defeating and counter-productive. Furthermore the argument has been made that one cannot have a position that is based on a negation alone. The only reason therefore for putting together an anthology of atheist writings which is called such is that some very thoughtful persons wrote eloquently on this aspect of the specific problematic of religion which was and still is present in our midst.

The main motive behind the publication of this book is to give rational tools to those who seek to counter the overwhelming influence and power of those religion-ists who dominate too many important institutions of power in our society, both po-litical and economic. The power elite of North America are either believers in god and religion, (some seek to be actually guided by such a belief system), or they have to publicly go through the motions of practicing religion because the institutions of such belief systems have much more power and influence than other social forces in our society like trade unions, cooperatives, left-of-centre political parties, the social movements labouring for gender equality and the rights of women ,and the protec-tion of the environment among many others. As a single force and body of organized opinion the religionists have power and influence out of all proportion to other movements. Among these, the fundamentalists, especially in the USA, have the pre-dominate influence. Need we add that in the last eight years, their political influence appears to have captured Washington and the White House? When one considers the many terrible decisions that have been made during this last period and the negative effect of these decisions on the rest of the world, the politics of religion have to be considered as a major factor to be countered.

Democracy vs. Theocracy

We know the place and role of the USA in the world. When we also realize that be-tween a quarter and a third of all Americans today are self-described Christian funda-mentalists, many of whom reject the separation of Church and State, we have a serious political problem at hand. It has become common for politicians of all stripes to evoke god in their pronouncements, leaving a door open to the conservative poli-ticians and political parties to declare that the USA is a 'Christian nation,' a declara-tion that appears nowhere in the American Declaration of Independence and Constitution. Never before have right-wing religious ideologues had such access to power in Washington – indeed, never has the country come closer to a religious gov-ernment than it has now. Even if a different mainstream political party takes over the

White House, the influence of these ideological theocrats will not easily diminish. And with the current reactionary government in control in Ottawa, the route to a theocracy is in progress in Canada as well even though it may take many decades.

The excesses of fundamentalism in the USA rank with any Shiite ayatollahs and the last two American presidential elections mark the deep transformation of the Republican Party into the first religious party in U.S. history. This does not mean that the USA and certainly not Canada are on the brink of being full-fledge theocracies. But we must fear that future social shocks, ranging from wars [note the messianic dimensions of the military goings and comings in both Iraq and Afghanistan] to the economic crisis, could provoke a situation in which those who seek to impose a religious government could suddenly rise to the top.

We have to bear in mind the roots of much of this development in the U.S. began slowly with the John Birch Society followed by the Christian militias of the 1990s, and what can be referred to as the Christian nationalists. Of particular interest is the history of the Christian Reconstruction, a radical theology whose backers seek to impose Old Testament law on the USA. The connections that run from Reconstruction's founding thinker Rushdoony all the way to the Bush White House is revealing. This make over of Christianity, from which Reconstructionism grew, and how it plays out in the right-wing mega-ministeries like D.James Kennedy and James Dobson is most instructive.

We should cease avoiding these dangerous trends and act with a sense of urgency. It makes no sense to fight religious authoritarianism abroad while letting it take over at home. The rise of religion is fundamentally a response to secular efforts to push religion out of the public square in the 1960s and 1970s. Consider the following: North America is dependent on oil, which drives much of American foreign policy; Christianity coupled with the southerniztion of American mainstream politics, has led to the transformation of the Republicans into a religious party. These facts; the soaring debt, recession and imperial hubris are likely to lead to the decline of American ascendancy.

Consider the *political* implications of the following:

According to several recent polls, 22 percent of Americans are certain that Jesus will return to earth sometime in the next fifty years. Another 22 percent believe that he will probably do so. This is likely the same 44 percent who go to church once a week or more, who believe that God literally promised the land of Israel to the Jews, and who want to stop teaching children about the biological fact of evolution. Believers of this sort constitute the most cohesive and motivated segment of the American electorate. Consequently, their views and prejudices now influence almost every decision of national importance. Political liberals seem to have drawn the wrong lesson from these developments and are now thumbing scripture wondering how best to ingratiate themselves to the legions of men and women in our country who vote mainly on the basis of religious dogma. More that 50 percent of Americans have a 'negative' or 'highly negative' view of people who do not believe in God; 70 percent think it important for presidential candidates to be 'strongly religious.' Because it is taboo to criticize a person's religious beliefs, political debate over questions of public policy, (stem-cell research, the ethics of assisted suicide and euthanasia, obscenity and free speech, gay marriage, etc.), generally get framed in terms appropriate to a theocracy. Unreason is now ascendant in the United States—in our schools, in our courts, and in each branch of the federal government. Only 28 percent of Americans believe in evolution; 72 percent believe in angels. Ignorance in this degree, concentrated in both the head and the belly of a lumbering super-power, is now a problem for the entire world (Sam Harris, *The End of Faith*, page 230).

After the Scopes trial, where in Dayton, Tennessee in 1925, the young school teacher John Thomas Scopes was acquitted of the charge of teaching evolution in his high school biology class, it appeared that the Christian fundamentalist interpretation of the earth's genesis had suffered a death blow. The last few decades have shown this to be not true. Indeed in recent decades, anti-evolutionism has been on the rise and is gaining ground, especially in the U.S. This creed is now called "creationism," a belief system which takes the Book of Genesis to be literal truth: an example is the Deluge (Noah's flood) sent by Jehovah to punish mankind, and which serves as a precursor to Armageddon (coming soon) and the thousand-year rule of Jesus and the Final Judgment. It's all very well for such beliefs to be held in private, but such forms of blind religious convictions are a worrisome threat to liberal democratic society as we know it. Fundamentalism of all sorts, creationism, intelligent design 'theory'—all pose serious threats, and rouse a level of intolerance attacking the Western intellectual tradition at its core, placing on the danger list the right of dissent, especially dissent that seeks to go to the very roots of a problem: that is radical dissent.

Religion as Politics and its Impact on Politics

There are many parts of the world where religious battles take place in the manner of Medieval and Reformation Europe. In Africa, for example, evangelical Christians, backed by American Church donated money, are pushing northwards clashing with Islamic fundamentalists who are backed by Saudi oil money, who are in turn pushing south. The Christian-Muslim split is only one form of religious competition in Nigeria. Events in Iraq have pitted Sunnis against the Shias; thousands of Iraqis have died in intra-Muslim fighting. On the Christian side, Catholics are in a tug of war with Protestant evangelists in various parts of Africa whose promise is immediate redemption. The many violent conflicts that surround these tensions may seem a trip back in time.

In fact, religious front-lines criss-cross the globe. Recall that the terrorist acts of 19 young Muslims in attacking New York and the USA was used as a pretext for everything worrisome that followed. The West's previous military interventions were supposedly to protect Muslims in Bosnia and Kosovo from the Christian Serbs and Croatians. The next war could be against the Islamic Republic of Iran. In the Middle East, even more people are claiming god on their side (with some of the most zealous sorts living a few kilometers from the conflict areas). In Myanmar (Burma) Buddhist monks nearly brought down a military regime, but in Sri Lanka they have prolonged bloody conflicts with Muslims. When India has an election, a bridge to Sri Lanka supposedly built by the god Ram may matter as much as a nuclear deal with the USA.

Religion and faith are again promoting and prolonging violence. Religion is not the exclusive cause of violence but as in the case of the Middle East once the religious arguments are put on the table, divisions become even more difficult to resolve. When one side believes that god granted it the West Bank, or that any more abortions is mass murder, a negotiated settlement over land and power becomes almost insurmountable.

Politicians like Iran's Mahmoud Ahmadinejad, or Osama bin Laden, in their extremist condemnations, fuel the passions of fanatics to extremes. When you add to this list the religious fanaticism of Franklin Graham who denounces Islam as evil or American conservatives like Newt Gingrich and Norman Podhoretz who talk openly about world wars between religions and civilizations, a spiral effect leads to violence. Religious fights have always attracted money and militarism, and continue to do so. Muslim enthusiasts have left Europe and elsewhere to join crusades in Kashmir, Chechnya and Iraq. India's Hindutva movement has also attracted fanatics from the Diaspora. All these migrants define themselves primarily through their religion.

Terrorist and counter-terrorist violence once was the battlefield of Marxist guerillas, middle-class Germans, Italians and Latin Americans, or the then secular Palestine Liberation Organization. More than ever Islam exists with sharpening divisions between Sunni and Shia. In its wake, national governments stand naked and, given their recent creation as States, vulnerable. Four threatening flashpoints for nuclear conflicts are Pakistan, India, Iran and Israel, with North Korea alongside as an example of a 'secular theocracy.' One can list a series of 21st century inter-denominational conflicts and religion-based terrorist attacks in Bali, Sulawesi (Indonesia), Philippines, Thailand, Sri Lanka, India/Kashmir, Pakistan, Afghanistan, Xinjiang (China), Chechnya (Russia), Moscow, Lebanon, Iraq, Saudi Arabia, Israel/Palestine, Somalia, Kenya, Ethiopia, Sudan, Egypt, Kosovo, Morocco, Britain, Spain, Algeria, Nigeria, New York, Washington, Mexico and Guatemala. If one is concerned about religion's effect on politics, there is no more discouraging place to visit than the tiny piece of land that is Israel-Palestine as Rabbi Yaacov Medan and Sheikh Yazid Khader each claim god to be on his side. From a territorial dispute four decades ago we are now facing an intractable fight between the children of Abraham, even though polls show that most people on both sides still want a two-State solution.

Throughout, other forces are often at work in these conflicts, such as tribalism or nationalism, but religion contributes a particular viciousness. Some 68,000 people in Sri Lanka have died since 1983. Outside interests are often present but in the end these bloody fights are local, an eye for an eye and a tooth for a tooth, the unbridled politics of revenge. The out and out theocracies are particularly barbaric, although the so-called secular States like Syria, Egypt, certain African States, and China are also brutal.

What needs to be noted is a new twist in the emergence of religion as politics: its growing political influence through political parties of god and thus through elections. This world-wide phenomenon is relatively new in the modern age.

Beside the Current Battle Lines

In the former Soviet Union, an officially godless society since its origins, religion in various forms is on a comeback trail in contemporary Russia with official tolerance; from the president (a former KGB officer) to lesser officials: priests are found blessing everything, everywhere.

In Western politics, too, religion, has forced itself back into public places. The American president begins each day on his knees and each cabinet meeting with a prayer. Susan Jacoby pointed out in her book *Freethinkers,* that the most dramatic presidential address in the USA in generations took place three days after 9/11 in the National Cathedral. President Bush, surrounded by Christian, Jewish and Muslim representatives spoke warmly about inclusiveness. Symptomatic of this situation is the propagandistic claim that the USA is indeed 'one nation under god.' While there are millions of non-believers in the country, there was not a single public word about them or by them about the content and purpose of the public display on this occasion. Religionists have their fingers on the nuclear button of Armageddon and direct the largest military machine in human history, with military bases all over the planet.

What of the post-Bush era? In early June 2007, during a nationally televised forum presidential candidates John Edwards, Barack Obama and Hilary Clinton testified to their faith, talking about the 'hand of God' (Edwards), forgiveness (Obama) and prayer (Clinton). While a Pew study shows that 49% of Americans believe that Christian conservatives have gone too far 'in trying to impose their religious values on the country' in challenging the separation of Church and State, secular and public education, and in demanding less rather than more political discussion of religion; nevertheless the Christian conservatives themselves take a very large place in the present political debates dealing with the future of American society.

The degree of all this is unusual in the Western world; however the degree of obsession with religion and flag-waving nationalism is at its most pronounced in the USA. Where else would we witness the construction of a $27 million lavish Creation Museum currently being built in Petersburg, Kentucky, which tells us that huge dinosaurs could have existed with humans shortly after time began in 4004 BCE, and that Noah managed to squeeze a male and female of all the world's animals into this boat of only 135 meters long? Where else in the Western world would we witness as reported in a *Newsweek* magazine poll earlier last year that 48% of those Americans surveyed believed that god created us in our present form in the past 10,000 years?

Politically the Christian fundamentalists have almost taken over the entire Republican Party. Among those elected there are 45 senators and 186 members of the House of Representatives who are given a 80%-100% score of approval by the most influential Christian advocacy groups: the Christian Coalition, Eagle Forum and the Family Resource Council, all right-wing fundamentalists. In addition, some 50% of chaplaincy appointments to the U.S. military come from this school of thought. And at a recent annual convention, National Religious Broadcasters representing some 5500 Christian broadcasters from radio and television, claimed to reach 141 million listeners and viewers across the U.S. Many of these statistics are referred to by Chris Hedges in his book *American Fascists: The Christian Right and the War on America*. The following questions should be asked: where is the American Left? Don't these values serve the interests of the American power elite and should therefore be confronted?

It has long been a centerpiece of 'progressive thought' that science, education and liberal democracy would put religion to rest. Not only has this not happened but on the contrary the numbers show that the proportion of people attached to the world's four biggest religions—Christianity, Islam, Buddhism and Hinduism—rose from 67% in 1900 to 73% in 2005 and may reach 80% by 2050 (source: World Christian Database).Although true stats on religion may be untrustworthy, there is clearly a dangerous trend.

More worrisome, it is the more fanatical forms of religion that are on the ascendancy, the sort that claim Adam and Eve met 6,300 years ago. Organized religion has always been at the service of the economic and political ruling class of society. While Pentecostalism is spreading among the destitute of the Brazilian favelas, the American evangelists tend to be educated and well-off. In India, Turkey and Pakistan religious parties of god have been driven by the local bourgeoisie.

Religion is becoming visible in many fields, from business to economic theory. When future historians look back to the early 21st century they probably will see religion as a formidable destructive force influencing political freedom, concepts of community, conflicts and wars. Although the reasons some people are religious may not have changed down through recent times, the role religion assumes in public life has. The place of religion has become plainly more evident in the last few decades. Recall when *Time* magazine ran a cover story in 1966 titled "Is God dead?" and three years later a human landed on the moon; the juxtaposition was pre-mature.

Religious politics began to arise in the early 1970s, at a time when the high aspirations of the 1960s stalled. The welfare State was targeted when Thatcherism filled the vacuum by going on the offensive, followed by Reaganism; uncertainty spread as avarice was celebrated, and the New Left movement fragmented into various parts not taking the time to mature with a fuller and complimentary agenda for social and political change. While the counter-culture danced around new tribal practices or turned to the mystical East, the secular humanists were unable to institute alternative celebratory rituals so the important sense of community was diluted. The spiritual vacuum was filled by the religionists with their standard and known symbols; at the same time their officially acknowledged holidays and symbols were slowly revitalized.

An Important Historic Split

During this period as the fundamentalists took more and more space in the Middle East, Iran, India and Pakistan, and in the U.S., Western democratic liberalism compounded a historic split. The split took place between the two founding revolutions of the West, an old sore that reopened. In France, the revolutionaries detested the Church, and the concept of god, all crucial forms of domination from their past. From this radical tradition followed a blunt, no-holds-barred attack on religion in all its forms. Following the American Revolution, the founding fathers saw a plurality of faiths, and took a more benign view. They divided Church and State to protect both from each other. Moderation and tolerance were meant to prevail in all interactions between believers and non-believers, at all levels of society and in all of its institutions. Enter the fundamentalists. This split between atheists and liberal secularists is reflected in the current debate over religion and society, and is also reflected in the style of the polemics of those who are part of the debate. There will be sirens all along calling for an alliance with the 'left religionists,' an alliance that has to be rigorously scrutinized. Coalitions can come and go, and reflect a need to fill the numbers for a protest march, petition or public demonstration of one form or another. But cooption into alliances which fudge fundamental choices must be carefully scrutinized. The dynamics of the relationship between liberal Christians and other religionists, and the fundamentalists are often moot. Unless and until liberal Christians repudiate dependence upon all sacred texts (and so far, they have not), their position is a back door into fundamentalism, because fundamentalists always take more seriously the principles that liberals are apparently willing to bargain away in order for an alliance to make religion palatable to fringe members and doubters. Whenever the institutions of religions are critiqued or threaten, the liberal religionists always side with the fundamentalists, witness the recent behaviour of Archbishop Rowan Williams of Canterbury.

Much of history suggests that atheists and religionists cannot work together when it comes to science and politics. The war between science and religion has a centuries old history. In the U.S. and Canada the cold war has become a hot war. What is refreshing is that we see the rise of a new crop of public intellectuals. We can recognize that the religionists continue to make the provocative moves that divide us, and if the faith-based initiatives of much of the American political class are any indication, they show no signs of ceasing these provocations any time soon. As long as personal religious beliefs remain strictly personal, people should be free to indulge. Is moral progress a delusion? Is evil a permanent reality? Atheists do not deny, as is suggested too often by book reviewers, that we humans have a spiritual nature which has nothing to do with religion. We should be humbled, perhaps to the point of spontaneous genuflection, says Sam Harris, by the knowledge that the ancient Greeks began to lay their Olympian myths to rest several hundred years before the birth of Christ.

Public Intellectuals and Public Debate

The sudden emergence of five remarkable public intellectuals and the public debate lancing the boil of silence is a significant event ushering in a new cultural and political period. Sam Harris, Richard Dawkins, Daniel Dennet, Christopher Hitchens, and Michel Onfray have triggered an earthquake. Two scientists, two philosophers and a journalist have claimed a colourful attention thanks to their best selling books and their many public lectures. We single out these five because they have broken the sound barrier loudly, although there are of course others who have and continue to contribute to the debate.

The particular success of the five reflects something significant about the slovenliness of the self-conscious non-religious, the humanists and secularists of different strides and the Left especially in North America. These strata of our society, too often comfortable in their university ivory towers, have been a timid minority, without a public voice, too polite and defensive, derided, ignored and rendered politically marginal at best. Meanwhile in the last four decades the zealous fundamentalists of monotheism have politicized themselves into a formidable force, here and on other continents. This anthology and the many other resources that have been brought to public attention are meant to help turn the tide of reaction.

The Parameters of this Book

In publishing this book we state plainly: our concern is mostly with Washington and the dominant public ideology that shapes Americanism and its impact upon the world. In the last decade the policies of the American political and corporate elite have generated a backlash fanning religious fundamentalism and fanaticism of one kind or another throughout the world. Washington is an all-powerful superpower, armed to the teeth, with many inside the corridors of power awaiting the glorious Armageddon.

Why the interest in the 'new atheists'? One reason is a concern about the rise of fundamentalism mainly but also religion in politics generally. There is an explicit political agenda at play, more oftentimes than not hidden from view. Some of this agenda is visible: opposing stem-cell research; gay marriage and abortion; championing State aid to religious schools and faith-based social programme, the list is long... The influences of all these issues are reflected in a Pew Research Center 2006 report on religion which reports that 69 percent of Americans believe that liberals have gone too far in separating Church from State. There is a possibility that in looking at fundamentalism abroad we fall off the political edge. The argument here is that fundamentalism is a danger amongst us here. We on the Left must be careful to not in any way cross the line into racism and xenophobia because our attention is so largely focused on fanaticism elsewhere.

There has to be the widest public debate on religion in all its aspects including the standard attempt to confuse it with spirituality. We have to conduct the debate about our deepest concerns—about ethics, and the seeming inevitability of some human suffering—in ways that are not irrational. We desperately need a public discourse that reflects critical thinking and intellectual honesty. We need to deal with our emotional and spiritual needs without embracing the preposterous and superstitious. We must acknowledge the need for community and hence of rituals with which to mark those transitions in every human life that demand attention and depth—birth, maturing from childhood, association and friendship, partnership, and death—without bowing to the old institutions of Church or State for purposes of 'legitimacy or legality.'

This must be done without lying to ourselves or our friends and families about atheism and our basic beliefs. Living without god(s) is not unlike living without masters. It requires creating a society of democratic participation by the largest number of citizens and thus creating the ecological city. It requires a society that is beyond being vulnerable and most unlike our own which is far too unequal, class-bound and thus deeply insecure. Thus we have to think both politically and philosophically. The crossroads of this thinking is ethics which once again takes centre place. We have to admit that the prospects in the short-run do not seem good, as we try to understand the nature of our failure, in the past and now.

We must not be surprised at the outright hostility or smug bemusement expressed by many liberals or progressive fellow travelers toward the renewed debate on atheism. The renewed or new critiques of religion have broken powerful taboos. There is an ever present commentary that we have gone or are going too far. Atheism and religion are subjects of current debate publicly and the Left must become engaged. It is equally important for the Left to make its own distinct contribution to this debate, hence this book.

We have included in this anthology excerpts from some of the great classics, many of which are hard to find. We have included some of the most outstanding and insightful excerpts from major persons of the early 20th century, followed by thinkers toward the latter part of the century and into the 21st century. We have peppered this exciting ensemble with short quotes from celebrity atheists to both amaze and amuse the reader who did not know that so and so was or is … and out of the closet.

We then include an epilogue which calls for a new Enlightenment as an open letter to the Left. Finally, the book ends with a resource guide of where to find more intellectual nourishment and support.

Enough to the obedience and submission demanded by god as characterized originally by the story of Adam and Eve. There they were, forbidden by the creator of the universe to partake from the tree of knowledge. They were ordered to be ignorant of good and evil and to have but one source of authority. The rest is a painful history for humanity. Another world is possible.

Dimitrios Roussopoulos
March 7, 2008

FROM THE EARLY CLASSICS

What, but the rapacity of the only men who exercised their reason, the priests, secured such vast property to the church, when a man gave his perishable substance to save himself from the dark torments of purgatory; and found it more convenient to indulge his depraved appetites, and pay an exorbitant price for absolution, than listen to the suggestions of reason, and work out his own salvation: in a word, was not the separation of religion from morality the work of the priests?
—*Mary Wollstonecraft, 18th century writer, philosopher, and feminist*

No man ever believes that the Bible means what it says; he is always convinced that it says what he means.
—*George Bernard Shaw, playwright, socialist activist, and polemical writer*

Let the human mind loose. It must be loose. It will be loose. Superstition and dogmatism cannot confine it.
—*John Adams Jr., 2nd President of the United States of America*

If God did not exist, it would be necessary to invent him.
—*Voltaire, novelist, deist and canonical philosopher of the French Enlightenment*

Atheism leaves a man to sense, to philosophy, to natural piety, to laws, to reputation; all of which may be guides to an outward moral virtue, even if religion vanished; but religious superstition dismounts all these and erects an absolute monarchy in the minds of men.
—*Francis Bacon, philosopher, statesman, and essayist*

Is God willing to prevent evil, but not able? Then he is not omnipotent. Is he able, but not willing? Then he is malevolent. Is he both able and willing? Then whence cometh evil? Is he neither able nor willing? Then why call him God?
—*Epicurus, ancient Greek philosopher*

Nothing shall warp me from the belief that every man is a lover of truth. There is no pure lie, no pure malignity in nature. The entertainment of the proposition of depravity is the last profligacy and profanation. There is no scepticism, no atheism but that. Could it be received into common belief, suicide would unpeople the planet.
—*Ralph Waldo Emerson, essayist, poet, and leader of the Transcendentalist movement*

I am for liberty of conscience in its noblest, broadest, and highest sense. But I cannot give liberty of conscience to the pope and his followers, the papists, so long as they tell me, through all their councils, theologians, and canon laws that their conscience orders them to burn my wife, strangle my children, and cut my throat when they find their opportunity.
—*Abraham Lincoln, 16th President of the United States*

1
Theologico-Political Treatise (1670)
Benedict de Spinoza

Men would never be superstitious, if they could govern all their circumstances by set rules, or if they were always favoured by fortune: but being frequently driven into straits where rules are useless, and being often kept fluctuating pitiably between hope and fear by the uncertainty of fortune's greedily coveted favours, they are consequently, for the most part, very prone to credulity. The human mind is readily swayed this way or that in times of doubt, especially when hope and fear are struggling for the mastery, though usually it is boastful, over-confident, and vain.

This as a general fact I suppose everyone knows, though few, I believe, know their own nature; no one can have lived in the world without observing that most people, when in prosperity, are so over-brimming with wisdom (however inexperienced they may be), that they take every offer of advice as a personal insult, whereas in adversity they know not where to turn, but beg and pray for counsel from every passer-by. No plan is then too futile, too absurd, or too fatuous for their adoption; the most frivolous causes will raise them to hope, or plunge them into despair—if anything happens during their fright which reminds them of some past good or ill, they think it portends a happy or unhappy issue, and therefore (though it may have proved abortive a hundred times before) style it a lucky or unlucky omen. Anything which excites their astonishment they believe to be a portent signifying the anger of the gods or of the Supreme Being, and, mistaking superstition for religion, account it impious not to avert the evil with prayer and sacrifice. Signs and wonders of this sort they conjure up perpetually, till one might think Nature as mad as themselves, they interpret her so fantastically.

Thus it is brought prominently before us, that superstition's chief victims are those persons who greedily covet temporal advantages; they it is, who (especially when they are in danger, and cannot help themselves) are wont with prayers and womanish tears to implore help from God: upbraiding Reason as blind, because she cannot show a sure path to the shadows they pursue, and rejecting human wisdom as vain; but believing the phantoms of imagination, dreams, and other childish absurdities, to be the very oracles of Heaven. As though God had turned away from the wise, and written His decrees, not in the mind of man but in the entrails of beasts, or left them to be proclaimed by the inspiration and instinct of fools, madmen, and birds. Such is the unreason to which terror can drive mankind!

Superstition, then, is engendered, preserved, and fostered by fear. If anyone desire an example, let him take Alexander, who only began superstitiously to seek guidance from seers, when he first learnt to fear fortune in the passes of Sysis (Curtius, v. 4); whereas after he had conquered Darius he consulted prophets no more, till a second time frightened by reverses. When the Scythians were provoking a battle, the Bactrians had deserted, and he himself was lying sick of his wounds, "he once more turned to superstition, the mockery of human wisdom, and bade Aristander, to whom he confided his credulity, inquire the issue of affairs with sacrificed victims." Very numerous examples of a like nature might be cited, clearly showing the fact, that only while under the dominion of fear do men fall a prey to superstition; that all the portents ever invested with the reverence of misguided religion are mere phantoms of dejected and fearful minds; and lastly, that prophets have most power among the people, and are most formidable to rulers, precisely at those times when the state is in most peril. I think this is sufficiently plain to all, and will therefore say no more on the subject.

The origin of superstition above given affords us a dear reason for the fact, that it comes to all men naturally, though some refer its rise to a dim notion of God, universal to mankind, and also tends to show, that it is no less inconsistent and variable than other mental hallucinations and emotional impulses, and further that it can only be maintained by hope, hatred, anger, and deceit; since it springs, not from reason, but solely from the more powerful phases of emotion. Furthermore, we may readily understand how difficult it is, to maintain in the same course men prone to every form of credulity. For, as the mass of mankind remains always at about the same pitch of misery, it never assents long to any one remedy, but is always best pleased by a novelty which has not yet proved illusive.

This element of inconsistency has been the cause of many terrible wars and revolutions; for, as Curtius well says (lib. iv. chap. 10): "The mob has no ruler more potent than superstition," and is easily led, on the plea of religion, at one moment to adore its kings as gods, and anon to execrate and abjure them as humanity's common bane. Immense pains have therefore been taken to counteract this evil by investing religion, whether true or false, with such pomp and ceremony, that it may rise superior to every shock, and be always observed with studious reverence by the whole people—a system which has been brought to great perfection by the Turks, for they consider even controversy impious, and so dog men's minds with dogmatic formulas, that they leave no room for sound reason, not even enough to doubt with.

But if, in despotic statecraft, the supreme and essential mystery be to hoodwink the subjects, and to mask the fear, which keeps them down, with the specious garb of religion, so that men may fight as bravely for slavery as for safety, and count it not shame but highest honour to risk their blood and their lives for the vainglory of a tyrant; yet in a free state no more mischievous expedient could be planned or attempted. Wholly repugnant to the general freedom are such devices as enthralling men's minds with prejudices, forcing their judgment, or employing any of the weapons of quasi-religious sedition; indeed, such seditions only spring up, when law enters the domain of speculative thought, and opinions are put on trial and condemned on the same footing as crimes, while those who defend and follow them are sacrificed, not to public safety, but to their opponents' hatred and cruelty. If deeds only could be made the grounds of criminal charges, and words were always allowed to pass free, such seditions would be divested of every semblance of justification, and would be separated from mere controversies by a hard and fast line.

Now, seeing that we have the rare happiness of living in a republic, where everyone's judgment is free and unshackled, where each may worship God as his conscience dictates, and where freedom is esteemed before all things dear and precious, I have believed that I should be undertaking no ungrateful or unprofitable task, in demonstrating that not only can such freedom be granted without prejudice to the public peace, but also, that without such freedom, piety cannot flourish nor the public peace be secure.

Such is the chief conclusion I seek to establish in this treatise; but, in order to reach it, I must first point out the misconceptions which, like scars of our former bondage, still disfigure our notion of religion, and must expose the false views about the civil authority which many have most impudently advocated, endeavoring to turn the mind of the people, still prone to heathen superstition, away from its legitimate rulers, and so bring us again into slavery. As to the order of my treatise I will speak presently, but first I will recount the causes which led me to write. I have often wondered, that persons who make a boast of professing the Christian religion, namely, love, joy, peace, temperance, and charity to all men, should quarrel with such rancorous animosity, and display daily towards one another such bitter hatred, that this, rather than the virtues they claim, is the readiest criterion of their faith. Matters have long since come to such a pass, that one can only pronounce a man Christian, Turk, Jew, or Heathen, by his general appearance and attire, by his frequenting this or that place of worship, or employing the phraseology of a particular sect—as for manner of life, it is in all cases the same. Inquiry into the cause of this anomaly leads me unhesitatingly to ascribe it to the fact, that the ministries of the Church are regarded by the masses merely as dignities, her offices as posts of emolument—in short, popular religion may be summed up as respect for ecclesiastics. The spread of this misconception inflamed every worthless fellow with an intense desire to enter holy orders, and thus the love of diffusing God's religion degenerated into sordid avarice and ambition. Every church became a theatre, where orators, instead of church teachers, harangued, caring not to instruct the people, but striving to attract admiration, to bring opponents to public scorn, and to preach only novelties and paradoxes, such as would tickle the ears of their congregation. This state of things necessarily stirred up an amount of controversy, envy, and hatred, which no lapse of time could appease; so that we can scarcely wonder that of the old religion nothing survives but its outward forms (even these, in the mouth of the multitude, seem rather adulation than adoration of the Deity), and that faith has become a mere compound of credulity and prejudices—aye, prejudices too, which degrade man from rational being to beast, which completely stifle the power of judgment between true and false, which seem, in fact, carefully fostered for the purpose of extinguishing the last spark of reason! Piety, great God! and religion are become a tissue of ridiculous mysteries; men, who flatly despise reason, who reject and turn away from understanding as naturally corrupt, these, I say, these of all men, are thought, O lie most horrible! to possess light from on High. Verily, if they had but one spark of light from on High, they would not insolently rave, but would learn to worship God more wisely, and would be as marked among their fellows for mercy as they now are for malice; if they were concerned for their opponents' souls, instead of for their own reputations, they would no longer fiercely persecute, but rather be filled with pity and compassion.

Furthermore, if any Divine light were in them, it would appear from their doctrine. I grant that they are never tired of professing their wonder at the profound mysteries of Holy Writ; still I cannot discover that they teach anything but speculations of Platonists and Aristotelians, to which (in order to save their credit for Christianity) they have made Holy Writ conform; not content to rave with the Greeks themselves, they want to make the prophets rave also; showing conclusively, that never even in sleep have they caught a glimpse of Scripture's Divine nature. The very vehemence of their admiration for the mysteries plainly attests, that their belief in the Bible is a formal assent rather than a living faith: and the fact is made still more apparent by their laying down beforehand, as a foundation for the study and true interpretation of Scripture, the principle that it is in every passage true and divine. Such a doctrine should be reached only after strict scrutiny and thorough comprehension of the Sacred Books (which would teach it much better, for they stand in need of no human fictions), and not be set up on the threshold, as it were, of inquiry.

As I pondered over the facts that the light of reason is not only despised, but by many even execrated as a source of impiety, that human commentaries are accepted as divine records, and that credulity is extolled as faith; as I marked the fierce controversies of philosophers raging in Church and State, the source of bitter hatred and dissension, the ready instruments of sedition and other ills innumerable, I determined to examine the Bible afresh in a careful, impartial, and unfettered spirit, making no assumptions concerning it, and attributing to it no doctrines, which I do not find clearly therein set down. With these precautions I constructed a method of Scriptural interpretation, and thus equipped proceeded to inquire What is prophecy? in what sense did God reveal Himself to the prophets, and why were these particular men chosen by Him? Was it on account of the sublimity of their thoughts about the Deity and nature, or was it solely on account of their piety? These questions being answered, I was easily able to conclude, that the authority of the prophets has weight only in matters of morality, and that their speculative doctrines affect us little.

2
Thoughts On Religion

Denis Diderot (1713–1784)

I   In religion, doubts, far from being acts of impiety, should be looked upon as good works when they issue from a man who humbly recognizes his ignorance, and when they are born of the fear of displeasing God by the abuse of reason

II   Admitting to a degree of conformity between man's reason and eternal reason —which is God—and then claiming that God demands the sacrifice of human reason, is to establish that he wants and doesn't want at the same time.

III   When God, from whom we receive reason, demands its sacrifice it is like a prestidigitator who takes back what he has given.

IV   If I renounce reason I no longer have a guide. I have to blindly accept a secondary principle and suppose that which is in question.

V   If reason is a gift from heaven, and the same thing can be said of faith, then heaven has given us two incompatible and contradictory presents.

VI   In order to remove this difficulty one must say that faith is a chimerical principle that doesn't exist in nature.

VII   Pascal, Nicole, and others have said: "That God should punish innocent children with eternal punishment for the guilty deeds of a father is a superior proposition and is not contrary to reason." But what then is a proposition contrary to reason if that which obviously expresses a blasphemy isn't one?

VIII   Lost in an immense forest during the night I only have a small light to guide me. An unknown man appears and says to me: "My friend, blow out your candle so you can better find your way." This unknown man is a theologian.

IX   If my reason comes from on high then it is the voice of heaven that speaks through it. I must listen to it.

X   Merit and lack of merit cannot be applied to the use of reason, because all the good will in the world cannot make a blind man discern colors. Unless I'm an imbecile I am forced to see evidence where it is, and the lack of evidence where it isn't. And imbecility is a misfortune and not a vice.

XI   The author of nature, who will not reward me for having been intelligent will not damn me for having been a fool.

XII   And he will not damn you for having been evil. After all, weren't you unhappy enough because you were evil?

XIII   Every virtuous act is accompanied by internal satisfaction, every criminal act by remorse. Yet without shame or remorse the spirit confesses its repugnance for this or that proposition. There is thus neither virtue nor crime in either believing or rejecting it.

XIV   If grace is necessary in order to do good, then of what use was Jesus Christ's death?

XV   If there are a hundred thousand damned beings for every one who is saved, then the devil always has the advantage, without having abandoned his son to death.

XVI   The Christian God is a father who makes much of his apples and very little of his children.

XVII   Take the fear of hell from a Christian and you take from him his belief.

XVIII   A true religion, interesting all men in all times and places, must be eternal, universal, and evident. None have these three characteristics. All are thus demonstrated false three times over.

XIX   Those facts that only a few men are able to witness are insufficient to demonstrate a religion that should be equally believed by everyone.

XX   The facts upon which religions are based are ancient and marvelous, that is to say, as suspect as is possible in proving that which is the most incredible.

XXI   Proving the Gospels by a miracle means proving an absurdity by something counter to nature.

XXII   But what will God do to those who didn't hear His son speak? Will He punish the deaf for not having heard?

XXIII   What will He do to those who, having heard tell of His religion were not able to understand it? Will he punish pygmies for not having been able to take giant steps?

XXIV   Why are the miracles of Jesus Christ true, while those of Aesculapius, Apollonius of Tyane, and Mohammed are false?

XXV   So all the Jews who were in Jerusalem were apparently converted upon seeing Jesus Christ's miracles? Not in the least. Far from believing in him they crucified him. We must agree that these Jews are men like no others. We have everywhere seen people led along by one sole false miracle, but Jesus Christ could do nothing with the Jewish people with an infinite number of true miracles.

XXVI   It is this miracle of Jewish incredulity that something should be made of, and not that of the resurrection.

XXVII It is as certain as two and two make four that Caesar existed. It is as certain that Jesus Christ existed as that Caesar did. It is thus as certain that Jesus Christ was resurrected as that he or Caesar existed. What logic! The existence of Jesus Christ and Caesar is not a miracle.

XXVIII We read in "The Life of M. Turenne" that a fire having broken out in a house the presence of the holy sacrament suddenly stopped the flames. But we also read in history that a monk having poisoned a consecrated host, a German Emperor had no sooner swallowed it than he died.

XXIX   There could be found in this something other than the appearance of bread and wine, or we would have to say that poison had been incorporated into the blood and body of Jesus Christ.

XXX   This body rots, this blood turns. This God is devoured by termites on the altar. Blind people, imbecilic Egyptian, open your eyes!

XXXI   The religion of Jesus Christ, announced by the ignorant, made the first Christians. The same religion, preached by savants and doctors, only makes unbelievers today.

XXXII It is objected that submission to a legislative authority dispenses one from reasoning. But where on the face of the earth is there a religion without such authority?

XXXIII It is childhood education that prevents a Mohammedan from having himself baptized. It is childhood education that prevents a Christian from being circumcised. It is the reason of the mature man that holds in equal contempt both baptism and circumcision.

XXXIV It is said in St. Luke that God the Father is greater than God the Son, pater major me est. Nevertheless, despite so clear a passage, the church pronounces anathema against the scrupulous believer who holds literally to the words of his father's testament.

XXXV   Since there is no passage in the scriptures that is more precise than this one, if the word of authority is able to dispose of the meaning of this passage as it wishes, then there are none we can say we fully understood and with which the church can't do what it pleases in the future.

XXXVI Tu es petrus, et super hunc petrum aedificabo ecclesiam mean. Is this the language of a God or a confused assemblage worthy of the Seigneur des accords?[1]

XXXVII In dolore paries (Genesis). You will give birth in pain, said God to the sinning woman. And what did female animals do to him that they too should give birth in pain?

XXXVIII   If pater major me est is to be understood literally Jesus Christ isn't God. If hoc est corpus meum is to be understood literally he gave himself to his apostles with his own hands, which is as absurd as saying St Denis kissed his own head after it was cut off.

XXXIX It is said that he withdrew to the Mount of Olives and prayed. And who did he pray to? He prayed to himself.

XL   "This God, who makes God die in order to appease God" is an excellent quote from Baron de la Hontan.[2] There is less evidence for and against Christianity in a hundred in-folio volumes than there is of the ridiculous in these two lines.

XLI   To say that man is a composite of force and weakness, of enlightenment and blindness, or small-mindedness and grandeur does not mean not putting him on trial, it rather defines him.

XLII   Either man is like God or nature made him, and God and nature do nothing that is evil.

XLIII   What we call "original sin" Ninon de l'Enclos called "an original sin."

XLIV   It is an unexampled impudence to cite the conformity of the writers of the Gospels when there are important facts in some of them that are not even mentioned in others.

XLV   Plato considered the Divinity under three aspects: goodness, wisdom, and power. You have to be blind not to see in this the trinity of the Christians. Almost three thousand years ago the philosopher of Athens called "logos" what we call the word.

XLVI   The divine persons are either three accidents or three substances. There is no middle way. If they are three accidents we are either atheists or deists. If they are three substances we are pagans.

XLVI   God the Father judges men to be deserving of His eternal vengeance. God the Son judges them deserving of His infinite pity. The Holy Ghost remains neutral. How can we make this Catholic verbiage agree with the unity of the divine will?

XLVIII A long time ago it was asked of theologians that they find a way to reconcile eternal punishment with God's infinite mercy. They haven't advanced a step.

XLIX And why punish a guilty man if there is no good to be obtained from his punishment?

L If we punish for ourselves alone we are both cruel and evil.

LI No good father would want to resemble the heavenly Father.

LII What proportionality is there between the offender and the offended? What proportionality between the offense and the punishment? A heap of foolishness and atrocities.

LIII And what causes Him to be so full of wrath, this God? And couldn't it be said that I am able do something for or against His glory, for or against His repose, for or against His happiness?

LIV They want God to burn those who are wicked—who can do nothing against him—in a fire that will continue without end, and yet they do not permit a father to deal a passing death to a son who compromised his life, his honor, and his fortune.

LV Oh Christians, you have two different ideas of good and evil, of truth and falsehood. You are thus either the most absurd of dogmatists or the most extreme of skeptics.

LVI All the evil of which we are capable is not all the evil that is possible, yet it is only he who can commit all the evil possible who also deserves eternal punishment. In order to make God into an infinitely vindictive being you transform an earthworm into an infinitely powerful being.

LVII Upon hearing a theologian exaggerate the act of a man who God was bawdy and slept with his neighbor—who God made obliging and beautiful, couldn't we say that the four corners of the world have been set on fire? My friend, listen to Marcus Aurelius and you will see that you anger your God for nothing but the illicit and voluptuous rubbing together of two intestines.

LVIII What these atrocious Christians translated as "eternal" only means "lasting" in Hebrew. The dogma of eternal punishment comes from the ignorance of a Hebraist and the ferocious humor of an interpreter.

LXIX That Jesus Christ, who is God, was tempted by the devil is a tale worthy of "The Thousand and One Nights."

LXI I would like a Christian, and especially a Jansenist, to make me understand the cui bono of the incarnation. And the number of the damned should not be infinitely inflated if we want to obtain some advantage from this dogma.

LXII   A young girl lived withdrawn from the world. One day she received the visit of a young man who was carrying a bird. She became pregnant and was asked who made the child. What a question! It was the bird.

LXIII   Why do Leida's swan and the tiny flames of Castor and Pollux make us laugh yet we don't laugh at the dove and the tongues of fire of the Gospels?

LXIV   In the first centuries there were sixty gospels that were almost equally believed. Fifty-six were rejected for puerility or ineptitude. Is there anything but this in those that were kept?

LXV   God gives a first law to man and then he abolishes that law. Is this not the conduct of a legislator who has made a mistake and who recognizes it as time passes? Would a perfect being change its mind?

LXVI   There are as many kinds of faith as there are religions in the world.

LXVII   All the sectarians in the world are nothing but heretical deists.

LXVIII   If man is unhappy without having been born guilty, might it not be that he is destined to enjoy eternal happiness without being able, by his very nature, to ever make himself worthy of it?

LXIX   This is what I think of Christian dogma. I will only say one word on its morality: It is that a Catholic who is father of a family, convinced that the maxims of the Gospels must be practiced under penalty of what is called hell, and given the extreme difficulty in reaching this degree of perfection, which human weakness prevents, I see nothing else to be done than for him to take his child by the foot and smash him against the ground, or to suffocate it at birth. By this act he saves it from the peril of damnation and assures him eternal happiness. And I maintain that this act, far from being criminal, should be considered infinitely praiseworthy, since it is founded upon paternal love, which demands that all good fathers do all the good possible for their children.

LXX   Are not the precepts of religion and society's laws, which prohibit the murder of innocents, in fact quite absurd and cruel, since in killing them we assure them infinite happiness and in letting them live we almost certainly destine them to eternal unhappiness?

LXXI   What is that, Monsieur de la Condamine? It would be permitted to inoculate your son to protect him from smallpox, but it isn't permitted to kill him to protect him from hell? Surely you jest.

LXXII   Satis triumphat veritas si apud paucos. Eosque bonos, accepta sit; nec ejus indoles placere multis.

The following two thoughts were taken from manuscripts of Diderot's at the Hermitage in St Petersburg. They deal with the same subject matter as the above, and the second has noted at its head "Philosophical thought."

> Formerly, on the island of Ternate no one, not even priests, was allowed to speak of religion. There was only one temple, and a law expressly forbade that there be a second one. There could be found there neither altars nor statues, nor images. A hundred priests, who enjoyed considerable revenue, worked in the temple. They neither sang nor spoke, but in an enormous silence pointed at a pyramid upon which was written these words: "Mortals, adore God, love your brothers and make yourselves useful to the nation."

> A man had been betrayed by his children, his wife, and his friends. Faithless friends had reversed his fortunes and plunged him into poverty. Penetrated by hatred and profound contempt for humanity he left society and took refuge alone in a cave. There, with his head in his hands, and meditating a vengeance proportional to his resentment, he said: "Those evil ones. What shall I do to punish them for their injustice and make them all as unhappy as they deserve to be? If only it were possible to imagine this…to attach them to a chimera upon which they'd place more importance than their lives and about which they could never be in agreement!" And then he ran from the cave, crying out: "God! God!" Echoes without number repeated around him: "God! God!" This fearsome name was carried from one pole to the other, and heard everywhere with amazement. At first men prostrated themselves, then they stood up, questioned, disputed, became bitter, anathematized, hated, killed each other. The fatal wish of the misanthrope was fulfilled. For such was in the past, and such shall be in the future the history of a being that is forever equally important and incomprehensible.

Notes

1. From an eighteenth century essay by Tabourot.

2. French seigneur of the 17th Century.

3
The System Of Nature (1770)
Paul-Henri Thiry, Baron d'Holbach

After having proved the existence of atheists, let us return to the calumnies that are showered upon them by the theists. According to Abbadie,[1] "an atheist cannot be virtuous: to him virtue is only a chimera; probity no more than a vain scruple; honesty nothing but foolishness; he knows no other law than his interest: where this sentiment prevails, conscience is only a prejudice; natural law only an illusion; right no more than an error; benevolence no longer has any foundation; the bonds of society are loosened; the ties of fidelity are removed; friend is ready to betray friend; the citizen to deliver up his country; the son to assassinate his father, in order to enjoy his inheritance, whenever they shall find occasion, and that authority or silence shall shield them from the arm of the secular power, which alone is to be feared. The most inviolable rights, and most sacred laws, must no longer be considered, except as dreams and visions."

Such, perhaps, would be the conduct, not of a feeling, thinking, reflecting being, susceptible of reason, but of a ferocious brute, an irrational wretch, who should not have any idea of the natural relations which subsist between beings, reciprocally necessary to each other's happiness. Can it actually be supposed that a man capable of experience, furnished with the faintest glimmerings of good sense, would lend himself to the conduct that is here ascribed to the atheist; that is to say, to a man who is sufficiently susceptible of reflection to undeceive himself by reasoning upon those prejudices which everyone strives to show him as important and sacred? Can it, I say, be supposed that any civilized society contains a citizen so completely blind as not to acknowledge his most natural duties, his dearest interests, the dangers he incurs in disturbing his fellow creatures or in following no other rule than his momentary appetites? Is not every human being who reasons in the least possible manner obliged to feel that society is advantageous to him; that he has need of assistance; that the esteem of his fellows is necessary to his own happiness; that he has everything to fear from the wrath of his associates; that the laws menace whoever shall dare to infringe them? Every man who has received a virtuous education, who has in his infancy experienced the tender cares of a parent, who has in consequence tasted the sweets of friendship, who has received kindness, who knows the worth of benevolence and equity, who feels the pleasure that the affection of our fellow creatures procures for us, who endures the inconveniences that result from their aversion and their scorn, is obliged to tremble at losing such manifest advantages, at incurring such imminent danger. Will not the hatred of others, the fear of punishment, his own contempt of himself, disturb his repose every time that, turning inwardly, he shall contemplate himself under the same perspective as does his neighbor? Is there then no remorse except for those who believe in a God? Is the idea that we are under the eye of a being of whom we have but vague notions more forcible than the thought that we are viewed by our fellow men; that we are viewed by ourselves; that we are compelled to be afraid; that we are under the cruel necessity of becoming despicable in our own eyes and blushing guiltily in thinking of our conduct and of the sentiments it must infallibly inspire?

This granted, we shall reply deliberately to this Abbadie, that an atheist is a man who understands nature and her laws, who understands his own nature, who knows what it imposes upon him. An atheist has experience, and this experience proves to him every moment that vice can injure him, that his most concealed faults, his most secret dispositions, may be detected and may display his character in open day. This experience proves to him that society is useful to his happiness, that his interest therefore demands he should attach himself to the country that protects him and enables him to enjoy in security the benefits of nature. Everything shows him that in order to be happy he must make himself beloved, that his father is for him the most certain of friends, that ingratitude would remove him from his benefactor, that justice is necessary to the maintenance of every association, and that no man, whatever may be his power, can be content with himself, when he knows he is an object of public hatred.

He who has maturely reflected upon himself, upon his own nature and upon that of his associates, upon his own needs, upon the means of procuring them, cannot prevent himself from becoming acquainted with his duties from discovering the obligations he owes to himself, as well as those he owes to others: he accordingly has morality; he has actual motives to comply with its dictates; he is obliged to feel that these duties are necessary; and if his reason be not disturbed by blind passions or by vicious habits, he will find that virtue is the surest road to felicity. The atheist or the fatalist build all their systems upon necessity: thus, their moral speculations, founded upon the nature of things, are at least much more permanent, much more invariable, than those which only rest upon a God whose aspect changes according to the various dispositions and passions of those contemplate him. The essence of things, and the immutable laws of nature, are not subject to fluctuation; the atheist is always compelled to call whatever injures himself either vice or folly; whatever injures others, crime; whatever is advantageous to society or contributes to its permanent happiness, virtue.

It will be obvious, then, that the principles of the atheist are much less liable to be shaken than those of the enthusiast, who bases his morality upon an imaginary being, the conception of which varies all too frequently, even within his own brain. If the atheist denies the existence of a God, he cannot deny his own existence, nor that of beings similar to himself, by whom he sees himself surrounded; he cannot doubt the relations that subsist between them; he cannot question the necessity of the duties that spring out of these relations; he cannot doubt the principles of morality, which is nothing but the science of the relations of beings living together in society.

If, however, satisfied with a barren, speculative knowledge of his duties, the atheist should not apply it to his conduct; if, borne along by criminal passions or habits, abandoned to shameful vices, at the mercy of a vicious temperament, he appears to forget his moral obligations, it by no means follows that he has no principles or that his principles are false. It can only be concluded that in the intoxication of his passions, in the confusion of his reason, he does not give activity to doctrines grounded upon truth; that he forgets his trustworthy principles in order to follow the propensities that mislead him.

Nothing is, perhaps, more common among men than a very marked discrepancy between the mind and the heart; that is to say, between the temperament, the passions, the habits, the caprices, the imagination, and the judgment, assisted by reflection. Nothing is more rare than to find these things working in harmony; it is, however, only when they do, that we see speculation influence practice. The most certain virtues are those which are founded upon the temperament of men. Indeed, do we not every day behold mortals in contradiction with themselves? Does not their more sober judgment unceasingly condemn the extravagances to which their passions deliver them up? In short, does not everything prove to us hourly that men, with the very best theory, have sometimes the very worst practice; that others with the most vicious theory frequently adopt the most estimable line of conduct? In the blindest and most appalling superstitions, in those that are most contrary to reason, we meet with virtuous men, the mildness of whose character, the sensibility of whose hearts, the excellence of whose temperament lead them back to humanity and to the laws of their nature, despite their mad theories. Among the adorers of the most cruel, vindictive, jealous God are found peaceable souls, enemies to persecution, violence, and cruelty; among the disciples of a God filled with mercy and clemency, are seen barbarous and inhuman monsters. Nevertheless, both the one and the other acknowledge that their gods ought to serve them for a model. Why, then, do they not in all things conform themselves? It is because the temperament of man is always stronger than his Gods; that the wickedest Gods cannot always corrupt an honest soul, and that the sweetest Gods cannot rectify hearts carried away by crime. The human constitution will always be more powerful than Religion; present objects, momentary interests, rooted habits, public opinion, have much more efficacy than imaginary beings or unintelligible theories, which themselves depend upon this constitution.

The point in question, then, is to examine if the principles of the atheist are true, and not whether his conduct is commendable. An atheist, having an excellent theory, founded upon nature, experience, and reason, who delivers himself up to excesses, dangerous to himself, injurious to society, is, without doubt, an inconsistent man. But he is not more to be feared than a religious zealot, who, believing in a good, equitable, perfect God, does not scruple to commit the most frightful devastations in his name. An atheistical tyrant would assuredly not be more to be dreaded than a fanatical despot. A skeptical philosopher, however, is not so mischievous as an enthusiastic priest, who fans the flame of discord among his fellow citizens. Would, then, an atheist clothed with power be equally dangerous as a persecuting king, or a savage inquisitor, or a whimsical devotee, or a morose bigot? These are assuredly more numerous in the world than atheists, whose opinions or whose vices are far from being in a position to influence society, since society is too filled with prejudice to wish to pay any attention to them. ...

Indeed, if men condescended to examine things coolly, they would find that the name of God has on this earth only served as a pretext for human passions. Ambition, imposture, and tyranny have often formed a league to avail themselves of its influence, in order to blind the people and bend them beneath the yoke. The monarch sometimes employs it to give a divine lustre to his person, the sanction of heaven to his rights, an oracular tone to his most unjust, most extravagant whims. The priest uses it to give currency to his pretensions, so that he may with impunity gratify his avarice, his pride, and his independence. The vindictive, enraged, superstitious being introduces the cause of his God so that he may give free scope to his fury, which he qualifies with zeal. In short, religion is dangerous, because it justifies and lends legitimacy and praise to the passions and crimes whose fruit it does not fail to gather: according to its ministers, everything is permitted to revenge the most high; thus the name of the Divinity is used to authorize and excuse the most injurious transgressions. The atheist, when he commits crimes, cannot, at least, pretend that it is his God who commands and approves them; this is the excuse that superstitious beings offer for their perversity, the tyrant for his persecutions, the priest for his cruelty and his sedition, the fanatic for his excesses, the penitent for his uselessness.

"It is not," says Bayle,[2] "the general opinions of the mind, but the passions, which determine us to act. Atheism is a system which will not make a good man wicked, nor will it make a wicked man good. Those," says the same author, "who embraced the sect of Epicurus did not become debauchees because they had adopted the doctrine of Epicurus; they only adopted the doctrine, then badly understood, because they were debauchees." In the same manner, a perverse man may embrace atheism, because he will flatter himself that this system will give full scope to his passions: he will nevertheless be deceived. Atheism, if well understood, is founded upon nature and upon reason, which never can, like superstition, either justify or expiate the crimes of the wicked.

From the diffusion of doctrines that make morality depend upon the existence and the will of God, and which are proposed to men for a model, there has unquestionably resulted very great inconvenience. Corrupt souls, in discovering how much each of these suppositions are erroneous or doubtful, give loose to the rein of their vices, and con- dude there are not more substantive motives for acting well; they imagine that virtue, like the Gods, is only an illusion; that there is no reason for practicing it in this world. Nevertheless, it must be evident that it is not as the creatures of God that we are bound to fulfill the duties of morality; it is as men, as sensible beings living together in society and seeking to secure for ourselves a happy existence, that we should feel the moral obligation. Whether a God exists or not, our duties will remain the same; our nature, if consulted, will incontestibly prove that vice is an evil and that virtue is an actual good.

If, then, there are found atheists who have denied the distinction between good and evil, or who have dared to strike at the foundations of morality, we ought to conclude that upon this point they have reasoned badly; that they have understood neither the nature of man, nor the true source of his duties; that they have falsely imagined that ethics, as well as theology, was only an ideal science, and that once the Gods were destroyed, there no longer remained any bonds to connect mortals. Nevertheless, the slightest reflection would have incontestibly proved to them that morality is founded upon immutable relations subsisting between sensible, intelligent, sociable beings; that without virtue, no society can maintain itself; that without putting the curb on his desires, no mortal can conserve himself. Men are constrained by their nature to love virtue and to dread crime, by the same necessity that obliges them to seek happiness and fly from sorrow: this nature compels them to make a distinction between those objects which please and those objects which injure them. Ask a man, who is sufficiently irrational to deny the difference between virtue and vice, if it would be indifferent to him to be beaten, robbed, insulted, treated with ingratitude, dishonored by his wife, insulted by his children, betrayed by his friend? His answer will prove to you that whatever he may say, he discriminates the actions of mankind; that the distinction between good and evil does not depend either upon the conventions of men, nor upon the ideas which they may have of divinity, nor upon the rewards or punishments that this divinity prepares for them in another life.

On the contrary, an atheist who should reason justly would feel himself more interested than another in practicing those virtues to which he finds his well-being attached in this world. If his views do not extend themselves beyond the limits of his present existence, he must, at least, desire to see his days roll on in happiness and in peace. Every man who, during the calm of his passions, falls back upon himself, will feel that his interest invites him to his own preservation; that his happiness demands he should take the necessary means to enjoy life peaceably, free of alarms and remorse. Man owes something to man, not because he would offend a God if he was to injure his fellow creature, but because in doing him an injury he would offend a man and violate the laws of equity, in the maintenance of which every human being finds himself interested...

The principles of atheism are not formed for the mass of the people, who are commonly under the tutelage of their priests; they are not calculated for those frivolous and dissipated minds who fill society with their vices and their uselessness; they will not gratify the ambitious, the intriguers, those restless beings who find their interest in making a disturbance: much less are they made for a great number of persons who, enlightened in other respects, have not sufficient courage to divorce themselves from the received prejudices.

So many causes unite to confirm man in those errors which he draws in with his mother's milk that every step that removes him from them costs him infinite pain. Those persons who are most enlightened frequently cling on some side to some universal prejudice. We feel ourselves, as it were, isolated: whenever we stand alone in our opinions, we no longer seem to speak the language of society; it requires courage to adopt a mode of thinking that is approved by so few. In those countries where human knowledge has made some progress, and where, besides, a certain freedom of thinking is enjoyed, one may easily find a great number of deists or skeptics, who, contented with having trampled underfoot the grosser prejudices of the illiterate, have not dared to go back to the source, and to bring divinity itself before the tribunal of reason. If these thinkers did not stop on the road, reflection would quickly prove to them that the God they have not the fortitude to examine is an equally injurious being, equally revolting to good sense, as any of those dogmas, mysteries, fables, and superstitious practices whose futility they have already acknowledged; they would feel, as we have already proved, that all these things are nothing more than the necessary consequences of those primitive conceptions by which men have made this divine phantom for themselves, and that in admitting this phantom, they no longer have any rational cause to reject the deductions which the imagination has drawn from it. A little attention would distinctly show them that it is precisely this phantom which is the true cause of all the evils of society; that those endless disputes, those bloody quarrels to which religion and the spirit of party every instant give birth are the inevitable effects of the importance they attach to an illusion, which is always ready to inflame their minds. In short, nothing is easier than to convince ourselves that an imaginary being, always portrayed in a terrifying aspect, must act vividly upon the imagination and sooner or later produce disputes, enthusiasm, fanaticism, and delirium.

Many persons acknowledge that the extravagances to which superstition lends activity are very real evils; many complain of the abuses of religion, but there are very few who feel that these abuses and these evils are the necessary consequences of the fundamental principles of all religion, which are founded upon the most grievous notions that one is compelled to make about deity. We daily see persons undeceived about religion, who nevertheless pretend that this religion *is necessary for the people;* that without it, they could not be controlled. But to reason thus, is it not to say that poison is beneficial to the people, that therefore it is proper to poison them in order to prevent them from abusing their power? Is it not in fact to pretend that it is advantageous to render them absurd, mad, extravagant; that they have need of hobgoblins to blind them, to make them giddy, to cause them to submit them to impostors or fanatics, who will avail themselves of their follies to disturb the universe? Again, is it indeed true that religion has had a truly useful influence over the morals of the people?

It is easy to see that it subjugates them without making them better; that it produces a herd of ignorant slaves whom panic terrors keep under the yoke of tyrants and priests; that it makes fools who know no other virtue save an appalling submission to futile customs, to which they attach a much greater value than to the actual virtues and moral duties whose existence has never been made known to them. If this religion does by chance restrain a few frightened individuals, it has no effect on the greater number, who suffer themselves to be borne along by the epidemical vices with which they are infected. It is in those countries where superstition has the greatest power that we always find the least morality. Virtue is incompatible with ignorance, superstition, slavery: slaves can only be restrained by the fear of punishment; ignorant children are only for a few moments intimidated by imaginary terrors. In order to mould men, in order to have virtuous citizens, we must instruct them, show them virtue, speak rationally with them, make them understand their interests, teach them to respect themselves and to fear shame, inspire within them the idea of true *honor,* make them understand the value of virtue and the motives for following it. How can we expect these happy effects from a religion that degrades them, or from a tyranny that proposes nothing more than to subjugate and divide them, and keep them in humiliation?

The false ideas that so many persons have of the utility of religion, which they at least judge to be calculated to restrain the people, arise from the fatal prejudice that it is a *useful error,* and that truths may be dangerous. This principle has complete efficacy to perpetuate the sorrows of the earth. Whoever shall have the courage to examine these things will without hesitation acknowledge that all the miseries of the human race are to be ascribed to his errors; that of these, religious error must be the most harmful of all, from the arrogance it inspires in sovereigns, the importance that is usually attached to it, the degradation it prescribes to subjects, the frenzies it excites among the people. We shall, therefore, be obliged to conclude that the superstitious errors of man are exactly those that, for the permanent interest of mankind, demand the most complete destruction, and that it is principally to their annihilation that the efforts of a sound philosophy ought to be directed. It is not to be feared that this attempt will produce disturbances or revolutions: the more freedom shall accompany the voice of truth, the more peculiar it will appear; the more simple it shall be, the less it will influence men, who are only smitten with the marvellous; even those individuals who seek after truth most ardently have frequently an irresistible inclination that urges them on, and incessantly disposes them to reconcile error with truth.

Here is, unquestionably, the true reason why atheism, whose principles have not hitherto been sufficiently developed, appears to alarm even those persons who are the most destitute of prejudice. They find too great an interval between vulgar superstition and an absolute lack of religion; they imagine they take a wise medium in compounding with error; they therefore reject the consequences, while admitting the principle; they preserve the shadow without foreseeing that, sooner or later, it must produce the same effects and, little by little, hatch the same follies in human minds. The majority of skeptics and reformers do no more than prune a cankered tree, to whose root they dare not apply the axe; they do not perceive that this tree will in the end produce the same fruit. Theology or religion will always be a heap of combustible matter brooded in the imagination of mankind; it will always finish by causing the most terrible explosions. As long as the sacerdotal order shall have the right to infect youth, to accustom them to tremble before mere words, to alarm nations with the name of a terrible God, so long will fanaticism be master of the human mind; imposture will, at its pleasure, cause discord in the nation. The simplest delusion, perpetually fed, modified, exaggerated by the imagination of men, will by degrees become a colossus, sufficiently powerful to overturn minds and overthrow empires. Deism is a system at which the human mind cannot make a long sojourn; founded upon error, it will, sooner or later, degenerate into the most absurd, the most dangerous superstition.

Notes

1. Jacques Abbadie was a 17th century philosopher who defended Christianity.
2. Pierre Bayle was a 17th century French writer whose critiques of Christian orthodoxy helped to launch the Enlightenment.

4
The Natural History Of Religion (1757)
David Hume

Impious Conceptions of The Divine Nature in Popular Religions of Both Kinds

The primary religion of mankind arises chiefly from an anxious fear of future events; and what ideas will naturally be entertained of invisible, unknown powers, while men lie under dismal apprehensions of any kind, may easily be conceived. Every image of vengeance, severity, cruelty, and malice must occur, and must augment the ghastliness and horror, which oppresses the amazed religionist. A panic having once seized the mind, the active fancy still farther multiplies the objects of terror; while that profound darkness, or, what is worse, that glimmering light, with which we are environed, represents the spectres of divinity under the most dreadful appearances imaginable. And no idea of perverse wickedness can be framed, which those terrified devotees do not readily, without scruple, apply to their deity.

This appears the natural state of religion, when surveyed in one light. But if we consider, on the other hand, that spirit of praise and eulogy, which necessarily has place in all religions, and which is the consequence of these very terrors, we must expect a quite contrary system of theology to prevail. Every virtue, every excellence, must be ascribed to the divinity, and no exaggeration will be deemed sufficient to reach those perfections, with which he is endowed. Whatever strains of panegyric can be invented, are immediately embraced, without consulting any arguments of phaenomena. It is esteemed a sufficient confirmation of them, that they give us more magnificent ideas of the divine objects of our worship and adoration.

Here therefore is a kind of contradiction between the different principles of human nature, which enter into religion. Our natural terrors present the notion of a devilish and malicious deity; our propensity to adulation leads us to acknowledge an excellent and divine. And the influence of these opposite principles are various, according to the different situation of the human understanding. ...

But as men farther exalt their idea of their divinity, it is their notion of his power and knowledge only, not of his goodness, which is improved. On the contrary, in proportion to the supposed extent of his science and authority, their terrors naturally augment; while they believe, that no secrecy can conceal them from his scrutiny, and that even the inmost recesses of their breast lie open before him. They must then be careful not to form expressly any sentiment of blame and disapprobation. All must be applause, ravishment, ecstacy. And while their gloomy apprehensions make them ascribe to him measures of conduct, which, in human creatures, would be highly blamed, they must still affect to praise and admire that conduct in the object of their devotional addresses. Thus it may safely be affirmed, that popular religions are really, in the conception of their more vulgar votaries, a species of demonism; and the higher the deity is exalted in power and knowledge, the lower of course is he depressed in goodness and benevolence; whatever epithets of praise may be bestowed on him by his amazed adorers. Among idolaters, the words may be false, and belie the secret opinion, but among more exalted religionists, the opinion itself contracts a kind of falsehood, and belies the inward sentiment. The heart secretly detests such measures of cruel and implacable vengeance; but the judgment dares not but pronounce them perfect and adorable. And the additional misery of this inward struggle aggravates all the other terrors, by which these unhappy victims to superstition are for ever haunted.

Lucian[1] observes that a young man, who reads the history of the gods in Homer or Hesiod, and finds their factions, wars, injustice, incest, adultery, and other immoralities so highly celebrated, is much surprised afterwards, when he comes into the world, to observe that punishments are by law inflicted on the same actions, which he had been taught to ascribe to superior beings. The contradiction is still perhaps stronger between the representations given us by some later religions and our natural ideas of generosity, lenity, impartiality, and justice; and in proportion to the multiplied terrors of these religions, the barbarous conceptions of the divinity are multiplied upon us. Nothing can preserve untainted the genuine principles of morals in our judgment of human conduct, but the absolute necessity of these principles to the existence of society. If common conception can indulge princes in a system of ethics, somewhat different from that which should regulate private persons; how much more those superior beings, whose attributes, views, and nature are so totally unknown to us? *Sunt superis sua* jura.[2] The gods have maxims of justice peculiar to themselves.

Bad Influence of Popular Religions on Morality

Here I cannot forbear observing a fact, which may be worth the attention of such as make human nature the object of their enquiry. It is certain, that, in every religion, however sublime the verbal definition which it gives of its divinity, many of the votaries, perhaps the greatest number, will still seek the divine favor, not by virtue and good morals, which alone can be acceptable to a perfect being, but either by frivolous observances, by intemperate zeal, by rapturous ecstasies, or by the belief of mysterious and absurd opinions. The least part of the *Sadder,* as well as of the *Pentateuch,*[3] consists in precepts of morality; and we may also be assured, that that part was always the least observed and regarded. When the old Romans were attacked with a pestilence, they never ascribed their sufferings to their vices, or dreamed of repentance and amendment. They never thought, that they were the general robbers of the world, whose ambition and avarice made desolate the earth, and reduced opulent nations to want and beggary. They only created a dictator, in order to drive a nail into a door; and by that means, they thought that they had sufficiently appeased their incensed deity.

In AEgina, one faction forming a conspiracy, barbarously and treacherously assassinated seven hundred of their fellow-citizens; and carried their fury so far, that, one miserable fugitive having fled to the temple, they cut off his hands, by which he clung to the gates, and carrying him out of holy ground, immediately murdered him. *By this impiety,* says Herodotus, (not by the other many cruel assassinations) *they offended the gods, and contracted an inexpiable guilt.*

Nay, if we should suppose, what never happens, that a popular religion were found, in which it was expressly declared, that nothing but morality could gain the divine favor; if an order of priests were instituted to inculcate this opinion, in daily sermons, and with all the arts of persuasion; yet so inveterate are the people's prejudices, that, for want of some other superstition, they would make the very attendance on these sermons the essentials of religion, rather than place them in virtue and good morals. The sublime prologue of Zaleucus's[4] laws inspired not the Locrians, so far as we can learn, with any sounder notions of the measures of acceptance with the deity, than were familiar to the other Greeks.

This observation, then, holds universally, but still one may be at some loss to account for it. It is not sufficient to observe, that the people, every where, degrade their deities into a similitude with themselves, and consider them merely as a species of human creatures, somewhat more potent and intelligent. This will not remove the difficulty. For there is no *man* so stupid, as that, judging by his natural reason, he would not esteem virtue and honesty the most valuable qualities, which any person could possess. Why not ascribe the same sentiment to his deity? Why not make all religion, or the chief part of it, to consist in these attainments?

Nor is it satisfactory to say, that the practice of morality is more difficult than that of superstition; and is therefore rejected. For, not to mention the excessive penances of the *Brachmans* and *Talapoins*[5]; it is certain, that the *Rhamadan*[6] of the Turks, during which the poor wretches, for many days, often in the hottest months of the year, and in some of the hottest climates of the world, remain without eating or drinking from the rising to the setting sun; this *Rhamadan,* I say, must be more severe than the practice of any moral duty, even to the most vicious and depraved of mankind. The four lents of the Muscovites, and the austerities of some Roman Catholics, appear more disagreeable than meekness and benevolence. In short, all virtue, when men are reconciled to it by ever so little practice, is agreeable, all superstition is forever odious and burthensome.

Perhaps, the following account may be received as a true solution of the difficulty. The duties, which a man performs as a friend or parent, seem merely owing to his benefactor or children; nor can he be wanting to these duties, without breaking through all the ties of nature and morality. A strong inclination may prompt him to the performance; a sentiment of order and moral obligation joins its force to these natural ties; and the whole man, if truly virtuous, is drawn to his duty, without any effort or endeavour. Even with regard to the virtues, which are more austere, and more founded on reflection, such as public spirit, filial duty, temperance, or integrity; the moral obligation, in our apprehension, removes all pretension to religious merit; and the virtuous conduct is deemed no more than what we owe to society and to ourselves. In all this, a superstitious man finds nothing, which he has properly performed for the sake of his deity, or which can peculiarly recommend him to the divine favor and protection. He considers not, that the most genuine method of serving the divinity is by promoting the happiness of his creatures. He still looks out for some more immediate service of the supreme Being, in order to allay those terrors, with which he is haunted. And any practice, recommended to him, which either serves to no purpose in life, or offers the strongest violence to his natural inclinations; that practice he will the more readily embrace, on account of those very circumstances, which should make him absolutely reject it. It seems the more purely religious, because it proceeds from no mixture of any other motive or consideration. And if, for its sake, he sacrifices much of his ease and quiet, his claim of merit appears still to rise upon him, in proportion to the zeal and devotion which he discovers. In restoring a loan, or paying a debt, his divinity is nowise beholden to him; because these acts of justice are what he was bound to perform, and what many would have performed, were there no god in the universe. But if he fast a day, or give himself a sound whipping this has a direct reference, in his opinion, to the service of God. No other motive could engage him to such austerities. By these distinguished marks of devotion, he has now acquired the divine favor; and may expect, in recompense, protection and safety in this world, and eternal happiness in the next.

Hence the greatest crimes have been found, in many instances, compatible with a superstitious piety and devotion; Hence, it is justly regarded as unsafe to draw any certain inference in favor of a man's morals, from the fervour or strictness of his religious exercises, even though he himself believe them sincere. Nay, it has been observed, that enormities of the blackest dye have been rather apt to produce superstitious terrors, and encrease the religious passion. Bomilcar, having formed a conspiracy for assassinating at once the whole senate of Carthage, and invading the liberties of his country, lost the opportunity, from a continual regard to omens and prophecies.[7] *Those who undertake the most criminal and most dangerous enterprizes are commonly the most superstitious;* as an ancient historian remarks on this occasion. Their devotion and spiritual faith rise with their fears. Catiline was not contented with the established deities and received rites of the national religion; his anxious terrors made him seek new inventions of this kind; which he never probably had dreamed of, had he remained a good citizen, and obedient to the laws of his country.[8]

To which we may add, that, after the commission of crimes, there arise remorses and secret horrors, which give no rest to the mind, but make it have recourse to religious rites and ceremonies, as expiations of its offences. Whatever weakens or disorders the internal frame promotes the interests of superstition. And nothing is more destructive to them than a manly, steady virtue, which either preserves us from disastrous, melancholy accidents, or teaches us to bear them. During such calm sunshine of the mind, these spectres of false divinity never make their appearance. On the other hand, while we abandon ourselves to the natural undisciplined suggestions of our timid and anxious hearts, every kind of barbarity is ascribed to the supreme Being, from the terrors with which we are agitated; and every kind of caprice, from the methods which we embrace in order to appease him. *Barbarity, caprice;* these qualities, however nominally disguised, we may universally observe, form the ruling character of the deity in popular religions. Even priests, instead of correcting these depraved ideas of mankind, have often been found ready to foster and encourage them. The more tremendous the divinity is represented, the more tame and submissive do men become his ministers. And the more unaccountable the measures of acceptance required by him, the more necessary does it become to abandon our natural reason, and yield to their ghostly guidance and direction. Thus it may be allowed, that the artifices of men aggravate our natural infirmities and follies of this kind, but never originally beget them. Their root strikes deeper into the mind, and springs from the essential and universal properties of human nature.

Notes

1. *Necyomantia,* 3. Lucian of Samosata, Greek humourist and satirist, author of *The Descent into Hades*.

2. "The gods have their own laws." Ovid, *Metamorphoses* 9.499.

3. *Sadder* refers to the Jewish sayings used at the Passover Seder. The Pentateuch is the first five books of the Bible.

4. Zaleucus, Ancient Greek lawmaker.

5. Brahmins are Hindu priests; Talapoins, Buddhist monks.

6. Ramedan is the Muslim moth of fasting.

7. Bomilcar, a 4th century BC Carthaginian general.

8. L. Sergius Catilina, a 1st century Roman.

5
The Age Of Reason (1796)

Thomas Paine

Revelation…,[1] so far as the term has relation between God and man, can only be applied to something which God reveals of his will to man; but though the power of the Almighty to make such a communication is necessarily admitted, because to that power all things are possible, yet, the thing so revealed (if any thing ever was revealed, and which, by the bye, it is impossible to prove) is revelation to the person only to whom it is made. His account of it to another is not revelation; and whoever puts faith in that account, puts it in the man from whom the account comes; and that man may have been deceived, or may have dreamed it; or he may be an impostor and may lie. There is no possible criterion whereby to judge of the truth of what he tells; for even the morality of it would be no proof of revelation. In all such cases, the proper answer should be, "When it is revealed to me, I will believe it to be revelation; but it is not and cannot be incumbent upon me to believe it to be revelation before; neither is it proper that I should take the word of man as the word of God, and put man in the place of God." This is the manner in which I have spoken of revelation in the former part of *The Age of Reason;* and which, whilst it reverentially admits revelation as a possible thing, because, as before said, to the Almighty all things are possible, it prevents the imposition of one man upon another, and precludes the wicked use of pretended revelation. But though, speaking for myself, I thus admit the possibility of revelation, I totally disbelieve that the Almigity ever did communicate any thing to man, by any mode of speech, in any language, or by any kind of vision, or appearance, or by any means which our senses are capable of receiving, otherwise than by the universal display of himself in the works of the creation, and by that repugnance we feel in ourselves to bad actions, and disposition to good ones.

The most detestable wickedness, the most horrid cruelties, and the greatest miseries, that have afflicted the human race, have had their origin in this thing called revelation, or revealed religion. It has been the most dishonourable belief against the character of the divinity, the most destructive to morality, and the peace and happiness of man, that ever was propagated since man began to exist. It is better, far better, that we admitted, if it were possible, a thousand devils to roam at large, and to preach publicly the doctrine of devils, if there were any such, than that we permitted one such impostor and monster as Moses, Joshua, Samuel, and the Bible prophets, to come with the pretended word of God in his mouth, and have credit among us.

Whence arose all the horrid assassinations of whole nations of men, women, and infants, with which the Bible is filled; and the bloody persecutions, and tortures unto death and religious wars, that since that time have laid Europe in blood and ashes; whence arose they, but from this impious thing called revealed religion, and this monstrous belief that God has spoken to man? The lies of the Bible have been the cause of the one, and the lies of the Testament [of] the other.

Some Christians pretend that Christianity was not established by the sword; but of what period of time do they speak? It was impossible that twelve men could begin with the sword: they had not the power; but no sooner were the professors of Christianity sufficiently powerful to employ the sword than they did so, and the stake and faggot too; and Mahomet could not do it sooner. By the same spirit that Peter cut off the ear of the high priest's servant (if the story be true) he would cut off his head, and the head of his master, had he been able. Besides this, Christianity grounds itself originally upon the [Hebrew] Bible, and the Bible was established altogether by the sword, and that in the worst use of it—not to terrify, but to extirpate. The Jews made no converts: they butchered all. The Bible is the sire of the [New] Testament, and both are called the *word of God*. The Christians read both books; the ministers preach from both books; and this thing called Christianity is made up of both. It is then false to say that Christianity was not established by the sword.

The only sect that has not persecuted are the Quakers; and the only reason that can be given for it is, that they are rather Deists than Christians. They do not believe much about Jesus Christ, and they call the scriptures a dead letter. Had they called them by a worse name, they had been nearer the truth.

It is incumbent on every man who reverences the character of the Creator, and who wishes to lessen the catalogue of artificial miseries, and remove the cause that has sown persecutions thick among mankind, to expel all ideas of a revealed religion as a dangerous heresy, and an impious fraud. What is it that we have learned from this pretended thing called revealed religion? Nothing that is useful to man, and every thing that is dishonourable to his Maker. What is it the Bible teaches us?—rapine, cruelty, and murder. What is it the Testament teaches us? to believe that the Almighty committed debauchery with a woman engaged to be married; and the belief of this debauchery is called faith.

As to the fragments of morality that are irregularly found thinly scattered in those books, they make no part of this pretended thing, revealed religion. They are the natural dictates of conscience, and the bonds by which society is held together, and without which it cannot exist; and are nearly the same in all religions, and in all societies. TheTestament teaches nothing new upon this subject, and where it attempts to exceed, it becomes mean and ridiculous. The doctrine of not retaliating injuries is much better expressed in Proverbs, which is a collection as well from the Gentiles as the Jews, than it is in the Testament. It is there said, (xxv. 21) *"If thine enemy be hungry, give him bread to eat; and if he be thirsty, give him water to drink:"* but when it is said, as in the Testament, *"If a man smite thee on the right cheek, turn to him the other also,"* it is assassinating the dignity of forbearance, and sinking man into a spaniel.

Loving of enemies is another dogma of feigned morality, and has besides no meaning. It is incumbent on man, as a moralist, that he does not revenge an injury; and it is equally as good in a political sense, for there is no end to retaliation; each retaliates on the other, and calls it justice: but to love in proportion to the injury, if it could be done, would be to offer a premium for a crime. Besides, the word *enemies is* too vague and general to be used in a moral maxim, which ought always to be demand defined, like a proverb. If a man be the enemy of another from mistake and prejudice, as in the case of religious opinions, and sometimes in politics, that man is different to an enemy at heart with a criminal intention; and it is incumbent upon us, and it contributes also to our own tranquillity, that we put the best construction upon a thing that it will bear. But even this erroneous motive in him makes no motive for love on the other part; and to say that we can love voluntarily, and without a motive, is morally and physically impossible.

Morality is injured by prescribing to it duties that, in the first place, are impossible to be performed, and if they could be would be productive of evil; or, as before said, be premiums for crime. The maxim of *doing as we would be done unto* does not include this strange doctrine of loving enemies; for no man expects to be loved himself for his crime or for his enmity.

Those who preach this doctrine of loving their enemies, are in general the greatest persecutors, and they act consistently by so doing for the doctrine is hypocritical, and it is natural that hypocrisy should act the reverse of what it preaches. For my own part, I disown the doctrine, and consider it as a feigned or fabulous morality; yet the man does not exist that can say I have persecuted him, or any man, or any set of men, either in the American Revolution, or in the French Revolution; or that I have, in any case, returned evil for evil. But it is not incumbent on man to reward a bad action with a good one, or to return good for evil; and wherever it is done, it is a voluntary act, and not a duty. It is also absurd to suppose that such doctrine can make any part of a revealed religion. We imitate the moral character of the Creator by forbearing with each other, for he forbears with all; but this doctrine would imply that he loved man, not in proportion as he was good, but as he was bad.

If we consider the nature of our condition here, we must see there is no occasion for such a thing as *revealed religion*. What is it we want to know? Does not the creation, the universe we behold, preach to us the existence of an Almighty power, that governs and regulates the whole? And is not the evidence that this creation holds out to our senses infinitely stronger than any thing we can read in a book, that any impostor might make and call the word of God? As for morality, the knowledge of it exists in every man's conscience.

Note

1. When Thomas Paine published his long essay "The Age of Reason," from whish this short piece is taken, he was publicly considered an atheist because of his harsh criticism of Christianity. However, he should more correctly be considered a deist. —Editor

6
A Refutation Of Deism (1814)
Percy Bysshe Shelley

Design must be proved before a designer can be inferred. The matter in controversy is the existence of design in the Universe, and it is not permitted to assume the contested premises and thence infer the matter in dispute. Insidiously to employ the words contrivance, design and adaptation before these circumstances are made apparent in the Universe, thence justly inferring a contriver, is a popular sophism against which it behoves us to be watchful.

To assert that motion is an attribute of mind, that matter is inert, that every combination is the result of intelligence is also an assumption of the matter in dispute.

Why do we admit design in any machine of human contrivance? Simply, because innumerable instances of machines having been contrived by human art are present to our mind, because we are acquainted with persons who could construct such machines; but if, having no previous knowledge of any artificial contrivance, we had accidentally found a watch upon the ground, we should have been justified in concluding that it was a thing of Nature, that it was a combination of matter with whose cause we were unacquainted, and that any attempt to account for the origin of its existence would be equally presumptuous and unsatisfactory.

The analogy which you attempt to establish between the contrivances of human art, and the various existences of the Universe, is inadmissible. We attribute these effects to human intelligence, because we know before hand that human intelligence is capable of producing them. Take away this knowledge, and the grounds of our reasoning will be destroyed. Our entire ignorance, therefore, of the Divine Nature leaves this analogy defective in its most essential point of comparison.

What consideration remains to be urged in support of the creation of the Universe by a supreme Being? Its admirable fitness for the production of certain effects, that wonderful consent of all its parts, that universal harmony by whose changeless laws innumerable systems of worlds perform their stated revolutions, and the blood is driven through the veins of the minutest animalcule that sports in the corruption of an insect's lymph: on this account did the Universe require an intelligent Creator, because it exists producing invariable effects, and inasmuch as it is admirably organised for the production of these effects, so the more did it require a creative intelligence.

Thus have we arrived at the substance of your assertion, "That whatever exists, producing certain effects, stands in need of a Creator, and the more conspicuous is its fitness for the production of these effects, the more certain will be our conclusion that it would not have existed from eternity, but must have derived its origin from an intelligent creator."

In what respect then do these arguments apply to the Universe, and not apply to God? From the fitness of the Universe to its end you infer the necessity of an intelligent Creator. But if the fitness of the Universe, to produce certain effects, be thus conspicuous and evident, how much more exquisite fitness to his end must exist in the Author of this Universe? If we find great difficulty from its admirable arrangement, in conceiving that the Universe has existed from all eternity, and to resolve this difficulty suppose a Creator, how much more dearly must we perceive the necessity of this very Creator's creation whose perfections comprehend an arrangement far more accurate and just.

The belief of an infinity of creative and created Gods, each more eminently requiring an intelligent author of his being than the foregoing, is a direct consequence of the premises which you have stated. The assumption that the Universe is a design, leads to a conclusion that there are infinity of creative and created Gods, which is absurd. It is impossible indeed to prescribe limits to learned error, when Philosophy relinquishes experience and feeling for speculation.

Until it is dearly proved that the Universe was created, we may reasonably suppose that it has endured from all eternity. In a case where two propositions are diametrically opposite, the mind believes that which is less incomprehensible: it is easier to suppose that the Universe has existed from all eternity, than to conceive an eternal being capable of creating it. If the mind sinks beneath the weight of one, is it an alleviation to encrease the intolerability of the burthen?

A man knows, not only that he now is, but that there was a time when he did not exist; consequently there must have been a cause. But we can only infer, from effects, causes exactly adequate to those effects. There certainly is a generative power which is effected by particular instruments; we cannot prove that it is inherent in these instruments, nor is the contrary hypothesis capable of demonstration. We admit that the generative power is incomprehensible, but to suppose that the same effects are produced by an eternal Omnipotent and Omniscient Being, leaves the cause in the same obscurity, but renders it more incomprehensible.

We can only infer from effects causes exactly adequate to those effects. An infinite number of effects demand an infinite number of causes, nor is the philosopher justified in supposing a greater connection or unity in the latter, than is perceptible in the former. The same energy cannot be at once the cause of the serpent and the sheep; of the blight by which the harvest is destroyed, and the sunshine by which it is matured; of the ferocious propensities by which man becomes a victim to himself, and of the accurate judgment by which his institutions are improved. The spirit of our accurate and exact philosophy is outraged by conclusions which contradict each other so glaringly.

The greatest, equally with the smallest motions of the Universe, are subjected to the rigid necessity of inevitable laws. These laws are the unknown causes of the known effects perceivable in the Universe. Their effects are the boundaries of our knowledge, their names the expressions of our ignorance. To suppose some existence beyond, or above them, is to invent a second and superfluous hypothesis to account for what has already been accounted for by the laws of motion and the properties of matter. I admit that the nature of these laws is incomprehensible, but the hypothesis of a Deity adds a gratuitous difficulty, which so far from alleviating those which it is adduced to explain, requires new hypotheses for the elucidation of its own inherent contradictions.

The laws of attraction and repulsion, desire and aversion, suffice to account for every phenomenon of the moral and physical world. A precise knowledge of the properties of any object, is alone requisite to determine its manner of action. Let the mathematician be acquainted with the weight and volume of a cannon ball, together with the degree of velocity and inclination with which is which it is impelled, and he will accurately delineate the course it must describe, and determine the force with which it will strike an object at a given distance. Let the influencing motive, present to the mind of any person be given, and the knowledge of his consequent conduct will result. Let the bulk and velocity of a comet be discovered, and the astronomer, by the accurate estimation of the equal and contrary actions of the centripetal and centrifugal forces, will justly predict the period of its return.

The anomalous motions of the heavenly bodies, their unequal velocities and frequent aberrations, are corrected by that gravitation by which they are caused. The illustrious Laplace[1] has shewn, that the approach of the Moon to the Earth, and the Earth to the Sun, is only a secular equation of a very long period, which has its maximum and minimum. The system of the Universe then is upheld solely by physical powers. The necessity of matter is the ruler of the world. It is vain philosophy which supposes more causes than are exactly adequate to explain the phenomena of things. ...

You assert that the construction of the animal machine, the fitness of certain animals to certain situations, the connexion between the organs of perception and that which is perceived; the relation between every thing which exists, and that which tends to preserve it in its existence, imply design. It is manifest that if the eye could not see, nor the stomach digest, the human frame could not preserve its present mode of existence. It is equally certain, however, that the elements of its composition, if they did not exist in one form, must exist in another; and that the combinations which they would form, must so long as they endured, derive support for their peculiar mode of being from their fitness to the circumstances of their situation.

It by no means follows, that because a being exists, performing certain functions, he was fitted by another being to the performance of these functions. So rash a conclusion would conduct, as I have before shewn, to an absurdity; and it becomes infinitely more unwarrantable from the consideration that the known laws of matter and motion, suffice to unravel, even in the present imperfect state of moral and physical science, the majority of those difficulties which the hypothesis of a Deity was invented to explain.

Doubtless no disposition of inert matter, or matter deprived of qualities, could ever have composed an animal, a tree, or even a stone. But matter deprived of qualities, is an abstraction, concerning which it is impossible to form an idea. Matter, such as we behold it, is not inert. It is infinitely active and subtile. Light, electricity and magnetism are fluids not surpassed by thought itself in tenuity and activity; like thought they are sometimes the cause and sometimes the effect of motion; and, distinct as they are from every other class of substances, with which we are acquainted, seem to possess equal claims with thought to the unmeaning distinction of immateriality.

The laws of motion and the properties of matter suffice to account for every phenomenon, or combination of phenomena exhibited in the Universe. That certain animals exist in certain climates, results from the consentaneity of their frames to the circumstances of their situation: let these circumstances be altered to a sufficient degree, and the elements of their composition must exist in some new combination no less resulting than the former from those inevitable laws by which the Universe is governed. ...

What then is this harmony, this order which you maintain to have required for its establishment, what it needs not for its maintenance, the agency of a supernatural intelligence? Inasmuch as the order visible in the Universe requires one cause, so does the disorder whose operation is not less dearly apparent demand another. Order and disorder are no more than modifications of our own perceptions of the relations which subsist between ourselves and external objects, and if we are justified in inferring the operation of a benevolent power from the advantages attendant on the former, the evils of the latter bear equal testimony to the activity of a malignant principle, no less pertinacious in inducing evil out of good, than the other is unremitting in procuring good from evil.

If we permit our imagination to traverse the obscure regions of possibility, we may doubtless imagine, according to the complexion of our minds, that disorder may have a relative tendency to unmingled good, or order be relatively replete with exquisite and subtle evil. To neither of these conclusions, which are equally presumptuous and unfounded, will it become the philosopher to assent. Order and disorder are expressions denoting our perceptions of what is injurious or beneficial to ourselves, or to the beings in whose welfare we are compelled to sympathize by the similarity of their conformation to our own.

A beautiful antelope panting under the fangs of a tiger, a defenceless ox, groaning beneath the butcher's axe, is a spectacle which instantly awakens compassion in a virtuous and unvitiated breast. Many there are, however, sufficiently hardened to the rebukes of justice and the precepts of humanity, as to regard the deliberate butchery of thousands of their species, as a theme of exultation and a source of honour, and to consider any failure in these remorseless enterprises as a defect in the system of things. The criteria of order and disorder are as various as those beings from whose opinions and feelings they result.

Populous cities are destroyed by earthquakes, and desolated by pestilence. Ambition is every where devoting its millions to incalculable calamity. Superstition, in a thousand shapes, is employed in brutalizing and degrading the human species, and fitting it to endure without a murmur the oppression of its innumerable tyrants. All this is abstractedly neither good nor evil because good and evil are words employed to designate that peculiar state of our own perceptions, resulting from the encounter of any object calculated to produce pleasure or pain. Exclude the idea of relation, and the words good and evil are deprived of import.

Earthquakes are injurious to the cities which they destroy, beneficial to those whose commerce was injured by their prosperity, and indifferent to others which are too remote to be affected by their influence. Famine is good to the corn-merchant, evil to the poor, and indifferent to those whose fortunes can at all times command a superfluity. Ambition is evil to the restless bosom it inhabits, to the innumerable victims who are dragged by its ruthless thirst for infamy, to expire in every variety of anguish, to the inhabitants of the country it depopulates, and to the human race whose improvement it retards; it is indifferent with regard to the system of the Universe, and is good only to the vultures and the jackals that track the conqueror's career, and to the worms who feast in security on the desolation of his progress. It is manifest that we cannot reason with respect to the universal system from that which only exists in relation to our own perceptions.

You allege some considerations in favor of a Deity from the universality of a belief in his existence. The superstitions of the savage, and the religion of civilized Europe appear to you to conspire to prove a first cause. I maintain that it is from the evidence of revelation alone that this belief derives the slightest countenance.

That credulity should be gross in proportion to the ignorance of the mind which it enslaves, is in strict consistency with the principles of human nature. The idiot, the child and the savage, agree in attributing their own passions and propensities to the inanimate substances by which they are either benefited or injured. The former become Gods and the latter Demons; hence prayers and sacrifices, by the means of which the rude Theologian imagines that he may confirm the benevolence of the one, or mitigate the malignity of the other. He has averted the wrath of a powerful enemy by supplications and submission; he has secured the assistance of his neighbour by offerings; he has felt his own anger subside before the entreaties of a vanquished foe, and has cherished gratitude for the kindness of another. Therefore does he believe that the elements will listen to his vows. He is capable of love and hatred towards his fellow beings, and is variously impelled by those principles to benefit or injure them. The source of his error is sufficiently obvious. When the winds, the waves and the atmosphere act in such a manner as to thwart or forward his designs, he attributes to them the same propensities of whose existence within himself he is conscious when he is instigated by benefits to kindness, or by injuries to revenge. The bigot of the woods can form no conception of beings possessed of properties differing from his own: it requires, indeed, a mind considerably tinctured with science, and enlarged by cultivation to contemplate itself, not as the centre and model of the Universe, but as one of the infinitely various multitude of beings of which it is actually composed.

There is no attribute of God which is not either borrowed from the passions and powers of the human mind, or which is not a negation. Omniscience, Omnipotence, Omnipresence, Infinity, Immutability, Incomprehensibility, and Immateriality, are all words which designate properties and powers peculiar to organised beings, with the addition of negations, by which the idea of limitation is excluded.[2]

That the frequency of a belief in God (for it is not Universal) should be any argument in its favor, none to whom the innumerable mistakes of men are familiar, will assert. It is among men of genius and science that Atheism alone is found, but among these alone is cherished an hostility to those errors, with which the illiterate and vulgar are infected.

How small is the proportion of whose who really believe in God, to the thousands who are prevented by their occupations from ever bestowing a serious thought upon the subject, and the millions who worship butterflies, bones, feathers, monkeys, calabashes and serpents. The word God, like other abstractions, signifies the agreement of certain propositions, rather than the presence of any idea. If we found our belief in the existence of God on the universal consent of mankind, we are duped by the most palpable of sophisms. The word God cannot mean at the same time an ape, a snake, a bone, a calabash, a Trinity, and a Unity. Nor can that belief be accounted universal against which men of powerful intellect and spotless virtue have in every age protested. ...

Intelligence is that attribute of the Deity, which you hold to be most apparent in the Universe. Intelligence is only known to us as a mode of animal being. We cannot conceive intelligence distinct from sensation and perception, which are attributes to organized bodies. To assert that God is intelligent, is to assert that he has ideas; and Locke has proved that ideas result from sensation. Sensation can exist only in an organized body, an organized body is necessarily limited both in extent and operation. The God of the rational Theosophist is a vast and wise animal. ...

Thus, from the principles of that reason to which you so rashly appealed as the ultimate arbiter of our dispute, have I shewn that the popular arguments in favor of the being of God are totally destitute of colour. I have shewn the absurdity of attributing intelligence to the cause of those effects which we perceive in the Universe, and the fallacy which lurks in the argument from design. I have shewn that order is no more than a peculiar manner of contemplating the operation of necessary agents, that mind is the effect, not the cause of motion, that power is the attribute, not the origin of Being. I have proved that we can have no evidence of the existence of a God from the principles of reason.

Notes

1. Pierre Simon, marquis de Laplace (1749-1827).

2. See *Le Sysèime de la Nature* by Holbach, page 15 in this book. —Editor

7
Immortality (1868–70)[1]
John Stuart Mill

The indications of immortality may be considered in two divisions: those which are independent of any theory respecting the Creator and his intentions, and those which depend upon an antecedent belief on that subject.

Of the former class of arguments speculative men have in different ages put forward a considerable variety, of which those in the Phaedon of Plato are an example; but they are for the most part such as have no adherents, and need not be seriously refuted, now. They are generally founded upon preconceived theories as to the nature of the thinking principle in man, considered as distinct and separable from the body, and on other preconceived theories respecting death. As, for example, that death, or dissolution, is always a separation of parts; and the soul being without parts, being simple and indivisible, is not susceptible of this separation. Curiously enough, one of the interlocutors in the Phaedon anticipates the answer by which an objector of the present day would meet this argument: namely, that thought and consciousness, though mentally distinguishable from the body, may not be a substance separable from it, but a result of it, standing in a relation to it (the illustration is Plato's) like that of a tune to the musical instrument on which it is played; and that the arguments used to prove that the soul does not die with the body, would equally prove that the tune does not die with the instrument, but survives its destruction and continues to exist apart. In fact, those moderns who dispute the evidences of the immortality of the soul, do not, in general, believe the soul to be a substance *per se*, but regard it as the name of a bundle of attributes, the attributes of feeling, thinking, reasoning, believing, willing, and these attributes they regard as a consequence of the bodily organization, which therefore, they argue, it is as unreasonable to suppose surviving when that organization is dispersed, as to suppose the colour or odour of a rose surviving when the rose itself has perished. Those, therefore, who would deduce the immortality of the soul from its own nature have first to prove that the attributes in question are not attributes of the body but of a separate substance. Now what is the verdict of science on this point? It is not perfectly conclusive either way. In the first place, it does not prove, experimentally, that any mode of organization has the power of producing feeling or thought. To make that proof good it would be necessary that we should be able to produce an organism, and try whether it would feel; which we cannot do; organisms cannot by any human means be produced, they can only be developed out of a previous organism. On the other hand, the evidence is well nigh complete that all thought and feeling has some action of the bodily organism for its immediate antecedent or accompaniment; that the specific variations and especially the different degrees of complication of the nervous and cerebral organization, correspond to differences in the development of the mental faculties; and though we have no evidence, except negative, that the mental consciousness ceases for ever when the functions of the brain are at an end, we do know that diseases of the brain disturb the mental functions and that decay or weakness of the brain enfeebles them. We have therefore sufficient evidence that cerebral action is, if not the cause, at least, in our present state of existence, a condition *sine qua non* of mental operations; and that assuming the mind to be a distinct substance, its separation from the body would not be, as some have vainly flattered themselves, a liberation from trammels and restoration to freedom, but would simply put a stop to its functions and remand it to unconsciousness, unless and until some other set of conditions supervenes, capable of recalling it into activity, but of the existence of which experience does not give us the smallest indication...

The belief, however, in human immortality, in the minds of mankind generally, is probably not grounded on any scientific arguments either physical or metaphysical, but on foundations with most minds much stronger, namely on one hand the disagreeableness of giving up existence, (to those at least to whom it has hitherto been pleasant) and on the other the general traditions of mankind. The natural tendency of belief to follow these two inducements, our own wishes and the general assent of other people, has been in this instance reinforced by the utmost exertion of the power of public and private teaching rulers and instructors having at all times, with the view of giving greater effect to their mandates whether from selfish or from public motives, encouraged to the utmost of their power the belief that there is a life after death, in which pleasures and sufferings far greater than on earth, depend on our doing or leaving undone while alive, what we are commanded to do in the name of the unseen powers. As causes of belief these various circumstances are most powerful. As rational grounds of it they carry no weight at all.

That what is called the consoling nature of an opinion, that is, the pleasure we should have in believing it to be true, can be a ground for believing it, is a doctrine irrational in itself and which would sanction half the mischievous illusions recorded in history or which mislead individual life. It is sometimes, in the case now under consideration, wrapped up in a quasi-scientific language. We are told that the desire of immortality is one of our instincts, and that there is no instinct which has not corresponding to it a real object fitted to satisfy it. Where there is hunger there is somewhere food, where there is sexual feeling there is somewhere sex, where there is love there is somewhere something to be loved, and so forth: in like manner since there is the instinctive desire of eternal life, eternal life there must be. The answer to this is patent on the very surface of the subject. It is unnecessary to go into any recondite considerations concerning instincts, or to discuss whether the desire in question is an instinct or not. Granting that wherever there is an instinct there exists something such as that instinct demands, can it be affirmed that this something exists in boundless quantity, or sufficient to satisfy the infinite craving of human desires? What is called the desire of eternal life is simply the desire of life; and does there not exist that which this desire calls for? Is there not life? And is not the instinct, if it be an instinct, gratified by the possession and preservation of life? To suppose that the desire of life guarantees to us personally the reality of life through all eternity, is like supposing that the desire of food assures us that we shall always have as much as we can eat through our whole lives and as much longer as we can conceive our lives to be protracted to.

The argument from tradition or the general belief of the human race, if we accept it as a guide to our own belief, must be accepted entire: if so we are bound to believe that the souls of human beings not only survive after death but show themselves as ghosts to the living for we find no people who have had the one belief without the other. Indeed it is probable that the former belief originated in the latter, and that primitive men would never have supposed that the soul did not die with the body if they had not fancied that it visited them after death. Nothing could be more natural than such a fancy; it is, in appearance, completely realized in dreams, which in Homer and in all ages like Homer's, are supposed to be real apparitions. To dreams we have to add not merely waking hallucinations but the delusions, however baseless, of sight and hearing, or rather the misinterpretations of those senses, sight or hearing supplying mere hints from which imagination paints a complete picture and invests it with reality. These delusions are not to be judged of by a modern standard: in early times the line between imagination and perception was by no means dearly defined; there was little or none of the knowledge we now possess of the actual course of nature, which makes us distrust or disbelieve any appearance which is at variance with known laws. In the ignorance of men as to what were the limits of nature and what was or was not compatible with it, no one thing seemed, as far as physical considerations went, to be much more improbable than another. In rejecting, therefore, as we do, and as we have the best reason to do, the tales and legends of the actual appearance of disembodied spirits, we take from under the general belief of mankind in a life after death, what in all probability was its chief ground and support, and deprive it of even the very little value which the opinion of rude ages can ever have as evidence of truth. If it be said that this belief has maintained itself in ages which have ceased to be rude and which reject the superstitions with which it once was accompanied, the same may be said of many other opinions of rude ages, and especially on the most important and interesting subjects, because it is on those subjects that the reigning opinion, whatever it may be, is the most sedulously inculcated upon all who are born into the world. This particular opinion, moreover, if it has on the whole kept its ground, has done so with a constantly increasing number of dissentients, and those especially among cultivated minds. Finally, those cultivated minds which adhere to the belief ground it, we may reasonably suppose, not on the belief of others, but on arguments and evidences; and those arguments and evidences, therefore, are what it concerns us to estimate and judge.

The preceding are a sufficient sample of the arguments for a future life which do not suppose an antecedent belief in the existence, or any theory respecting the attributes of the Godhead. It remains to consider what arguments are supplied by such lights, or such grounds of conjecture, as natural theology affords, on those great questions.

We have seen that these lights are but faint; that of the existence of a Creator they afford no more than a preponderance of probability; of his benevolence a considerably less preponderance; that there is, however, some reason to think that he cares for the pleasures of his creatures, but by no means that this is his sole care, or that other purposes do not often take precedence of it. His intelligence must be adequate to the contrivances apparent in the universe, but need not be more than adequate to them, and his power is not only not proved to be infinite, but the only real evidences in natural theology tend to show that it is limited, contrivance being a mode of overcoming difficulties, and always supposing difficulties to be overcome.

We have now to consider what inference can legitimately be drawn from these premises, in favor of a future life. It seems to me, apart from express revelation, none at all.

The common arguments are, the goodness of God; the improbability that he would ordain the annihilation of his noblest and richest work, after the greater part of its few years of life had been spent in the acquisition of faculties which time is not allowed him to turn to fruit; and the special improbability that he would have implanted in us an instinctive desire of eternal life, and doomed that desire to complete disappointment.

These might be arguments in a world the constitution of which made it possible without contradiction to hold it for the work of a Being at once omnipotent and benevolent. But they are not arguments in a world like that in which we live. The benevolence of the divine Being may be perfect, but his power being subject to unknown limitations, we know not that he could have given us what we so confidently assert that he must have given; *could* (that is) without sacrificing something more important. Even his benevolence, however justly inferred, is by no means indicated as the interpretation of his whole purpose, and since we cannot tell how far other purposes may have interfered with the exercise of his benevolence, we know not that he *would,* even if he could have granted us eternal life. With regard to the supposed improbability of his having given the wish without its gratification, the same answer may be made; the scheme which either limitation of power, or conflict of purposes, compelled him to adopt, may have *required* that we should have the wish although it were not destined to be gratified. One thing, however, is quite certain in respect to God's government of the world; that he either could not, or would not, grant to us every thing we wish. We wish for life, and he has granted some life: that we wish (or some of us wish) for a boundless extent of life and that it is not granted, is no exception to the ordinary modes of his government. Many a man would like to be a Croesus or an Augustus Caesar, but has his wishes gratified only to the moderate extent of a pound a week or the Secretaryship of his Trades Union. There is, therefore, no assurance whatever of a life after death, on grounds of natural religion.

Note
1. From John Stuart Mill (1806-1873), *Three Essays on Religion: Nature, The Utility of Religion, and Theism* (1874), pp. 196-99, 203-10.

8
Evangelical Teaching (1855)
George Eliot

Given, a man with moderate intellect, a moral standard not higher than the average, some rhetorical affluence and great glibness of speech, what is the career in which, without the aid of birth or money, he may most easily attain power and reputation in English society? Where is that Goshen of mediocrity in which a smattering of science and learning will pass for profound instruction, where platitudes will be accepted as wisdom, bigoted narrowness as holy zeal, unctuous egoism as God-given piety? Let such a man become an evangelical preacher; he will then find it possible to reconcile small ability with great ambition, superficial knowledge with the prestige of erudition, a middling morale with a high reputation for sanctity. Let him shun practical extremes and be ultra only in what is purely theoretic: let him be stringent on predestination, but latitudinarian on fasting unflinching in insisting on the eternity of punishment, but diffident of curtailing the substantial comforts of time; ardent and imaginative on the pre- millennial advent of Christ, but cold and cautious towards every other infringement of the *status quo*. Let him fish for souls not with the bait of inconvenient singularity, but with the drag-net of comfortable conformity. Let him be hard and literal in his interpretation only when he wants to hurl texts at the heads of unbelievers and adversaries, but when the letter of the Scriptures presses too closely on the genteel Christianity of the nineteenth century, let him use his spiritualizing alembic and disperse it into impalpable ether. Let him preach less of Christ than of Antichrist; let him be less definite in showing what sin is than in showing who is the Man of Sin, less expansive on the blessedness of faith than on the accursedness of infidelity. Above all, let him set up as an interpreter of prophecy, and rival Moore's Almanack in the prediction of political events, tickling the interest of hearers who are but moderately spiritual by showing how the Holy Spirit has dictated problems and charades for their benefit, and how, if they are ingenious enough to solve these, they may have their Christian graces nourished by learning precisely to whom they may point as the "horn that had eyes," "the lying prophet," and the "unclean spirits." In this way he will draw men to him by the strong cords of their passions, made reason-proof by being baptized with the name of piety. In this way he may gain a metropolitan pulpit; the avenues to his church will be as crowded as the passages to the opera; he has but to print his prophetic sermons and having taken a horse's tail for his standard, and that the French are the very frogs predicted in the Revelation.

Pleasant to the clerical flesh under such circumstances is the arrival of Sunday! Somewhat at a disadvantage during the week, in the presence of working-day interests and lay splendours, on Sunday the preacher becomes the cynosure of a thousand eyes, and predominates at once over the Amphitryon with whom he dines, and the most captious member of his church or vestry. He has an immense advantage over all other public speakers. The platform orator is subject to the criticism of hisses and groans. Counsel for the plaintiff expects the retort of counsel for the defendant. The honorable gentleman on one side of the House is liable to have his facts and figures shown up by his honourable friend on the opposite side. Even the scientific or literary lecturer, if he is dull or incompetent, may see the best part of his audience slip quietly out one by one. But the preacher is completely master of the situation: no one may hiss, no one may depart. Like the writer of imaginary conversations, he may put what imbecilities he pleases into the mouths of his antagonists, and swell with triumph when he has refuted them. He may riot in gratuitous assertions, confident that no man will contradict him; he may exercise perfect free-will in logic, and invent illustrative experience; he may give an evangelical edition of history with the inconvenient facts omitted; all this he may do with impunity, certain that those of his hearers who are not sympathizing are not listening. For the Press has no band of critics who go the round of the churches and chapels, and are on the watch for a slip or defect in the preacher, to make a "feature" in their article: the clergy are practically, the most irresponsible of all talkers. For this reason, at least, it is well that they do not always allow their discourses to be merely fugitive, but are often induced to *fix* them in that black and white in which they are open to the criticism of any man who has the courage and patience to treat them with thorough freedom of speech and pen.

It is because we think this criticism of clerical teaching desirable for the public good that we devote some pages to Dr. John Cumming (1807-1881). He is, as every one knows, a preacher of immense popularity, and of the numerous publications in which he perpetuates his pulpit labours, all circulate widely, and some, according to their title- page, have reached the sixteenth thousand. Now our opinion of these publications is the very opposite of that given by a newspaper eulogist: we do *not* "believe that the repeated issues of Dr. Cumming's thoughts are having a beneficial effect on society," but the reverse; and hence, little inclined as we are to dwell on his pages, we think it worth while to do so, for the sake of pointing out in them what we believe to be profoundly mistaken and pernicious. Of Dr. Cumming personally we know absolutely nothing: our acquaintance with him is confined to a perusal of his works; our judgement of him is founded solely on the manner in which he has written himself down on his pages. We know neither how he looks nor how he lives. We are ignorant whether, like Saint Paul, he has a bodily presence that is weak and contemptible, or whether his person is as florid and as prone to amplification as his style. For aught we know, he may not only have the gift of prophecy but may bestow the profits of all his works to feed the poor, and be ready to give his own body to be burned with as much alacrity as he infers the everlasting burning of Roman Catholics and Puseyites. Out of the pulpit he may be a model of justice, truthfulness, and the love that thinketh no evil; but we are obliged to judge of his charity by the spirit we find in his sermons, and shall only be glad to learn that his practice is, in many respects, an amiable *non sequitur* from his teaching. …

One of the most striking characteristics of Dr. Cumming's writings is *unscrupulosity of statement*. His motto apparently is, *Christianitatem, quocunque modo, Christianitatem*; and the only system he includes under the term Christianity is Calvinistic Protestantism. Experience has so long shown that the human brain is a congenial nidus for inconsistent beliefs that we do not pause to inquire how Dr. Cumming, who attributes the conversion of the unbelieving to the Divine Spirit, can think it necessary to co-operate with that Spirit by argumentative white lies. Nor do we for a moment impugn the genuineness of his zeal for Christianity, or the sincerity of his conviction that the doctrines he preaches are necessary to salvation; on the contrary, we regard the flagrant unveracity found on his pages as an indirect result of that conviction—as a result, namely, of the intellectual and moral distortion of view which is inevitably produced by assigning to dogmas, based on a very complex structure of evidence, the place and authority of first truths. A distinct appreciation of the value of evidence—in other words, the intellectual perception of truth is more closely allied to truthfulness of statement, or the moral quality of veracity, than is generally admitted. That highest moral habit, the constant preference of truth, both theoretically and practically, pre-eminently demands the co-operation of the intellect with the impulses—as is indicated by the fact that it is only found in anything like completeness in the highest class of minds. And it is commonly seen that, in proportion as religious sects believe themselves to be guided by direct inspiration rather than by a spontaneous exertion of their faculties, their sense of truthfulness is misty and confused. No one can have talked to the more enthusiastic Methodists and listened to their stories of miracles without perceiving that they require no other passport to a statement than that it accords with their wishes and their general conception of God's dealings; nay, they regard as a symptom of sinful scepticism an inquiry into the evidence for a story which they think unquestionably tends to the glory of God, and in retailing such stories, new particulars, further tending to His glory, are "borne in" upon their minds. Now, Dr. Cumming, as we have said, is no enthusiastic pietist: within a certain circle within the mill of evangelical orthodoxy—his intellect is perpetually at work; but that principle of sophistication which our friends the Methodists derive from the predominance of their pietistic feelings is involved for him in the doctrine of verbal inspiration; what is for them a state of emotion submerging the intellect is with him a formula imprisoning the intellect, depriving it of its proper function the free search for truth and making it the mere servant-of-all-work to a foregone conclusion. Minds fettered by this doctrine no longer inquire concerning a proposition whether it is attested by sufficient evidence, but whether it accords with Scripture; they do not search for facts, as such, but for facts that will bear out their doctrine. They become accustomed to reject the more direct evidence in favour of the less direct, and where adverse evidence reaches demonstration they must resort to devices and expedients in order to explain away contradiction. It is easy to see that this mental habit blunts not only the perception of truth, but the sense of truthfulness, and that the man whose faith drives him into fallacies treads close upon the precipice of falsehood.

We have entered into this digression for the sake of mitigating the inference that is likely to be drawn from that characteristic of Dr. Cumming's works to which we have pointed. He is much in the same intellectual condition as that professor of Padua, who, in order to disprove Galileo's discovery of Jupiter's satellites, urged that as there were only seven metals there could not be more than seven planets—a mental condition scarcely compatible with candour. And we may well suppose that if the professor had held the belief in seven planets, and no more, to be a necessary condition of salvation, his mental vision would have been so dazed that even if he had consented to look through Galileo's telescope, his eyes would have reported in accordance with his inward alarms rather than with the external fact. So long as a belief in propositions is regarded as indispensable to salvation, the pursuit of truth *as such* is not possible, any more than it is possible for a man who is swimming for his life to make meteorological observations on the storm which threatens to overwhelm him. The sense of alarm and haste, the anxiety for personal safety, which Dr. Cumming insists upon as the proper religious attitude, unmans the nature, and allows no thorough, calm thinking, no truly noble, disinterested feeling. Hence, we by no means suspect that the unscrupulosity of statement with which we charge Dr. Cumming extends beyond the sphere of his theological prejudices: religion apart, he probably appreciates and practices veracity. ...

In marshalling the evidences of Christianity Dr. Cumming directs most of his arguments against opinions that are either totally imaginary, or that belong to the past rather than to the present; while he entirely fails to meet the difficulties actually felt and urged by those who are unable to accept Revelation. There can hardly be a stronger proof of misconception as to the character of free-thinking in the present day than the recommendation of *Leland's Short and Easy Method with the Deists*[4]—a method which is unquestionably short and easy for preachers disinclined to consider their stereotyped modes of thinking and arguing, but which has quite ceased to realize those epithets in the conversion of Deists. Yet Dr. Cumming not only recommends this book, but takes the trouble himself to write a feebler version of its arguments. For example, on the question of the genuineness and authenticity of the New Testament writings, he says:

> If, therefore, at a period long subsequent to the death of Christ, a number of men had appeared in the world, drawn up a book which they christened by the name of Holy Scripture, and recorded these things which appear in it as facts when they were only the fancies of their own imagination, surely the *Jews* would have instantly reclaimed that no such events transpired, that no such person as Jesus Christ appeared in their capital, and that *their* crucifixion of Him, and their alleged evil treatment of His apostles, were mere fictions.[1]

It is scarcely necessary to say that, in such argument as this, Dr. Cumming is beating the air. He is meeting a hypothesis which no one holds, and totally missing the real question. The only type of "infidel" whose existence Dr. Cumming recognizes is that fossil personage who "calls the Bible a lie and a forgery." He seems to be ignorant—or he chooses to ignore the fact—that there is a large body of eminently instructed and earnest men who regard the Hebrew and Christian Scriptures as a series of historical documents, to be dealt with according to the rules of historical criticism; and that an equally large number of men, who are not historical critics, find the dogmatic scheme built on the letter of the Scriptures opposed to their profoundest moral convictions. Dr. Cumming's infidel is a man who, because his life is vicious, tries to convince himself that there is no God, and that Christianity is an imposture, but who is all the while secretly conscious that he is opposing the truth, and cannot help "letting out" admissions "that the Bible is the Book of God." We are favoured with the following "Creed of the Infidel":

> I believe that there is no God, but that matter is God, and God is matter; and that it is no matter whether there is any God or not. I believe also that the world was not made, but that the world made itself, or that it had no beginning, and that it will last for ever. I believe that man is a beast; that the soul is the body, and that the body is the soul; and that after death there is neither body nor soul. I believe that there is no religion, that *natural religion is the only religion, and all religion unnatural.* I believe not in Moses; I believe in the first philosophers. I believe not in the evangelists; I believe in Chubb, Collins, Toland, Tindal, and Hobbes. I believe in Lord Bolingbroke, and I believe not in Saint Paul. I believe not in revelation; *I believe in tradition; I believe in the Talmud; I believe in the Koran;* I believe not in the Bible. I believe in Socrates; I believe in Confucius; I believe in Mahomet; I believe not in Christ. And lastly, *I believe* in all unbelief.

The intellectual and moral monster whose creed is this complex web of contradictions is, moreover, according to Dr. Cumming, a being who unites much simplicity and imbecility with his Satanic hardihood, much tenderness of conscience with his obdurate vice. Hear the "proof":

> I once met with an acute and enlightened infidel, with whom I reasoned day after day, and for hours together; I submitted to him the internal, the external, and the experimental evidences, but made no impression on his scorn and unbelief. At length I entertained a suspicion that there was something morally, rather than intellectually wrong, and that the bias was not in the intellect, but in the heart; one day therefore I said to him—'I must now state my conviction, and you may call me uncharitable, but duty compels me: you are living in some known and gross sin: *The man's countenance became pale; he bowed and left me.*[2]

Here we have the remarkable psychological phenomenon of an "acute and enlightened" man who, deliberately purposing to indulge in a favourite sin, and regarding the Gospel with scorn and unbelief, is nevertheless so much more scrupulous than the majority of Christians that he cannot "embrace sin and the Gospel simultaneously"; who is so alarmed at the Gospel in which he does not believe that he cannot be easy without trying to crush it; whose acuteness and enlightenment suggest to him, as a means of crushing the Gospel, to argue from day to day with Dr. Cumming and who is withal so naive that he is taken by surprise when Dr. Cumming, failing in argument, resorts to accusation, and so tender in conscience that, at the mention of his sin, he turns pale and leaves the spot. If there be any human mind in existence capable of holding Dr. Cumming's "Creed of the Infidel," of at the same time believing in tradition and "believing in all unbelief," it must be the mind of the infidel just described, for whose existence we have Dr. Cumming's *ex officio* word as a theologian; and to theologians we may apply what Sancho Panza says of the bachelors of Salamanca, that they never tell lies except when it suits their purpose.

The total absence from Dr. Cumming's theological mind of any demarcation between fact and rhetoric is exhibited in another passage, where he adopts the dramatic form:

> Ask the peasant on the hills—and *I have asked amid the mountains of Braemar and Deeside*—'How do you know that this book is divine, and that the religion you profess is true? You never read Paley?' 'No, I never heard of him! 'You have never read Butler?' 'No, I have never heard of him! 'Nor Chalmers?' 'No, I do not know him! 'You have never read any books on evidence?' 'No, I have read no such books! Then, how do you know this book is true?' 'Know it! Tell me that the Dee, the Clunie, and the Garrawalt, the streams at my feet, do not run; that the winds do not sigh amid the gorges of these blue hills; that the sun does not kindle the peaks of Loch-na-Gar,—tell me my heart does not beat, and I will believe you; but do not tell me the Bible is not divine. I have found its truth illuminating my footsteps; its consolations sustaining my heart. May my tongue cleave to my mouth's roof, and my right hand forget its cunning, if I ever deny what is my deepest inner experience, that this blessed book is the Book of God.[3]

Dr. Cumming is so slippery and lax in his mode of presentation that we find it impossible to gather whether he means to assert that this is what a peasant on the mountains of Braemar *did* say, or that it is what such a peasant *would* say: in the one case, the passage may be taken as a measure of his truthfulness; in the other, of his judgement.

His own faith, apparently, has not been altogether intuitive, like that of his rhetorical peasant, for he tells us that he has himself experienced what it is to have religious doubts. "I was tainted while at the University by this spirit of scepticism. I thought Christianity might not be true. The very possibility of its being true was the thought I felt I must meet and settle. Conscience could give me no peace till I had settled it. I read, and I have read from that day, for fourteen or fifteen years, till this, and now I am as convinced, upon the dearest evidence, that this book is the Book of God, as that I now address you." This experience, however, instead of impressing on him the fact that doubt may be the stamp of a truth-loving mind—that *sunt quibus non credidisse honor est, et fidei futurae pignus*—seems to have produced precisely the contrary effect. It has not enabled him even to conceive the condition of a mind "perplext in faith but pure in deed," craving light, yearning for a faith that will harmonize and cherish its highest powers and aspirations, but unable to find that faith in dogmatic Christianity. His own doubts apparently were of a different kind. Nowhere in his pages have we found a humble, candid, sympathetic attempt to meet the difficulties that may be felt by an ingenuous mind. Everywhere he supposes that the doubter is hardened, conceited, consciously shutting his eyes to the light—a fool who is to be answered according to his folly—that is, with ready replies made up of reckless assertions, of apocryphal anecdotes, and, where other resources fail, of vituperative imputations. As to the reading which he has prosecuted for fifteen *years either* it has left him totally ignorant of the relation which his own religious creed bears to the criticism and philosophy of the nineteenth century, *or* he systematically blinks that criticism and that philosophy; and instead of honestly and seriously endeavouring to meet and solve what he knows to be the real difficulties, contents himself with setting up popinjays to shoot at, for the sake of confirming the ignorance and winning the cheap admiration of his evangelical hearers and readers. Like the Catholic preacher who, after throwing down his cap and apostrophizing it as Luther, turned to his audience and said, "You see this heretical fellow has not a word to say for himself," Dr. Cumming, having drawn his ugly portrait of the infidel, and put arguments of a convenient quality into his mouth, finds a "short and easy method" of confounding this "croaking frog."

In his treatment of infidels, we imagine he is guided by a mental process which may be expressed in the following syllogism: Whatever tends to the glory of God is true; it is for the glory of God that infidels should be as bad as possible; therefore, whatever tends to show that infidels are as bad as possible is true. All infidels, he tells us, have been men of "gross and licentious lives." Is there not some well-known unbeliever—David Hume, for example—of whom even Dr. Cumming's readers may have heard as an exception? No matter. Some one suspected that he was *not* an exception; and as that suspicion tends to the glory of God, it is one for a Christian to entertain.[4] If we were unable to imagine this kind of self-sophistication, we should be obliged to suppose that, relying on the ignorance of his evangelical disciples, he fed them with direct and conscious falsehoods. "Voltaire," he informs them, "declares there is no God"; he was "an antitheist—that is, one who deliberately and avowedly opposed and hated God; who swore in his blasphemy that he would dethrone Him"; and "advocated the very depths of the lowest sensuality." With regard to many statements of a similar kind, equally at variance with truth, in Dr. Cumming's volumes, we presume that he has been misled by hearsay or by the second-hand character of his acquaintance with free-thinking literature. An evangelical preacher is not obliged to be well read. Here, however, is a case which the extremist supposition of educated ignorance will not reach. Even books of "evidences" quote from Voltaire the line,

> Si Dieu n'existait pas, il faudrait l'inventer.

Even persons fed on the mere whey and buttermilk of literature must know that in philosophy Voltaire was nothing if not a theist—must know that he wrote not against God, but against Jehovah, the God of the Jews, whom he believed to be a false God—must know that to say Voltaire was an atheist on this ground is as absurd as to say that a Jacobite opposed hereditary monarchy because he declared the Brunswick family had no title to the throne. That Dr. Cumming should repeat the vulgar fables about Voltaire's death is merely what we might expect from the specimens we have seen of his illustrative stories. A man whose accounts of his own experience are apocryphal is not likely to put borrowed narratives to any severe test.

The alliance between intellectual and moral perversion is strikingly typified by the way in which he alternates from the unveracious to the absurd, from misrepresentation to contradiction. Side by side with the adduction of "facts" such as those we have quoted, we find him arguing on one page that the doctrine of the Trinity was too grand to have been conceived by man, and was *therefore* Divine; and on another page, that the Incarnation *had* been preconceived by man, and is *therefore* to be accepted as Divine. But we are less concerned with the fallacy of his "ready replies" than with their falsity; and even of this we can only afford space for a very few specimens. Here is one: "There is a *thousand times* more proof that the Gospel of John was written by him than there is that the 'Anabasis' was written by Xenophon, or the 'Ars Poetica' by Horace." If Dr. Cumming had chosen Plato's Epistles or Anacreon's Poems, instead of the "Anabasis" or the "Ars Poetica," he would have reduced the extent of the falsehood, and would have furnished a ready reply, which would have been equally effective with his Sunday-school teachers and their disputants. Hence we conclude this prodigality of misstatement, this exuberance of mendacity, is an effervescence of zeal *in majorem gloriam Dei.* Elsewhere he tells us that "the idea of the author of the 'Vestiges' is that man is the development of a monkey, that the monkey is the embryo man; so that *if you keep a baboon long enough, it will develop itself into a* man."[5] How well Dr. Cumming has qualified himself to judge of the ideas in "that very unphilosophical book," as he pronounces it, may be inferred from the fact that he implies the author of the "Vestiges" to have *originated* the nebular hypothesis.

In the volume from which the last extract is taken, even the hardihood of assertion is surpassed by the suicidal character of the argument. It is called *The Church before the Flood*, and is devoted chiefly to the adjustment of the question between the Bible and Geology. Keeping within the limits we have prescribed to ourselves, we do not enter into the matter of this discussion; we merely pause a little over the volume in order to point out Dr. Cumming's mode of treating the question. He first tells us that "the Bible has not a single scientific error in it"; that "*its slightest intimations of scientific principles or natural phenomena have in every instance been demonstrated to be exactly and strictly true*"; and he asks:

> How is it that Moses, with no greater education than the Hindoo or the ancient philosopher, has written his book, touching science at a thousand points, so accurately that scientific research has discovered no flaws in it; and yet in those investigations which have taken place in more recent centuries, it has not been shown that he has committed one single error, or made one solitary assertion which can be proved by the maturest science, or by the most eagle-eyed philosopher, to be incorrect, scientifically or historically?

According to this, the relation of the Bible to science should be one of the strong points of apologists for revelation: the scientific accuracy of Moses should stand at the head of their evidences; and they might urge with some cogency that, since Aristotle, who devoted himself to science, and lived many ages after Moses, does little else than err ingeniously, this fact, that the Jewish lawgiver, though touching science at a thousand points, has written nothing that has not been "demonstrated to be exactly and strictly true," is an irrefragable proof of his having derived his knowledge from a supernatural source. How does it happen, then, that Dr. Cumming forsakes this strong position? How is it that we find him, some pages further on, engaged in reconciling Genesis with the discoveries of science, by means of imaginative hypotheses and feats of "interpretation"? Surely that which has been demonstrated to be exactly and strictly true does not require hypothesis and critical argument, in order to show that it may *possibly* agree with those very discoveries by means of which its exact and strict truth has been demonstrated. And why should Dr. Cumming suppose, as we shall presently find him supposing, that men of science hesitate to accept the Bible because it appears to contradict their discoveries? By his own statement, that appearance of contradiction does not exist; on the contrary, it has been demonstrated that the Bible precisely agrees with their discoveries. Perhaps, however, in saying of the Bible that its "slightest intimations of scientific principles or natural phenomena have in every instance been demonstrated to be exactly and strictly true," Dr. Cumming merely means to imply that theologians have found out a way of explaining the Biblical text so that it no longer, in their opinion, appears to be in contradiction with the discoveries of science. One of two things, therefore: either, he uses language without the slightest appreciation of its real meaning; or, the assertions he makes on one page are directly contradicted by the arguments he urges on another.

Dr. Cumming's principles—or, we should rather say, confused notions—of Biblical interpretation, as exhibited in this volume, are particularly significant of his mental calibre. He says[6]:

> Men of science, who are full of scientific investigation, and enamoured of scientific discovery, will hesitate before they accept a book which, they think, contradicts the plainest and the most unequivocal disclosures they have made in the bowels of the earth, or among the stars of the sky. To all these we answer, as we have already indicated, there is not the least dissonance between God's written book and the most mature discoveries of geological science. One thing, however, there may be: *there may be a contradiction between the discoveries of geology and our preconceived interpretations of the Bible.* But this is not because the Bible is wrong, but because our interpretation is wrong. (The italics in all cases are our own.)

Elsewhere he says:

> It seems to me plainly evident that the record of Genesis, when read fairly, and not in the light of our prejudices, and *mind you, the essence of Popery is to read the Bible in the light of our opinions, instead of viewing our opinions in the light of the Bible, in its plain and obvious sense,*— falls in perfectly with the assertion of geologists.

On comparing these two passages, we gather that when Dr. Cumming, under stress of geological discovery, assigns to the Biblical text a meaning entirely different from that which, on his own showing, was universally ascribed to it for more than three thousand years, he regards himself as "viewing his opinions in the light of the Bible in its plain and obvious sense"! Now he is reduced to one of two alternatives: either, he must hold that the "plain and obvious meaning" lies in the sum of knowledge possessed by each successive age the Bible being an elastic garment for the growing thought of mankind; or, he must hold that some portions are amenable to this criterion, and others not so. In the former case, he accepts the principle of interpretation adopted by the early German rationalists; in the latter case, he has to show a further criterion by which we can judge what parts of the Bible are elastic and what rigid. If he says that the interpretation of the text is rigid wherever it treats of doctrines necessary to salvation, we answer, that for doctrines to be necessary to salvation they must first be true; and in order to be true, according to his own principle, they must be founded on a correct interpretation of the Biblical text. Thus he makes the necessity of doctrines to salvation the criterion of infallible interpretation, and infallible interpretation the criterion of doctrines being necessary to salvation. He is whirled round in a circle, having, by admitting the principle of novelty in interpretation, completely deprived himself of a basis. That he should seize the very moment in which he is most palpably betraying that he has no test of Biblical truth beyond his own opinion, as an appropriate occasion for flinging the rather novel reproach against Popery that its essence is to "read the Bible in the light of our opinions," would be an almost pathetic self-exposure, if it were not disgusting. Imbecility that is not even meek, ceases to be pitiable, and becomes simply odious.

Parenthetic lashes of this kind against Popery are very frequent with Dr. Cumming, and occur even in his more devout passages, where their introduction must surely disturb the spiritual exercises of his hearers. Indeed, Roman Catholics fare worse with him even than infidels. Infidels are the small vermin the mice to be bagged *en passant.* The main object of his chase the rats which are to be nailed up as trophies—are the Roman Catholics. Romanism is the masterpiece of Satan. But reassure yourselves! Dr. Cumming has been created. Antichrist is enthroned in the Vatican; but he is stoutly withstood by the Boanerges of Crown Court. The personality of Satan, as might be expected, is a very prominent tenet in Dr. Cumming's discourses; those who doubt it are, he thinks, "generally specimens of the victims of Satan as a triumphant seducer"; and it is through the medium of this doctrine that he habitually contemplates Roman Catholics. They are the puppets of which the Devil holds the strings. It is only exceptionally that he speaks of them as fellow men, acted on by the same desires, fears, and hopes as himself; his rule is to hold them up to his hearers as foredoomed instruments of Satan, and vessels of wrath. If he is obliged to admit that they are "no shams," that they are "thoroughly in earnest" that is because they are inspired by hell, because they are under an "infranatural" influence. If their missionaries are found wherever Protestant missionaries go, this zeal in propagating their faith is not in them a consistent virtue, as it is in Protestants, but a "melancholy fact," affording additional evidence that they are instigated and assisted by the Devil. And Dr. Cumming is inclined to think that they work miracles, because that is no more than might be expected from the known ability of Satan who inspires them.[7] He admits, indeed, that "there is a fragment of the Church of Christ in the very bosom of that awful apostasy,"[8] and that there are members of the Church of Rome in glory; but this admission is rare and episodical—is a declaration, pro forma, about as influential on the general disposition and habits as an aristocrat's profession of democracy.

This leads us to mention another conspicuous characteristic of Dr. Cumming's teaching—the *absence of genuine charity*. It is true that he makes large profession of tolerance and liberality within a certain circle; he exhorts Christians to Unity; he would have Churchmen fraternize with Dissenters, and exhorts these two branches of God's family to defer the settlement of their differences till the millennium. But the love thus taught is the love of the *clan,* which is the correlative of antagonism to the rest of mankind. It is not sympathy and helpfulness towards men as men, but towards men as Christians, and as Christians in the sense of a small minority. Dr. Cumming's religion may demand a tribute of love, but it gives a charter to hatred; it may enjoin charity, but it fosters all uncharitableness. If I believe that God tells me to love my enemies, but at the same time hates His own enemies and requires me to have one will with Him, which has the larger scope, love or hatred? And we refer to those pages of Dr. Cumming's in which he opposes Roman Catholics, Puseyites, and infidels—pages which form the larger proportion of what he has published—for proof that the idea of God which both the logic and spirit of his discourses keep present to his hearers is that of a God who hates His enemies, a God who teaches love by fierce denunciations of wrath—a God who encourages obedience to His precepts by elaborately revealing to us that His own government is in precise opposition to those precepts. We know the usual evasions on this subject. We know Dr. Cumming would say that even Roman Catholics are to be loved and succored as men; that he would help even that "unclean spirit," Cardinal Wiseman, out of a ditch. But who that is in the slightest degree acquainted with the action of the human mind will believe that any genuine and large charity can grow out of an exercise of love which is always to have an *arrière-pensée* of hatred? Of what quality would be the conjugal love of a husband who loved his spouse as a wife, but hated her as a woman? It is reserved for the regenerate mind, according to Dr. Cumming's conception of it, to be "wise, amazed, temperate and furious, loyal and neutral, in a moment." Precepts of charity uttered with faint breath at the end of a sermon are perfectly futile, when all the force of the lungs has been spent in keeping the hearer's mind fixed on the conception of his fellow men, not as fellow sinners and fellow sufferers, but as agents of hell, as automata through whom Satan plays his game upon earth, not on objects which call forth their reverence, their love, their hope of good even in the most strayed and perverted, but on a minute identification of human things with such symbols as the scarlet whore, the beast out of the abyss, scorpions whose sting is in their tails, men who have the mark of the beast, and unclean spirits like frogs. You might as well attempt to educate a child's sense of beauty by hanging its nursery with the horrible and grotesque pictures in which the early painters represented the Last Judgement, as expect Christian graces to flourish on that prophetic interpretation which Dr. Cumming offers as the principal nutriment of his flock. Quite apart from the critical basis of that interpretation, quite apart from the degree of truth there may be in Dr. Cumming's prognostications—questions into which we do not choose to enter—his use of prophecy must be *a priori* condemned, in the judgement of right-minded persons, by its results as testified in the net moral effect of his sermons. The best minds that accept Christianity as a divinely inspired system believe that the great end of the Gospel is not merely the saving but the educating of men's souls, the creating within them of holy dispositions, the subduing of egoistical pretensions, and the perpetual enhancing of the desire that the will of God—a will synonymous with goodness and truth may be done on earth. But what relation to all this has a system of interpretation which keeps the mind of the Christian in the position of a spectator at a gladiatorial show, of which Satan is the wild beast in the shape of the great red dragon, the two thirds of mankind the victims the whole provided and got up by God for the edification of the saints? The demonstration that the Second Advent is at hand, if true, can have no really holy, spiritual effect; the highest state of mind inculcated by the Gospel is resignation to the disposal of God's providence—"Whether we live, we live unto the Lord; whether we die, we die unto the Lord" not an eagerness to see a temporal manifestation which shall confound the enemies of God and give exaltation to the saints; it is to dwell in Christ by spiritual communion with His nature, not to fix the date when He shall appear in the sky. Dr. Cumming's delight in shadowing forth the downfall of the Man of Sin, in prognosticating the battle of Gog and Magog, and in advertising the premillennial Advent, is simply the transportation of political passions on to a so-called religious platform; it is the anticipation of the triumph of "our party," accomplished by our principal men being "sent for" into the clouds. Let us be understood to speak in all seriousness. If we were in search of amusement, we should not seek for it by examining Dr. Cumming's works in order to ridicule them. We are simply discharging a disagreeable duty in delivering our opinion that, judged by the highest standard even of orthodox Christianity, they are little calculated to produce

A closer walk with God, A calm and heavenly frame.[9]

but are more likely to nourish egoistic complacency and pretension, a hard and condemnatory spirit towards one's fellow men, and a busy occupation with the minutia of events, instead of a reverent contemplation of great facts and a wise application of great principles. It would be idle to consider Dr. Cumming's theory of prophecy in any other light, as a philosophy of history or a specimen of Biblical interpretation; it bears about the same relation to the extension of genuine knowledge as the astrological "house" in the heavens bears to the true structure and relations of the universe...

One more characteristic of Dr. Cumming's writings, and we have done. This is the *perverted moral judgement* that everywhere reigns in them. Not that this perversion is peculiar to Dr. Cumming; it belongs to the dogmatic system which he shares with all evangelical believers. But the abstract tendencies of systems are represented in very different degrees, according to the different characters of those who embrace them; just as the same food tells differently on different constitutions: and there are certain qualities in Dr. Cumming that cause the perversion of which we speak to exhibit itself with peculiar prominence in his teaching. A single extract will enable us to explain what we mean:

> The 'thoughts' are evil. If it were possible for human eye to discern and to detect the thoughts that flutter round the heart of an unregenerate man—to mark their hue and their multitude it would be found that they are indeed 'evil! We speak not of the thief, and the murderer, and the adulterer, and such-like, whose crimes draw down the cognizance of earthly tribunals, and whose unenviable character it is to take the lead in the paths of sin; but we refer to the men who are marked out by their practice of many of the seemliest moralities of life by the exercise of the kindliest affections, and the interchange of the sweetest reciprocities—and of these men, if unrenewed and unchanged, we pronounce that their thoughts are evil. To ascertain this, we must refer to the object around which our thoughts ought continually to circulate. The Scriptures assert that this object is *the glory of God;* that for this we ought to think, to act, and to speak; and that in thus thinking, acting, and speaking, there is involved the purest and most endearing bliss. Now it will be

found true of the most amiable men that with all their good society and kindliness of heart, and all their strict and unbending integrity, they never or rarely think of the glory of God. The question never occurs to them Will this redound to the glory of God? Will this make His name more known, His being more loved, His praise more sung? And just inasmuch as their every thought comes short of this lofty aim, in so much does it come short of good, and entitle itself to the character of evil. If the glory of God is not the absorbing and the influential aim of their thoughts, then they are evil; but God's glory never enters into their minds. They are amiable, because it chances to be one of the constitutional tendencies of their individual character, left uneffaced by the Fall; and *they are just and upright, because they have perhaps no occasion to be otherwise, or find it subservient to their interests to maintain such a character.*[10]

Again we read:

There are traits in the Christian character which the mere worldly man cannot understand. He can understand the outward morality, but he cannot understand the inner spring of it; he can understand Dorcas's liberality to the poor, but he cannot penetrate the ground of Dorcas's liberality. *Some men give to the poor because they are ostentatious, or because they think the poor will ultimately avenge their neglect; but the Christian gives to the poor, not only because he has sensibilities like other men*, but because inasmuch as ye did it to the least of these my brethren, ye did it unto me.[11]

Before entering on the more general question involved in these quotations, we must point to the clauses we have marked with italics, where Dr. Cumming appears to express sentiments which, we are happy to think, are not shared by the majority of his brethren in the faith. Dr. Cumming, it seems, is unable to conceive that the natural man can have any other motive for being just and upright than that it is useless to be otherwise, or that a character for honesty is profitable; according to his experience, between the feelings of ostentation and selfish alarm and the feeling of love to Christ, there lie no sensibilities which can lead a man to relieve want. Granting, as we should prefer to think, that it is Dr. Cumming's exposition of his sentiments which is deficient rather than his sentiments themselves, still, the fact that the deficiency lies precisely here, and that he can overlook it not only in the haste of oral delivery but in the examination of proof-sheets is strongly significant of his mental bias—of the faint degree in which he sympathizes with the disinterested elements of human feeling, and of the fact, which we are about to dwell upon, that those feelings are totally absent from his religious theory. Now, Dr. Cumming invariably assumes that, in fulminating against those who differ from him, he is standing on a moral elevation to which they are compelled reluctantly to look up; that his theory of motives and conduct is in its loftiness and purity a perpetual rebuke to their low and vicious desires and practice. It is time he should be told that the reverse is the fact; that there are men who do not merely cast a superficial glance at his doctrine, and fail to see its beauty or justice, but who, after a close consideration of that doctrine, pronounce it to be subversive of true moral development, and therefore positively noxious. Dr. Cumming is fond of showing-up the teaching of Roman- ism, and accusing it of undermining true morality: it is time he should be told that there is a large body, both of thinkers and practical men, who hold precisely the same opinion of his own teaching—with this difference, that they do not regard it as the inspiration of Satan, but as the natural crop of a human mind where the soil is chiefly made up of egoistic passions and dogmatic beliefs.

Dr. Cumming's theory, as we have seen, is that actions are good or evil according as they are prompted or not prompted by an exclusive reference to the "glory of God." God, then, in Dr. Cumming's conception, is a Being who has no pleasure in the exercise of love and truthfulness and justice, considered as affecting the well-being of His creatures; He has satisfaction in us only in so far as we exhaust our motives and dispositions of all relation to our fellow beings, and replace sympathy with men by anxiety for the "glory of God." The deed of Grace Darling, when she took a boat in the storm to rescue drowning men and women, was not good if it was only compassion that nerved her arm and impelled her to brave death for the chance of saving others; it was only good if she asked herself—Will this redound to the glory of God? The man who endures tortures rather than betray a trust, the man who spends years in toil in order to discharge an obligation from which the law declares him free, must be animated not by the spirit of fidelity to his fellow man, but by a desire to make "the name of God more known." The sweet charities of domestic life—the ready hand and the soothing word in sickness, the forbearance towards frailties, the prompt helpfulness in all efforts and sympathy in all joys aresimply evil if they result from a "constitutional tendency," or from dispositions disciplined by the experience of suffering and the perception of moral loveliness. A wife is not to devote herself to her husband out of love to him and a sense of the duties implied by a close relation—she is to be a faithful wife for the glory of God; if she feels her natural affections welling up too strongly, she is to repress them; it would not do to act from natural affection she must think of the glory of God. A man is to guide his affairs with energy and discretion, not from an honest desire to fulfil his responsibilities as a member of society and a father, but that "God's praise may be sung." Dr. Cumming's Christian pays his debts for the glory of God: were it not for the coercion of that supreme motive, it would be evil to pay them. A man is not to be just from a feeling of justice; he is not to help his fellow men out of good will to his fellow men; he is not to be a tender husband and father out of affection: all his natural muscles and fibres are to be torn away and replaced by a patent steel-spring—anxiety for the "glory of God."

Happily, the constitution of human nature forbids the complete prevalence of such a theory. Fatally powerful as religious systems have been, human nature is stronger and wider than religious systems, and though dogmas may hamper, they cannot absolutely repress its growth: build walls round the living tree as you will, the bricks and mortar have by and by to give way before the slow and sure operation of the sap. But next to that hatred of the enemies of God which is the principle of persecution, there perhaps has been no perversion more obstructive of true moral development than this substitution of a reference to the glory of God for the direct promptings of the sympathetic feelings. Benevolence and justice are strong only in proportion as they are directly and inevitably called into activity by their proper objects: pity is strong only because we are strongly impressed by suffering and only in proportion as it is compassion that speaks through the eyes when we soothe, and moves the arm when we succour, is a deed strictly benevolent. If the soothing or the succour be given because another being wishes or approves it, the deed ceases to be one of benevolence, and becomes one of deference, of obedience, of self-interest, or vanity. Accessory motives may aid in producing an *action,* but they presuppose the weakness of the direct motive; and conversely, when the direct motive is strong, the action of accessory motives will be excluded. If then, as Dr. Cumming inculcates, the glory of God is to be "the absorbing and the influential aim" in our thoughts and actions, this must tend to neutralize the human sympathies; the stream of feeling will be diverted from its natural current in order to feed an artificial canal. The idea of God is really moral in its influence—it really cherishes all that is best and loveliest in man—only when God is contemplated as sympathizing with the pure elements of human feeling, as possessing infinitely all those attributes which we recognize to be moral in humanity. In this light, the idea of God and the sense of His presence intensify all noble feeling, and encourage all noble effort, on the same principle that human sympathy is found a source of strength: the brave man feels braver when he knows that another stout heart is beating time with his; the devoted woman who is wearing out her years in patient effort to alleviate suffering or save vice from the last stages of degradation finds aid in the pressure of a friendly hand which tells her that there is one who understands her deeds, and in her place would do the like. The idea of a God who not only sympathizes with all we feel and endure for our fellow men, but who will pour new life into our too languid love, and give firmness to our vacillating purpose, is an extension and multiplication of the effects produced by human sympathy; and it has been intensified for the better spirits who have been under the influence of orthodox Christianity, by the contemplation of Jesus as "God manifest in the flesh." But Dr. Cumming's God is the very opposite of all this: He is a God who, instead of sharing and aiding our human sympathies, is directly in collision with them; who, instead of strengthening the bond between man and man, by encouraging the sense that they are both alike the objects of His love and care, thrusts Himself between them and forbids them to feel for each other except as they have relation to Him. He is a God who, instead of adding His solar force to swell the tide of those impulses that tend to give humanity a common life in which the good of one is the good of all, commands us to check those impulses, lest they should prevent us from thinking of His glory. It is in vain for Dr. Cumming to say that we are to love man for God's sake: with the conception of God which his teaching presents, the love of man for God's sake involves, as his writings abundantly show, a strong principle of hatred. We can only love one being for the sake of another when there is an habitual delight in associating the idea of those two beings that is, when the object of our indirect love is a source of joy and honour to the object of our direct love. But, according to Dr. Cumming's theory, the majority of mankind the majority of his neighbours are in precisely the opposite relation to God. His soul has no pleasure in them: they belong more to Satan than to Him; and if they contribute to His glory, it is against their will. Dr. Cumming, then, can only love *some* men for God's sake; the rest he must in consistency *hate* for God's sake.

There must be many, even in the circle of Dr. Cumming's admirers, who would be revolted by the doctrine we have just exposed, if their natural good sense and healthy feeling were not early stifled by dogmatic beliefs, and their reverence misled by pious phrases. But as it is, many a rational question, many a generous instinct, is repelled as the suggestion of a supernatural enemy, or as the ebullition of human pride and corruption. This state of inward contradiction can be put an end to only by the conviction that the free and diligent exertion of the intellect, instead of being a sin, is a part of their responsibility—that Right and Reason are synonymous. The fundamental faith for man is faith in the result of a brave, honest, and steady use of all his faculties:

Let knowledge grow from more to more,
But more of reverence in us dwell;
That mind and soul according well
May make one music as before,
But vaster.[12]

Before taking leave of Dr. Cumming, let us express a hope that we have in no case exaggerated the unfavourable character of the inferences to be drawn from his pages. His creed often obliges him to hope the worst of men, and to exert himself in proving that the worst is true; but thus far we are happier than he. We have no theory which requires us to attribute unworthy motives to Dr. Cumming, no opinions, religious or irreligious, which can make it a gratification to us to detect him in delinquencies. On the contrary, the better we are able to think of him as a man, while we are obliged to disapprove him as a theologian, the stronger will be the evidence for our conviction, that the tendency towards good in human nature has a force which no creed can utterly counteract, and which ensures the ultimate triumph of that tendency over all dogmatic perversions.

Notes

1. *Manual of Christian Evidences*, John Cumming (1847), p. 81.

2. *Manual of Christian Evidences*, John Cumming (1847), p. 254.

3. [William Paley (1743-1805); Thomas Chalmers (1780-1847).

4. See *Manual of Christian Evidences*, p. 73.

5. Robert Chambers (1802-1871).

6. *Christ Before the Flood*, John Cumming, p. 93.

7. *Signs of the Times*, John Cumming, p. 38.

8. *Apocalyptic Sketches*, John Cumming, p. 243.

9. William Cowper, *Olney Hymns* (1779), no. 1.

10. *Occasional Discourses*, vol. i, John Cumming, p. 8.

11. Ibid., p. 236.

12. Alfred, Lord Tennyson, *In Memoriam: A. H. H.* (1850), Prologue, stanza 7.

9
The Spirit Of Rationalism In Europe (1865)[1]
W.E.H. Lecky

To those who have appreciated the great truth that a Radical political change neces-sarily implies a corresponding change in the mental habits of society, the process which I have traced will furnish a decisive evidence of the declining influence of dog-matic theology. That vast department of thought and action which is comprised un-der the name of politics was once altogether guided by its power. It is now passing from its influence rapidly, universally, and completely. The classes that are most pen-etrated with the spirit of special dogmas were once the chief directors of the policy of Europe. They now form a baffled and desponding minority, whose most cherished political principles have been almost universally abandoned, who are struggling faintly and ineffectually against the ever-increasing spirit of the age, and whose ideal is not in the future but in the past. It is evident that a government never can be really like a railway company, or a literary society, which only exercises an influence over secular affairs. As long as it determines the system of education that exists among its subjects, as long as it can encourage or repress the teaching of particular doctrines, as long as its foreign policy brings it into collision with governments which still make the maintenance of certain religious systems a main object of their policy, it will nec-essarily exercise a gigantic influence upon belief. It cannot possibly be uninfluential, and it is difficult to assign limits to the influence that it may exercise. If the men who compose it (or the public opinion that governs them) be pervaded by an in-tensely-realised conviction that the promulgation of a certain system of doctrine is incomparably the highest of human interests, that to assist that promulgation is the main object for which they were placed in the world, and should be the dominant motive of their lives, it will be quite impossible for these men, as politicians, to avoid interfering with theology. Men who are inspired by an absorbing passion will inevita-bly gratify it if they have the power. Men who sincerely desire the happiness of mankind will certainly use to the uttermost the means they possess of promoting what they feel to be beyond all comparison the greatest of human interests. If by giving a certain direction to education they could avert fearful and general physical suffering, there can be no doubt that they would avail themselves of their power. If they were quite certain that the greatest possible suffering was the consequence of deviating from a particular class of opinions, they could not possibly neglect that consideration in their laws. This is the conclusion we should naturally draw from the nature of the human mind, and it is most abundantly corroborated by experience.[2] In order to ascertain the tendencies of certain opinions, we should not confine ourselves to those exceptional intellects who, having perceived the character of their age, have spent their lives in endeavoring painfully and laboriously to wrest their opinions in conformity with them. We should rather observe the position which large bodies of men, governed by the same principles, but living under various circumstances and in different ages, naturally and almost unconsciously occupy. We have ample means of judging in the present case. We see the general tone which is adopted on political subjects by the clergy of the most various creeds, by the religious newspapers, and by the politicians who represent that section of the community which is most occupied with dogmatic theology. We see that it is a tendency distinct from and opposed to the tendencies of the age. History tells us that it was once dominant in politics, that it has been continuously and rapidly declining, and that it has declined most rapidly and most steadily in those countries in which the development of intellect has been most active. All over Europe the priesthood are now associated with a policy of toryism, of reaction, or of obstruction. All over Europe the organs that represent dogmatic interests are in permanent opposition to the progressive tendencies around them, and are rapidly sinking into contempt. In every country in which a strong political life is manifested, the secularisation of politics is the consequence. Each stage of that movement has been initiated and effected by those who are most indifferent to dogmatic theology, and each has been opposed by those who are most occupied with theology.

And as I write these words, it is impossible to forget that one of the great problems on which the thoughts of politicians are even now concentrated is the hopeless decadence of the one theocracy of modern Europe, of the great type and representative of the alliance of politics and theology. That throne on which it seemed as though the changeless Church had stamped the impress of her own perpetuity—that throne which for so many centuries of anarchy and confusion had been the Sinai of a protecting and an avenging law—that throne which was once the centre and the archetype of the political system of Europe, the successor of Imperial Rome, the inheritor of a double portion of her spirit, the one power which seemed removed above all the vicissitudes of politics, the iris above the cataract, unshaken amid so much turmoil and so much change; that throne has in our day sunk into a condition of hopeless decrepitude, and has only prolonged its existence by the confession of its impotence. Supported by the bayonets of a foreign power, and avowedly incapable of self-existence, it is no longer a living organism, its significance is but the significance of death. There was a time when the voice that issued from the Vatican shook Europe to its foundations, and sent forth the proudest armies to the deserts of Syria. There was a time when all the valour and all the chivalry of Christendom would have followed the banner of the Church in any field and against any foe. Now a few hundred French, and Belgians, and Irish are all who would respond to its appeal. Its august antiquity, the reverence that centres around its thief, the memory of the unrivalled influence it has exercised, the genius that has consecrated its past, the undoubted virtues that have been displayed by its rulers, were all unable to save the papal government from a decadence the most irretrievable and the most hopeless. Reforms were boldly initiated, but they only served to accelerate its ruin. A repressive policy was attempted, but it could not arrest the progress of its decay. For nearly a century, under every ruler and under every system of policy, it has been hopelessly, steadily, and rapidly declining. At last the influences that had so long been corroding it attained their triumph. It fell before the Revolution, and has since been unable to exist, except by the support of a foreign army. The principle of its vitality has departed.

No human pen can write its epitaph, for no imagination can adequately realise its glories. In the eyes of those who estimate the greatness of a sovereignty, not by the extent of its territory, or by the valour of its soldiers, but by the influence which it has exercised over mankind, the papal government has had no rival, and can have no successor. But though we may not fully estimate the majesty of its past, we can at least trace the causes of its decline. It fell because it neglected the great truth that a government to be successful must adapt itself to the ever-changing mental condition of society; that a policy which in one century produces the utmost prosperity, in another leads only to ruin and to disaster. It fell because it represented the union of politics and theology, and because the intellect of Europe has rendered it an anachronism by pronouncing their divorce. It fell because its constitution was essentially and radically opposed to the spirit of an age in which the secularisation of politics is the measure and the condition of all political prosperity.

The secularisation of politics is, as we have seen, the direct consequence of the declining influence of dogmatic theology. I have said that it also reacts upon and influences its cause. The creation of a strong and purely secular political feeling diffused through all classes of society, and producing an ardent patriotism, and a passionate and indomitable love of liberty, is sufficient in many respects to modify all the great departments of thought, and to contribute largely to the formation of a distinct type of intellectual character.

It is obvious, in the first place, that one important effect of a purely secular political feeling will be to weaken the intensity of sectarianism. Before its existence sectarianism was the measure by which all things and persons were contemplated. It exercised an undivided control over the minds and passions of men, absorbed all their interests, and presided over all their combinations. But when a purely political spirit is engendered, a new enthusiasm is introduced into the mind, which first divides the affections and at last replaces the passion that had formerly been supreme. Two different enthusiasms, each of which makes men regard events in a special point of view, cannot at the same time be absolute. The habits of thought that are formed by the one, will necessarily weaken or efface the habits of thought that are formed by the other. Men learn to classify their fellows by a new principle. They become in one capacity the cordial associates of those whom in another capacity they had long regarded with unmitigated dislike. They learn to repress and oppose in one capacity those whom in another capacity they regard with unbounded reverence. Conflicting feelings are thus produced which neutralise each other; and if one of the two increases, the other is proportionately diminished. Every war that unites for secular objects nations of different creeds, every measure that extends political interests to classes that had formerly been excluded from their range, has therefore a tendency to assuage the virulence of sects. ...

But probably the most important, and certainly the most beneficial, effect of political life is to habituate men to a true method of enquiry. Government in a constitutional country is carried on by debate, all the arguments on both sides are brought forward with unrestricted freedom, and every newspaper reports in full what has been said against the principles it advocates by the ablest men in the country. Men may study the debates of Parliament under the influence of a strong party bias, they may even pay more attention to the statements of one party than to those of the other, but they never imagine that they can form an opinion by an exclusive study of what has been written on one side. The two views of every question are placed in juxtaposition, and every one who is interested in the subject examines both. When a charge is brought against any politician, men naturally turn to his reply before forming an opinion, and they feel that any other course would be not only extremely foolish, but also extremely dishonest. This is the spirit of truth as opposed to the spirit of falsehood and imposture, which in all ages and in all departments of thought has discouraged men from studying opposing systems, lamented the circulation of adverse arguments, and denounced as criminal those who listen to them. Among the higher order of intellects, the first spirit is chiefly cultivated by those philosophical studies which discipline and strengthen the mind for research. But what philosophy does for a very few, political life does, less perfectly, indeed, but still in a great degree, for the many. It diffuses abroad not only habits of acute reasoning, but also, what is far more important, habits of impartiality and intellectual fairness, which will at last be carried into all forms of discussion, and will destroy every system that refuses to accept them. Year after year, as political life extends, we find each new attempt to stifle the expression of opinion received with an increased indignation, the sympathies of the people immediately enlisted on behalf of the oppressed teacher, and the work which is the object of condemnation elevated in public esteem often to a degree that is far greater than it deserves. Year after year the conviction becomes more general, that a provisional abnegation of the opinions of the past and a resolute and unflinching impartiality are among the highest duties of the enquirer, and that he who shrinks from such a research is at least morally bound to abstain from condemning the opinions of his neighbour.

If we may generalise the experience of modern constitutional governments, it would appear that this process must pass through three phases. When political life is introduced into a nation that is strongly imbued with sectarianism, this latter spirit will at first dominate over political interests, and the whole scope and tendency of government will be directed by theology. After a time the movement I have traced in the present chapter will appear. The secular element will emerge into light. It will at length obtain an absolute ascendency, and, expelling theology successively from all its political strongholds, will thus weaken its influence over the human mind. Yet in one remarkable way the spirit of sectarianism will still survive: it will change its name and object, transmigrate into political discussion, and assume the form of an intense party-spirit. The increasing tendency, however, of political life seems to be to weaken or efface this spirit, and in the more advanced stages of free government it almost disappears. A judicial spirit is fostered which leads men both in politics and theology to eclecticism, to judge all questions exclusively on the ground of their intrinsic merits, and not at all according to their position in theological or political systems. To increase the range and intensity of political interests is to strengthen this tendency; and every extension of the suffrage thus diffuses over a wider circle a habit of thought that must eventually modify theological belief. If the suffrage should ever be granted to women, it would probably, after two or three generations, effect a complete revolution in their habits of thought, which by acting upon the first period of education would influence the whole course of opinion.

Notes

1. W.E.H. Lecky (1838-1903), an intellectual historian whose principal work was History of the Rise and Influence of the Spririt of Rationalism in Europe (1865) of which the essay included here consists of pp.126-32, 133-36.

2. This has been very clearly noticed in one of the ablest modern books in defence of the Tory theory. "At the point where Protestantism becomes vicious, where it receives the first tinge of latitudinarianism, and begins to join hands with infidelity by superseding the belief of an objective truth in religion, necessary for salvation; at that very spot it likewise assumes an aspect of hostility to the union of church and State." (Gladstone, on *Church and State*, p. 188.)

10
The Christian Church And Women (1885)
Elizabeth Cady Stanton

The grand ideas of Confucius, Zoroaster, Buddha, Mohammed, Jesus, have been slowly transforming the world from the reign of brute force to moral power, and science has been as slowly emancipating mankind from their fears of the unknown; but the Christian Church has steadily used its influence against progress, science, the education of the masses and freedom for woman. It is often asserted that woman owes all the advantages of the position she occupies to-day to Christianity, but the facts of history show that the Christian Church has done nothing specifically for woman's elevation. In the general march of civilization she has necessarily reaped the advantage of man's higher development; but we must not claim for Christianity all that has been achieved by science, discovery and invention.

If we admit that the truth it has taught, as an offset to its many errors, has been one of the factors in civilization, we shall concede all that can be fairly claimed. The prolonged slavery of woman is the darkest page in human history; and she has touched the depths of misery since in Bethlehem the Magi gathered round the child in the manger, who was hailed as the Savior of mankind. But the life and teachings of Jesus, all pointing to the complete equality of the human family, were too far in advance of his age to mould its public opinion. We must distinguish between the teachings attributed to Jesus and those of the Christian Church. One represents the ideal the race is destined to attain; the other, the popular sentiment of its time.

Had Jesus lived in Russia in the nineteenth century, he would have been exiled as a Nihilist for his protests against tyranny and his sympathy with the suffering masses. He would have been driven from Germany as a socialist, from France as a communist, and imprisoned as a blasphemer in England and America, had he taught in London and New York the radical ideas he proclaimed in Palestine.

I speak of the Christian Church, Catholic and Protestant, of the priesthood, the bulls of its popes, the decrees of its councils, the articles and resolutions of its general assemblies, presbyteries, synods, conferences, which, all summed up, compose the canon law, which has held Christendom during what are called the Dark Ages until now under its paralyzing influence, moulding civil law and social customs and plunging woman into absolute slavery.

The worst features of the canon law reveal themselves to-day in woman's condition as dearly as they did fifteen hundred years ago. The clergy in their pulpits teach the same doctrines in regard to her from the same texts, and echo the same old platitudes and false ideas promulgated for centuries by ecclesiastical councils. According to Church teaching, woman was an after-thought in the creation, the author of sin, being at once in collusion with Satan. Her sex was made a crime; marriage a condition of slavery, owing obedience; maternity a curse; and the true position of all womankind one of inferiority and subjection to all men; and the same ideas are echoed in our pulpits today.

England and America are the two nations in which the Christian religion is dominant; yet, by their ethics taught in the pulpit, the ideal woman is comparatively more degraded than in pagan nations. I say comparatively, for, because of the various steps of progress in education, science, invention and art, woman is now more fully the equal of man in these countries than in any other nation or period of the world. And yet the old ideas taught by the Church in the Dark Ages of her inferiority and depravity are still maintained; and, just in proportion as women are the equals of the men by their side, the more keenly they feel every invidious distinction based on sex. To those not conversant with the history of the Christian Church and the growth of the canon law, it may seem a startling assertion; but it is, nevertheless, true that the Church has done more to degrade woman than all other adverse influences put together. And it has done this by playing the religious emotions (the strongest feelings of her nature) to her own complete subjugation. The same religious conscience that carried the widows to the funeral pyres of their husbands now holds some women in the Turkish seraglios, others in polygamy under the Mormon theocracy, and others in the Christian churches, in which, while rich women help to build and support them, they may not speak or vote or enjoy any of the honors conferred on men, and all alike are taught that their degradation is of divine ordination, and thus their natural feelings of self-respect are held in abeyance to what they are taught to believe is God's will. Out of the doctrine of original sin grew the crimes and miseries of asceticism, celibacy, and witchcraft, woman becoming the helpless victim of all the delusions generated in the brain of man.

Having decided that she was the author of sin and the medium through whom the devil would effect the downfall of the Church, godly men logically inferred that the greater the distance from themselves and all womankind, the nearer they were to God and heaven. With this idea, they fought against all woman's influence, both good and evil. At one period, they crucified all natural affections for mother, sister, wife and daughter, and continued a series of persecutions that blackened the centuries with the most horrible crimes.

This more than any other one influence was the cause of that general halt in civilization, that retrogressive movement of the Dark Ages, for which no historian has satisfactorily accounted. At no period of the world was the equilibrium of the masculine and feminine elements of humanity so disturbed. The result was moral chaos—just what would occur in the material world, if it were possible to destroy the equilibrium of the positive and negative electricity or of the centripetal and centrifugal force.

For the supposed crimes of heresy and witchcraft hundreds of women endured such persecutions and tortures that the most stolid historians are said to have wept in recording them; and no one can read them today but with a bleeding heart. And, as the Christian Church grew stronger, woman's fate grew more helpless. Even the Reformation and Protestantism brought no relief, the clergy being all along their most bitter persecutors, the inventors of the most infernal tortures. Hundreds and hundreds of fair young girls, innocent as the angels in heaven, hundreds and hundreds of old women, weary and trembling with the burdens of life, were hunted down by emissaries of the Church, dragged into the courts, with the ablest judges and lawyers of England, Scotland and America on the bench, and tried for crimes that never existed but in the wild, fanatical imaginations of religious devotees. Women were accused of consorting with devils and perpetuating their diabolical propensities. Hundreds of these children of hypothetical origin were drowned, burned and tortured in the presence of their mothers, to add to their death agonies. These things were not done by savages or pagans; they were done by the Christian Church. Neither were they confined to the Dark Ages, but permitted by law in England far into the eighteenth century. The clergy everywhere sustained witchcraft as Bible doctrine, until the spirit of rationalism laughed the whole thing to scorn, and science gave mankind a more cheerful view of life.

So large a place as the nature and position of woman occupied in the councils of the Church that the Rev. Charles Kingsley facetiously remarked that the Christian Church was swamped by hysteria from the third to the sixteenth century. Speaking of witchcraft, Lecky says the Reformation was the signal for a fresh outburst of the superstition in England; and there, as elsewhere, its decline was represented by the clergy as the direct consequence and the exact measure of the progress of religious skepticism. In Scotland, where the reformed ministers exercised greater influence than in any other country, and where the witch trials fell almost entirely into their hands, the persecution was proportionately atrocious. Preobably the ablest defender of the belief was Joseph Glanvill (1636-80), a clergyman of the English Establishment; and one of the most influential was Richard Baxter (1651-91), the greatest of the Puritans. It spread with Puritanism into the New World, and the executions in Massachusetts form one of the darkest pages in American history. The greatest religious leader of the last century, John Wesley, was among the latest of its supporters. He said giving up witchcraft was giving up the Bible. Skepticism on the subject of witches first arose among those who were least governed by the Church, advanced with the decline of the influence of the clergy, and was commonly branded by them as a phase of infidelity. One remarkable fact stands out in the history of witchcraft; and that is, its victims were chiefly women. Scarce one wizard to a hundred witches was ever burned or tortured.

Although the ignorance and crimes of the race have ever fallen most heavily on woman, yet in the general progress of civilization she has had some share. As man became more enlightened, she of necessity enjoyed the results; but to no form of popular religion has woman ever been indebted for one pulsation of liberty. Obedience and subjection have been the lessons taught her by all alike.

Lecky, in his *History of Rationalism* and his *European Morals,* gives facts sufficient to convince any woman of common sense that the greatest obstacle in the way of the freedom and elevation of her sex has been, and is, the teaching of the Church in regard to her rights and duties. Women have ever been the chief victims in the persecutions of the Church amid all its awful tragedies, and on them have fallen the heaviest penalties of the canon law. But the canon law did not confine itself to social relations; it laid its hand with withering touch on the civil law, and blighted many personal and property rights accorded women under the Roman Code. Speaking of the Roman Code before the introduction of Christianity (Gaius), Sir Henry Maine (1822-88) says:

> The jurisconsults had evidently at this time assumed the equality of the sexes as a principle to the code of equity. The situation of the Roman woman, whether married or single, became one of great personal and property independence, but Christianity tended somewhat from the very first to narrow this remarkable liberty. The prevailing state of religious sentiment may explain why modern jurisprudence has adopted these rules concerning the posi-

tion of woman, which belong peculiarly to an imperfect civilization. No society which preserves any tincture of Christian institutions is likely to restore to married women the personal liberty conferred on them by middle Roman law. Canon law has deeply injured civilization.

Rev. Charles Kingsley (1819-1875) says:

> Whoever wishes to gain insight into that great institution, Canon Law, can do so most effectively by studying Common Law in regard to woman. There will never be a good world for woman until the last remnant of Canon Law is civilized off the face of the earth. Meanwhile, all the most pure and high-minded women in England and Europe have been brought up under the shadow of the Canon Law, and have accepted it, with the usual divine self-sacrifice, as their destiny by law of God and nature, and consider their own womanhood outraged, when it, their tyrant, is meddled with.

Women accept their position under the shadow of the canon law for the best of reasons they know nothing about it. And, if they should undertake to explore it, they would waste their lives in the effort.

This is one of the peculiarities of woman's position; she knows nothing of the laws, either canon or civil, under which she lives; and such churchmen as the Rev. Morgan Dix (1862-1908) are determined she never shall. Nero was thought the chief of tyrants because he made laws and hung them up so high the people could not read them.

As the result of the canon law, what is woman's position in the State and the Church today? We have weman disenfranchised, with no voice in the government under which she lives, denied until recently the right to enter colleges or professions, laboring at half-price in the world of work; a code of morals that makes man's glory woman's shame; a civil code that makes her in marriage a nonentity, her person, her children, her earnings the property of her husband. In adjusting this institution of marriage, woman has never yet in the history of the world had one word to say. The relation has been absolutely established and perpetuated without her consent. We have thus far had the man marriage. He has made all the laws concerning it to suit his own convenience and love of power. He has tried every possible form of it, and is as yet satisfied with none of his experiments. If an inhabitant of some other planet could suddenly light in one of our law libraries, and read over our civil and criminal codes, he would be at a loss to know what kind of beings women are, so anomalous is the position we hold, with some rights partially recognized in one place and wholly obliterated in another. In the criminal code, we find no feminine pronouns. All criminals are designated as "he," "his," "him." We might suppose our fathers thought women were too pure and angelic ever to commit crimes, if we did not find in the law reports, cases in which women had been imprisoned and hanged as "he," "his," "him." And yet, when it comes to privileges we are excluded, because the laws and constitutions do not contain the feminine pronouns "she," "hers," "her." We are a kind of half human, half animal being, like those wonderful questioning sphinxes we see in the Old World.

And we present very much the same appearance in the Church. Go into any little country town, and the chief excitement among the women is found in fairs, donation parties, festivals, church building and decorating. The women are the chief, untiring, pertinacious beggars for the church. They compose the vast majority of the congregation. Rich women give large sums to clear church debts, to educate young men for the ministry, and to endow theological seminaries. Poorer women decorate the temples for Christmas and Easter, make surplices and gowns, embroider table covers for the altar, and slippers for the rector; and all alike think they are serving God in sustaining the church and the priesthood.

In return, the whole tone of Church teaching in regard to woman is, to the last degree, contemptuous and degrading.

Perchance the very man educated by some sewing society of women will ascend the pulpit, and take his text in 1 Corinthians xiv. 34, 35: "Let your women keep silence in the churches; for it is not permitted unto them to speak; but they are commanded to be under obedience, as also saith the law. And if they will learn anything, let them ask their husbands at home, for it is a shame for women to speak in the church." Ephesians v. 23: "Wives, submit yourselves unto your own husbands, as unto the Lord. For the husband is the head of the wife, even as Christ is the head of the Church." 1 Timothy ii. 11, 12, 13: "Let the women learn in silence with all subjection. But I suffer not a woman to teach nor to usurp authority over the man… For Adam was first formed, then Eve." 1 Corinthians xi, 8, 9: "For the man is not of the woman, but the woman of the man. Neither was the man created for the woman but the woman for the man."

In all the great cathedrals in England and in some here in New York, boys from ten to fifteen chant the hymns of praise that woman's lips may not profane, while they, oblivious to these insults to their sex, swell the listening crowd, and worship the very God who they are told made them slaves, and cursed them with sufferings that time can never mitigate.

While in England, I visited the birthplace of Dean Arthur Penrhyn Stanley (1815-81). The old homestead was occupied by a curate and his two daughters. They escorted us all over the place—in the school where poor children were taught, in the old church where the dean had long preached. "Do you see that table cover in the altar?" said one of the daughters. "Sister and I worked that." "Did you spread it on the table?" said I. "Oh, no," said she; "no woman is allowed to enter this enclosure." "Why?" said I. "Oh! it is too sacred." "But," said I, "men go there; and it is said that women are purer, more delicate, refined, and naturally religious than they are." "Yes, but women are not allowed." "Shall I explain the reason to you?" I replied. "Yes," she said, with a look of surprise. "Well," said I, "it is because the Church believes that woman brought sin into the world, that she was the cause of man's fall from holiness, that she was cursed of God, and has ever since been in collusion with the devil. Hence, the Church has considered her unfit to sing in the choir or enter the Holy of Holies." She looked very thoughtful, and said, "I never supposed these old customs had such significance." "Yes," I replied, "every old custom, every fashion, every point of etiquette, is based on some principle, and women ignorantly submit to many degrading customs, because they do not understand their origin."

These indignities have their root in the doctrine of original sin, gradually developed in the canon law—a doctrine never taught in the primitive Christian Church. In spite of the life, character and teachings of Jesus, ever proclaiming the essential equality and oneness of the whole human family, the priesthood, claiming apostolic descent, so interprets Christianity as to make it the basis of all religious and political disqualifications for women, sustaining the rights of man alone.

The offices woman held during the apostolic age she has been gradually deprived of through ecclesiastical enactments. Although, during the first four hundred years of the Christian Church, women were the chosen companions of Jesus and his followers, doing their utmost to spread the new faith, as preachers, elders, deacons, these facts are carefully excluded from all the English translations of the Scriptures; while woman's depravity, inferiority and subordination are dwelt upon wherever the text will admit of it. Under all the changes in advancing civilization for the last fifteen hundred years, this one idea of woman has been steadily promulgated; and today, in the full blaze of the sunlight of the late years of the nineteenth century, it is echoed in the pulpit by nearly every sect and in the halls of legislation by political leaders.

Whatever oppressions man has suffered, they have invariably fallen more heavily on woman. Whatever new liberties advancing civilization has brought to man, ever the smallest measure has been accorded to woman, as a result of church teaching. The effect of this is seen in every department of life.

There is nothing so cheap as womanhood in the commerce of the world. You can scarcely take up a paper that does not herald some outrage on woman, from the dignified matron on her way to church to the girl of fourteen gathering wild flowers on her way to school. I hold men in high places responsible for the actions of the lower orders. The sentiments and opinions expressed by clergymen and legislators mould the morals of the highway. So long as the Church and the State, in their creeds and codes, make woman an outcast, she will be the sport of the multitudes. Whatever can be done to dignify her in the eyes of man will be a shield and helmet for her protection. If the same respect the masses are educated to feel for cathedrals, altars, symbols and sacraments was extended to the mothers of the race, as it should be, all these distracting problems, in which their interests are involved, would be speedily settled. You cannot go so low down in the scale of being as to find men who would enter our churches to desecrate the altars or toss about the emblem of the sacrament, because they have been educated with a holy reverence for these things. But where are any lessons of reverence for woman taught to the multitude?

And yet is she not, as the mother of the race, more exalted than sacraments, symbols, altars, and vast cathedral domes? Are not the eternal principles of justice engraven on her heart more sacred than canons, creeds and codes written on parchment by Jesuits, bishops, cardinals and popes? Yet where shall we look for lessons of honor and respect to her?

Do our sons in the law schools rise from their studies of the invidious statutes and opinions of jurists in regard to women with a higher respect for their mothers? By no means. Every line of the old common law of England on which the American system of jurisprudence is based, touching the interests of woman, is, in a measure, responsible for the wrongs she suffers today.

Do our sons in their theological seminaries rise from their studies of the Bible, and the popular commentaries on the passages of Scripture concerning woman's creation and position in the scale of being, with an added respect for their mothers? By no means. They come ofttimes fresh from the perusal of what they suppose to be God's will and law, fresh from communion with the unseen, perhaps with the dew of inspiration on their lips, to preach anew the subjection of one-half the race to the other.

A very striking fact, showing the outrages women patiently endure through the perversion of their religious sentiments by crafty priests, is seen in the treatment of the Hindu widow, the civil law in her case, as in so many others, being practically annulled by theological dogmas.

"The most liberal of the Hindu schools of jurisprudence,"[1] says Maine, "that prevailing in Bengal proper, gives a childless widow the enjoyment of her husband's property under certain restrictive conditions during her life"; and in this it agrees with many bodies of unwritten local custom. If there are male children, they succeed at once; but if there are none the widow comes in for her life before the collateral relatives. At the present moment, marriages among the upper classes of Hindus being very commonly infertile, a considerable portion of the soil of the wealthiest Indian provinces is in the hands of childless widows as tenants for life. But it was exactly in Bengal proper that the English, on entering India, found the suttee, or widow-burning, not merely an occasional, but a constant and almost universal practice with the wealthier classes; and, as a rule, it was only the childless widow, and never the widow with minor children, who burnt herself on her husband's funeral pyre. There is no question that there was the closest connection between the law and the religious custom; and the widow was made to sacrifice herself, in order that her tenancy for life might be gotten rid of. The anxiety of her family that the rite should be performed, which seemed so striking to the first English observers of the practice, was in fact explained by the coarsest motives; but the Brahmins who exhorted her to the sacrifice were undoubtedly influenced by a purely professional dislike to her enjoyment of property. The ancient rule of the civil law, which made her a tenant for life, could not be gotten rid of; but it was combated by the modern institution, which made it her duty to devote herself to a frightful death. The reasoning on this subject, current even in comparatively ancient times, is thus given in the Mitakshava: "The wealth of a regenerate man is designed for religious uses; and a woman's succession to such property is unfit, because she is not competent to the performance of religious rites." Thus the liberal provisions of the civil law were disposed of by burning the widow, and she was made willing for the sacrifice by a cultivated sense of religious duty. What is true in this case is true of women in all ages. They have been trained by their religion to sacrifice themselves, body and soul, for the men of their families and to build up the churches. We do not burn the bodies of women today; but we humiliate them in a thousand ways, and chiefly by our theologies. So long as the pulpits teach woman's inferiority and subjection, she can never command that honor and respect of the ignorant classes needed for her safety and protection. There is nothing more pathetic in all history than the hopeless resignation of woman to the outrages she has been taught to believe are ordained of God.

Note

1. *Early History of Institutions,* Lecture XI., on the Property of Married Women, Sir Henry Maine.

11
Humanity's Gain From Unbelief (1889)
Charles Bradlaugh

As an unbeliever, I ask leave to plead that humanity has been a real gainer from scepticism, and that the gradual and growing rejection of Christianity—like the rejection of the faiths which preceded it—has, in fact, added, and will add, to man's happiness and well-being. I maintain that, in physics, science is the outcome of scepticism, and that general progress is impossible without scepticism on matters of religion. I mean by religion, every form of belief which accepts or asserts the supernatural. I write as a Monist, and use the word "nature" as meaning all phenomena, every phenomenon, all that is necessary for the happening of any and every phenomenon. Every religion is constantly changing, and at any given time is the measure of the civilization attained by what Francois-Pierre-Guillaume Guizot (1787-1874) described as the *juste milieu* of those who profess it. Each religion is slowly, but certainly, modified in its dogma and practice by the gradual development of the peoples amongst whom it is professed. Each discovery destroys in whole or part some theretofore-cherished belief. No religion is suddenly rejected by any people; it is, rather, gradually outgrown. None see a religion die; dead religions are like dead languages and obsolete customs; the decay is long, and, like the glacier-march, is only perceptible to the careful watcher by comparisons extending over long periods. A superseded religion may often be traced in the festivals, ceremonies, and dogmas of the religion which has replaced it. Traces of obsolete religions may often be found in popular customs, in old-wives' stories, and in children's tales.

It is necessary, in order that my plea should be understood, that I should explain what I mean by Christianity; and in the very attempt at this explanation there will, I think, be found strong illustration of the value of unbelief. Christianity in practice may be gathered from its more ancient forms represented by the Roman Catholic and the Greek churches, or from the various churches which have grown up in the last few centuries. Each of these churches calls itself Christian. Some of them deny the right of the others to use the word Christian. Some Christian churches treat, or have treated, other Christian churches as heretics or unbelievers. The Roman Catholics and the Protestants in Great Britain and Ireland have, in turn, been terribly cruel one to the other, and the ferocious laws of the seventeenth and eighteenth centuries enacted by the English Protestants against English and Irish Papists are a disgrace to civilization. These penal laws, enduring longest in Ireland, still bear fruit in much of the political mischief and agrarian crime of today. It is only the tolerant indifference of scepticism that has repealed, one after the other, most of the laws directed by the Established Christian Church against Papists and Dissenters, and also against Jews and heretics. Church-of-England clergymen have in the past gone to great lengths in denouncing non-conformity; and even in the present day an effective sample of such denunciatory bigotry may be found in a sort of orthodox catechism written by the Rev. E A. Grace, of Great Barling, Essex, the popularity of which is vouched for by the fact that it has gone through ten editions. This catechism for little children teaches that "dissent is a great sin" and that Dissenters "worship God according to their own evil and corrupt imaginations, and not according to his revealed will, and therefore their worship is idolatrous." Church-of-England Christians and dissenting Christians, when fraternizing amongst themselves, often publicly draw the line at Unitarians, and positively deny that these have any sort of right to call themselves Christians.

In the first half of the seventeenth century, Quakers were flogged and imprisoned in England as blasphemers, and the early Christian settlers in New England, escaping from the persecution of Old-World Christians, showed scant mercy to the followers of Fox and Penn. It is customary, in controversy, for those advocating the claims of Christianity to include all good done by men in nominally Christian countries, as if such good were the result of Christianity, while they contend that the evil which exists prevails in spite of Christianity. I shall try to make out that the ameliorating march of the last few centuries has been initiated by the heretics of each age, though I quite concede that the men and women denounced and persecuted as infidels by the pious of one century are frequently classed as saints by the pious of a later generation.

What, then, is Christianity? As a system or scheme of doctrine, Christianity may, I submit, not unfairly be gathered from the Old and New Testaments. It is true that some Christians to-day desire to escape from submission to part, at any rate, of the Old Testament; but this very tendency seems to me to be part of the result of the beneficial heresy for which I am pleading. Man's humanity has revolted against Old-Testament barbarism, and, therefore, he has attempted to dissociate the Old

Testament from Christianity. Unless Old and New Testaments are accepted as God's revelation to man, Christianity has no higher claim than any other of the world's many religions—if no such claim can be made out for it apart from the Bible. And though it is quite true that some who deem themselves Christians put the Old Testament completely in the background, this is, I allege, because they are outgrowing their Christianity. Without the doctrine of the atoning sacrifice of Jesus, Christianity, as a religion, is naught; but unless the story of Adam's fall is accepted, the redemption from the consequences of that fall cannot be believed. Both in Great Britain and in the United States the Old and New Testaments are forced on the people as part of Christianity, for it is blasphemy at common law to deny the scriptures of the Old and New Testaments to be of divine authority, and such denial is punishable with fine and imprisonment, or even worse. The rejection of Christianity intended throughout this paper is, therefore, the rejection of the Old and New Testaments as being of divine revelation. It is the rejection alike of the authorized teachings of the Church of Rome and of the Church of England, as these may be found in the Bible; the creeds, the encyclicals, the prayer-book, the canons, and the homilies of either or both of these churches. It is the rejection of the Christianity of Luther, of Calvin, and of Wesley.

A ground frequently taken by Christian theologians is that the progress and civilization of the world are due to Christianity, and the discussion is complicated by the fact that many eminent servants of humanity have been nominal Christians of one or other of the sects. My allegation will be that the special service rendered to human progress by these exceptional men has not been in consequence of their adhesion to Christianity, but in spite of it; and that the specific points of advantage to human kind have been in ratio of their direct opposition to precise Biblical enactments. Take one dear gain to humanity consequent on unbelief—i.e., the abolition of slavery in some countries, the abolition of the slave-trade in most civilized countries, and the tendency to its total abolition. I am unaware of any religion in the world which in the past forbade slavery. The professors of Christianity for ages supported it; the Old Testament repeatedly sanctioned it by special laws; the New Testament has no repealing declaration. Though we are at the close of the nineteenth century of the Christian era, it is only during the past three-quarters of a century that the battle for freedom has been gradually won. It is scarcely a quarter of a century since the famous emancipation amendment was carried to the United States Constitution; and it is impossible for any well-informed Christian to deny that the abolition movement in North America was most steadily and bitterly opposed by the religious bodies in the various States. Henry Wilson, in his *Rise and Fall of the Slave-Power in America;* Samuel J. May, in his *Recollections of the Anti-Slavery Conflict,* and J. Greenleaf Whittier, in his poems, alike are witnesses that the Bible and pulpit, the church and its great influence, were used against abolition and in favor of the slaveowner. I know that Christians in the present day often declare that Christianity had a large share in bringing about the abolition of slavery, and this because men professing Christianity were Abolitionists. I plead that those so-called Christian Abolitionists were men and women whose humanity—recognizing freedom for all—was, in this, in direct conflict with Christianity. It is not yet fifty years since the European Christian Powers jointly agreed to abolish the slave trade. What of the effect of Christianity on these Powers in the centuries which had preceded? The heretic Condorcet pleaded powerfully for freedom, whilst Christian France was still slave-holding. For many centuries Christian Spain and Christian Portugal held slaves. Puerto Rico freedom is not of long date, and Cuban emancipation is even yet newer. It was a Christian king, Charles V., and a Christian friar, who founded in Spanish America the slave-trade between the Old World and the New. For some 1,800 years almost all Christians kept slaves, bought slaves, sold slaves, bred slaves, stole slaves. Pious Bristol and godly Liverpool, less than one hundred years ago, openly grow rich on the traffic. During the ninth century Greek Christians sold slaves to the Saracens. In the eleventh century prostitutes were publicly sold in Rome as slaves, and the profit went to the church.

It is said that William Wilberforce (1759-1833) was a Christian, but, at any rate, his Christianity was strongly diluted with unbelief. As an Abolitionist, he did not believe Leviticus, c. 25, v. 44-46; he must have rejected Exodus, c. 21, v. 2-6; he could not have accepted the many permissions and injunctions by the Bible Deity to his chosen people to capture and hold slaves. In the House of Commons on the 18th of February, 1796, Wilberforce reminded that Christian assembly that infidel and anarchic France had given liberty to the Africans, whilst Christian and monarchic England was "obstinately continuing a system of cruelty and injustice." Wilberforce, whilst advocating the abolition of slavery, found the whole influence of the English court and the great weight of the Episcopal bench against him. George III., a most Christian king, regarded abolition theories with abhorrence, and the Christian House of Lords was utterly opposed to granting freedom to the slave. When Christian missionaries, some sixty-two years ago, preached to Demerara negroes under the rule of Christian England, they were treated by Christian judges, holding commission from Christian England, as criminals for so preaching. A Christian commissioned officer, member of the Established Church of England, signed the auction notices for the sale of slaves as late as the year 1824. In the evidence before a Christian court-martial a missionary is charged with having tended to make the negroes dissatisfied with their condition as slaves, and with having promoted discontent and dissatisfaction amongst the slaves against their lawful masters. For this the Christian judges sentenced the Demerara Abolitionist missionary to be hanged by the neck till he was dead. The judges belonged to the Established Church; the missionary was a Methodist. In this the Church-of-England Christians in Demerara were no worse than Christians of other sects. Their Roman Catholic Christian brethren in St. Domingo fiercely attacked the Jesuits as criminals, because they treated the negroes as though they were men and women, in encouraging "two slaves to separate their interest and safety from that of the gang," whilst orthodox Christians let them couple promiscuously and breed for the benefit of the owners, like any other of their plantation cattle. In 1823 the *Royal Gazette* (Christian) of Demerara said: "We shall not suffer you to enlighten our slaves, who are by law our property, till you can demonstrate that, when they are made religious and knowing, they will continue to be our slaves."

When William Lloyd Garrison, the pure-minded and most earnest Abolitionist, delivered his first anti-slavery address in Boston, Massachusetts, the only building he could obtain in which to speak was the infidel hall owned by Abner Kneeland, the "infidel" editor of the *Boston Investigator,* who had been sent to jail for blasphemy. All the Christian sects had, in turn, refused Mr. Lloyd Garrison the use of the buildings they severally controlled. Lloyd Garrison told me, himself, how honored deacons of a Christian church joined in an actual attempt to hang him. When abolition was advocated in the United States in 1790, the representative from South Carolina was able to plead that the Southern clergy "did not condemn either slavery or the slave-trade," and Mr. Jackson, the representative from Georgia, pleaded that "from Genesis to Revelation" the current was favorable to slavery. Elias Hicks, the brave Abolitionist Quaker, was denounced as an atheist, and less than twenty years ago a Hicksite Quaker was expelled from one of the Southern American legislatures because of the reputed irreligion of these Abolitionist "Friends." When the Fugitive-Slave Law was under discussion in North America, large numbers of clergymen, of nearly every denomination, were found ready to defend this infamous act. Samuel James May, the famous Abolitionist, was driven from the pulpit as irreligious, solely because of his attacks on slave-holding. Northern clergymen tried to induce "silver-tongued" Wendell Phillips to abandon his advocacy of abolition. Southern pulpits rang with praises for the murderous attack on Charles Sumner. The slayers of Elijah Lovejoy were highly-reputed Christian men.

Guizot, notwithstanding that he tries to claim that the Church exerted its influence to restrain slavery, says *(European Civilization,* Vol. I., p. 110):

> It has often been repeated that the abolition of slavery among modern people
> is entirely due to Christians. That, I think, is saying too much. Slavery existed
> for a long period in the heart of Christian society, without its being particu-
> larly astonished or irritated. A multitude of causes, and a great development
> in other ideas and principles of civilization, were necessary for the abolition
> of this iniquity of all iniquities.

And my contention is that this "development in other ideas and principles of civilization" was long retarded by governments in which the Christian Church was dominant. The men who advocated liberty were imprisoned, racked, and burned, so long
as the Church was strong enough to be merciless. The Rev. Francis Minton, Rector of
Middlewich, in his recent earnest volume[1] on the struggles of labor, admits that

> ...a few centuries ago slavery was acknowledged throughout Christendom to
> have the divine sanction...Neither the exact cause nor the precise time of the
> decline of the belief in the righteousness of slavery can be defined. It was,
> doubtless, due to a combination of causes, one probably being as indirect as
> the recognition of the greater economy of free labor. With the decline of the
> belief, the abolition of slavery took place.

The institution of slavery was actually existent in Christian Scotland in the seventeenth century, where the white coal-workers and salt- workers of East Lothian were
chattels, as were their negro brethren in the Southern States thirty years since, and
"went to those who succeeded to the property of the works, and they could be sold,
bartered, or pawned."[2] There is, says J. M. Robertson, "no trace that the Protestant
clergy of Scotland ever raised a voice against the slavery which grew up before their
eyes. And it was not until 1799, after Republican and irreligious France had set the example, that it was legally abolished."

Take the further gain to humanity consequent on the unbelief, or rather disbelief, in witchcraft and wizardry. Apart from the brutality by Christians towards those
suspected of witchcraft, the hindrance to scientific initiative or experiment was incal-
culably great so long as belief in magic obtained. The inventions of the past two centuries, and especially those of this nineteenth century, might have benefited
mankind much earlier and much more largely but for the foolish belief in witchcraft
and the shocking ferocity exhibited towards those suspected of necromancy. After

quoting a large number of cases of trial and punishment for witchcraft from official records in Scotland, J. M. Robertson says:

> The people seem to have passed from cruelty to cruelty, precisely as they became more and more fanatical, more and more devoted to their church, till, after many generations, the slow spread of human science began to counteract the ravages of superstition, the clergy resisting reason and humanity to the last.

The Rev. Mr. Minton[3] concedes that it is "the advance of knowledge which has rendered the idea of Satanic agency, through the medium of witchcraft, grotesquely ridiculous." He admits that "for more than fifteen hundred years the belief in witchcraft was universal in Christendom," and that "the public mind was saturated with the idea of Satanic agency in the economy of nature." He adds: "If we ask why the world now rejects what was once so unquestioningly believed, we can only reply that advancing knowledge has gradually undermined the belief."

In a letter recently sent to the *Pall Mall Gazette* against modem Spiritualism, Professor Huxley declares "that the older form of the same fundamental delusion—the belief in possession and in witchcraft—gave rise, in the fifteenth, sixteenth, and seventeenth centuries, to persecutions by Christians of innocent men, women, and children, more extensive, more cruel, and more murderous than any to which the Christians of the first three centuries were subjected by the authorities of pagan Rome." And Professor Huxley adds:

> No one deserves much blame for being deceived in these matters. We are all intellectually handicapped in youth by the incessant repetition of the stories about possession and witchcraft in both the Old and the New Testament. The majority of us are taught nothing which will help us to observe accurately, and to interpret observations with due caution.

The English statute-book under Elizabeth and under James was disfigured by enactments against witchcraft passed under pressure from the Christian churches, which acts have only been repealed in consequence of the disbelief in the Christian precept, "Thou shalt not suffer a witch to live." The statute 1 James I., c. 12, condemned to death "all persons invoking any evil spirits, or consulting, covenanting with, entertaining, employing, feeding, or rewarding any evil spirit," or generally practising any "infernal arts." This was not repealed until the eighteenth century was far advanced. Edison's phonograph would, two hundred and eighty years ago, have insured martyrdom for the inventor; the utilization of electric force to transmit messages around the world would have been clearly the practice of an infernal art. At least, we may plead that unbelief has healed the bleeding feet of science and made the road free for her upward march.

Is it not also fair to urge the gain to humanity which has been apparent in the wiser treatment of the insane consequent on the unbelief in the Christian doctrine that these unfortunates were either examples of demoniacal possession or of special visitation of Deity? For centuries, under Christianity, mental disease was most ignorantly treated. Exorcism, shackles, and the whip were the penalties, rather than the curatives, for mental maladies. From the heretical departure of Phillipe Pinel (1745-1826), at the close of the last century, to the position of Henry Maudsley (1835-1918) today, every step illustrates the march of unbelief. Take the gain to humanity in the unbelief, not yet complete, but now largely preponderant, in the dogma that sickness, pestilence, and famine were manifestations of divine anger, the results of which could neither be avoided nor prevented. The Christian churches have done little or nothing to dispel this superstition. The official and authorized prayers of the principal denominations even today reaffirm it. Modern study of the laws of health, experiments in sanitary improvements, more careful application of medical knowledge, have proved more efficacious in preventing or diminishing plagues and pestilence than have the intervention of the priest or the practice of prayer. Those in England who hold the old faith that prayer will suffice to cure disease are today termed "peculiar people," and are occasionally indicted for manslaughter, when their sick children die, because the parents have trusted to God instead of appealing to the resources of science.

It is certainly clear gain to astronomical science that the church which tried to compel Galileo to unsay the truth, has been overborne by the growing unbelief of the age, even though our little children are yet taught that Joshua made the sun and moon stand still, and that for Hezekiah the sun-dial reversed its record. As Buckle, arguing for the morality of scepticism, says[4]:

> As long as men refer the movements of the comets to the immediate finger of God, and as long as they believe that an eclipse is one of the modes by which the Deity expresses his anger, they will never be guilty of the blasphemous presumption of attempting to predict such supernatural appearances. Before they could dare to investigate the causes of the mysterious phenomena, it is necessary that they should believe, or, at all events, that they should suspect, that the phenomena themselves were capable of being explained by the human mind.

As in astronomy, so in geology, the gain of the knowledge to humanity has been almost solely in measure of the rejection of the Christian theory, a century since almost universally held, that the world was created six thousand years ago, or, at any rate, that by the sin of the first man, Adam, death commenced about that period. Ethnology and anthropology have only been possible in so far as, adopting the regretful words of Sir William Jones (1746-1794), "intelligent and virtuous persons are inclined to doubt the authenticity of the documents delivered by Moses concerning the primitive world."

Surely it is clear gain to humanity that unbelief has sprung up against the divine right of kings; that men no longer believe that the monarch is "God's anointed," or that "the powers that be are ordained of God." In the struggles for political freedom, the weight of the church was mostly thrown on the side of the tyrant. The homilies of the Church of England declare that "even the wicked rulers have their power and authority from God," that "such subjects as are disobedient or rebellious against their princes, disobey God and procure their own damnation." It can scarcely be necessary to argue to the citizens of the United States of America that the origin of their liberties was in the rejection of this faith in the divine right of George III. Will any one, save the most bigoted, contend that it is not certain gain to humanity to spread unbelief in the terrible doctrine that eternal torment is the probable fate of the great majority of the human family? Is it not gain to have diminished the faith that it was the duty of the wretched and the miserable to be content with the lot in life which Providence had awarded them?

If it stood alone, it would be almost sufficient to plead, as justification for heresy, the approach towards equality and liberty for the utterance of all opinions achieved because of growing unbelief. At one period in Christendom each government acted as though only one religious faith could be true, and as though the holding, or, at any rate, the making known, of any other opinion was a criminal act deserving punishment. Under the one word, "infidel," even as late as Sir Edward Coke (1552-1634), were classed together all who were not Christians, even though they were Mohommedans, Brahmans, or Jews. All who did not accept the Christian faith were sweepingly denounced as infidels and, therefore, *hors de la loi*. One hundred and forty-five years since, the Attorney General, pleading in our highest court, said:[5] "What is the definition of an infidel? Why, one who does not believe in the Christian religion. Then a Jew is an infidel." And English history for several centuries prior to the Commonwealth shows how, habitually and most atrociously, Christian kings, Christian courts, and Christian churches persecuted and harassed these infidel Jews.

There was a time in England when Jews were such infidels that they were not even allowed to be sworn as witnesses. In 1740, a legacy left for establishing an assembly for the reading of the Jewish Scriptures was held to be void[6] because it was "for the propagation of the Jewish law in contradiction to the Christian religion." It is only in very modern times that municipal rights have been accorded in England to Jews. It is barely thirty years since they have been allowed to sit in Parliament. In 1801, the late Mr. Newdegate, in debate,[7] objected "that they should have sitting in that House an individual who regarded our Redeemer as an impostor." Lord Chief Justice Raymond has shown[8] how it was that Christian intolerance was gradually broken down:

> A Jew may sue at this day, but heretofore he could not; for then they were looked upon as enemies, but now commerce has taught the world more humanity.

Lord Coke treated the infidel as one who, in law, had no right of any kind, with whom no contract need be kept, to whom no debt was payable. The plea of "alien infidel," as answer to a claim, was actually pleaded in court as late as 1737.[9] In a solemn judgment Lord Coke says:

> All infidels are, in law, *perpetui inimici*, for between them, as with the devils whose subjects they be, and the Christians, there is perpetual hostility.

Twenty years ago the law of England required the writer of any periodical, publication, or pamphlet under sixpence in price to give sureties for eight hundred pounds against the publication of blasphemy. I was the last person prosecuted, in 1868, for non-compliance with that law, which was repealed by Mr. Gladstone in 1869. Up till the 23d of December, 1888, an infidel in Scotland was only allowed to enforce any legal claim in court on condition that, if challenged, he denied his infidelity. If he lied and said that he was a Christian, he was accepted, despite his lying. If he told the truth and said that he was an unbeliever, then he was practically an outlaw, incompetent to give evidence for himself or for any other. Fortunately, all this was changed by the royal assent to the Oaths Act on the 24th of December. Has not humanity clearly gained a little in this struggle through unbelief?

For more than a century and a half the Roman Catholic had, in practice, harsher measure dealt out to him by the English Protestant Christian than was, even during that period, the fate of the Jew or the unbeliever. If the Roman Catholic would not take the oath of abjuration, which, to a sincere Romanist, was impossible, he was, in effect, an outlaw, and the "jury-packing," so much complained of to-day in Ireland, is one of the survivals of the old, bad time when Roman Catholics were thus, by law, excluded from the jury-box.

The *Scotsman* of January 5, 1889, notes that, in 1860, the Rev. Dr. Robert Lee, of Greyfriars, gave a course of Sunday evening lectures on Biblical Criticism, in which he showed the absurdity and untenableness of regarding every word in the Bible as inspired, and adds:

> We well remember the awful indignation such opinions inspired, and it is refreshing to contrast them with the calmness with which they are now received. Not only from the pulpits of the city, but from the press (misnamed religious) were his doctrines denounced. And one eminent U.P. minister went the length of publicly praying for him, and for the students under his care. It speaks volumes for the progress made since then, when we think that, in all probability, Dr. Charteris, Dr. Lee's successor in the chair, differs, in his teaching, from the Confession of Faith much more widely than Dr. Lee ever did, and yet he is considered supremely orthodox, whereas the stigma of heresy was attached to the other all his life.

And this change and gain to humanity are due to the gradual progress of unbelief alike inside and outside the churches. Take, from differing churches, two recent illustrations. The late Principal, Dr. Lindsay Alexander, a strict Calvinist, in his important work on *Biblical Theology,* claims that "all the statements of Scripture are alike to be deferred to, as presenting to us the mind of God." Yet the Reverend Doctor of Divinity also says:

> We find in their writings [i.e., in the writings of the sacred authors] statements which no ingenuity can reconcile with what modern research has shown to be the scientific truth.

At the last Southwell Diocesan Church-of-England Conference, at Derby, the Bishop of the Diocese presiding, the Rev. J. G. Richardson said of the Old Testament that

> ...it was no longer honest, or even safe, to deny that this noble literature, rich in all the elements of moral or spiritual grandeur, given so the Church had always taught and would always teach under the inspiration of Almighty God, was sometimes mistaken in its science, was sometimes inaccurate in its history, and sometimes relative and accommodatory in its morality. It resumed theories of the physical world which science has abandoned and could never resume; it contained passages of narrative which devout and temperate men

pronounced discredited both by external and internal evidence; it praised, or justified, or approved, or condoned, or tolerated conduct which the teaching of Christ and the conscience of the Christian alike condemned.

Or—as I should urge the gain to humanity by unbelief is that the "teaching of Christ" has been modified, enlarged, widened, and humanized, and that "the conscience of the Christian" is, in quantity and quality, made fitter for the ever-increasing additions of knowledge of these later and more heretical days.

Notes

1. *Capital and Wages,* p. 19.

2. *Perversion of Scotland,* p. 197.

3. *Capital and Wages,* pp. 15,16.

4. *History of Civilization,* Vol. I., p. 345. Henry Thomas Buckle (1821-1862), British historian.

5. Omychund vs. Barker, 1 Atkyns, 29.

6. D'Costa vs. D'Pays, Amb., 228.

7. 3 Hansard, cxvi., 381.

8. 1 Lord Raymond's Reports, 282, Wells vs. Williams.

9. Ramkijsenseat vs. Barker, 1 Atkyns, 51.

10.Coke's reports, Calvin's case.

12
Miracle (1895)
Anatole France

We should not say: there are no miracles, because none has ever been proved. This always leaves it open to the Orthodox to appeal to a more complete state of knowledge. The truth is, no miracle can, from the nature of things, be stated as an established fact; to do so will always involve drawing a premature conclusion. A deeply rooted instinct tells us that whatever Nature embraces in her bosom is conformable to her laws, either known or occult. But, even supposing he could silence this presentiment of his, a man will never be in a position to say: "Such and such a fact is outside the limits of Nature." Our researches will never carry us as far as that. Moreover, if it is of the essence of miracle to elude scientific investigation, every dogma attesting it invokes an intangible witness that is bound to evade our grasp to the end of time.

This notion of miracles belongs to the infancy of the mind, and cannot continue when once the human intellect has begun to frame a systematic picture of the universe. The wise Greeks could not tolerate the idea. Hippocrates said, speaking of epilepsy: "This malady is called divine; but all diseases are divine, and all alike come from the gods." There he spoke as a natural philosopher. Human reason is less assured of itself nowadays. What annoys me above all is when people say: "We do not believe in miracles, because no miracle is proved."

Happening to be at Lourdes, in August, I paid a visit to the grotto where innumerable crutches were hung up in token of a cure. My companion pointed to these trophies of the sick-room and hospital ward, and whispered in my ear:

One wooden leg would be more to the point.

It was the word of a man of sense; but speaking philosophically, the wooden leg would be no whit more convincing than a crutch. If an observer of a genuinely scientific spirit were called upon to verify that a man's leg, after amputation, had suddenly grown again as before, whether in a miraculous pool or anywhere else, he would not cry: "Lo! a miracle." He would say this:

> An observation, so far unique, points us to a presumption that under conditions still undetermined, the tissues of a human leg have the property of reorganizing themselves like a crab's or lobster's claws and a lizard's tail, but much more rapidly. Here we have a fact of nature in apparent contradiction with several other facts of the like sort. The contradiction arises from our ignorance, and clearly shows that the science of animal physiology must be reconstituted, or to speak more accurately, that it has never yet been properly constituted. It is little more than two hundred years since we first had any true conception of the circulation of the blood. It is barely a century since we learned what is implied in the act of breathing.

I admit it would need some boldness to speak in this strain. But the man of science should be above surprise. At the same time, let us hasten to add, none of them has ever been put to such a proof, and nothing leads us to apprehend any such prodigy. Such miraculous cures as the doctors have been able to verify to their satisfaction are all quite in accordance with physiology. So far the tombs of the Saints, the magic springs and sacred grottoes, have never proved efficient except in the case of patients suffering from complaints either curable or susceptible of instantaneous relief. But were a dead man revived before our eyes, no miracle would be proved, unless we knew what life is and death is, and that we shall never know.

What is the definition of a miracle? We are told: a breach of the laws of nature. But we do not know the laws of nature; how, then, are we to know whether a particular fact is a breach of these laws or no?

"But surely we know some of these laws?

"True, we have arrived at some idea of the correlation of things. But failing as we do to grasp all the natural laws, we can be sure of none, seeing they are mutually interdependent.

"Still, we might verify our miracle in those series of correlations we *have* arrived at.

"No, not with anything like philosophical certainty. Besides, it is precisely those series we regard as the most stable and best determined which suffer least interruption from the miraculous. Miracles never, for instance, try to interfere with the mechanism of the heavens. They never disturb the course of the celestial bodies, and never advance or retard the calculated date of an eclipse. On the contrary, their favourite field is the obscure domain of pathology as concerned with the internal organs, and above all nervous diseases. However, we must not confound a question of fact with one of principle. In principle the man of science is ill-qualified to verify a supernatural occurrence. Such verification presupposes a complete and final knowledge of nature, which he does not possess, and will never possess, and which no one ever did possess in this world. It is just because I would not believe our most skilful oculists as to the miraculous healing of a blind man that *a fortiori* I do not believe Matthew or Mark either, who were not oculists. A miracle is by definition unidentifiable and unknowable."

The savants cannot in any case certify that a fact is in contradiction with the universal order, that is with the unknown ordinance of the Divinity. Even God could do this only by formulating a pettifogging distinction between the general manifestations and the particular manifestations of His activity, acknowledging that from time to time He gives little timid finishing touches to His work and condescending to the humiliating admission that the cumbersome machine He has set agoing needs every hour or so, to get it to jog along indifferently well, a push from its contriver's hand.

Science is well fitted, on the other hand, to bring back under the data of positive knowledge facts which seemed to be outside its limits. It often succeeds very happily in accounting by physical causes for phenomena that had for centuries been regarded as supernatural. Cures of spinal affections were confidently believed to have taken place at the tomb of the Deacon Paris at Saint-Medard and in other holy places. These cures have ceased to surprise since it has become known that hysteria occasionally simulates the symptoms associated with lesions of the spinal marrow.

The appearance of a new star to the mysterious personages whom the Gospels call the "Wise Men of the East" (I assume the incident to be authentic historically) was undoubtedly a miracle to the astrologers of the Middle Ages, who believed that the firmament, in which the stars were stuck like nails, was subject to no change whatever. But, whether real or supposed, the star of the Magi has lost its miraculous character for us, who know that the heavens are incessantly perturbed by the birth and death of worlds, and who in 1866 saw a star suddenly blaze forth in the Corona Borealis, shine for a month, and then go out.

It did not proclaim the Messiah; all it announced was that, at an infinitely remote distance from our earth, an appalling conflagration was burning up a world in a few days, or rather had burnt it up long ago, for the ray that brought us the news of this disaster in the heavens had been on the road for five hundred years and possibly longer.

The miracle of Bolsena is familiar to everybody, immortalized as is in one of Raphael's *Stanze* at the Vatican. A sceptical priest was celebrating Mass; the host, when he broke it for Communion, appeared bespattered with blood. It is only within the last ten years that the Academies of Science would not have been sorely puzzled to explain so strange a phenomenon. Now no one thinks of denying it, since the discovery of a microscopic fungus, the spores of which, having germinated in the meal or dough, offer the appearance of clotted blood. The naturalist who first found it, rightly thinking that here were the red blotches on the wafer in the Bolsena miracle, named the fungus *micrococcus prodigiosus*.

There will always be a fungus, a star, or a disease that human science does not know of; and for this reason it must always behoove the philosopher, in the name of the undying ignorance of man, to deny every miracle and say of the most startling wonders, the host of Bolsena, the star in the East, the cure of the paralytic and the like: either it is not, or it is; and if it is, it is part of nature and therefore natural.

13
Autobiography (1876)[1]
Charles Darwin

During these two years [October 1836 to January 1839] I was led to think much about religion. Whilst on board the *Beagle* I was quite orthodox, and I remember being heartily laughed at by several of the officers (though themselves orthodox) for quoting the Bible as an unanswerable authority on some point of morality. I suppose it was the novelty of the argument that amused them. But I had gradually come by this time, i.e., 1836 to 1839, to see that the Old Testament was no more to be trusted than the sacred books of the Hindoos. The question then continually rose before my mind and would not be banished, is it credible that if God were now to make a revelation to the Hindoos, he would permit it to be connected with the belief in Vishnu, Siva, etc., as Christianity is connected with the Old Testament? This appeared to me utterly incredible.

By further reflecting that the clearest evidence would be requisite to make any sane man believe in the miracles by which Christianity is supported—and that the more we know of the fixed laws of nature the more incredible do miracles become, that the men at that time were ignorant and credulous to a degree almost incomprehensible by us—that the Gospels cannot be proved to have been written simultaneously with the events, that they differ in many important details, far too important, as it seemed to me, to be admitted as the usual inaccuracies of eye-witnesses; by such reflections as these, which I give not as having the least novelty or value, but as they influenced me, I gradually came to disbelieve in Christianity as a divine revelation. The fact that many false religions have spread over large portions of the earth like wild-fire had some weight with me.

But I was very unwilling to give up my belief; I feel sure of this, for I can well remember often and often inventing day-dreams of old letters between distinguished Romans, and manuscripts being discovered at Pompeii or elsewhere, which confirmed in the most striking manner all that was written in the Gospels. But I found it more and more difficult, with free scope given to my imagination, to invent evidence which would suffice to convince me. Thus disbelief crept over me at a very slow rate, but was at last complete. The rate was so slow that I felt no distress.

Although I did not think much about the existence of a personal God until a considerably later period of my life, I will here give the vague conclusions to which I have been driven. The old argument from design in Nature, as given by Paley, which formerly seemed to me so conclusive, fails, now that the law of natural selection has been discovered. We can no longer argue that, for instance, the beautiful hinge of a bivalve shell must have been made by an intelligent being, like the hinge of a door by man. There seems to be no more design in the variability of organic beings, and in the action of natural selection, than in the course which the wind blows. But I have discussed this subject at the end of my book on the *Variation of Domesticated Animals and Plants,* and the argument there given has never, as far as I can see, been answered.

But passing over the endless beautiful adaptations which we everywhere meet with, it may be asked how can the generally beneficent arrangement of the world be accounted for? Some writers indeed are so much impressed with the amount of suffering in the world, that they doubt, if we look to all sentient beings, whether there is more of misery or of happiness; whether the world as a whole is a good or bad one. According to my judgment happiness decidedly prevails, though this would be very difficult to prove. If the truth of this conclusion be granted, it harmonizes well with the effects which we might expect from natural selection. If all the individuals of any species were habitually to suffer to an extreme degree, they would neglect to propagate their kind; but we have no reason to believe that this has ever, or at least often occurred. Some other considerations, moreover, lead to the belief that all sentient beings have been formed so as to enjoy, as a general rule, happiness.

Every one who believes, as I do, that all the corporeal and mental organs (excepting those which are neither advantageous nor disadvantageous to the possessor) of all beings have been developed through natural selection, or the survival of the fittest, together with use or habit, will admit that these organs have been formed so that their possessors may compete successfully with other beings, and thus increase in number. Now an animal may be led to pursue that course of action which is most beneficial to the species by suffering, such as pain, hunger, thirst, and fear; or by pleasure, as in eating and drinking, and in the propagation of the species; or by both means combined, as in the search for food. But pain or suffering of any kind, if long continued, causes depression and lessens the power of action, yet is well adapted to make a creature guard itself against any great or sudden evil. Pleasurable sensations, on the other hand, may be long continued without any depressing effect; on the contrary, they stimulate the whole system to increased action. Hence it has come to pass that most or all sentient beings have been developed in such a manner, through natural selection, that pleasurable sensations serve as their habitual guides. We see this in the pleasure from exertion, even occasionally from great exertion of the body or mind, in the pleasure of our daily meals, and especially in the pleasure derived from sociability, and from loving our families. The sum of such pleasures as these, which are habitual or frequently recurrent, give, as I can hardly doubt, to most sentient beings an excess of happiness over misery, although many occasionally suffer much. Such suffering is quite compatible with the belief in natural selection, which is not perfect in its action, but tends only to render each species as successful as possible in the battle for life with other species, in wonderfully complex and changing circumstances.

That there is much suffering in the world no one disputes. Some have attempted to explain this with reference to man by imagining that it serves for his moral improvement. But the number of men in the world is as nothing compared with that of all other sentient beings, and they often suffer greatly without any moral improvement. This very old argument from the existence of suffering against the existence of an intelligent First Cause seems to me a strong one; whereas, as just remarked, the presence of much suffering agrees well with the view that all organic beings have been developed through variation and natural selection.

At the present day the most usual argument for the existence of an intelligent God is drawn from the deep inward conviction and feelings which are experienced by most persons.

Formerly I was led by feelings such as those just referred to (although I do not think that the religious sentiment was ever strongly developed in me), to the firm conviction of the existence of God, and of the immortality of the soul. In my Journal I wrote that whilst standing in the midst of the grandeur of a Brazilian forest, "it is not possible to give an adequate idea of the higher feelings of wonder, admiration, and devotion, which fill and elevate the mind." I well remember my conviction that there is more in man than the mere breath of his body. But now the grandest scenes would not cause any such convictions and feelings to rise in my mind. It may be truly said that I am like a man who has become colour-blind, and the universal belief by men of the existence of redness makes my present loss of perception of not the least value as evidence. This argument would be a valid one if all men of all races had the same inward conviction of the existence of one God; but we know that this is very far from being the case. Therefore I cannot see that such inward convictions and feelings are of any weight as evidence of what really exists. The state of mind which grand scenes formerly excited in me, and which was intimately connected with a belief in God, did not essentially differ from that which is often called the sense of sublimity; and however difficult it may be to explain the genesis of this sense, it can hardly be advanced as an argument for the existence of God, any more than the powerful though vague and similar feelings excited by music.

With respect to immortality, nothing shows me [so clearly] how strong and almost instinctive a belief it is, as the consideration of the view now held by most physicists, namely, that the sun with all the planets will in time grow too cold for life, unless indeed some great body dashes into the sun, and thus gives it fresh life. Believing as I do that man in the distant future will be a far more perfect creature than he now is, it is an intolerable thought that he and all other sentient beings are doomed to complete annihilation after such long-continued slow progress. To those who fully admit the immortality of the human soul, the destruction of our world will not appear so dreadful.

Another source of conviction in the existence of God, connected with the reason, and not with the feelings, impresses me as having much more weight. This follows from the extreme difficulty or rather impossibility of conceiving this immense and wonderful universe, including man with his capacity of looking far backwards and far into futurity, as the result of blind chance or necessity. When thus reflecting I feel compelled to look to a First Cause having an intelligent mind in some degree analogous to that of man; and I deserve to be called a Theist. This conclusion was strong in my mind about the time, as far as I can remember, when I wrote the *Origin of Species*; and it is since that time that it has very gradually, with many fluctuations, become weaker. But then arises the doubt, can the mind of man, which has, as I fully believe, been developed from a mind as low as that possessed by the lowest animals, be trusted when it draws such grand conclusions?

I cannot pretend to throw the least light on such abstruse problems. The mystery of the beginning of all things is insoluble by us; and I for one must be content to remain an Agnostic.

Notes
1. This essay appears in *The Life and Letters of Charles Darwin*.

14
The Antichrist (1888)
Friedrich Nietzsche

47

The thing that sets us apart is not that we are unable to find God, either in history, or in nature, or behind nature—but that we regard what has been honoured as God, not as "divine," but as pitiable, as absurd, as injurious; not as a mere error, but as a *crime against life*... We deny that God is God... If any one were to *show* us this Christian God, we'd be still less inclined to believe in him. In a formula: *dens, qualem Paulus creavit, dei negatio.* Such a religion as Christianity, which does not touch reality at a single point and which goes to pieces the moment reality asserts its rights at any point, must be inevitably the deadly enemy of the "wisdom of this world," which is to say, of *science*—*and* it will give the name of good to whatever means serve to poison, calumniate and *cry down* all intellectual discipline, all lucidity and strictness in matters of intellectual conscience, and all noble coolness and freedom of the mind. "Faith," as an imperative, vetoes science—in *praxi,* lying at any price... Paul *well knew* that lying—that "faith"—was necessary; later on the church borrowed the fact from Paul.

The God that Paul invented for himself, a God who "reduced to absurdity" "the wisdom of this world" (especially the two great enemies of superstition, philology and medicine), is in truth only an indication of Paul's resolute *determination* to accomplish that very thing himself: to give one's own will the name of God, *thora*[1]—that is essentially Jewish. Paul *wants* to dispose of the "wisdom of this world": his enemies are the *good* philologians and physicians of the Alexandrine school—on them he makes his war. As a matter of fact no man can be a *philologian* or a physician without being also *Antichrist.* That is to say, as a philologian a man sees *behind* the "holy books," and as a physician he sees *behind* the physiological degeneration of the typical Christian. The physician says "incurable"; the philologian says "fraud."

48

Has any one ever clearly understood the celebrated story at the beginning of the Bible—of God's mortal terror of *science?* No one, in fact, has understood it. This priest-book *par excellence* opens, as is fitting, with the great inner difficulty of the priest: *he* faces only one great danger; *ergo,* "God" faces only one great danger.

The old God, wholly "spirit," wholly the high-priest, wholly perfect, is promenading his garden: he is bored and trying to kill time. Against boredom even gods struggle in vain.[2] What does he do? He creates man—man is entertaining... But then he notices that man is also bored. God's pity for the only form of distress that invades all paradises knows no bounds: so he forthwith creates other animals. God's first mistake: to man these other animals were not entertaining—he sought dominion over them; he did not want to be an "animal" himself. So God created woman. In the act he brought boredom to an end—and also many other things! Woman was the *second* mistake of God. "Woman, at bottom, is a serpent, Heva"—every priest knows that; "from woman comes every evil in the world" every priest knows that, too. *Ergo,* she is also to blame for *science...* It was through woman that man learned to taste of the tree of knowledge. What happened?

The old God was seized by mortal terror. Man himself had been his *greatest* blunder; he had created a rival to himself; science makes men godlike—it is all up with priests and gods when man becomes scientific! Moral: science is the forbidden *per se*; it alone is forbidden. Science is the *first* of sins, the germ of all sins, the *original* sin. *This is all there is of morality.* "*Thou* shalt *not* know": the rest follows from that—God's mortal terror, however, did not hinder him from being shrewd. How is one to *protect* one's self against science? For a long while this was the capital problem. Answer: out of paradise with man! Happiness, leisure, foster thought—and all thoughts are bad thoughts! Man *must* not think. And so the priest invents distress, death, the mortal dangers of childbirth, all sorts of misery, old age, decrepitude, above all, *sickness* nothing but devices for making war on science! The troubles of man don't *allow* him to think... Nevertheless how terrible!—the edifice of knowledge begins to tower aloft, invading heaven, shadowing the gods—what is to be done? The old God invents *war;* he separates the peoples; he makes men destroy one another (—the priests have always had need of war...). War—among other things, a great disturber of science! —Incredible! Knowledge, *deliverance from the priests,* prospers in spite of war. So the old God comes to his final resolution: "Man has become scientific—there *is no help for it: he must be drowned!*"

49

I have been understood. At the opening of the Bible there is the *whole* psychology of the priest. The priest knows of only one great danger: that is science the sound comprehension of cause and effect. But science flourishes, on the whole, only under favourable conditions—a man must have time, he must have an *overflowing* intellect, in order to "know"… "*Therefore,* man must be made unhappy," this has been, in all ages, the logic of the priest. It is easy to see just *what,* by this logic, was the first thing to come into the world: "sin." The concept of guilt and punishment, the whole "moral order of the world," was set up *against* science— *against* the deliverance of man from priests… Man must *not* look outward; he must look inward. He must *not* look at things shrewdly and cautiously, to learn about them; he must not look at all; he must *suffer*… And he must suffer so much that he is always in need of the priest. Away with physicians! *What is needed is a Saviour.*—The concept of guilt and punishment, including the doctrines of "grace," of "salvation," of "forgiveness"—lies through and through, and absolutely without psychological reality—were devised to destroy man's *sense of causality:* they are an attack upon the concept of cause and effect! And *not* an attack with the fist, with the knife, with honesty in hate and love! On the contrary, one inspired by the most cowardly, the most crafty, the most ignoble of instincts! An attack of *priests!* An attack of *parasites!* The vampirism of pale, subterranean leeches!… When the natural consequences of an act are no longer "natural," but are regarded as produced by the ghostly creations of superstition by "God," by "spirits," by "souls"—and reckoned as merely "moral" consequences, as rewards, as punishments, as hints, as lessons, then the whole groundwork of knowledge is destroyed then *the greatest of crimes against humanity has been perpetrated.* I repeat that sin, man's self-desecration *par excellence,* was invented in order to make science, culture, and every elevation and ennobling of man impossible; the priest *rules* through the invention of sin.—

50

In this place I can't permit myself to omit a psychology of "belief," of the "believer," for the special benefit of "believers." If there remain any today who do not yet know how *indecent* it is to be "believing"—or how much a sign of *decadence,* of a broken will to live, then they will know it well enough tomorrow. My voice reaches even the deaf. It appears, unless I have been incorrectly informed, that there prevails among Christians a sort of criterion of truth that is called "proof by power." "Faith makes blessed: *therefore* it is true."—It might be objected right here that blessedness is not demonstrated, it is merely *promised:* it hangs upon "faith" as a condition—one *shall* be blessed *because* one believes… But what of the thing that the priest promises to the believer, the wholly transcendental "beyond"—how is *that* to be demonstrated? The "proof by power," thus assumed, is actually no more at bottom than a belief that the effects which faith promises will not fail to appear. In a formula: "I believe that faith makes for blessedness—therefore, it is true."… But this is as far as we may go. This "therefore" would be *absurdum* itself as a criterion of truth. But let us admit, for the sake of politeness, that blessedness by faith may be demonstrated (*not* merely hoped for, and *not* merely promised by the suspicious lips of a priest): even so, *could* blessedness—in a technical term, *pleasure ever* be a proof of truth? So little is this true that it is almost a proof against truth when sensations of pleasure influence the answer to the question "What is true?" or, at all events, it is enough to make that "truth" highly suspicious. The proof by "pleasure" is a proof *of* pleasure nothing more; why in the world should it be assumed that *true* judgments give more pleasure than false ones, and that, in conformity to some preestablished harmony, they necessarily bring agreeable feelings in their train? The experience of all disciplined and profound minds teaches *the contrary.* Man has had to fight for every atom of the truth, and has had to pay for it almost everything that the heart, that human love, that human trust cling to. Greatness of soul is needed for this business: the service of truth is the hardest of all services.—What, then, is the meaning of *integrity* in things intellectual? It means that a man must be severe with his own heart, that he must scorn "beautiful feelings," and that he makes every Yea and Nay a matter of conscience! —Faith makes blessed: *therefore,* it lies.

51

The fact that faith, under certain circumstances, may work for blessedness, but that this blessedness produced by an *idee fixe* by no means makes the idea itself true, and the fact that faith actually moves no mountains, but instead *raises them* up where there were none before: all this is made sufficiently clear by a walk through a *lunatic asylum. Not,* of course, to a priest: for his instincts prompt him to the lie that sickness finds sickness *necessary,* just as the Greek spirit had need of a superabundance of health, the actual ulterior purpose of the whole system of salvation of the church is to *make* people ill. And the church itself— doesn't it set up a Catholic lunatic asylum as the ultimate ideal? The whole earth as a madhouse? The sort of religious man that the church *wants* is a typical *decadent;* the moment at which a religious crisis dominates a people is always marked by epidemics of nervous disorder; the "inner world" of the religious man is so much like the "inner world" of the overstrung and exhausted that it is difficult to distinguish between them; the "highest" states of mind, held up before mankind by Christianity as of supreme worth, are actually epileptoid in form: the church has granted the name of holy only to lunatics or to gigantic frauds *in majorem dei honorem*. Once I ventured to designate the whole Christian system of training in penance and salvation (now best studied in England) as a method of producing a *folie circulaire* upon a soil already prepared for it, which is to say, a soil thoroughly unhealthy. Not every one may be a Christian: one is not "converted" to Christianity—one must first be sick enough for it…We others, who have the *courage* for health *and* likewise for contempt, we may well despise a religion that teaches misunderstanding of the body! that refuses to rid itself of the superstition about the soul! that makes a "virtue" of insufficient nourishment! that combats health as a sort of enemy, devil, temptation! that persuades itself that it is possible to carry about a "perfect soul" in a cadaver of a body, and that, to this end, had to devise for itself a new concept of "perfection," a pale, sickly, idiotically ecstatic state of existence, so-called "holiness"—a holiness that is itself merely a series of symptoms of an impoverished, enervated and incurably disordered body!… The Christian movement, as a European movement, was from the start no more than a general uprising of all sorts of outcast and refuse elements (who now, under cover of Christianity, aspire to power). It does *not* represent the decay of a race; it represents, on the contrary, a conglomeration of *decadent* products from all directions, crowding together and seeking one another out. It was *not,* as has been thought, the corruption of antiquity, of *noble* antiquity, which made Christianity possible; one cannot too sharply challenge the learned imbecility which today maintains that theory. At the time when the sick and rotten Chandala ("untouchable") classes in the whole *imperium* were Christianized, the *contrary type,* the nobility, reached its finest and ripest development. The majority became master; democracy, with its Christian instincts, *triumphed*… Christianity was not "national," it was not based on race, it appealed to all the varieties of men disinherited by life, it had its allies everywhere. Christianity has the rancour of the sick at its very core: the instinct against the *healthy,* against *health.* Everything that is well-consti- tuted, proud, gallant and, above all, beautiful gives offence to its ears and eyes. Again I remind you of Paul's priceless saying: "And God hath chosen the *weak* things of the world, the *foolish* things of the world, the *base* things of the world, and things which are *despised*"[3]: *this* was the formula; *in hoc signo* the *decadence* triumphed—*God on the cross*—is man always to miss the frightful inner significance of this symbol? Everything that suffers, everything that hangs on the cross, is *divine*…

We all hang on the cross, consequently *we* are divine… We alone are divine… Christianity was thus a victory: a nobler attitude of mind was destroyed by it—Christianity remains to this day the greatest misfortune of humanity.

52

Christianity also stands in opposition to all *intellectual* well-being, sick reasoning is the only sort that it *can* use as Christian reasoning it takes the side of everything that is idiotic; it pronounces a curse upon "intellect," upon the superbia of the healthy intellect. Since sickness is inherent in Christianity, it follows that the typically Christian state of "faith" *must* be a form of sickness too, and that all straight, straightforward and scientific paths to knowledge *must* be banned by the church as *forbidden* ways. Doubt is thus a sin from the start… The complete lack of psychological cleanliness in the priest—revealed by a glance at him—is a phenomenon resulting from *decadence*; one may observe in hysterical women and in rachitic children how regularly the falsification of instincts, delight in lying for the mere sake of lying, and incapacity for looking straight and walking straight are symptoms of *decadence.* "Faith" means the will to avoid knowing what is true. The pietist, the priest of either sex, is a fraud *because* he is sick: his instinct *demands* that the truth shall never be allowed its rights on any point. "Whatever makes for illness is *good*; whatever issues from abundance, from superabundance, from power, is *evil*": so argues the believer. The *impulse to lie*—it is by this that I recognize every foreordained theologian. Another characteristic of the theologian is his *unfitness for philology.* What I here mean by philology is, in a general sense, the art of reading with profit—the capacity for absorbing facts *without* interpreting them falsely, and *without* losing caution, patience and subtlety in the effort to understand them. Philology as *ephexislo*[4] in interpretation: whether one be dealing with books, with newspaper reports, with the most fateful events or with weather statistics, not to mention the "salvation of the soul"… The way in which a theologian, whether in Berlin or in Rome, is ready to explain, say, a "passage of Scripture," or an experience, or a victory by the national army, by turning upon it the high illumination of the Psalms of David, is always so *daring* that it is enough to make a philologian run up a wall. But what shall he do when pietists and other such cows from Swabia use the "finger of God" to convert their miserably commonplace and huggermugger existence into a miracle of "grace," a "providence" and an "experience of salvation"? The most modest exercise of the intellect, not to say of decency, should certainly be enough to convince these interpreters of the perfect childishness and unworthiness of such a misuse of the divine digital dexterity. However small our piety, if we ever encountered a god who always cured us of a cold in the head at just the right time, or got us into our carriage at the very instant heavy rain began to fall, he would seem so absurd a god that he'd have to be abolished even if he existed. God as a domestic servant, as a letter carrier, as an almanac-man—at bottom, he is a mere name for the stupidest sort of chance... "Divine Providence," which every third man in "educated Germany" still believes in, is so strong an argument against God that it would be impossible to think of a stronger. And in any case it is an argument against Germans!

62

With this I come to a conclusion and pronounce my judgment. I *condemn* Christianity; I bring against the Christian church the most terrible of all the accusations that an accuser has ever had in his mouth. It is, to me, the greatest of all imaginable corruptions; it seeks to work the ultimate corruption, the worst possible corruption. The Christian church has left nothing untouched by its depravity; it has turned every value into worthlessness, and every truth into a lie, and every integrity into baseness of soul. Let any one dare to speak to me of its "humanitarian" blessings! Its deepest necessities range it against any effort to abolish distress; it lives by distress; it *creates* distress to make *itself* immortal... For example, the worm of sin: it was the church that first enriched mankind with this misery! The "equality of souls before God"—this fraud, this pretext for the *rancour* of all the base-minded—this explosive concept, ending in revolution, the modern idea, and the notion of overthrowing the whole social order—this is *Christian* dynamite... The "humanitarian" blessings of Christianity forsooth! To breed out of *humanitas* a self-contradiction, an art of self-pollution, a will to lie at any price, an aversion and contempt for all good and honest instincts! All this, to me, is the "humanitarianism" of Christianity! Parasitism as the *only* practice of the church; with its anaemic and "holy" ideals, sucking all the blood, all the love, all the hope out of life; the beyond as the will to deny all reality; the cross as the distinguishing mark of the most subterranean conspiracy ever heard of, against health, beauty, well-being, intellect, *kindness* of soul *against life itself*...

This eternal accusation against Christianity I shall write upon all walls, wherever walls are to be found—I have letters that even the blind will be able to see... I call Christianity the one great curse, the one great intrinsic depravity, the one great instinct of revenge, for which no means are venomous enough, or secret, subterranean and *small* enough—I call it the one immortal blemish upon the human race...

And mankind reckons *time* from the *dies nefastus* when this fatality befell from the *first* day of Christianity! —*Why not rather from its last? From today? The transvaluation of all values!*

Notes

1. Or Torah.

2. 1920 translation by H.L. Mencken.

3. I Corinthians i, 27, 28. [Mencken's note]

4. To the ancient Greeks scepticism was also occasionally called ephecticism. [Mencken's note]

15
God In The Constitution
Robert G. Ingersoll

All governments derive their just powers from the consent of the governed.

In this country [the USA] it is admitted that the power to govern resides in the people themselves; that they are the only rightful source of authority. For many centuries before the formation of our Government, before the promulgation of the Declaration of Independence, the people had but little voice in the affairs of nations. The source of authority was not in this world; kings were not crowned by their subjects, and the sceptre was not held by the consent of the governed. The king sat on his throne by the will of God, and for that reason was not accountable to on high. God was a supreme autocrat in heaven, whose will was law, and the king was a supreme autocrat on earth whose will was law. The God in heaven had inferior beings to do his will, and the king on earth had certain favorites and officers to do his. These officers were accountable to him, and he was responsible to God.

The Feudal system was supposed to be in accordance with the divine plan. The people were not governed by intelligence, but by threats and promises, by rewards and punishments. No effort was made to enlighten the common people; no one thought of educating a peasant—of developing the mind of a laborer. The people were created to support thrones and altars. Their destiny was to toil and obey—to work and want. They were to be satisfied with huts and hovels, with ignorance and rags, and their children must expect no more. In the presence of the king they fell upon their knees, and before the priest they groveled in the very dust. The poor peasant divided his earnings with the state, because he imagined it protected his body; he divided his crust with the church, believing that it protected his soul. He was the prey of Throne and Altar—one deformed his body, the other his mind—and these two vultures fed upon his toil. He was taught by the king to hate the people of other nations, and by the priest to despise the believers in all other religions. He was made the enemy of all people except his own. He had no sympathy with the peasants of other lands, enslaved and plundered like himself. He was kept in ignorance, because education is the enemy of superstition, and because education is the foe of that egotism often mistaken for patriotism.

The intelligent and good man holds in his affections the good and true of every land—the boundaries of countries are not the limitations of his sympathies. Caring nothing for race, or color, he loves those who speak other languages and worship other gods. Between him and those who suffer, there is no impassable gulf. He salutes the world, and extends the hand of friendship to the human race. He does not bow before a provincial and patriotic god—one who protects his tribe or nation, and abhors the rest of mankind.

Through all the ages of superstition, each nation has insisted that it was the peculiar care of the true God, and that it alone had the true religion—that the gods of other nations were false and fraudulent, and that other religions were wicked, ignorant and absurd. In this way the seeds of hatred had been sown, and in this way have been kindled the flames of war. Men have had no sympathy with those of a different complexion, with those who knelt at other altars and expressed their thoughts in other words and even a difference in garments placed them beyond the sympathy of others. Every peculiarity was the food of prejudice and the excuse for hatred.

The boundaries of nations were at last crossed by commerce. People became somewhat acquainted, and they found that the virtues and vices were quite evenly distributed. At last, subjects became somewhat acquainted with kings, peasants had the pleasure of gazing at princes, and it was dimly perceived that the differences were mostly in rags and names.

In 1776 our fathers endeavored to retire the gods from politics. They declared that "all governments derive their just powers from the consent of the governed." This was a contradiction of the then political ideas of the world; it was, as many believed, an act of pure blasphemy—a renunciation of the Deity. It was in fact a declaration of the independence of the earth. It was a notice to all churches and priests that thereafter mankind would govern and protect themselves. Politically it tore down every altar and denied the authority of every "sacred book," and appealed from the Providence of God to the Providence of Man.

Those who promulgated the Declaration adopted a Constitution for the great Republic.

What was the office or purpose of that Constitution?

Admitting that all power came from the people, it was necessary, first, that certain means be adopted for the purpose of ascertaining the will of the people, and second, it was proper and convenient to designate certain departments that should exercise certain powers of the Government. There must be the legislative, the judicial and the executive departments. Those who make laws should not execute them. Those who execute laws should not have the power of absolutely determining their meaning or their constitutionality. For these reasons, among others, a Constitution was adopted.

This Constitution also contained a declaration of rights. It marked out the limitations of discretion, so that in the excitement of passion, men shall not go beyond the point designated in the calm moment of reason.

When man is unprejudiced, and his passions subject to reason, it is well he should define the limits of power, so that the waves driven by the storm of passion shall not overbear the shore.

A constitution is for the government of man in this world. It is the chain the people put upon their servants, as well as upon themselves. It defines the limit of power and the limit of obedience.

It follows, then, that nothing should be in a constitution that cannot be enforced by the power of the state that is, by the army and navy. Behind every provision of the Constitution should stand the force of the nation. Every sword, every bayonet, every cannon should be there.

Suppose, then, that we amend the Constitution and acknowledge the existence and supremacy of God—what becomes of the supremacy of the people, and how is this amendment to be enforced? A constitution does not enforce itself. It must be carried out by appropriate legislation. Will it be a crime to deny the existence of this constitutional God? Can the offender be proceeded against in the criminal courts? Can his lips be closed by the power of the state? Would not this be the inauguration of religious persecution?

And if there is to be an acknowledgment of God in the Constitution, the question naturally arises as to which God is to have this honor. Shall we select the God of the Catholics—he who has established an infallible church presided over by an infallible pope, and who is delighted with certain ceremonies and placated by prayers uttered in exceedingly common Latin? Is it the God of the Presbyterian with the Five Points of Calvinism, who is ingenious enough to harmonize necessity and responsibility, and who in some way justifies himself for damning most of his own children? Is it the God of the Puritan, the enemy of joy—of the Baptist, who is great enough to govern the universe, and small enough to allow the destiny of a soul to depend on whether the body it inhabited was immersed or sprinkled?

What God is it proposed to put in the Constitution? Is it the God of the Old Testament, who was a believer in slavery and who justified polygamy? If slavery was right then, it is right now; and if Jehovah was right then, the Mormons are right now. Are we to have the God who issued a commandment against all art who was the enemy of investigation and of free speech? Is it the God who commanded the husband to stone his wife to death because she differed with him on the subject of religion? Are we to have a God who will re-enact the Mosaic code and punish hundreds of offences with death? What court, what tribunal of last resort, is to define this God, and who is to make known his will? In his presence, laws passed by men will be of no value. The decisions of courts will be as nothing. But who is to make known the will of this supreme God? Will there be a supreme tribunal composed of priests?

Of course all persons elected to office will either swear or affirm to support the Constitution. Men who do not believe in this God, cannot so swear or affirm. Such men will not be allowed to hold any office of trust or honor. A God in the Constitution will not interfere with the oaths or affirmations of hypocrites. Such a provision will only exclude honest and conscientious unbelievers. Intelligent people know that no one knows whether there is a God or not. The existence of such a Being is merely a matter of opinion. Men who believe in the liberty of man, who are willing to die for the honor of their country, will be excluded from taking any part in the administration of its affairs. Such a provision would place the country under the feet of priests.

To recognize a Deity in the organic law of our country would be the destruction of religious liberty. The God in the Constitution would have to be protected. There would be laws against blasphemy, laws against the publication of honest thoughts, laws against carrying books and papers in the mails in which this constitutional God should be attacked. Our land would be filled with theological spies, with religious eavesdroppers, and all the snakes and reptiles of the lowest natures, in this sunshine of religious authority, would uncoil and crawl.

It is proposed to acknowledge a God who is the lawful and rightful Governor of nations; the one who ordained the powers that be. If this God is really the Governor of nations, it is not necessary to acknowledge him in the Constitution. This would not add to his power. If he governs all nations now, he has always controlled the affairs of men. Having this control, why did he not see to it that he was recognized in the Constitution of the United States? If he had the supreme authority and neglected to put himself in the Constitution, is not this, at least, *prima facie* evidence that he did not desire to be there?

For one, I am not in favor of the God who has "ordained the powers that be." What have we to say of Russia—of Siberia? What can we say of the persecuted and enslaved? What of the kings and nobles who live on the stolen labor of others? What of the priest and cardinal and pope who wrest, even from the hand of poverty, the single coin thrice earned?

Is it possible to flatter the Infinite with a constitutional amendment? The Confederate States acknowledged God in their constitution, and yet they were overwhelmed by a people in whose organic law no reference to God is made. All the kings of the earth acknowledge the existence of God, and God is their ally; and this belief in God is used as a means to enslave and rob, to govern and degrade the people whom they call their subjects.

The Government of the United States is secular. It derives its power from the consent of man. It is a Government with which God has nothing whatever to do—and all forms and customs, inconsistent with the fundamental fact that the people are the source of authority, should be abandoned. In this country there should be no oaths—no man should be sworn to tell the truth, and in no court should there be any appeal to any supreme being. A rascal by taking the oath appears to go in partnership with God, and ignorant jurors credit the firm instead of the man. A witness should tell his story, and if he speaks falsely should be considered as guilty of perjury. Governors and Presidents should not issue religious proclamations. They should not call upon the people to thank God. It is no part of their official duty. It is outside of and beyond the horizon of their authority. There is nothing in the Constitution of the United States to justify this religious impertinence.

For many years priests have attempted to give to our Government a religious form. Zealots have succeeded in putting the legend upon our money: "In God We Trust;" and we have chaplains in the army and navy, and legislative proceedings are usually opened with prayer. All this is contrary to the genius of the Republic, contrary to the Declaration of Independence, and contrary really to the Constitution of the United States. We have taken the ground that the people can govern themselves without the assistance of any supernatural power. We have taken the position that the people are the real and only rightful source of authority. We have solemnly declared that the people must determine what is politically right and what is wrong, and that their legally expressed will is the supreme law. This leaves no room for national superstition no room for patriotic gods or supernatural beings—and this does away with the necessity for political prayers.

The government of God has been tried. It was tried in Palestine several thousand years ago, and the God of the Jews was a monster of cruelty and ignorance, and the people governed by this God lost their nationality. Theocracy was tried through the Middle Ages. God was the Governor—the pope was his agent, and every priest and bishop and cardinal was armed with credentials from the Most High—and the result was that the noblest and best were in prisons, the greatest and grandest perished at the stake. The result was that vices were crowned with honor, and virtues whipped naked through the streets. The result was that hypocrisy swayed the sceptre of authority, while honesty languished in the dungeons of the Inquisition.

The government of God was tried in Geneva when John Calvin was his representative; and under this government of God the flames climbed around the limbs and blinded the eyes of Michael Servetus, because he dared to express an honest thought.[1] This government of God was tried in Scotland, and the seeds of theological hatred were sown, that bore, through hundreds of years, the fruit of massacre and assassination. This government of God was established in New England, and the result was that Quakers were hanged or burned the laws of Moses re-enacted and the "witch was not suffered to live." The result was that investigation was a crime, and the expression of an honest thought a capital offence. This government of God was established in Spain, and the Jews were expelled, the Moors were driven out, Moriscoes were exterminated, and nothing left but the ignorant and bankrupt worshipers of this monster. This government of God was tried in the United States when slavery was regarded as a divine institution, when men and women were regarded as criminals because they sought for liberty by flight, and when others were regarded as criminals because they gave them food and shelter. The pulpit of that day defended the buying and selling of women and babes, and the mouths of slave-traders were filled with passages of Scripture, defending and upholding the traffic in human flesh.

We have entered upon a new epoch. This is the century of man. Every effort to really better the condition of mankind has been opposed by the worshipers of some God. The church in all ages and among all peoples has been the consistent enemy of the human race. Everywhere and at all times, it has opposed the liberty of thought and expression. It has been the sworn enemy of investigation and of intellectual development. It has denied the existence of facts, the tendency of which was to undermine its power. It has always been carrying fagots to the feet of Philosophy. It has erected the gallows for Genius. It has built the dungeon for Thinkers. And today the orthodox church is as much opposed as it ever was to the mental freedom of the human race.

Of course, there is a distinction made between churches and individual members. There have been millions of Christians who have been believers in liberty and in the freedom of expression—millions who have fought for the rights of man but churches as organizations have been on the other side. It is true that churches have fought churches, that Protestants battled with the Catholics for what they were pleased to call the freedom of conscience; and it is also true that the moment these Protestants obtained the civil power, they denied this freedom of conscience to others.

Let me show you the difference between the theological and the secular spirit. Nearly three hundred years ago, one of the noblest of the human race, Giordano Bruno,[2] was burned at Rome by the Catholic Church, that is to say, by the "Triumphant Beast." This man had committed certain crimes, he had publicly stated that there were other worlds than this—other constellations than ours. He had ventured the supposition that other planets might be peopled. More than this, and worse than this, he had asserted the heliocentric theory—that the earth made its annual journey about the sun. He had also given it as his opinion that matter is eternal. For these crimes he was found unworthy to live, and about his body were piled the fagots of the Catholic Church. This man, this genius, this pioneer of the science of the nineteenth century, perished as serenely as the sun sets. The Infidels of today find excuses for his murderers. They take into consideration the ignorance and brutality of the times. They remember that the world was governed by a God who was then the source of all authority. This is the charity of Infidelity—of philosophy. But the church of to-day is so heartless, is still so cold and cruel, that it can find no excuse for the murdered.

This is the difference between Theocracy and Democracy—between God and man.

If God is allowed in the Constitution, man must abdicate. There is no room for both. If the people of the great Republic become superstitious enough and ignorant enough to put God in the Constitution of the United States, the experiment of self-government will have failed, and the great and splendid declaration that "all governments derive their just powers from the consent of the governed" will have been denied, and in its place will be found this: All power comes from God; priests are his agents, and the people are their slaves.

Religion is an individual matter, and each soul should be left entirely free to form its own opinions and to judge of its accountability to a supposed supreme being. With religion, government has nothing whatever to do. Government is founded upon force, and force should never interfere with the religious opinions of men. Laws should define the rights of men and their duties toward each other, and these laws should be for the benefit of man in this world.

A nation can neither be Christian nor Infidel—a nation is incapable of having opinions upon these subjects. If a nation is Christian, will all the citizens go to heaven? If it is not, will they all be damned? Of course it is admitted that the majority of citizens composing a nation may believe or disbelieve, and they may call the nation what they please. A nation is a corporation. To repeat a familiar saying, "it has no soul." There can be no such thing as a Christian corporation. Several Christians may form a corporation, but it can hardly be said that the corporation thus formed was included in the atonement. For instance: Seven Christians form a corporation—that is to say, there are seven natural persons and one artificial: can it be said that there are eight souls to be saved?

No human being has brain enough, or knowledge enough, or experience enough, to say whether there is, or is not, a God. Into this darkness Science has not yet carried its torch. No human being has gone beyond the horizon of the natural. As to the existence of the supernatural, one man knows precisely as much, and exactly as little as another. Upon this question, chimpanzees and cardinals, apes and popes, are upon exact equality. The smallest insect discernible only by the most powerful microscope is as familiar with this subject as the greatest genius that has been produced by the human race.

Governments and laws are for the preservation of rights and the regulation of conduct. One man should not be allowed to interfere with the liberty of another. In the metaphysical world there should be no interference whatever. The same is true in the world of art. Laws cannot regulate what is or is not music, what is or what is not beautiful and constitutions cannot definitely settle and determine the perfection of statues, the value of paintings, or the glory and subtlety of thought. In spite of laws and constitutions the brain will think. In every direction consistent with the well-being and peace of society, there should be freedom. No man should be compelled to adopt the theology of another; neither should a minority, however small, he forced to acquiesce in the opinions of a majority, however large.

If there be an infinite Being, he does not need our help we need not waste our energies in his defence. It is enough for us to give to every other human being the liberty we claim for ourselves. There may or may not be a Supreme Ruler of the universe but we are certain that man exists, and we believe that freedom is the condition of progress; that it is the sunshine of the mental and moral world, and that without it man will go back to the den of savagery, and will become the fit associate of wild and ferocious beasts.

We have tried the government of priests, and we know that such governments are without mercy. In the administration of theocracy, all the instruments of torture have been invented. If any man wishes to have God recognized in the Constitution of our country, let him read the history of the Inquisition, and let him remember that hundreds of millions of men, women and children have been sacrificed to placate the wrath, or win the approbation of this God.

There has been in our country a divorce of church and state. This follows as a natural sequence of the declaration that "governments derive their just powers from the consent of the governed." The priest was no longer a necessity. His presence was a contradiction of the principle on which the Republic was founded. He represented, not the authority of the people, but of some "Power from on High," and to recognize this other Power was inconsistent with free government. The founders of the Republic at that time parted company with the priests, and said to them: "You may turn your attention to the other world—we will attend to the affairs of this." Equal liberty was given to all. But the ultra theologian is not satisfied with this—he wishes to destroy the liberty of the people—he wishes a recognition of his God as the source of authority, to the end that the church may become the supreme power.

But the sun will not be turned backward. The people of the United States are intelligent. They no longer believe implicitly in supernatural religion. They are losing confidence in the miracles and marvels of the Dark Ages. They know the value of the free school. They appreciate the benefits of science. They are believers in education, in the free play of thought, and there is a suspicion that the priest, the theologian, is destined to take his place with the necromancer, the astrologer, the worker of magic, and the professor of the black art.

We have already compared the benefits of theology and science. When the theologian governed the world, it was covered with huts and hovels for the many, palaces and cathedrals for the few. To nearly all the children of men, reading and writing were unknown arts. The poor were clad in rags and skins, they devoured crusts, and gnawed bones. The day of Science dawned, and the luxuries of a century ago are the necessities of to-day. Men in the middle ranks of life have more of the conveniences and elegancies than the princes and kings of the theological times. But above and over all this, is the development of mind. There is more of value in the brain of an average man of to-day—of a master-mechanic, of a chemist, of a naturalist, of an inventor, than there was in the brain of the world four hundred years ago.

These blessings did not fall from the skies. These benefits did not drop from the outstretched hands of priests. They were not found in cathedrals or behind altars, neither were they searched for with holy candles. They were not discovered by the closed eyes of prayer, nor did they come in answer to superstitious supplication. They are the children of freedom, the gifts of reason, observation and experience and for them all, man is indebted to man.

Let us hold fast to the sublime declaration of Lincoln. Let us insist that this, the Republic, is "A government of the people, by the people, and for the people."

Notes
1. Michael Servetus (1511?-1553).
2. Giordano Bruno (1548-1600).

16
The Essence of Religion in General (1841)[1]
Ludwig Feuerbach

What we have so far maintained concerning the general relationship between man and his object, and between man and sensuous objects, is particularly true of man's relationship to the religious object.

In view of its relation to the objects of the senses, the consciousness of the object can be distinguished from self-consciousness; but, in the case of the religious object, consciousness and self-consciousness directly coincide. A sensuous object exists apart from man, but the religious object exists within him—it is itself an inner, intimate object, indeed, the closest object, and hence an object which forsakes him as little as his self-consciousness or conscience. "God," says. Augustine, for example, "is nearer, more closely related to us and therefore more easily known by us than sensuous and physical things."[2] Strictly speaking, the object of the senses is in itself indifferent, having no relevance to our disposition and judgment. But the object of religion is a distinguished object—the most excellent, the first, the highest being. It essentially presupposes a critical judgment—the discrimination between the divine and the non-divine, between that which is worthy of adoration and that which is not.[3] It is in this context, therefore, that the following statement is unconditionally true: the object of man is nothing else than his objective being itself. As man thinks, as is his understanding of things, so is his God; so much worth as a man has, so much and no more has his God. The consciousness of God is the self-consciousness of man; the knowledge of God is the self-knowledge of man. Man's notion of himself is his notion of God, just as his notion of God is his notion of himself—the two are identical. What is God to man, that is man's own spirit, man's own soul; what is man's spirit, soul, and heart—that is his God. God is the manifestation of man's inner nature, his expressed self; religion is the solemn unveiling of man's hidden treasures, the avowal of his innermost thoughts, the open confession of the secrets of his love.

But if religion, i.e., the consciousness of God, is characterised as the self-consciousness of man, this does not mean that the religious man is directly aware that his consciousness of God is his self-consciousness, for it is precisely the absence of such an awareness that is responsible for the peculiar nature of religion. Hence, in order to eliminate this misunderstanding, it would be better to say that religion is the first, but indirect, self-consciousness of man. That is why religion precedes philosophy everywhere, in the history of mankind as well as in the history of the individual. Man transposes his essential being outside himself before he finds it within himself. His own being becomes the object of his thought first as another being. Religion is the essential being of man in his infancy; but the child sees his essential being, namely, man outside himself, as a child; a man is object to himself as another man. Hence, the historical development occurring within religions takes the following course: What an earlier religion regarded as objective, is now recognised as subjective; i.e., what was regarded and worshiped as God, is now recognised as something human. From the standpoint of a later religion, the earlier religion turns out to be idolatry: Man is seen to have worshiped his own essence. Man has objectified himself, but he has not yet recognised the object as his own essential being—a step taken by later religion. Every progress in religion means therefore, a deepening of man's knowledge of himself. But every religion, while designating older religions as idolatrous, looks upon itself as exempted from their fate. It does so necessarily, for otherwise it would no longer be religion; it sees only in other religions what is the fault—if a fault it can be called—of religion as such. Because its object, its content, is a different one, because it has superseded the content of earlier religions, it presumes to be exalted above the necessary and eternal laws that constitute the essence of religion; it gives itself to the illusion that its object, its content, is superhuman. However, the hidden nature of religion, which remains opaque to religion itself, is transparent to the thinker who makes it the object of his thought. And our task consists precisely in showing that the antithesis of the divine and human is illusory; that is, that it is nothing other than the antithesis between the essential being of man and his individual being, and that consequently the object and the content of the Christian religion are altogether human.

Religion, at least the Christian religion, is the expression of how man relates to himself, or more correctly, to his essential being; but he relates to his essential being as to another being. The Divine Being is nothing other than the being of man himself, or rather, the being of man abstracted from the limits of the individual man or the real, corporeal man, and objectified, i.e., contemplated and worshiped as another being, as a being distinguished from his own. All determinations of the Divine Being are, therefore, determinations of the being of man.[4]

In relation to the predicates—attributes or determinations—of God, this is admitted without hesitation, but by no means admitted in relation to the subject of these predicates, in relation to the being in which they are grounded. The negation of the subject is taken to mean the negation of religion, atheism, but not the negation of the predicates. That which has no determinations, also has no effect upon me; that which has no effect upon me, also does not exist for me. To eliminate all determinations of a being is the same as to eliminate that being itself. A being without determinations is a being that cannot be an object of thought; it is a nonentity. Where man removes all determinations from God, God is reduced to a negative being, to a being that is not a being. To a truly religious man, however, God is not a being without determinations, because he is a definite, real being to him. Hence, the view that God is without determinations, that he cannot be known, is a product of the modern era, of modern unbelief.

Just as reason can be, and is, determined as finite only where man regards sensual enjoyment, religious feeling, aesthetic contemplation, or moral sentiment as the absolute, the true, so the view as to the unknowability or indeterminateness of God can be fixed as a dogma only where this object commands no interest for cognition, where reality alone claims the interest of man or where the real alone has for him the significance of being an essential, absolute, divine object, but where at the same time this purely worldly tendency is contradicted by a still-existing remnant of old religiosity. By positing God as unknowable, man excuses himself to what is still left of his religious conscience for his oblivion of God, his surrender to the world. He negates God in practice—his mind and his senses have been absorbed by the world—but he does not negate him in theory. He does not attack his existence; he leaves it intact. But this existence neither affects nor incommodes him, for it is only a negative existence, an existence without existence; it is an existence that contradicts itself—a being that, in view of its effects, is indistinguishable from non-being. The negation of determinate, positive predicates of the Divine Being is nothing else than the negation of religion, but one which still has an appearance of religion, so that it is not recognised as a negation—it is nothing but a subtle, sly atheism. The alleged religious horror of limiting God by determinate predicates is only the irreligious wish to forget all about God, to banish him from the mind. He who is afraid to be finite is afraid to exist. All real existence, that is, all existence that really is existence, is qualitative, determinate existence. He who seriously, truly believes in the existence of

God is not disturbed even by grossly sensuous qualities attributed to God. He who regards the fact of his existence as an insult, he who recoils from that which is gross, may just as well give up existing. A God to whom his determinateness is an insult lacks the courage and strength to exist. Determinateness is the fire, the oxygen, the salt of existence. An existence in general, an existence without qualities, is an insipid and preposterous existence. But there is nothing more, and nothing less, in God than what religion puts in him. Only when man loses his taste for religion, that is, when religion itself becomes insipid, does God become an insipid existence.

Moreover, there is yet a milder way of denying the divine predicates than the direct one just described. One admits that the predicates of the Divine Being are finite and, more particularly, human determinations, but one rejects the idea of rejecting them. One even defends them on the ground that they are necessary for man; that being man, he cannot conceive God in any way other than human. One argues that although these determinations have no meaning in relation to God, the fact is that God, if he is to exist for man, can appear to man in no other way than he does, namely, as a being with human attributes. However, this distinction between what God is in himself and what he is for man destroys the peace of religion as well as being an unfeasible and unfounded distinction. It is not at all possible for me to know whether God as he is in and for himself is something different from what he is for me. The manner in which he exists for me is also the totality of his existence for me. The determinations in terms of which he exists for me contain also the "in-itself-ness" of his being, his essential nature itself; he exists for me in a way in which he can exist for me alone. The religious man is completely satisfied with how he sees God in relation to himself—and he knows nothing of any other relation—for God is to him what he can be to man at all. In the distinction made above, man transgresses the boundaries of himself, his being and its absolute measure, but this transcending is only an illusion. For I can make the distinction between the object as it is in itself and the object as it is for me only where an object can really appear different from what it actually appears to me. I cannot make such a distinction where the object appears to me as it does according to my absolute measure; that is, as it must appear to me. It is true that my conception can be subjective; that is, one which is not bound by the essential constitution of my species. However, if my conception corresponds to the measure of my species, the distinction between what something is in itself and what it is for me ceases; for in that case this conception is itself an absolute one. The measure of the species is the absolute measure, law, and criterion of man. Yet religion has the conviction that its conceptions and determinations of God are such as every man ought to have if he is to have true conceptions, that these are conceptions necessitated by human nature, that they are indeed objective, conforming to the nature of God. To every religion, the gods of other religions are only conceptions of God; but its own conception of God is itself its God—God as it conceives him to be, God genuinely and truly so, God as he is in himself. Religion is satisfied only with a complete and total God—it will not have merely an appearance of God, it can be satisfied with nothing less than God himself, God in person. Religion abandons itself if it abandons God in his essential being; it is no longer true if it renounces its possession of the true God. Scepticism is the archenemy of religion. But the distinction between object and concept, between God as he is in himself and as he is for me, is a sceptical, that is, irreligious distinction.

That which is subsumed by man under the concept of "being-in-itself," that which he regards as the most supreme being or as the being of which he can conceive none higher, that is the Divine Being. How can he therefore still ask, what this being is in itself? If God were an object to the bird, he would be an object to it only as a winged being—the bird knows nothing higher, nothing more blissful than the state of being winged. How ludicrous would it be if this bird commented: "God appears to me as a bird, but I do not know what he is in himself." The highest being to the bird is the "bird-being." Take from it its conception of "bird-being," and you take from it its conception of the highest being. How, therefore, could the bird ask whether God in himself were winged? To ask whether God is in himself what he is for me, is to ask whether God is God; it is to raise oneself above God and to rebel against him.

Given, therefore, the situation in which man is seized by the awareness that religious predicates are mere anthropomorphisms, his faith has also come under the sway of doubt and unbelief. And if this awareness does not lead him to the formal negation of the predicates and thence to the negation of the being in which they are grounded, it is only due to an inconsistency for which his faint-heartedness and irresolute intellect are responsible. If you doubt the objective truth of the predicates, you must also doubt the objective truth of the subject to which they belong. If your predicates are anthropomorphisms, their subject, too, is an anthropomorphism. If love, goodness, and personality are human determinations, the being which constitutes their source and, according to you, their presupposition is also an anthropomorphism; so is the existence of God; so is the belief that there is a God—in short, all presuppositions that are purely human. What tells you that the belief in a God at all is not an indication of the limitedness of man's mode of conception? Higher beings—and you assume that such beings exist—are perhaps so blissful in themselves, so at unity with themselves that they are not exposed to a tension between themselves and a higher being. To know God and not to be God, to know blissfulness and not to enjoy it, is to be in conflict with oneself, is to be delivered up to unhappiness.[5]

You believe in love as a divine attribute because you yourself love, and believe that God is a wise and benevolent being because you know nothing better in yourself than wisdom and benevolence. You believe that God exists, that therefore he is a subject or an essence—whatever exists is also an essence, whether it is defined as a substance, a person, or in any other way—because you yourself exist, are yourself an essence. You know no higher human good than to love, to be wise and good. Equally, you know no other happiness than to exist, to be a being, for your consciousness of good and happiness derives itself from your consciousness of being and existing yourself. God to you exists, is a being for the same reason that he is to you a wise, blissful, and benevolent being. The distinction between the divine attributes and the divine essence is only this. To you the essence, the existence does not appear as an anthropomorphism, because the fact of your own being brings with it the necessity of conceiving the existence of God, whereas the attributes appear to you as anthropomorphisms, because their necessity—the necessity that God is wise, good, just, etc.—is not an immediate necessity identical with the being of man, but is mediated by his self-consciousness, by the activity of his thought. I may be wise or unwise, good or bad, but I am a being—I exist. Man's existence is to him the first datum, the sustaining ground of his conceptions, the presupposition of all his predicates. Hence, man is prepared to concede that the predicates of God are anthropomorphic, but not the existence of God; to him it is a settled, inviolable, absolutely certain, and objective truth. And yet, this distinction is only an apparent one. The necessity of the subject lies only in the necessity of the predicate. Your being is the being of man; the certainty and reality of your existence lie in the certainty and reality of your human attributes. What the subject is—its being—lies only in the predicate; the predicate is the truth of the subject; the subject is only the personified, existing predicate. The distinction between subject and object corresponds to the distinction between existence and essence. The negation of the predicate is therefore the negation of the subject. What remains of the being of man if you take away its attributes? Even in the language of ordinary life one speaks of the divine not in terms of its essence, but in terms of its attributes—providence, wisdom, omnipotence.

The certainty of the existence of God, which has been held by man to be more certain than even his own existence, depends therefore on the certainty of the attributes of God—it does not have the character of immediate certainty. To the Christian, only the existence of a Christian God is a certainty, just as to the pagan only that of a pagan god is certain. The pagan did not doubt the existence of Jupiter, because Jupiter as a divine being was not repulsive to him. He could not conceive of a god with any other attributes, because these attributes were to him a certainty, a divine truth. The truth of the predicate alone ensures the existence of the subject.

That which man conceives to be true is also that which he immediately conceives to be real because, originally, only the real is true to him—true in opposition to that which is merely conceived, dreamed, or imagined. The concept of being, of existence, is the original concept of truth. In other words, man originally makes truth dependent on existence, but only later existence dependent on truth. Now God is the essence of man, regarded by him as the highest truth. But God, or religion—both are the same—varies according to the determination in terms of which man comprehends his essence, in terms of which he regards it as the highest being. This determination, which is decisive for man's idea of God, is to him the truth and, precisely for that reason, also the highest existence, or existence itself. For strictly speaking, only the highest existence is existence, and deserves this name. Therefore, God is a really existing being for the same reason that he is this particular being. The attribute or determination of God is nothing else than the essential attribute of man himself, and the thus-determined man is what he is, has his existence, his reality, in his determinateness. You cannot take away from a Greek the quality of being a Greek without taking away his existence. Hence, it is of course true that for a particular religion—that is, relatively—the certainty of the existence of God is immediate; for just as arbitrarily or necessarily the Greek was Greek, so necessarily were his gods Greek beings, so necessarily were they really existing beings. In view of its understanding of the world and man, religion is identical with the essence of man. However, it is not man who stands above the conceptions essential to his being; rather, it is these conceptions that stand above him. They animate, determine, and govern him. This goes to show that the necessity to prove, and the possibility to doubt, how and whether existence is related to being or quality is abolished. That which I sever from my being can only be doubtful. How could I therefore doubt God who is my essence? To doubt God would be to doubt myself. Only when God is conceived abstractly, when his predicates are arrived at through philosophical abstraction, does the distinction or separation arise between subject and predicate, existence and essence—only then does the illusion arise that the existence or the subject is something different from the predicate, something immediate, indubitable, or distinct from the predicate which is subject to doubt. But this is only an illusion. A God whose predicates are abstract also has an abstract existence. Existence, being, is as varied as the qualities predicated of it.

The identity of subject and predicate is borne out clearly by the course taken by religion in its development, a course which is identical with that taken by human culture. As long as man is a mere natural being, his God is a mere natural deity. Mere man lives in houses, he encloses his gods in temples. A temple expresses the value which man attaches to beautiful buildings. Temples in honour of religion are in truth temples in honour of architecture. With man's progress to culture from a state of primitive savagery, with the distinction between what is proper and what is improper for man, there also arises the distinction between what is proper and what is improper for God. God expresses man's notion of majesty, highest dignity, religious sentiment, and highest feeling of propriety. Only at a later stage did the culturally more advanced artists of Greece embody in their statues of gods the concepts of dignity, spiritual grandeur, rest without movement, and serenity. But why did they regard these qualities as divine attributes? Because they held these attributes in themselves to be divine. Why did they exclude all repulsive and low emotions? Because they regarded these emotions as something improper, undignified, unhuman, and, consequently, ungodlike. The Homeric gods eat and drink—this means that eating and drinking are divine pleasures. Physical strength is a quality of the Homeric gods—Zeus is the strongest of all gods. Why? Because physical strength in itself was something glorious and divine to the Greeks. The highest virtue to ancient Germans was the virtue of the warrior; that is why their highest god was the god of war—Odin; that is why war to them was "the primeval or the oldest law." The first, true divine being is not the quality of divinity, but the divinity or the deity of quality. In other words, that which theology and philosophy have so far regarded as God, as the absolute and essential, is not God; but that which they did not regard as God, is precisely God—quality, determination, and reality par excellence. A true atheist, that is, an atheist in the ordinary sense, is therefore he alone to whom the predicates of the Divine Being—for example, love, wisdom, and justice—are nothing, not he to whom only the subject of these predicates is nothing. And the negation of the subject is by no means also necessarily the negation of the predicates as they are in themselves. The predicates have a reality of their own, have an independent significance; the force of what they contain compels man to recognise them. They prove their truth to man directly through themselves. They are their own proof and evidence. Goodness, justice, and wisdom do not become chimeras if the existence of God is a chimera, nor do they become truths simply because the existence of God is a truth. The concept of

God depends on the concept of justice, kindness, and wisdom—a God who is not kind, not just, and not wise is no God. But these concepts do not depend on the concept of God. That a quality is possessed by God does not make it divine; God possesses it, because it is in itself divine, because without it God would be a defective being. Justice, wisdom, and, in fact, every determination which constitutes the divinity of God, is determined and known through itself; but God is known and determined by the predicates. Only in the case where I think that God and justice are identical, that God is immediately the reality of the idea of justice or of any other quality, do I think of God as self-determined. But if God, the subject, is that which is determined, and the quality or the predicate is that which determines him, then the predicate, and not the subject, in truth deserves the primacy of being, the status of divinity.

Only when it happens that a number of contradictory qualities are combined into one being, which is then conceived in the form of a person, that is, when personality is particularly emphasised, does one forget the origin of religion, does one forget that that which reflective thought looks upon as the predicate distinguishable or separable from the subject was originally the true subject. Thus, the Greeks and the Romans deified the accidents as substances; virtues, mental states, and emotions, were as independent beings. Man, particularly the religious man, is the measure of all things, of all reality. Whatever impresses man, whatever makes a particular impression on his mind—and it may be merely some strange, inexplicable sound or note—he hypostatises into a particular deity. Religion encompasses all the objects of the world; think of anything existing, and you will find that it has been the object of religious veneration. Nothing is to be found in the essence and consciousness of religion that is not there in the being of man, that is not there in his consciousness of himself and the world. Religion has no particular content of its own. Even the emotions of fear and dread had their temples in Rome. The Christians, too, hypostatised their mental states into beings and qualities of things, their dominant emotions into powers dominating the world. In short, they hypostatised the qualities of their being—whether known or unknown to them—into self-subsisting beings. Devils, goblins, witches, ghosts, angels, etc., continued to be sacred truths as long as the religious disposition held its uninterrupted sway over mankind.

In order not to acknowledge the identity of the divine and human predicates, and hence of the divine and human essence, one takes recourse to the idea that God, as an infinite being, has an infinite plenitude of various predicates, of which we know only some in this world, and indeed, those that are similar or analogous to our own;

but the others, by virtue of which God is a totally different being from the being of man or from anything similar to it, we shall only know in the future—in the world hereafter. However, an infinite plenitude or multitude of predicates which are truly different—and so different that the knowledge of the one does not immediately posit and lead to the knowledge of the other—realises its truth only in an infinite plenitude or multitude of different beings or individuals. Thus, the being of man is infinitely rich in different kinds of predicates, but precisely for that reason it is infinitely rich in different kinds of individuals. Each new man is, so to say, a new predicate, a new talent added to mankind. Mankind possesses as many qualities, as many powers, as the number of its members. Although the individual partakes of the same power that is inherent in all men, it is so constituted in him that it appears to be a new and unique power. The secret of the inexhaustible plenitude of the divine determinations is, therefore, nothing else than the secret of the being of man which is infinitely diverse, infinitely determinable, and—precisely for these reasons—sensuous. Only in sensuousness, only in space and time, does an infinite being—a being that is really infinite and plentiful in predicates—exist. Where there are truly different predicates, there are truly different times. One man is an excellent musician, an excellent writer, and an excellent physician; but he cannot make music, write, and cure at one and the same time. Time, and not the Hegelian dialectic, is the power by means of which antitheses and contradictions are united in one and the same being. However, the infinite plurality of different predicates must remain an unreal conception if it is seen in conjunction with the concept of God, but in disjunction with the being of man. Thus, it must remain a fantasy—a conception of sensuousness, lacking the essence and truth of sensuousness. Thus, it must remain a conception that stands in direct contradiction with the Divine Being as an intellectual—that is, abstract, simple, and unique being—for the predicates of God are of such a nature that possessing one implies possessing all the others, because there is no real difference between them. If, therefore, the present predicates do not involve the future ones, the present God does not involve the future God, then the future God does not involve the present—they are two different beings.[6] But this distinction contradicts the unity, uniqueness, and simplicity of God. Why is a certain predicate a predicate of God? Because it is of divine nature, that is, because it expresses no limitation, no defect. Why are other predicates so? Because, however different they may be among themselves, they concur in this: They equally express perfection and unlimitedness. Hence, I can imagine innumerable predicates of God, because they must all concur in the abstract concept of the Godhead, because they must have in common that which makes every single predicate into a divine attribute or predicate. This is the case with Spinoza. He speaks of an infinite plurality of the attributes of the divine substance, but he does not name any besides thought and extension, Why? Because it is a matter of complete indifference to know them; because they are, indeed, in themselves indifferent and superfluous; because despite these innumerable predicates, I would still be saying the same as with the two predicates of thought and extension. Why is thought an attribute of substance? Because according to Spinoza, it is comprehended through itself, because it is something that cannot be divided, that is, perfect and infinite. Why extension or matter? Because they express the same thing in relation to themselves. That means that substance can have an indefinite number of predicates, because it is not their determinateness, their difference, but their non-difference, their sameness, which makes them attributes of substance. Or rather, substance has such an infinite number of predicates, only because—and this is, indeed, strange—it has really no predicate, no definite, real predicate. The indeterminate One existing in thought is supplemented by the indeterminate, manifoldness existing in the imagination. Because the predicate is not *multum,* it is *multa.* In truth, the positive predicates are thought and extension. With these two, infinitely more is said than with nameless innumerable predicates; for they say something definite; they enable me to know something. But substance is too indifferent, too passionless to be enthusiastic about, or be on the side of, something; in order to be something, it prefers to be nothing.

Now, if it is accepted that whatever the subject or being involves lies solely in its determinations—in other words, the predicate is the true subject—it is also clear that if the divine predicates are determinations of the being of man, their subject, too, is the being of man. The divine predicates are general, on the one hand, but personal, on the other. The general ones are metaphysical, but they provide religion with ultimate points of reference, with a foundation; they are not the characteristic determinations of religion. It is the personal predicates alone on which the essence of religion is grounded, in which the divine nature of religion is objectified. Such personal predicates are, for example, that God is a Person, that he is the moral Lawgiver, the Father of men, the Holy One, the Just, the Merciful. It is obvious from these and other determinations—or at least it will be clear later—that as personal determinations these predicates are purely human determinations, and that, consequently, man's relationship to God in religion is his relationship to his own being. For these predicates are to religion not man's conceptions or images of God distinct from God as he is in himself, but truths and realities. Religion knows nothing of anthropomorphisms—anthropomorphisms are not anthropomorphisms to it. The essence of religion is precisely that it regards the attributes of God as the being of God. That these attributes are images is shown only by the intellect, which reflects on religion and, while defending them, denies them before its own tribunal. But in the view of religion, God is a real Father, real Love, real Mercy; for it takes him to be a real, living, personal attribute. Indeed, these and corresponding determinations are precisely those that are most offensive to the intellect, and which it denies in its reflection on religion. Subjectively, religion is emotion; objectively also, emotion is to it an attribute of the Divine Being. It regards even anger as not unworthy of God, provided that nothing evil is associated with it.

But it is important to note here—and the phenomenon in question is an extremely remarkable one, characterising the innermost essence of religion—that the more human the being of God is, the greater is the apparent difference between God and man; that is, the more is the identity of the human and the Divine Being denied by theology or the self-reflection of religion, and the more is the human—taken in the sense in which it is as such the object of man's consciousness—depreciated.[7] The reason for this is to be found in the following: because the positive and essential basis of the conception or determination of God can only be human, the conception of man as an object of consciousness can only be negative, that is, hostile to man. In order to enrich God, man must become poor; that God may be all, man must be nothing. But he also does not need to be anything for himself, because everything for himself, everything he takes from himself, is not lost, but preserved in God. Since man has his being in God, why then should he have it in and for himself? Why should it be necessary to posit and have the same thing twice? What man withdraws from himself, what he lacks in himself, he only enjoys in an incomparably higher and richer measure in God.

As a consequence of their vow of chastity, the monks repressed sexual love in themselves; but, for that matter, they had in the Virgin Mary the image of woman; in God, in heaven, the image of love. The more an ideal, imagined woman was the object of their real love, the more easily could they dispense with woman in flesh and blood. The greater the significance they attached to the annihilation of sensuality, the greater was for them the significance of the heavenly Virgin: She occupied in their mind a place even more prominent than that of Christ or God. The more the sensuous is denied, the more sensuous is the God to whom it is sacrificed. Whatever is sacrificed to God is something particularly cherished, but also something that is particularly pleasing to God. That which is the highest to man is also the highest to his God; that which pleases man pleases God also. The Hebrews did not sacrifice to Jehovah unclean, loathsome animals, but those they valued most; those they ate themselves were also the food of God.[8] Where, therefore, the denial of sensuousness leads to its hypostatisation as a certain being, or to its transformation into an offering pleasing to God, there the highest value is attached to sensuousness; there the renounced sensuousness is restored precisely through the fact that God takes the place of the sensuous being that has been renounced. The nun weds herself to God; she has a heavenly bridegroom, and the monk, a heavenly bride. But the heavenly virgin is obviously the form in which a general truth concerning the essence of religion appears. Man affirms in God what he denies in himself.[9] Religion abstracts from man, from the world. But it can abstract only from defects and limits, whether real or imaginary; it can abstract only from the illusory but not from the real, positive being of the world and man. Hence, it must reincorporate into its negation and abstraction that wherefrom it abstracts, or believes to abstract. And thus, in fact, religion unconsciously places in God all that it consciously denies, provided, of course, that the negated is something essential, true, and, consequently, something that cannot be negated. Thus, in religion man negates his reason—he knows nothing of God through his own reason; his thoughts are only earthly; he can only believe in what God reveals. But, for that matter, the thoughts of God are human and earthly; like man, he has plans in his head—he makes allowance for the circumstances and intellectual powers of man, like a teacher for his pupils' capacity to understand; he calculates exactly the effect of his gifts and revelations; he keeps an eye on man in all his doings; he knows everything—even the most earthly, the meanest, or the worst. In short, man denies his knowledge, his thought, that he may place them in God. Man renounces himself as a person only to discover God, the omnipotent and the infinite, as a personal being; he denies human honour, the human ego, only to have a God that is selfish, egoistic, who seeks in everything only himself, his honour, his advantage, only to have a God whose sole concern is the gratification of his own selfishness, the enjoyment of his own ego.[10] Religion further denies goodness as a quality of man's being; man is wicked, corrupt, and incapable of good; but, in contrast, God is only good—the good being. It is demanded of man to conceive the good as God, but does this not make goodness an essential determination of man? If I am absolutely, i.e., by nature wicked and unholy, how can holiness and goodness be the objects of my thought—no matter whether these objects are given to me internally or externally? If my heart is wicked, my understanding corrupt, how can I perceive and feel the holy to be holy, the good to be good? How can I perceive a beautiful painting as beautiful if my soul is by nature ugly, and hence incapable of perceiving aesthetic beauty? Even if I am not a painter and do not have the power to produce something beautiful out of myself, my feeling and understanding are aesthetic since I perceive beauty in the world outside. Either the good does not exist for man, or if it does, it reveals the holiness and goodness of the being of man. That which is absolutely against my nature, with which I have nothing in common, I also cannot think or feel. Holiness stands in contrast to me as an individual, but in unity with my human essence the holy is a reproach to my sinfulness; in it I recognise myself as a sinner, but in my idea of holiness I also know that I am not, and I reproach myself for not being what I ought to be, what I can be according to my nature. An ought without the possibility of conforming to it is a ludicrous chimera which cannot take hold of the mind. But in so far as I acknowledge goodness as my essential determination, as my law, I acknowledge it, consciously or unconsciously, as my own nature. A being other than mine, and differing from me according to its nature, does not concern me. I can perceive sin as sin only if I perceive it as involving me in a contradiction with myself; that is, as a contradiction between my personality and essence, as a contradiction of the divine; that is, of a being other than mine, the feeling of sin is inexplicable, meaningless.

The distinction between Augustinianism and Pelagianism consists only of this: what the former expresses in the form characteristic to religion, the latter expresses in the form characteristic to rationalism. Both say the same thing, both see the good as belonging to man; but Pelagianism does it directly, in a rationalistic, moral form, whereas Augustinianism does it indirectly, in a mystical, that is, religious form.[11] That which is ascribed to the God of man is in truth ascribed to man himself; that which man predicates of God, he in truth predicates of himself. Augustinianism would only then be true—and true, indeed, in a sense opposed to Pelagianism—if the devil were the God of man, if man, aware that be was himself a devil, worshiped and celebrated the devil as the highest expression of his own being. But as long as man worships a good being as God, that long does he behold his own goodness in God.

The doctrine of the fundamental corruption of man's nature and the doctrine that man is incapable of good are identical, and concur in the view that, in truth, man is unable to do anything by himself and through his own power.

The denial of human power and activity would be true only if man also denied the existence of moral activity in God; that is, if he were to say with the Oriental nihilist or pantheist: the Divine Being is absolutely without will, inactive, indifferent, and ignorant of the distinction between good and evil. But he who defines God as an active being—and, indeed, as morally active, as a moral and critical being, as a being that loves, works, and rewards good, and punishes, rejects, and condemns evil—he who so defines God only apparently denies human activity. In actual fact, he regards it as the highest, the most real activity. He who attributes action to man declares human activity to be divine. He says: a God who does not act, that is, does not act morally or humanly, is no God. He therefore makes the notion of God dependent on the notion of activity, or rather human activity, for he knows of none higher.

Man—and this is the secret of religion—objectifies[12] his being, and then again makes himself the object of this objectified being, transformed into a subject, a person. He thinks of himself as an object, but as an object of an object, as an object to another being. Thus, here man is an object to God. That man is good or evil is not indifferent to God. No! God is keenly and deeply concerned whether man is good; he wants him to be good and blissful—and both necessarily belong together. The reduction of human activity to nothingness is thus retracted by the religious man through the fact that he turns his sentiments and actions into an object of God, man into a purpose of God—that which is an object in mind is a purpose in action—and the divine activity into a means of man's salvation. God acts, that man may be good and felicitous. Thus, while in appearance the greatest humiliation is inflicted upon man, in truth he is exalted to the highest. Thus, in and through God, the aim of man is man himself. It is true that the aim of man is God, but the aim of God is nothing except the moral and eternal salvation of man; that means that the aim of man is man himself. The divine activity does not distinguish itself from the human.

How could the divine activity work on me as its object, indeed, work in me, if it were essentially foreign to me? How could it have a human aim, the aim to make man better and happy, if it were not itself human? Does not the aim determine the act? When man makes it his goal to morally improve himself, his resolutions and projects are divine; but, equally, when God has in view the salvation of man, both his aims and his corresponding activity are human. Thus, in God man confronts his own activity as an object. But because he regards his own activity as existing objectively and as distinct from himself, he necessarily receives the impulse, the urge, to act not from himself, but from this object. He looks upon his being as existing outside himself, and he looks upon it as the good; hence it is self-evident, a tautology, that he receives the impulse to good from where he deposits it.

God is the most subjective, the very own being of man, but set apart from himself. That means that he cannot derive his actions purely out of himself, or that all good comes from God. The more subjective, the more human God is the more man exteriorises his subjectivity, his humanity, because God is in reality the exteriorised self of man which he, however, reappropriates. As the activity of the arteries drives the blood into the extremities, and the action of the veins leads it back again, as life basically consists in a constant systole and diastole, so is it also in religion. In the religious systole man's being departs from itself into an outward projection; man disowns, rejects himself; in the religious diastole his heart again embraces his rejected being. God alone is the being whose actions originate within himself, whose activity flows out of himself—thus operates the repelling force in religion; God is the being who acts in me, with me, through me, upon me, and for me; he is the principle of my salvation, of my good sentiments and actions, and hence my own good principle and essence—thus operates the attracting force in religion.

The course of religious development, as delineated in general above, consists more specifically in this, that man progressively appropriates to himself what he had attributed to God. In the beginning, man posits his essence completely and without distinction outside himself. This is illustrated particularly by his belief in revelation. That which to a later epoch or to a culturally advanced people is revealed by reason or nature is, revealed to an earlier epoch, or to a culturally backward people, by God. All human urges, however natural—even the urge for cleanliness—were conceived by the Israelites as positive divine commandments. This example again shows us that man's image of God is the more debased and the more commonly human the more man denies himself. Can the degradation, the self-abnegation of man sink to lower depths than when he denies himself even the power and ability to fulfil by himself, out of his own resources, the requirements of ordinary decency?[13] In comparison, the Christian religion distinguished the urges and emotions of man according to their character and content. It made only the good emotions, only the good sentiments, and only the good thoughts the revelations and workings of God, that is, his sentiments, emotions, and thoughts; for what God reveals is a determination of God himself; that which fills the heart overflows the lips; the nature of the effect reveals the nature of the cause; the character of the revelation points to the character of the being that reveals itself. A God who reveals himself only in good sentiments is himself a God whose essential quality is only moral goodness. The Christian religion separated inward moral purity from external physical purity; the Israelite religion identified the two.[14] In contrast to the Israelite, the Christian religion is the religion of criticism and freedom. The Israelite recoiled from doing anything that was not commanded by God; even in external things he was without will; even his food fell within the jurisdiction of religious authority. On the other hand, the Christian religion left all these external things to the autonomy of man, that is, it posited in man what the Israelite posited outside himself—in God. Israel is the most perfect embodiment of religions positivism; that is, of the type of religion that posits the essential being of man out-side man. As compared with the Israelite, the Christian is an *esprit fort,* a free spirit. That is how things change. What yesterday still passed for religion, has ceased to be so today; and what is regarded as atheism today will be religion tomorrow.

Notes

1. From the book *The Essence of Christianity.*

2. *De Genes! ad litteram,* Lib., V, c. 16.

3. "You do not realise that it is easier to know than to worship God."—Minucius Felix, *Octavianus,* c. 24.

4. "The perfections of God are the perfections of our own soul, but God possesses them bound-lessly... We possess only some powers, some knowledge, some good; but God possess them in their entirety and perfection." (Leibniz, *Théodicée,* Préface.) "Everything by which the human soul is distinguished is inherent also in the Divine Being. Everything which is excluded from God also does not belong to the essential determinations of the soul." (St. Gregorius Nyss, *de anima,* Lips. 1837, p. 42.) "The most excellent and important among all forms of knowledge is therefore self-knowledge; for if one knows himself he can also know God." (Clemens Alexandrinus, *Paedag.,* Lib., iii, c. l.)

5. Hence in the world hereafter the conflict between God and man ceases. There, man is no longer man—at the most, only in fantasy. He no longer has a will of his own, no longer has a will that is distinguished from that of God; consequently, he also no longer has a being that is specifically his own—and what kind of a being is a being without will? In the world hereafter man is one with God; there, the antithesis between God and man vanishes. But where there is only God, there is no longer God. Where there is nothing contrasting majesty, there is also no majesty.

6. For religious belief there is no other difference between the present and the future God than that the former is an object of belief, conception, and fantasy, whereas the latter is an object of the immediate; i.e., of personal and sensuous conception. He is the same God both here and in the world hereafter, but here he is opaque, whereas in the other world he is transparent.

7. However great may the similarity between the creator and the creature be conceived, the dissimi-larity between both must be conceived even greater. (Later. Conc. Can. 2. Summa Omn. Conc. Carranza. Antw. 1559, p. 326.) The last distinction between man and God, between the finite and the infinite being in general, to which the religio-speculative imagination soars is the distinction between something and nothing, between *ens* and *nonens*; for only in nothingness is all commu-nity with other beings annulled.

8. *Cibus Dei,* Leviticus iii, 2.

9. "He who despises himself," says Anselm, "is honoured by God. He who dislikes himself is liked by God. Therefore, be small in your own eyes so that you may be big in the eyes of God; for you shall be the more valued by God, the more contemptuous you are of men." (Anselm, Opp., Parisiis 1721, p. 191.)

10. "God can only love himself, can think only of himself, can only work for himself. In making man, God pursues his own advantage, his own glory." (Vide P. Bayle, *Ein Beitrag zur Geschichte der Philo. u. Mensch.*)

11. Pelagianism negates God and religion—"by ascribing too much power to the will, they weaken the power of pious prayer." (Augustinus, *de natura et gratia contra Pelagium,* c. 58.) It has only the Creator, i.e., Nature, as its basis, not the Saviour, the God proper of religion—in short, it negates God, but, in return, elevates man into God, in so far as it makes man a being who does not need God, who is self-sufficient and independent. (On this point, see *Luther Against Erasmus and Augustine, 1.* c., c. 33.) Augustinianism negates man, but, in return, it lowers God to the level of man, even to the disgrace of a death on the cross for the sake of man. The former puts man in the place of God; the latter puts God in the place of man. Both lead to the same result; the distinction between them is only apparent, a pious illusion. Augustinianism is only reversed Pelagianism—that which the latter posits as subject, the former posits as object.

12. Man's religious, namely, original, self-objectification is, moreover, to be distinguished from that occurring in reflection and speculation; the latter is arbitrary, the former necessary—as necessary as art and language. In the course of time, theology naturally coincides with religion.

13. Deuteronomy xxiii: 12, 13.

14. See, for example, Genesis xxxv: 2; Leviticus xi: 44 and xx: 26 Also, the *Commentary* of Le Clerc on these passages.

17
God And The State
Michael Bakunin (and other anarchists)

Anarchists prize freedom above all else, therefore the cry "Neither God or Master." In seeking a free society, anarchists work to reduce to the past of sources and centers of authority based on violence, repression and oppression. All anarchists are atheists but not all atheists are anarchists. Michael Bakunin wrote *Federalism, Socialism, and Anti-Theologism* (1867) as a critique of Jean-Jacques Rousseau's *Theory of the State*. His *God and the State* was written in 1871, and consisted of a chapter called "Authority and Science," and a chapter called "Man, Society, and Freedom." What follows is an array of quotes, primarily from Bakunin, but quotes from Pierre-Joseph Proudhon and Emma Goldman are also included.

> The lust for power of a few individuals originally, and of several social classes later, established slavery and conquest as the dominant principle, and implanted this terrible idea of divinity in the heart of society. Thereafter no society was viewed as feasible without these two institutions, the Church and the State, at its base. These two social scourges are defended by all their doctrinaire apologists.
>
> No sooner did these institutions appear in the world than two ruling classes—the priests and the aristocrats—promptly organized themselves and lost no time in indoctrinating the enslaved people with the idea of the utility, indispensability, and sacredness of the Church and the State.
> —Michael Bakunin, *God and the State*, 1871

> God being everything, the real world and man are nothing. God being truth, justice and infinite life, man is falsehood, inequality, and death. God being master, man is the slave.
> —Michael Bakunin, *God and the State*, 1871

We cannot, we ought not make the least concession to theology, because in that mystic and rigorously consistent alphabet, he who begins with A must fatally arrive at Z, and he who wants to adore God must renounce his liberty and his human dignity.

God exists; hence man is a slave. Man is intelligent, just, free; hence God does not exist. We defy anyone to avoid this circle; and now let all choose.
—Michael Bakunin, *Federalism, Socialism, and Anti-Theologism*, 1867

With all due deference to all the semi-philosophers and to all the so-called religious thinkers, we say: *The existence of God implies the abdication of human reason and justice; it is the negation of human liberty, and it necessarily ends in both theoretical and absolute slavery.*
—Michael Bakunin, *Federalism, Socialism, and Anti-Theologism*, 1867

Christianity is precisely the religion par excellence, because it exhibits and manifests to the fullest extent the very nature and essence of every religious system, *which is the impoverishment, enslavement, and annihilation of humanity for the benefit of divinity.*
—Michael Bakunin, *God and the State*, 1871

Whoever says revelation says revealers, messiahs, prophets, priests, and legislators inspired by God himself; and these once recognized as the representatives of divinity or truth… necessarily exercise absolute power.
—Michael Bakunin, *God and the State*, 1871

Divine morality is the absolute negation of human morality. Divine morality found its perfect expression in the Christian maxim: "Thou shalt love God more than thyself and thou shalt love thy neighbor as much as thyself." Which implies the sacrifice of both oneself, and one's neighbor to God. One can admit the sacrifice of oneself, this being an obvious act of sheer folly, but the sacrifice of one's fellow-man is from the human point of view absolutely immoral. And why am I forced toward this inhuman sacrifice? For the salvation of my own soul; that is the last word of Christianity.

The individual in possession of his immortal soul and his inner liberty independent of society—the modern saint—has *material* need of society, without feeling the slightest need of society from a moral point of view. But what should we call a relationship which, being motivated only by material needs,

is not sanctioned or backed up by some moral need? Evidently there is only one name for it: *exploitation.*
—Michael Bakunin, *The Knouto-German Empire*, 1871

Religion is a collective insanity, the more powerful because it is traditional folly, and because its origins are lost in the more remote antiquity.

Whenever a chief of State speaks of God, be he William I, the Knouto-Germanic emperor, or (Ulysses S) Grant, the President of the great republic, be sure that he is getting ready to shear once more this people-flock.

A jealous lover of human liberty, deeming it the absolute condition of all that we admire and respect in humanity, I reverse the phrase of Voltaire, and say, *if God really existed, it* would be necessary to abolish him.
—Michael Bakunin, *God and the State*, 1871

People go to church as they go to the tavern, in order to stupefy themselves, to forget their misery, to see themselves in their imagination, for a few minutes at least, free and happy, as happy as others, the well-to-do people. Give them a human existence, and they will never go into a tavern or a church. And it is only the Social Revolution that can and will give them such an existence.
—Michael Bakunin, *A Circular Letter to My Friends in Italy*, October,1871

All religion with their gods were never anything but the creation of the credulous fancy of men who has not yet reached the level of pure reflection and free thought based upon science. Consequently, the religious Heaven was nothing but a mirage in which man, exalted by faith, long ago encountered his own image enlarged and reversed—that is, deified.

All religions are founded on blood, for all, as is known, test essentially on the idea of sacrifice—that is, on the perpetual immolation of humanity to the insatiable vengeance of divinity. In this blood mystery, man is always the victim, and the priest—a man also, but one privileged by grace—is the divine executioner.

Everywhere... religious or philosophical idealism (the one being simply the more or less free interpretation of the other) serves today as the banner of bloody and brutal material force, of shameless material exploitation.
—Michael Bakunin, *The Knouto-Germanic Empire*, 1871

By what right could God still say to me: "Be holy even as I am holy"? "Lying spirit" I would reply, "thou foolish God, thy reign is past. Seek new victims among the beans… Eternal father, Jupiter, Jehovah, we have learned to know they ways. Thou art, thou wast, and ever will be, the envier of Adam and the tormentor of Prometheus.

—Pierre-Joseph Proudhon, *System of Economic Contradictions*, 1846

For my part, I say that the first duty of the thinking, freeman is ceaselessly to banish the idea of God from his mind and consciousness. For God, if he exists, is essentially hostile to our nature, and we in no way depend on his authority… Each step in our progress represents one more victory in which we annihilate the Deity.

—Pierre-Joseph Proudhon, *System of Economic Contradictions*, 1846

God is stupidity and cowardice; God is hypocrisy and falsehood. God is tyranny and poverty; God is evil. For as long as men bow before altars, mankind will remain damned, the slave of kings and priests… Get thee hence, O God.

—Pierre-Joseph Proudhon, *System of Economic Contradictions*, 1846

I do not believe in God because I believe in man. Whatever his mistakes, man has for thousands of years been working to undo the botched job your God has made.

—Emma Goldman, speech to a church congregation, Detroit, 1897

18
Introduction To A Contribution To The Critique Of Hegel's Philosophy Of Right
Karl Marx

For Germany, the *criticism of religion* has been essentially completed, and the criticism of religion is the prerequisite of all criticism.

The *profane* existence of error is compromised as soon as its *heavenly oratio pro aris et focis* ["speech for the altars and hearths"] has been refuted. Man, who has found only the *reflection* of himself in the fantastic reality of heaven, where he sought a superman, will no longer feel disposed to find the *mere appearance* of himself, the non-man [*Unmensch*], where he seeks and must seek his true reality.

The foundation of irreligious criticism is: *man makes religion*, religion does not make man. Religion is, indeed, the self-consciousness and self-esteem of man who has either not yet won through to himself, or has already lost himself again. But man is no abstract being squatting outside the world. Man is the world of man—state, society. This state and this society produce religion, which is an *inverted consciousness of the world*, because they are an *inverted world*. Religion is the general theory of this world, its encyclopaedic compendium, its logic in popular form, its spiritual *point d'honneur*, its enthusiasm, its moral sanction, its solemn complement, and its universal basis of consolation and justification. It is the *fantastic realization* of the human essence since the *human essence* has not acquired any true reality. The struggle against religion is, therefore, indirectly the struggle *against that world* whose spiritual *aroma* is religion.

Religious suffering is, at one and the same time, the *expression* of real suffering and a *protest* against real suffering. Religion is the sigh of the oppressed creature, the heart of a heartless world, and the soul of soulless conditions. It is the *opium* of the people.[1]

The abolition of religion as the illusory happiness of the people is the demand for their real happiness. To call on them to give up their illusions about their condition is to call on them to *give up a condition that requires illusions*. The criticism of religion is, therefore, *in embryo, the criticism of that vale of tears* of which religion is the *halo*.

Criticism has plucked the imaginary flowers on the chain not in order that man shall continue to bear that chain without fantasy or consolation, but so that he shall throw off the chain and pluck the living flower. The criticism of religion disillusions man, so that he will think, act, and fashion his reality like a man who has discarded his illusions and regained his senses, so that he will move around himself as his own true Sun. Religion is only the illusory Sun which revolves around man as long as he does not revolve around himself.

It is, therefore, the *task of history*, once the *other-world of truth* has vanished, to establish the *truth of this world*. It is the immediate *task of philosophy*, which is in the service of history, to unmask self-estrangement in its *unholy forms* once the *holy form* of human self-estrangement has been unmasked. Thus, the criticism of Heaven turns into the criticism of Earth, the *criticism of religion* into the *criticism of law*, and the *criticism of theology* into the *criticism of politics*.

The following expositiontion—a contribution to this undertaking—concerns itself not directly with the original but with a copy, with the German philosophy of the state and of law. The only reason for this is that it is concerned with *Germany*.

If we were to begin with the German *status quo* itself, the result—even if we were to do it in the only appropriate way, i.e., negatively—would still be an *anachronism*. Even the negation of our present political situation is a dusty fact in the historical junk room of modern nations. If I negate powdered pigtails, I am still left with unpowdered pigtails. If I negate the situation in Germany in 1843, then according to the French calendar I have barely reached 1789, much less the vital centre of our present age.

Indeed, German history prides itself on having travelled a road which no other nation in the whole of history has ever travelled before, or ever will again. We have shared the restorations of modern nations without ever having shared their revolutions. We have been restored, firstly, because other nations dared to make revolutions, and, secondly, because other nations suffered counter-revolutions; on the one hand, because our masters were afraid, and, on the other, because they were not afraid. With our shepherds to the fore, we only once kept company with freedom, on the day of its internment.

One school of thought that legitimizes the infamy of today with the infamy of yesterday, a school that stigmatizes every cry of the serf against the knout as mere rebelliousness once the knout has aged a little and acquired a hereditary significance and a history, a school to which history shows nothing but its *a posteriori*, as did the God of Israel to his servant Moses, the *historical school of law*—this school would have invented German history were it not itself an invention of that history. A Shylock, but a cringing Shylock, that swears by its bond, its historical bond, its Christian-Germanic bond, for every pound of flesh cut from the heart of the people.

Good-natured enthusiasts, Germanomaniacs by extraction and free-thinkers by reflexion, on the contrary, seek our history of freedom beyond our history in the ancient Teutonic forests. But, what difference is there between the history of our freedom and the history of the boar's freedom if it can be found only in the forests? Besides, it is common knowledge that the forest echoes back what you shout into it. So peace to the ancient Teutonic forests!

War on the German state of affairs! By all means! They are *below the level of history, they are beneath any criticism*, but they are still an object of criticism like the criminal who is below the level of humanity but still an object for the *executioner*. In the struggle against that state of affairs, criticism is no passion of the head, it is the head of passion. It is not a lancet, it is a weapon. Its object is its *enemy*, which it wants not to refute but to *exterminate*. For the spirit of that state of affairs is refuted. In itself, it is no object *worthy of thought*, it is an existence which is as despicable as it is despised. Criticism does not need to make things clear to itself as regards this object, for it has already settled accounts with it. It no longer assumes the quality of an *end-in-itself*, but only of a *means*. Its essential pathos is indignation, its essential work is denunciation.

It is a case of describing the dull reciprocal pressure of all social spheres one on another, a general inactive ill-humor, a limitedness which recognizes itself as much as it mistakes itself, within the frame of government system which, living on the preservation of all wretchedness, is itself nothing but *wretchedness in office*.

What a sight! This infinitely proceeding division of society into the most manifold races opposed to one another by petty antipathies, uneasy consciences, and brutal mediocrity, and which, precisely because of their reciprocal ambiguous and distrustful attitude are all, without exception although with various formalities, treated by their *rulers* as *conceded existences*. And they must recognize and acknowledge as a concession of heaven the very fact that they are *mastered, ruled, possessed*! And, on the other side, are the rulers themselves, whose greatness is in inverse proportion to their number!

Criticism dealing with this content is criticism in a *hand-to-hand* fight, and in such a fight the point is not whether the opponent is a noble, equal, *interesting* opponent, the point is to strike him. The point is not to let the Germans have a minute for self-deception and resignation. The actual pressure must be made more pressing by adding to it consciousness of pressure, the shame must be made more shameful by publicizing it. Every sphere of German society must be shown as the *partie honteuse* of German society: these petrified relations must be forced to dance by singing their own tune to them! The people must be taught to be terrified at itself in order to give it courage. This will be fulfilling an imperative need of the German nation, and the needs of the nations are in themselves the ultimate reason for their satisfaction.

This struggle against the limited content of the German *status quo* cannot be without interest even for the *modern* nations, for the German *status quo* is the *open completion of the ancien régime* and the *ancien régime* is the *concealed deficiency of the modern state*. The struggle against the German political present is the struggle against the past of the modern nations, and they are still burdened with reminders of that past. It is instructive for them to see the *ancien régime*, which has been through its *tragedy* with them, playing its *comedy* as a German revenant. *Tragic* indeed was the pre-existing power of the world, and freedom, on the other hand, was a personal notion; in short, as long as it believed and had to believe in its own justification. As long as the *ancien régime*, as an existing world order, struggled against a world that was only coming into being, there was on its side a historical error, not a personal one. That is why its downfall was tragic.

On the other hand, the present German regime, an anachronism, a flagrant contradiction of generally recognized axioms, the nothingness of the *ancien régime* exhibited to the world, only imagines that it believes in itself and demands that the world should imagine the same thing. If it believed in its own *essence*, would it try to hide that essence under the *semblance* of an alien essence and seek refuge in hypocrisy and sophism? The modern *ancien régime* is rather only the *comedian* of a world order whose true heroes are dead. History is thorough and goes through many phases when carrying an old form to the grave. The last phases of a world-historical form is its *comedy*. The gods of Greece, already tragically wounded to death in Aeschylus's tragedy *Prometheus Bound*, had to re-die a comic death in Lucian's *Dialogues*. Why this course of history? So that humanity should part with its past *cheerfully*. This *cheerful* historical destiny is what we vindicate for the political authorities of Germany.

Meanwhile, once modern politico-social reality itself is subjected to criticism, once criticism rises to truly human problems, it finds itself outside the German *status quo*, or else it would reach out for its object below its object. An example. The relation of industry, of the world of wealth generally, to the political world is one of the major problems of modern times. In what form is this problem beginning to engage the attention of the Germans? In the form of *protective duties*, of the *prohibitive system*, or *national economy*. Germanomania has passed out of man into matter, and thus one morning our cotton barons and iron heroes saw themselves turned into patriots. People are, therefore, beginning in Germany to acknowledge the sovereignty of monopoly on the inside through lending it sovereignty on the outside. People are, therefore, now about to begin, in Germany, what people in France and England are about to end. The old corrupt condition against which these countries are revolting in theory, and which they only bear as one bears chains, is greeted in Germany as the dawn of a beautiful future which still hardly dares to pass from crafty theory to the most ruthless practice. Whereas the problem in France and England is: *Political economy*, or the *rule of society over wealth*; in Germany, it is: National economy, or the *mastery of private property over nationality*. In France and England, then, it is a case of abolishing monopoly that has proceeded to its last consequences; in Germany, it is a case of proceeding to the last consequences of monopoly. There is an adequate example of the German form of modern problems, an example of how our history, like a clumsy recruit, still has to do extra drill on things that are old and hackneyed in history.

If, therefore, the whole German development did not exceed the German political development, a German could at the most have the share in the problems-of-the-present that a Russian has. But, when the separate individual is not bound by the limitations of the nation, the nation as a whole is still less liberated by the liberation of one individual. The fact that Greece had a Scythian among its philosophers did not help the Scythians to make a single step towards Greek culture.

Luckily, we Germans are not Scythians.

As the ancient peoples went through their pre-history in imagination, in mythology, so we Germans have gone through our post-history in thought, in philosophy. We are philosophical contemporaries of the present without being its historical contemporaries. German philosophy is the ideal prolongation of German history. If therefore, instead of of the *oeuvres incompletes* of our real history, we criticize the *oeuvres posthumes* of our ideal history, *philosophy*, our criticism is in the midst of the questions of which the present says: *that is the question*. What, in progressive nations, is a *practical* break with modern state conditions, is, in Germany, where even those conditions do not yet exist, at first a critical break with the philosophical reflexion of those conditions.

German philosophy of right and state is the only German history which is *al pari* with the official modern present. The German nation must therefore join this, its dream-history, to its present conditions and subject to criticism not only these existing conditions, but at the same time their abstract continuation. Its future cannot be *limited* either to the immediate negation of its real conditions of state and right, or to the immediate implementation of its ideal state and right conditions, for it has the immediate negation of its real conditions in its ideal conditions, and it has almost *outlived* the immediate implementation of its ideal conditions in the contemplation of neighboring nations. Hence, it is with good reason that the practical political part in Germany demands the negation of philosophy.

It is wrong, not in its demand but in stopping at the demand, which it neither seriously implements nor can implement. It believes that it implements that negation by turning its back to philosophy and its head away from it and muttering a few trite and angry phrases about it. Owing to the limitation of its outlook, it does not include philosophy in the circle of German reality or it even fancies it is beneath German practice and the theories that serve it. You demand that real life embryos be made the starting-point, but you forget that the real life embryo of the German nation has grown so far only inside its cranium. In a word—*You cannot abolish philosophy without making it a reality*.

The same mistake, but with the factors *reversed*, was made by the theoretical party originating from philosophy.

In the present struggle it saw *only the critical struggle of philosophy against the German world*; it did not give a thought to the fact that *philosophy up to the present* itself belongs to this world and is its completion, although an ideal one. Critical towards its counterpart, it was uncritical towards itself when, proceeding from the *premises* of philosophy, it either stopped at the results given by philosophy or passed off demands and results from somewhere else as immediate demands and results of philosophy—although these, provided they are justified, can be obtained only by the *negation of philosophy up to the present*, of philosophy as such. We reserve ourselves the right to a more detailed description of this section: *It thought it could make philosophy a reality without abolishing it*.

The criticism of the *German philosophy of state and right*, which attained its most consistent, richest, and last formulation through *Hegel*, is both a critical analysis of the modern state and of the reality connected with it, and the resolute negation of the whole manner of the *German consciousness in politics and right* as *practiced* hereto, the most distinguished, most universal expression of which, raised to the level of *science*, is the *speculative philosophy* of right itself. If the speculative philosophy of right, that abstract extravagant *thinking* on the modern state, the reality of which remains a thing of the beyond, if only beyond the Rhine, was possible only in Germany; inversely the German thought-image of the modern state which makes abstraction of real man, was possible only because and insofar as the modern state itself makes abstraction of real man, or satisfies the whole of man only in imagination. In politics, the Germans thought what other nations did. Germany was their *theoretical conscience*. The abstraction and presumption of its thought was always in step with the one-sidedness and lowliness of its reality. If, therefore, the *status quo of German statehood* expresses the *completion* of the *ancien régime*, the completion of the thorn in the flesh of the modern state, the *status quo* of German state science expresses the *incompletion of the modern state*, the defectiveness of its flesh itself.

Already as the resolute opponent of the previous form of *German* political consciousness the criticism of speculative philosophy of right strays, not into itself, but into *problems* which there is only one means of solving—*practice*.

It is asked: can Germany attain a practice *à la hauteur des principles*—i.e., a *revolution* which will raises: it not only to the official level of modern nations, but to the height of humanity which will be the near future of those nations?

The weapon of criticism cannot, of course, replace criticism of the weapon, material force must be overthrown by material force; but theory also becomes a material force as soon as it has gripped the masses. Theory is capable of gripping the masses as soon as it demonstrates *ad hominem*, and it demonstrates *ad hominem* as soon as it becomes radical. To be radical is to grasp the root of the matter. But, for man, the root is man himself. The evident proof of the radicalism of German theory, and hence of its practical energy, is that is proceeds from a resolute *positive* abolition of religion. The criticism of religion ends with the teaching that *man is the highest essence for man*—hence, with the *categoric imperative to overthrow all relations* in which man is a debased, enslaved, abandoned, despicable essence, relations which cannot be better described than by the cry of a Frenchman when it was planned to introduce a tax on dogs: "Poor dogs! They want to treat you as human beings!"

Even historically, theoretical emancipation has specific practical significance for Germany. For Germany's *revolutionary* past is theoretical, it is the *Reformation*. As the revolution then began in the brain of the *monk*, so now it begins in the brain of the *philosopher*.

Luther, we grant, overcame bondage out of *devotion* by replacing it by bondage out of *conviction*. He shattered faith in authority because he restored the authority of faith. He turned priests into laymen because he turned laymen into priests. He freed man from outer religiosity because he made religiosity the inner man. He freed the body from chains because he enchained the heart.

But, if Protestantism was not the true solution of the problem, it was at least the true setting of it. It was no longer a case of the layman's struggle against the *priest* outside himself but of his struggle against his *own priest inside himself*, his priestly nature. And if the Protestant transformation of the German layman into priests emancipated the lay popes, the *princes*, with the whole of their priestly clique, the privileged and philistines, the philosophical transformation of priestly Germans into men will emancipate the *people*. But, *secularization* will not stop at the *confiscation of church estates* set in motion mainly by hypocritical Prussia any more than emancipation stops at princes. The Peasant War, the most radical fact of German history, came to grief because of theology. Today, when theology itself has come to grief, the most unfree fact of German history, our *status quo*, will be shattered against philosophy. On the eve of the Reformation, official Germany was the most unconditional slave of Rome. On the eve of its revolution, it is the unconditional slave of less than Rome, of Prussia and Austria, of country junkers and philistines.

Meanwhile, a major difficulty seems to stand in the way of a radical German revolution. For revolutions require a *passive* element, a material basis. Theory is fulfilled in a people only insofar as it is the fulfilment of the needs of that people. But will the monstrous discrepancy between the demands of German thought and the answers of German reality find a corresponding discrepancy between civil society and the state, and between civil society and itself? Will the theoretical needs be immediate practical needs? It is not enough for thought to strive for realization, reality must itself strive towards thought.

But Germany did not rise to the intermediary stage of political emancipation at the same time as the modern nations. It has not yet reached in practice the stages which it has surpassed in theory. How can it do a *somersault*, not only over its own limitations, but at the same time over the limitations of the modern nations, over limitations which it must in reality feel and strive for as for emancipation from its real limitations? Only a revolution of radical needs can be a radical revolution and it seems that precisely the preconditions and grounds for such needs are lacking.

If Germany has accompanied the development of the modern nations only with the abstract activity of thought without taking an effective share in the real struggle of that development, it has, on the other hand, shared the *sufferings* of that development, without sharing in its enjoyment, or its partial satisfaction. To the abstract activity on the one hand corresponds the abstract suffering on the other. That is why Germany will one day find itself on the level of European decadence before ever having been on the level of European emancipation. It will be comparable to a *fetish worshipper* pining away with the diseases of Christianity.

If we now consider the *German governments*, we find that because of the circumstances of the time, because of Germany's condition, because of the standpoint of German education, and, finally, under the impulse of its own fortunate instinct, they are driven to combine the *civilized shortcomings of the modern state world*, the advantages of which we do not enjoy, with the *barbaric deficiencies of the ancien régime*, which we enjoy in full; hence, Germany must share more and more, if not in the reasonableness, at least in the unreasonableness of those state formations which are beyond the bounds of its *status quo*. Is there in the world, for example, a country which shares so naively in all the illusions of constitutional statehood without sharing in its realities as so-called constitutional Germany? And was it not perforce the notion of a German government to combine the tortures of censorship with the tortures of the French September laws [1835 anti-press laws] which provide for freedom of the press? As you could find the gods of all nations in the Roman Pantheon, so you will find in the Germans' Holy Roman Empire all the sins of all state forms. That this eclecticism will reach a so far unprecedented height is guaranteed in particular by the *political-aesthetic gourmanderie* of a German king who intended to play all the roles of monarchy, whether feudal or democratic, if not in the person of the people, at least in his *own* person, and if not for the people, at least for *himself*. Germany, as the *deficiency of the political present constituted a world of its ow*n, will not be able to throw down the specific German limitations without throwing down the general limitation of the political present.

It is not the *radical* revolution, not the *general human* emancipation which is a utopian dream for Germany, but rather the partial, the *merely* political revolution, the revolution which leaves the pillars of the house standing. On what is a partial, a merely political revolution based? On *part of civil society* emancipating itself and attaining *general* domination; on a definite class, proceeding from its *particular situation*; undertaking the general emancipation of society. This class emancipates the whole of society, but only provided the whole of society is in the same situation as this class—e.g., possesses money and education or can acquire them at will.

No class of civil society can play this role without arousing a moment of enthusiasm in itself and in the masses, a moment in which it fraternizes and merges with society in general, becomes confused with it and is perceived and acknowledged as its *general representative*, a moment in which its claims and rights are truly the claims and rights of society itself, a moment in which it is truly the social head and the social heart. Only in the name of the general rights of society can a particular class vindicate for itself general domination. For the storming of this emancipatory position, and hence for the political exploitation of all sections of society in the interests of its own section, revolutionary energy and spiritual self-feeling alone are not sufficient. For the *revolution of a nation*, and the *emancipation of a particular class* of civil society to co-incide, for one estate to be acknowledged as the estate of the whole society, all the defects of society must conversely be concentrated in another class, a particular estate must be the estate of the general stumbling-block, the incorporation of the general limitation, a particular social sphere must be recognized as the notorious crime of the whole of society, so that liberation from that sphere appears as general self-liberation. For one estate to be *par excellence* the estate of liberation, another estate must conversely be the obvious estate of oppression. The negative general significance of the French nobility and the French clergy determined the positive general significance of the nearest neighboring and opposed class of the *bourgeoisie*.

But no particular class in Germany has the constituency, the penetration, the courage, or the ruthlessness that could mark it out as the negative representative of society. No more has any estate the breadth of soul that identifies itself, even for a moment, with the soul of the nation, the geniality that inspires material might to political violence, or that revolutionary daring which flings at the adversary the defiant words: *I am nothing but I must be everything*. The main stem of German morals and honesty, of the classes as well as of individuals, is rather that *modest egoism* which asserts its limitedness and allows it to be asserted against itself. The relation of the various sections of German society is therefore not dramatic but epic. Each of them begins to be aware of itself and begins to camp beside the others with all its particular claims not as soon as it is oppressed, but as soon as the circumstances of the time, without the section's own participation, creates a social substratum on which it can in turn exert pressure. Even the *moral self-feeling of the German middle class* rests only on the consciousness that it is the common representative of the philistine mediocrity of all the other classes. It is therefore not only the German kings who accede to the throne *mal à propos*, it is every section of civil society which goes through a defeat before it celebrates victory and develops its own limitations before it overcomes the limitations facing it, asserts its narrow-hearted essence before it has been able to assert its magnanimous essence; thus the very opportunity of a great role has passed away before it is to hand, and every class, once it begins the struggle against the class opposed to it, is involved in the struggle against the class below it. Hence, the higher nobility is struggling against the monarchy, the bureaucrat against the nobility, and the bourgeois against them all, while the proletariat is already beginning to find itself struggling against the bourgeoisie. The middle class hardly dares to grasp the thought of emancipation from its own standpoint when the development of the social conditions and the progress of political theory already declare that standpoint antiquated or at least problematic.

In France, it is enough for somebody to be something for him to want to be everything; in Germany, nobody can be anything if he is not prepared to renounce everything. In France, partial emancipation is the basis of universal emancipation; in Germany, universal emancipation is the *conditio sine qua non* of any partial emancipation. In France, it is the reality of gradual liberation that must give birth to complete freedom, in Germany, the impossibility of gradual liberation. In France, every class of the nation is a political idealist and becomes aware of itself at first not as a particular class but as a representative of social requirements generally. The role of *emancipator* therefore passes in dramatic motion to the various classes of the French nation one after the other until it finally comes to the class which implements social freedom no longer with the provision of certain conditions lying outside man and yet created by human society, but rather organizes all conditions of human existence on the premises of social freedom. On the contrary, in Germany, where practical life is as spiritless as spiritual life is unpractical, no class in civil society has any need or capacity for general emancipation until it is forced by its *immediate* condition, by *material* necessity, by its *very chains*.

Where, then, is the positive possibility of a German emancipation?

Answer: In the formulation of a class with radical chains, a class of civil society which is not a class of civil society, an estate which is the dissolution of all estates, a sphere which has a universal character by its universal suffering and claims no *particular right* because no *particular wrong*, but *wrong generally*, is perpetuated against it; which can invoke no *historical*, but only *human*, title; which does not stand in any one-sided antithesis to the consequences but in all-round antithesis to the premises of German statehood; a sphere, finally, which cannot emancipate itself without emancipating itself from all other spheres of society and thereby emancipating all other spheres of society, which, in a word, is the *complete loss* of man and hence can win itself only through the *complete re-winning of man*. This dissolution of society as a particular estate is the *proletariat*.

The proletariat is beginning to appear in Germany as a result of the rising *industrial* movement. For, it is not the *naturally arising* poor but the *artificially impoverished*, not the human masses mechanically oppressed by the gravity of society, but the masses resulting from the *drastic dissolution* of society, mainly of the middle estate, that form the proletariat, although, as is easily understood, the naturally arising poor and the Christian-Germanic serfs gradually join its ranks.

By heralding the *dissolution of the hereto existing world order*, the proletariat merely proclaims the *secret of its own existence*, for it is the factual dissolution of that world order. By demanding the *negation of private property*, the proletariat merely raises to the rank of a principle of society what society has raised to the rank of its principle, what is already incorporated in it as the negative result of society without its own participation. The proletarian then finds himself possessing the same right in regard to the world which is coming into being as the *German king* in regard to the world which has come into being when he calls the people his people, as he calls the horse his horse. By declaring the people his private property, the king merely proclaims that the private owner is king.

As philosophy finds its material weapon in the proletariat, so the proletariat finds its spiritual weapon in philosophy. And once the lightning of thought has squarely struck this ingenuous soil of the people, the emancipation of the *Germans* into *men* will be accomplished.

Let us sum up the result: The only liberation of Germany which is practically possible is liberation from the point of view of that theory which declares man to be the supreme being for man. Germany can emancipate itself from the Middle Ages only if it emancipates itself at the same time from the partial victories over the *Middle Ages*. In Germany, *no* form of bondage can be broken without breaking all forms of bondage. Germany, which is renowned for its *thoroughness*, cannot make a revolution unless it is a *thorough* one. The *emancipation of the German* is the *emancipation of man*. The *head* of this emancipation is *philosophy*, its *heart* the *proletariat*. Philosophy cannot realize itself without the transcendence [*Aufhebung*] of the proletariat, and the proletariat cannot transcend itself without the realization [*Verwirklichung*] of philosophy.

When all the inner conditions are met, the *day of the German resurrection* will be heralded by the *crowing of the cock of Gaul*.

Notes

1. In the 19th century, opium was widely used for medical purposes as a painkiller, and did not connote a *delusionary* state of consciousness. Thus it is in the sense of making suffering bearable, not the sense of a drug-induced delusion that Marx uses the term here. Possible misunderstanding is promoted in some translations which render this phrase as the "opium *for* the people" rather than "of" the people.

FROM THE EARLY 20th CENTURY CLASSICS

There are no dangerous thoughts; thinking itself is dangerous.
—*Hannah Arendt, political theorist*

The fact that a believer is happier than a skeptic is no more to the point than the fact that a drunken man is happier than a sober one.
—*George Bernard Shaw, playwright*

You never see animals going through the absurd and often horrible fooleries of magic and religion…Dogs do not ritually urinate in the hope of persuading heaven to do the same and send down rain. Asses do not bray a liturgy to cloudless skies. Nor do cats attempt, by abstinence from cat's meat, to wheedle the feline spirits into benevolence. Only man behaves with such gratuitous folly. It is the price he has to pay for being intelligent but not, as yet, quite intelligent enough.
—*Aldous Huxley, writer and humanist*

I don't agree with those who think that the conflict is simply between two religions, namely Christianity and Islam…To me, the key conflict is between irrational blind faith and rational, logical minds.
—*Taslima Nasrin, physician, author, and feminist, as of November 2007, exiled in a secret location for her outspoken critiques of Islam*

All your Western theologies, the whole mythology of them, are based on the concept of God as a senile delinquent.
—*Tennessee Williams, playwright*

For those who believe in God, most of the big questions are answered. But for those of us who can't readily accept the God formula, the big answers don't remain stone-written. We adjust to new conditions and discoveries. We are pliable. Love need not be a command or faith a dictum. I am my own God. We are here to unlearn the teachings of the church, state and our education system. We are here to drink beer. We are here to kill war. We are here to laugh at the odds and live our lives so well that Death will tremble to take us.
—*Charles Bukowski, poet and novelist*

Nowhere is it written that the Good exists, that we must be honest, that we must not lie; because the fact is we are on a plane where there are only men. Dostoievsky said, "If God didn't exist, everything would be possible." That is the very starting point of existentialism. Indeed, everything is permissible if God does not exist, and as a result man is forlorn, because neither within him nor without does he find anything to cling to. He can't start making excuses for himself.
—*Jean-Paul Sartre, philosopher and activist, credited with popularizing Existentialism*

19
The Philosophy Of Atheism (1916)
Emma Goldman

To give an adequate exposition of the philosophy of Atheism, it would be necessary to go into the historical changes of the belief in a Deity, from its earliest beginning to the present day. But that is not within the scope of the present paper. However, it is not out of place to mention, in passing, that the concept God, Supernatural Power, Spirit, Deity, or in whatever other term the essence of Theism may have found expression, has become more indefinite and obscure in the course of time and progress. In other words, the God idea is growing more impersonal and nebulous in proportion as the human mind is learning to understand natural phenomena and in the degree that science progressively correlates human and social events.

God, today, no longer represents the same forces as in the beginning of His existence; neither does He direct human destiny with the same iron hand as of yore. Rather, the God idea expresses a sort of spiritualistic stimulus to satisfy the fads and fancies of every shade of human weakness. In the course of human development the God idea has been forced to adapt itself to every phase of human affairs, which is perfectly consistent with the origin of the idea itself.

The conception of gods originated in fear and curiosity. Primitive man, unable to understand the phenomena of nature and harassed by them, saw in every terrifying manifestation some sinister force expressly directed against him; and as ignorance and fear are the parents of all superstition, the troubled fancy of primitive man wove the God idea.

Very aptly, the world-renowned atheist and anarchist, Michael Bakunin, says in his great work *God and the State*:

All religions, with their demi-gods, and their prophets, their messiahs and their saints, were created by the prejudiced fancy of men who had not attained the full development and full possession of their faculties. Consequently, the religious heaven is nothing but the mirage in which man, exalted by ignorance and faith, discovered his own image, but enlarged and reversed that is, divinised. The history of religions, of the birth, grandeur, and the decline of the gods who had succeeded one another in human belief, is nothing, therefore, but the development of the collective intelligence and conscience of mankind. As fast as they discovered, in the course of their historically-progressive advance, either in themselves or in external nature, a quality, or even any great defect whatever, they attributed them to their gods, after having exaggerated and enlarged them beyond measure, after the manner of children, by an act of their religious fancy... With all due respect, then, to the metaphysicians and religious idealists, philosophers, politicians or poets: the idea of God implies the abdication of human reason and justice; it is the most decisive negation of human liberty, and necessarily ends in the enslavement of mankind, both in theory and practice.[1]

Thus the God idea revived, readjusted, and enlarged or narrowed, according to the necessity of the time, has dominated humanity and will continue to do so until man will raise his head to the sunlit day, unafraid and with an awakened will to himself. In proportion as man learns to realize himself and mold his own destiny, theism becomes superfluous. How far man will be able to find his relation to his fellows will depend entirely upon how much he can outgrow his dependence upon God.

Already there are indications that theism, which is the theory of speculation, is being replaced by Atheism, the science of demonstration; the one hangs in the metaphysical clouds of the Beyond, while the other has its roots firmly in the soil. It is the earth, not heaven, which man must rescue if he is truly to be saved.

The decline of theism is a most interesting spectacle, especially as manifested in the anxiety of the theists, whatever their particular brand. They realize, much to their distress, that the masses are growing daily more atheistic, more anti-religious; that they are quite willing to leave the Great Beyond and its heavenly domain to the angels and sparrows; because more and more the masses are becoming engrossed in the problems of their immediate existence.

How to bring the masses back to the God idea, the spirit, the First Cause, etc.: that is the most pressing question to all theists. Metaphysical as all these questions seem to be, they yet have a very marked physical background, inasmuch as religion, "Divine Truth," rewards and punishments are the trade-marks of the largest, the most corrupt and pernicious, the most powerful and lucrative industry in the world, not excepting the industry of manufacturing guns and munitions. It is the industry of befogging the human mind and stifling the human heart. Necessity knows no law; hence the majority of theists are compelled to take up every subject, even if it has no bearing upon a deity or revelation or the Great Beyond. Perhaps they sense the fact that humanity is growing weary of the hundred and one brands of God.

How to raise this dead level of theistic belief is really a matter of life and death for all denominations. Therefore their tolerance; but it is a tolerance not of understanding, but of weakness. Perhaps that explains the efforts fostered in all religious publications to combine variegated religious philosophies and conflicting theistic theories into one denominational trust. More and more, the various concepts "of the only true God, the only pure spirit, the only true religion" are tolerantly glossed over in the frantic effort to establish a common ground to rescue the modern mass from the "pernicious" influence of atheistic ideas.

It is characteristic of theistic "tolerance" that no one really cares what the people believe in, just so they believe or pretend to believe. To accomplish this end, the crudest and vulgarest methods are being used. Religious endeavor meetings and revivals with Billy Sunday[2] as their champion—methods which must outrage every refined sense, and which in their effect upon the ignorant and curious often tend to create a mild state of insanity not infrequently coupled with erotomania. All these frantic efforts find approval and support from the earthly powers; from the Russian despot to the American President; from Rockefeller and Wanamaker down to the pettiest business man. They know that capital invested in Billy Sunday, the YMCA, Christian Science, and various other religious institutions will return enormous profits from the subdued, tamed, and dull masses.

Consciously or unconsciously, most theists see in gods and devils, heaven and hell, reward and punishment, a whip to lash the people into obedience, meekness and contentment. The truth is that theism would have lost its footing long before this but for the combined support of Mammon and power. How thoroughly bankrupt it really is, is being demonstrated in the trenches and battlefields of Europe today.

Have not all theists painted their Deity as the god of love and goodness? Yet after thousands of years of such preachments the gods remain deaf to the agony of the human race. Confucius cares not for the poverty, squalor and misery of the people of China. Buddha remains undisturbed in his philosophical indifference to the famine and starvation of the outraged Hindoos; Jahve continues deaf to the bitter cry of Israel; while Jesus refuses to rise from the dead against his Christians who are butchering each other.

The burden of all song and praise, "unto the Highest" has been that God stands for justice and mercy. Yet injustice among men is ever on the increase; the outrages committed against the masses in this country alone would seem enough to overflow the very heavens. But where are the gods to make an end to all these horrors, these wrongs, this inhumanity to man? No, not the gods, but MAN must rise in his mighty wrath. He, deceived by all the deities, betrayed by their emissaries, he, himself, must undertake to usher in justice upon the earth.

The philosophy of Atheism expresses the expansion and growth of the human mind. The philosophy of theism, if we can call it philosophy, is static and fixed. Even the mere attempt to pierce these mysteries represents, from the theistic point of view, non-belief in the all embracing omnipotence, and even a denial of the wisdom of the divine powers outside of man. Fortunately, however, the human mind never was, and never can be, bound by fixities. Hence it is forging ahead in its restless march towards knowledge and life. The human mind is realizing "that the universe is not the result of a creative fiat by some divine intelligence, out of nothing, producing a masterpiece in perfect operation," but that it is the product of chaotic forces operating through aeons of time, of clashes and cataclysms, of repulsion and attraction crystallizing through the principle of selection into what the theists call "the universe guided into order and beauty." As Joseph McCabe well points out in his *Existence of God*: "a law of nature is not a formula drawn up by a legislator, but a mere summary of the observed facts—a 'bundle of facts'." Things do not act in a particular way because there is a law, but we state the 'law' because they act in that way."[3]

The philosophy of Atheism represents a concept of life without any metaphysical Beyond or Divine Regulator. It is the concept of an actual, real world with its liberating, expanding and beautifying possibilities, as against an unreal world, which, with its spirits, oracles, and mean contentment, has kept humanity in helpless degradation.

It may seem a wild paradox, and yet it is pathetically true, that this real, visible world and our life should have been so long under the influence of metaphysical speculation, rather than of physical demonstrable forces. Under the lash of the theistic idea, this earth has served no other purpose than as a temporary station to test man's capacity for immolation to the will of God. But the moment man attempted to ascertain the nature of that will, he was told that it was utterly futile for "finite human intelligence" to get beyond the all-powerful infinite will. Under the terrific weight of this omnipotence, man has been bowed into the dust—a will-less creature, broken and swarting in the dark. The triumph of the philosophy of Atheism is to free man from the nightmare of gods; it means the dissolution of the phantoms of the beyond. Again and again the light of reason has dispelled the theistic nightmare, but poverty, misery and fear have recreated the phantoms— though whether old or new, whatever their external form, they differed little in their essence. Atheism, on the other hand, in its philosophic aspect refuses allegiance not merely to a definite concept of God, but it refuses all servitude to the God idea, and opposes the theistic principle as such. Gods in their individual function are not half as pernicious as the principle of theism which represents the belief in a supernatural, or even omnipotent, power to rule the earth and man upon it. It is the absolutism of theism, its pernicious influence upon humanity, its paralyzing effect upon thought and action, which Atheism is fighting with all its power.

The philosophy of Atheism has its root in the earth, in this life; its aim is the emancipation of the human race from all God-heads, be they Judaic, Christian, Mohammedan, Buddhistic, Brahministic, or what not. Mankind has been punished long and heavily for having created its gods; nothing but pain and persecution have been man's lot since gods began. There is but one way out of this blunder: Man must break his fetters which have chained him to the gates of heaven and hell, so that he can begin to fashion out of his reawakened and illumined consciousness a new world upon earth.

Only after the triumph of the Atheistic philosophy in the minds and hearts of man will freedom and beauty be realized. Beauty as a gift from heaven has proved useless. It will, however, become the essence and impetus of life when man learns to see in the earth the only heaven fit for man. Atheism is already helping to free man from his dependence upon punishment and reward as the heavenly bargain-counter for the poor in spirit.

Do not all theists insist that there can be no morality, no justice, honesty or fidelity without the belief in a Divine Power? Based upon fear and hope, such morality has always been a vile product, imbued partly with self-righteousness, partly with hypocrisy. As to truth, justice, and fidelity, who have been their brave exponents and daring proclaimers? Nearly always the godless ones: the Atheists: they lived, fought, and died for them. They knew that justice, truth, and fidelity are not conditioned in heaven, but that they are related to and interwoven with the tremendous changes going on in the social and material life of the human race; not fixed and eternal, but fluctuating, even as life itself. To what heights the philosophy of Atheism may yet attain, no one can prophesy. But this much can already be predicted: only by its regenerating fire will human relations be purged from the horrors of the past.

Thoughtful people are beginning to realize that moral precepts, imposed upon humanity through religious terror, have become stereotyped and have therefore lost all vitality. A glance at life today, at its disintegrating character, its conflicting interests with their hatreds, crimes, and greed, suffices to prove the sterility of theistic morality.

Man must get back to himself before he can learn his relation to his fellows. Prometheus chained to the Rock of Ages is doomed to remain prey to the vultures of darkness. Unbind Prometheus, and you dispel the night and its horrors.

Atheism in its negation of gods is at the same time the strongest affirmation of man, and through man, the eternal yea to life, purpose, and beauty.

Notes

1. Mikhail Bakunin (1814-1876), *L'Empire Knouto-Germanique et la revolution sociale* (1871).

2. Billy Sunday (1862-1935), American evangelist.

3. *The Existence of God* (1913) by Joseph McCabe (1867-1955).

20
On The Scopes Trial (1925)[1]
H.L. Mencken

Homo Neandertalensis

The so-called religious organizations which now lead the war against the teaching of evolution are nothing more, at bottom, than conspiracies of the inferior man against his betters. They mirror very accurately his congenital hatred of knowledge, his bitter enmity to the man who knows more than he does, and so gets more out of life. Certainly it cannot have gone unnoticed that their membership is recruited, in the overwhelming main, from the lower orders, that no man of any education or other human dignity belongs to them. What they propose to do, at bottom and in brief, is to make the superior man infamous: by mere abuse if it is sufficient, and if it is not, then by law.

Such organizations, of course, must have leaders; there must be men in them whose ignorance and imbecility are measurably less abject than the ignorance and imbecility of the average. These super-Chandala often attain to a considerable power, especially in democratic states. Their followers trust them and look up to them; sometimes, when the pack is on the loose, it is necessary to conciliate them. But their puissance cannot conceal their incurable inferiority. They belong to the mob as surely as their dupes, and the thing that animates them is precisely the mob's hatred of superiority. Whatever lies above the level of their comprehension is of the devil. A glass of wine delights civilized men; they themselves, drinking it, would get drunk. *Ergo,* wine must be prohibited. The hypothesis of evolution is credited by all men of education; they themselves can't understand it. *Ergo,* its teaching must be put down.

This simple fact explains such phenomena as the Tennessee buffoonery. Nothing else can. We must think of human progress, not as of something going on in the race in general, but as of something going on in a small minority, perpetually beleaguered in a few walled towns. Now and then the horde of barbarians outside breaks through, and we have an armed effort to halt the process. That is, we have a Reformation, a French Revolution, a war for democracy, a Great Awakening. The minority is decimated and driven to cover. But a few survive and a few are enough to carry on.

The inferior man's reasons for hating knowledge are not hard to discern. He hates it because it is complex—because it puts an unbearable burden upon his meager capacity for taking in ideas. Thus his search is always for short cuts. All superstitions are such short cuts. Their aim is to make the unintelligible simple, and even obvious. So on what seem to be higher levels. No man who has not had a long and arduous education can understand even the most elementary concepts of modern pathology. But even a hind at the plow can grasp the theory of chiropractic in two lessons. Hence the vast popularity of chiropractics among the submerged and of osteopathy, Christian Science and other such quackeries with it. They are idiotic, but they are simple—and every man prefers what he can understand to what puzzles and dismays him.

The popularity of Fundamentalism among the inferior orders of men is explicable in exactly the same way. The cosmogonies that educated men toy with are all inordinately complex. To comprehend their veriest outlines requires an immense stock of knowledge, and a habit of thought. It would be as vain to try to teach to peasants or to the city proletariat as it would be to try to teach them to streptococci. But the cosmogony of Genesis is so simple that even a yokel can grasp it. It is set forth in a few phrases. It offers, to an ignorant man, the irresistible reasonableness of the nonsensical. So he accepts it with loud hosannas, and has one more excuse for hating his betters.

Malone The Victor, Even Though Court Sides with Opponents, Says Mencken

… Bryan… sat through [Malone's speech] in his usual posture, with his palm-leaf fan flapping energetically and his hard, cruel mouth shut tight. The old boy grows more and more pathetic. He has aged greatly during the past few years and begins to look elderly and enfeebled. All that remains of his old fire is now in his black eyes. They glitter like dark gems, and in their glitter there is immense and yet futile malignancy. That is all that is left of the Peerless Leader of thirty years ago. Once he had one leg in the White House and the nation trembled under his roars.[2] Now he is a tinpot pope in the coca-cola belt and a brother to the forlorn pastors who belabor half-wits in galvanized iron tabernacles behind the railroad yards. His own speech was a grotesque performance and downright touching in its imbecility. Its climax came when he launched into a furious denunciation of the doctrine that man is a mammal. It seemed a sheer impossibility that any literate man should stand up in public and discharge any such nonsense. Yet the poor old fellow did it. Darrow stared incredulous. Malone sat with his mouth wide open. Hays indulged himself one of his sardonic chuckles. Stewart and Bryan *fils* looked extremely uneasy, but the old mountebank ranted on.[3] To call a man a mammal, it appeared, was to flout the revelation of God. The certain effect of the doctrine would be to destroy morality and promote infidelity. The defense let it pass. The lily needed no gilding.

There followed some ranting about the Leopold-Loeb case,[4] culminating in the argument that learning was corrupting—that the colleges by setting science above Genesis were turning their students into murderers. Bryan alleged that Darrow had admitted the fact in his closing speech at the Leopold-Loeb trial, and stopped to search for the passage in a printed copy of the speech. Darrow denied making any such statement, and presently began reading what he actually had said on the subject. Bryan then proceeded to denounce Nietzsche, whom he described as an admirer and follower of Darwin. Darrow challenged the fact and offered to expound what Nietzsche really taught. Bryan waved him off.

The effect of the whole harangue was extremely depressing. It quickly ceased to be an argument addressed to the court—Bryan, in fact, constantly said "My friends" instead of "Your Honor"—and became a sermon at the camp-meeting. All the familiar contentions of the Dayton divines appeared in it—that learning is dangerous, that nothing is true that is not in the Bible, that a yokel who goes to church regularly knows more than any scientist ever heard of. The thing went to fantastic lengths. It became a farrago of puerilities without coherence or sense. I don't think the old man did himself justice. He was in poor voice and his mind seemed to wander. There was far too much hatred in him for him to be persuasive.

The crowd, of course, was with him. It has been fed upon just such balderdash for years. Its pastors assault it twice a week with precisely the same nonsense. It is chronically in the position of a populace protected by an espionage act in time of war. That is to say, it is forbidden to laugh at the arguments of one side and forbidden to hear the case of the other side. Bryan has been roving around in the tall grass for years and he knows the bucolic mind. He knows how to reach and inflame its basic delusions and superstitions. He has taken them into his own stock and adorned them with fresh absurdities. Today he may well stand as the archetype of the American rustic. His theology is simply the elemental magic that is preached in a hundred thousand rural churches fifty-two times a year.

These Tennessee mountaineers are not more stupid than the city proletariat; they are only less informed. If Darrow, Malone and Hays could make a month's stumping tour in Rhea county I believe that fully a fourth of the population would repudiate fundamentalism, and that not a few of the clergy now in practice would be restored to their old jobs on the railroad. Malone's speech yesterday probably shook a great many true believers; another like it would fetch more than one of them. But the chances are heavily against them ever hearing a second. Once this trial is over, the darkness will close in again, and it will take long years of diligent and thankless effort to dispel it—if, indeed, it is ever dispelled at all. ...

Aftermath

The Liberals, in their continuing discussion of the late trial of the infidel Scopes at Dayton, Tenn., run true to form. That is to say, they show all their habitual lack of humor and all their customary furtive weakness for the delusions of *Homo neandertalensis*. I point to two of their most enlightened organs: the eminent New York *World* and the gifted *New Republic*. The *World* is displeased with Mr. Darrow because, in his appalling cross-examination of the mountebank Bryan, he did some violence to the theological superstitions that millions of Americans cherish. The *New Republic* denounces him because he addressed himself, not to "the people of Tennessee" but to the whole country, and because he should have permitted "local lawyers" to assume "the most conspicuous position in the trial."

Once more, alas, I find myself unable to follow the best Liberal thought. What the *World's* contention amounts to, at bottom, is simply the doctrine that a man engaged in combat with superstition should be very polite to superstition. This, I fear, is nonsense. The way to deal with superstition is not to be polite to it, but to tackle it with all arms, and so rout it, cripple it, and make it forever infamous and ridiculous. Is it, perchance, cherished by persons who should know better? Then their folly should be brought out into the light of day, and exhibited there in all its hideousness until they flee from it, hiding their heads in shame.

True enough, even a superstitious man has certain inalienable rights. He has a right to harbor and indulge his imbecilities as long as he pleases, provided only he does not try to inflict them upon other men by force. He has a right to argue for them as eloquently as he can, in season and out of season. He has a right to teach them to his children. But certainly he has no right to be protected against the free criticism of those who do not hold them. He has no right to demand that they be treated as sacred. He has no right to preach them without challenge. Did Darrow, in the course of his dreadful bombardment of Bryan, drop a few shells, incidentally, into measurably cleaner camps? Then let the garrisons of those camps look to their defenses. They are free to shoot back. But they can't disarm their enemy.

The meaning of religious freedom, I fear, is sometimes greatly misapprehended. It is taken to be a sort of immunity, not merely from governmental control but also from public opinion. A dunderhead gets himself a long-tailed coat, rises behind the sacred desk, and emits such bilge as would gag a Hottentot. Is it to pass unchallenged? If so, then what we have is not religious freedom at all, but the most intolerable and outrageous variety of religious despotism. Any fool, once he is admitted to holy orders, becomes infallible. Any half-wit, by the simple device of ascribing his delusions to revelation, takes on an authority that is denied to all the rest of us.

I do not know how many Americans entertain the ideas defended so ineptly by poor Bryan, but probably the number is very large. They are preached once a week in at least a hundred thousand rural churches, and they are heard too in the meaner quarters of the great cities. Nevertheless, though they are thus held to be sound by millions, these ideas remain mere rubbish. Not only are they not supported by the known facts; they are in direct contravention of the known facts. No man whose information is sound and whose mind functions normally can conceivably credit them. They are the products of ignorance and stupidity, either or both.

What should be a civilized man's attitude toward such superstitions? It seems to me that the only attitude possible to him is one of contempt. If he admits that they have any intellectual dignity whatever, he admits that he himself has none. If he pretends to a respect for those who believe in them, he pretends falsely, and sinks almost to their level. When he is challenged he must answer honestly, regardless of tender feelings. That is what Darrow did at Dayton, and the issue plainly justified the fact. Bryan went there in a hero's shining armor, bent deliberately upon a gross crime against sense. He came out a wrecked and preposterous charlatan, his tail between his legs. Few Americans have ever done so much for their country in a whole lifetime as Darrow did in two hours.

Notes

1. This essay consists of three newspaper articles written about the Scopes Trial (see Introduction of this book, p.xiii). Malone was one of the defense attorneys. —Editor

2. William Jennings Bryan (1860-1925).

3. Bryan's son, William Jennings Bryan Jr., was assisting his father in the case.

4. Richard Loeb and Nathan Leopold, seventeen and eighteen years of age, were accused of murdering a fourteen-year-old boy; Darrow defended them.

21
The Lord's Day Alliance (1928)
Clarence Darrow

Among the various societies that are engaged in the business of killing pleasure, the Lord's Day Alliance of New York deserves a place of honor. If any poor mortal is caught enjoying life on Sunday its agents gleefully hie themselves to the nearest legislature and urge a law to stop the fun. Their literature and periodicals tell very plainly the kind of business they are in. This association of crape-hangers seems to be especially interested in the State of New York, which contains about one-tenth of the population of the Union, and among them an unusually large number of foreigners and other heathen who have not been taught the proper regard for the sanctity of the Sabbath.

The activities of this Alliance in New York still leave them ample time to watch the sinners in the other states and bring to book the wicked who are bent on having pleasure on the holy Sabbath Day. In their own language, the work is "in the interests of the preservation and promotion of the Lord's Day as the American Christian Sabbath to oppose all adverse measures seeking to weaken the law and to seek the passage of such measures as would tend to strengthen it." The Alliance informs us that "in the last four years it has furnished sixty-seven addresses per month, on an average. During this time over three hundred and twenty institute meetings have been held for the study of the Sabbath question. Several million pages of literature have been distributed." It "also furnishes press articles and syndicate matter for the newspapers." Imagine an institute spending so much time in the study of the Sabbath question! If they have learned anything on that subject it is not revealed in their tracts.

These Lord's Day folk seek to protect the day "in the interest of the home and the church," "to exalt Jesus Christ who is Lord of the Sabbath Day and to spread the knowledge of the will of God that His Kingdom may come and His will may be done." Though the organization is still young it points to a long list of glorious achievements. We are informed that "no adverse measure affecting the Sabbath has passed

Albany during this time, although forty-two such measures have been introduced in the legislature... A representative of our organization has been present on each occasion to oppose any such adverse measures." It boasts that it "opposed the opening of the State Fair in 1925 on Sunday, by vigorous protest to the members of the Commission and the Attorney General." The result was a ruling from the Attorney General sustaining the law. Of course, so long as no one could go to the fair on Sunday the people were obliged to go to church. It "has defeated annually an average of forty commercial and anti-Sunday bills in our legislature and has brought about the closing of the First and Second-Class Post-Offices on Sunday... As a result, thousands are in our churches each Sunday." It has been "thanked by President Coolidge for the services rendered hundreds of thousands of government employees in the District of Columbia and elsewhere throughout the nation." What further honor could anybody get on earth? It has "accepted the challenge and in scores of places defeated... commercialized amusement forces which have declared a nation-wide fight to the finish for Sunday movies and are even proposing to enlist the aid of the churches in their unholy campaign." It succeeded in "changing the date of the gigantic air carnival to which admission was charged, from Sunday, August 2, 1925, to Saturday, August 1, 1925, held at Bolling Field, Washington." No one but a parson has the right to charge for his performance on Sunday. Through its request "the War Department issued orders on November 2, 1925, covering every military post in the United States, banning Sunday public air carnivals and maneuvers." It is "now leading a country-wide movement for the enactment of a Sunday rest law for the District of Columbia. Washington needs and must have a Sunday rest law." It informs us that the "day must be kept above the Dollar, Christ above Commercialism on the Lord's Day, the person must have the right of way over the Pocketbook on our American Sunday."

Surely this is a great work and deserves the active support and sympathy of all people who are really interested in driving pleasure-seekers from golf grounds, automobile trips, baseball parks, moving-picture houses and every other form of pleasure on Sunday. It is possible that for lack of any other place to go, some of them might be compelled to park themselves in church. If America does not succeed in bringing back the ancient Puritan Sabbath with its manifold blessings, it will not be the fault of the Lord's Day Alliance.

As a part of this noble work the organization publishes various pamphlets and leaflets and scatters them broadcast through the land. As a rule, these pamphlets are the effusions of more or less obscure parsons. These preachers have special knowledge of God's plans and God's will. Their sermonettes are conflicting in their statements and utterly senseless in their assertions. The sentries of the Alliance on guard at the state capitals and in the national Congress, while these wise bodies are in session, have no doubt succeeded in coercing spineless members of legislative bodies to yield to their will and their parade of votes; and thus spread considerable gloom over the United States on the Sabbath Day.

These Lord's Day Alliance gentlemen are not only religious but scientific. For instance, they publish a pamphlet written by one Dr. A. Haegler, of Basel, Switzerland, in which he says that experiments have shown that during a day's work a laborer expends more oxygen than he can inhale. True, he catches up with a large part of this deficiency through the night time, but does not regain it all. It follows, of course, that if he keeps on working six days a week, for the same time each day, he will be out a considerable amount of oxygen, and the only way he can make it up is to take a day off on Sunday and go to church. This statement seems to be flawless to the powerful intellects who put out this literature. Any person who is in the habit of thinking might at once arrive at the conclusion that if the workman could not take in enough oxygen gas in the ordinary hours of work and sleep he might well cut down his day's work and lengthen his sleep and thus start even every morning. This ought to be better than running on a shortage of gas all through the week. Likewise, it must occur to most people that there are no two kinds of labor that consume the same amount of oxygen gas per day, and probably no two human systems that work exactly alike. Then, too, if the workman ran behind on his oxygen gas in the days when men worked from ten to sixteen hours a day he might break even at night, since working hours have been reduced to eight or less, with a Saturday half-holiday thrown in. It might even help the situation to raise the bedroom window at night. These matters, of course, do not occur to the eminent doctor who wrote the pamphlet and the scientific gentlemen who send it out. To them the silly statement proves that a man needs to take a day off on Sunday and attend church in order that he may catch up on his oxygen. To them it is perfectly plain that for catching up on oxygen the church has a great advantage over the golf links or the baseball park, or any other place where the wicked wish to go. This, in spite of the fact that in crowded buildings the oxygen might be mixed with halitosis.

The exact proof that these parsons marshal for showing that the need of a Sunday rest is manifest in the nature of things is marvelous. If the need of Sunday rest was meant to be shown by natural law it seems as if this should have been clearly indicated, especially if the righteous God had determined to punish Sunday violations with death and hell. There was no reason why the Creator should have been content to leave the proof to a revelation said to have been made in a barbarous age to an unknown man, hidden in the clouds on the top of a high mountain peak. Humans would not have graven such an important message on a tablet of stone and then insisted that the tablet should be destroyed before any being except Moses had set eye upon it. Even God should not ask for faith that amounts to credulity and gross superstition.

A deity could have written the Sabbath requirements plain on the face of nature. For instance, he might have made the waves be still on the seventh day of the week; the grass might have taken a day off and rested from growing until Monday morning; the wild animals of the forest and glen might have refrained from fighting and eating and chasing and maiming and have been made to close their eyes on the Sabbath Day, and to have kept peace and tranquility. The earth might have paused in its course around the sun or stood still on its axis. It should have been as important to make this gesture in homage of the day as it was to help Joshua hold the sun in leash that a battle might be prolonged. If nature had made plain provision for the Sabbath Day it would be patent to others as well as to the medicine men who insist that the Sabbath Day was made for their profit alone.

But let us pass from the realm of science, where pastors never did especially shine, into a field where they are more likely to excel. Here it is fairly easy to see what it is all about. The Reverend Robert C. McQuilkin, Pastor at Orange, New Jersey, furnishes a pamphlet for The Lord's Day Alliance. Read what the Doctor says:

> God claims the Sabbath for himself in a very unique, distinctive way as a day of rest and worship. He again and again commands you to spend its hours in the conservation of our spiritual power in the exercise of public and private worship. To spend this holy day in pleasure or unnecessary secular labor is to *rob God*. We have got to be careful how we take the hours of the Sabbath for secular study or work, for God will surely bring us to judgment concerning the matter. Church attendance is a definite obligation, a debt which we owe to God.

Here is where the Alliance seems to strike pay dirt! What reason has God to claim the Sabbath for Himself, and why is God robbed if a man should work on Sunday? It can hardly be possible that the puny insects that we call men could disturb God in His Sunday rest. Is it not a little presumptuous even to parsons, to say that a debt to the church is a debt to God?

To emphasize the importance of leaving the Sabbath to the preachers, we are warned of the fate of the sinner who profanes the Sabbath by work or play. The Lord's

Day Alliance has issued a little folder on which there is the following heading in large letters: THE IMPORTANCE OF THE DEATH PENALTY. Under it is printed this timely caution: "Six days shall work be done, but on the seventh day is a Sabbath of solemn rest, holy to Jehovah; whosoever doeth any work on the Sabbath Day shall surely be put to death. Exodus 31-15." The pamphlet also states that a wealthy business man is furnishing the money for the distribution of this sheet. If this barbarous statement represents the views of the Lord's Day Alliance then what is the mental caliber of the Congressmen, members of the legislatures, judges, and the public that are influenced by their ravings? Can anyone but an idiot have any feeling but contempt for men who seek to scare children and old women with such infamous stuff?

Let us see what the Bible says on this important subject. In Exodus 20:8-11 we find not only the commandment which was delivered to Moses in reference to the Sabbath, but the reasons for such a commandment:

> Remember the Sabbath Day to keep it holy. Six days shalt thou labor and do all thy work; but the seventh day is the Sabbath of the Lord thy God. In it thou shalt do no work, thou, nor thy son, nor thy daughter, nor thy man servant nor thy maid servant nor thy cattle which is within thy gates; *for in six days the Lord made heaven and earth, the sea and all that is in them and rested the seventh day, wherefore the Lord blessed the Sabbath Day and hallowed it.*

It is plain from this commandment that the Sabbath was not instituted in obedience to any natural law or so that man might catch up on his supply of oxygen, but because the Lord in six days had performed the herculean task of creating the universe out of nothing, and took a day off to rest on the seventh. Therefore, every man must rest on the seventh, no matter whether he has been working and is tired or not. This is made even more binding in Exodus 35:2:

> Six days shall work be done; upon the seventh day there shall be to you a holy day, the Sabbath of the rest of the Lord. Whosoever doeth work therein shall be put to death.

In view of the commands of God, certainly his special agents on the earth cannot be blamed for cruelty, no matter what ferocious doctrine they may preach. In Numbers 28:9-10, in connection with various offerings that the Law required on the Sabbath, a provision is made for meat offerings and drink offerings. The meat offerings enjoin the sacrifice of lambs by fire as "a sweet savor unto the Lord," and then the Lord provides that the pastor shall further:

Sacrifice on the Sabbath Day two lambs of first year without spot and two-tenths of a part of an ephah of fine flour for a meal-offering, mingled with oil and the drink offering thereof: this is the burnt-offering of every Sabbath, besides the continual burnt-offering and his drink offering.

It is evident that the lambs less than one year old, without spot, were to be burned because they were so young and innocent and would therefore make such a "sweet savor unto the Lord." Nothing is lacking in this smell but mint sauce. If Moses is to be obeyed on pain of hell in his command to abstain from work or play on the Sabbath why is the rest of the program any less sacred? How can the holy parsons release their congregations from the sacrifice of the two spotless lambs and the two- tenths of an ephah of fine flour mingled with oils?

In the Fifteenth Chapter of Numbers, it is related that while the children of Israel were in the wilderness they found a man gathering sticks on the Sabbath Day. The Hebrews were evidently at a loss to know what should be done with him for this most heinous offense, so they put him in "ward" to await the further orders of the Lord. It is then related, "and the Lord said unto Moses: The man shall surely be put to death; all the congregation shall stone him with stones without the camp. And all the congregation brought him without the camp and stoned him to death with stones: *as Jehovah commanded Moses.*" In spite of manifold texts like this there are persons who protest that they love this bloody, barbarous, tribal God of the Jews. The literature of the Alliance clearly indicates that its sponsors would follow this command of Jehovah at the present time if they could only have their way.

Dr. McQuilkin further tells us that the defenders of the day have often been too superficial in their contentions on behalf of this holy Sabbath; that they should soft-pedal the "thou shalt nots" and "we should thunder our 'thou shalts' into the ears of the foolish, wicked men who for the sake of pleasure or financial profit would rob their fellow men or themselves of the precious rest God had given them for the cultivation and nurture of their immortal souls. Such men," he continues, "must be identified with murderers and suicides." The common punishment for murder is death, and suicide *is* death, therefore Dr. McQuilkin, with the rest of his associates and with his God, believes in the death penalty for working or playing on the Sabbath.

How one involuntarily loves this righteous Dr. McQuilkin of Orange, New Jersey. He must be a man whose love and understanding oozes from every pore of his body. No doubt the people of Orange who are burdened with sorrow or sin bring their sore troubles and lay them on his loving breast. I am sure that little children in their grief rush to his outstretched arms for solace and relief.

The Reverend Doctor McQuilkin makes short work of the idea that you cannot make people good by law. In fact, that seems to him to be the only way to make them good. Therefore people and enterprises that commercialize Sundays by baseball games and moving pictures, who "whine about the impossibility of making people good by law, ought to go either to school or to jail." Probably the pastor would be in favor of the jail. The Reverend Doctor is very much exercised about his idea that the Sabbath should be spent in cultivating our "spiritual nature." From the gentle and kindly character of the doctor's utterances, one judges that he must spend several days a week cultivating his "spiritual nature."

The godly doctor is indeed earnest about the church-going. He says, "God will surely bring us to judgment in the matter of staying away from church, for church attendance is a definite obligation, a debt which we owe to God." The doctor has a naive way of mixing up himself and his private business affairs with the Lord.

Could it be possible that the Reverend Doctor McQuilkin's serious case of rabies might be due to vacant pews? Such cases are related in the following extract from a very disheartening paragraph put out by the Lord's Day Alliance in a folder entitled "Let's Save Our American Christian Sabbath."

> A significant part of this falling away from old American ideals has been the neglect of the churches—life among Christian people dropping to a lower plane [sic] on Sunday. The lure of pleasure and the drift to seven-day slavery within a few years have utterly changed the character of the day. The average attendance at Sunday morning services, taken for all the churches of New York State—counting large city churches as well as small country ones—has steadily dropped until it has now reached only *fifty-three* persons. This amounts to but little more than one fourth of their total enrolled membership! The old days of tithes are gone! Lack of support is making the situation more and more critical and many churches have had to be abandoned. Is the church to survive? *Are we to remain a Christian nation?*

This is indeed distressing. I can well imagine the feeling of chagrin that steals over the parson when he talks to fifty persons on a Sunday morning. Here are the few parishioners, solemn-visaged and sitting impatiently in their pews while a joyous crowd rolls by in automobiles on their road to hell. I cannot help thinking of the parson on a Sunday morning, telling the same story over and over again to his half hundred listeners.

I have seen this pastor and this congregation in the country church and the city church. What have they in common with the world today? Who are these faithful fifty? One-third of them, at least, are little boys and girls, twisting and turning and yawning and fussing in their stiff, uncomfortable clothes, in the hard church pews. Then there are the usual fat old women, wearing their Sunday finery. Their faces are dull and heavy and altogether unlovely. They no longer think of the world; they are looking straight into space at the Promised Land. They hold a hymn book or a Bible in their time-worn hands. Perhaps there are ten full grown men in church; two or three of these look consumptive; one or two are merchants who think that being at church will help them sell prunes; the rest are old and tottering. It has been long years since a new thought or even an old one has found lodgment in their atrophied brains. They are decrepit and palsied and done; so far as life and the world are concerned, they are already dead. One feels sympathetic toward the old. But why should the aged, who have lived their lives, grumble and complain about youth with its glow and ambition and hope? Why should they sit in the fading light and watch the world go by and vainly reach out their bony hands to hold it back?

Aside from the Lord's Day Alliance's way of appealing to the law to make people go to church, I can think of only two plans to fill the pews. First, to abandon a large number of the churches and give the parsons a chance to find some useful and paying job. Secondly, to get more up-to-date, human and intelligent preachers into the church pulpits.

The literature issued by the Alliance shows great concern about Sunday newspapers. These papers consume a great deal of valuable time on the Sabbath Day. They are in no way the proper literature for Sunday reading. Automobile trips, too, are an abomination on the Sabbath. One pamphlet records approval of the conduct of the "venerable" John D. Paton who even refused to use street-cars on Sunday while visiting in America. He kept his appointments by long walks, sometimes even having to run between engagements. This sounds to me strangely like work. Still it might have been necessary in order to get the proper amount of oxygen gas.

Playing golf on Sunday is a sacrilegious practice. A whole leaflet is prepared by Dr. Jefferson on golf. "No one ought to play golf on Sunday... The golf player may need oxygen but he should not forget his caddie." The doctor calls our attention to the fact that men in the days of Moses were mindful of even the least of these. How our parsons do love Moses and his murderous laws! We are told that a caddie works, that it is not play to trudge after a golf ball with a bag of dubs on his back. The leaflets say that the caddie does not work on Sunday for fun but for money, and it "isn't a manly thing for the golf player to hire him to work on Sunday." We are told that "there are now over one hundred thousand caddies on the golf links every Sunday.

These caddies are making a living." Of course this picture is pathetic. It is too bad that the Lord's Day Alliance cannot get these hundred thousand caddies discharged. Then possibly some of them would go to church on Sunday. They might even drop a nickel in the contribution box.

Does anyone believe that if the caddies were offered the same money for going to church that they get for hunting golf balls they would choose the church? It takes a bright boy to be a caddie.

The caddies do not inspire all the tears; we are told that chauffeurs and railroad employees are necessary to take the players to and from the golf links. This, no doubt true. Still, we have seen chauffeurs sitting in automobiles outside a church where they had driven their employers to get their souls saved. On our suburban railroads there are many trains put in service on Sunday to take people to and from church, but these have not come under the ban of the Lord's Day Alliance. Its complaint is that so few trains are needed for this blessed work.

There is some logic in this folder. We are told that "if golf is allowable on Sunday, then, so is tennis, baseball, basketball, football, bowling and all other games which our generation is fond of." "You can't forbid one without forbidding the others," says the Alliance. We heartily agree with the Reverend Doctor on this particular question.

No one needs to go to ball games or movies or play golf on Sunday unless he wants to spend his time that way. I have never seen anybody who objected to the members of the Lord's Day Alliance or any others from abstaining from all kinds of work and all sorts of play and every method of enjoyment on Sunday.

Dr. Robert E. Speer of Englewood, New Jersey, is very definite and specific as to the proper way to spend Sunday and the sort of recreation man should naturally enjoy on this holy day. Dr. Speer says, "God wants the worship of the Lord's Day and he wants us to have the indispensable comforts and pleasure of it." One would think that Dr. Speer got daily messages from God. "We need the day for meditation and prayer and plans for better living." No one questions the good doctor's right to satisfy his needs in such way as seems necessary and pleasurable for him. All that I contend for is that I, too, shall decide these questions for myself. Dr. Speer says:

> There are some things deadly in their power to spoil it (referring to the Sabbath). One is the Sunday newspapers... I pass by all that may be denounced as defiling in it... There is harm enough in its "wallow of secularity"... Look at the men who feed their minds and souls on Sunday with this food. They miss the calm and holy peace, the glowing divinity of the day.

It is just conceivable that one might read a Sunday newspaper and still have time for "the glowing divinity of the day," to glow long enough to satisfy every desire.

Dr. Speer condemns those who berate the quality of the sermons preached on Sunday and informs us that the wisest man can learn something from the poorest preacher, although he neglects to say just what. He tells us that a country preacher's sermon is superior to the country editor's writings or the country lawyer's speeches. This may be true. It is, at all events, true to Dr. Speer, and there is no reason in the world why he should not hunt up the "poorest preacher" that he can find and listen to him on every Sunday. No doubt Dr. Speer might learn something from him.

Dr. Speer disapproves of riding on railroad trains on Sunday if it can be avoided. "Certainly no one should take long railroad journeys on Sunday." He tells us, "Sunday golf, newspapers, and all that sort of thing are bad and weakening in their influence. These are particular evidence of the trend of the man who thus abandons his birthright." The doctor is more definite in his beautiful picture of just what one ought to do on the Sabbath Day. On this subject he says:

> I do not believe that anyone who grew up in a truly Christian home in which the old ideas prevailed can have any sympathy with this modern abuse of the old-fashioned observance of Sunday. There, on Sunday, the demands of the week were laid aside. The family gathered over the Bible and the Catechism. There was a quiet calm through the house. Innumerable things rendered it a marked day, as distinct from other days, and probably it ended with a rare walk with the father at the son's side and some sober talk over what is abiding and what is of eternal worth.

We could hazard a guess that the reason that the mother was not present on this joyful occasion was because she was at home washing the dishes from a big Sunday dinner that she had prepared.

It is entirely possible that Dr. Speer's picture of the ideal Sabbath is a good picture. Doubtless it is good to him. Still, hidden in my mind and recalled by Dr. Speer's alluring language, is the memory of his ideal Presbyterian Sunday. This was a day of unmitigated pain. No spirit of life or joy relieved the boredom and torture of the endless hours. The day meant misery to all the young. Even now I can feel the blank despair that overcame youth and hope as we children left our play on Saturday night and sadly watched the sun go down and the period of gloom steal across the world. Why should Dr. Speer and the other dead seek to force that sort of a Sabbath upon men and women who want to take in their oxygen gas in the baseball bleachers, or the golf links?

From Dr. Speer's picture of the ideal Sabbath I infer that he is a Presbyterian. This opinion has been confirmed by reference to *Who's Who*. I find that for long years he has been a Presbyterian preacher, not only in America, but he has carried the blessed gospel even into China that the heathen of that benighted land might not live and die without the consoling knowledge of eternal hell.

Dr. Speer's beautiful picture of the old-time Christian Sabbath describes "the family gathered over the Bible and the Catechism." I, too, sat under the ministrations of a Presbyterian preacher and was duly instructed in the Westminster Catechism. In spite of the aversion and terror that its reference inspired, I took down the book to read once more the horrible creed of the twisted and deformed minds who produced this monstrosity which has neither sense, meaning, justice nor mercy, but only malignant depravity. A devilish creed which shocks every tender sentiment of the human mind. I am inclined to think from their internal evidence that most of the sermonettes circulated by the Lord's Day Alliance had their origin in the warped minds of the Presbyterian clergy. I would hazard a bet that the tender, gentle, loving Dr. McQuilkin is a Presbyterian. I sought to confirm this belief by consulting *Who's Who*, but found that the editors had stupidly left out his name. Still I am convinced that he is a Presbyterian.

When one thinks of this organization with its senseless leaflets, its stern endeavors, its blank despair, its half-shut eyes blinking at life, one is reminded of the frogs in the green scum-covered pond in the woods who sit on their haunches in the dark and croak all day. No doubt these frogs believe that the germ infested pond is a sacred pool. They are oblivious of the rolling, living ocean that lies just beyond.

Dr. Speer, like all the other members of the Lord's Day Alliance, is very sure that one of the chief occupations of Sunday should be attending church. But what church, pray? We are informed that any preacher is better to listen to and read from than any editor, lawyer or other person. Most of us have heard all sorts of preachers. We have listened to some whose churches could only be filled if the Lord's Day Alliance should succeed and make it an offense punishable by death not to go to church. We have heard preachers who had something to say and could say it well. There is as much difference in the views and ability of preachers as in other men. Would Dr. Speer think that we should go to hear the Fundamentalists or the Unitarians? Should we listen to the Holy Rollers or the Modernists?

There are few men outside of the Lord's Day Alliance who would care to listen to their favorite preacher for a *full day* and there are few preachers who would undertake to talk for a whole day. What, then, must one do for the rest of the time? One simply cannot sleep *all* day on Sunday.

In all this literature we are constantly urged to preserve our "American Sabbath." Is there any special holiness that lurks around an "American Sabbath"? Are not European Christians as competent to determine the right way to employ their time on Sundays as American Christians? The Lord's Day folk say that reading the Sunday newspapers, playing golf, riding in automobiles, and witnessing baseball games and movies is "un-American." This compound word has been used to cover a multitude of sins. What it means nobody knows. It is bunkum meant to serve every cause, good and bad alike. By what license does the Lord's Day Alliance call its caricature of Sunday an "American Sabbath"? On what grounds does it urge it as against the European Sabbath? Is this nightmare which the Lord's Day Alliance is so anxious to force upon the United States a product of America? Everyone knows that Sunday, with the rest of the Christian religion, came to us from Europe. The weird ideas of the Lord's Day Alliance are European. When and how it came to us is worth finding out.

Jesus and His disciples did not believe in the Jewish Sabbath. They neither abstained from work nor play. St. Paul, specially, condemned the setting apart of days and said to his disciples, "Ye observe days and months and times and years. I am afraid of ye lest I have bestowed upon ye labor in vain."

The early fathers did not approve of any such day as the Lord's Day Alliance insists shall be fastened upon America. St. Jerome and his group attended church services on Sunday, but otherwise pursued their usual occupations. St. Augustine calls Sunday a festal day and says that the Fourth Commandment is in no literal sense binding upon Christianity. Even Luther and Calvin enjoined no such a day upon the Christians as these moderns wish to fasten upon America that the churches may be filled. The righteous John Knox "played bowls" on Sunday, and in his voluminous preaching used no effort to make Sunday a day of gloom wherein people should abstain from work and play. It was not until 1595 that an English preacher of Suffolk first insisted that the Jewish Sabbath should be maintained. The controversy over this question lasted for a hundred years and resulted in a law proscribing every kind of Sunday recreation, even "vainly and profanely walking for pleasure." England soon reacted against this blue Sabbath and permitted trading, open theatres and frivolity in the afternoon and evening. Under the leadership of the Church of England the Sabbath no longer was a day of gloom and despair.

The real American Sabbath was born in Scotland after the death of John Knox. It fits the stern hills, the bleak moors and the unfriendly climate of this northern land. It was born of fear and gloom and it lives by fear and gloom. Early in the Seventeenth Century, Scotland adopted this stern theory of the Jewish Sabbath and applied it ruthlessly. The Westminster Confession was adopted by the General Assembly of the Kirk of Scotland in 1647 and has remained the formal standard of faith to the present day. Ordinary recreations were disallowed. Books and music were forbidden except such as were recognized as religious in a narrow sense. No recreation but whiskey-drinking remained. This Presbyterian Sabbath of Scotland was brought to New England by the early settlers of America and is, in fact, a Scotch Sabbath—not an American Sabbath.

Even in spite of the natural gloom and cold of Scotland, Sunday strictness has been greatly modified there in the last fifty years. It is not the present Scotch Sabbath that these modern Puritans insist on forcing upon America. It is the old, ferocious, Scotch Sabbath of the Westminster Confession. It was brought from a land of gloom into a land of sunshine, and the Lord's Day Alliance prefers the gloom and hardness of this outworn, out-lived Scotch Sabbath to the sunshine and joy that comes with a fertile soil, a mild climate and natural human emotions.

It is almost unbelievable that a handful of men without reason or humanity should be able to force their cruel dogmas upon the people. Not one in twenty of the residents of the United States believes in the Sabbath of the Lord's Day Alliance. Our cities, villages, and even country districts, protest against the bigotry and intolerance of The Lord's Day Alliance and their kind. Still, in spite of this, by appeal to obsolete statutes, religious prejudice, crass ignorance and unfathomable fanaticism, they carry on their mighty campaign of gloom.

After long years of effort, with the lazy, cowardly public that does not want to be disturbed, the Legislature of New York, in the face of the opposition of the Lord's Day Alliance, managed to pass a law providing that incorporated cities and towns should have the right to legalize baseball games and moving picture shows on Sunday after two o'clock in the afternoon and charge an admission fee for seeing the entertainment. Why after two o'clock? The answer is perfectly plain: It is possible that someone might be forced into church in the morning if there was nowhere else to go. Were the hours after two o'clock any less sacred in the laws of Moses and the prophets than the hours before two o'clock? Or was the Legislature induced to pass this law simply to give the minister a privilege that it grants to no one else?

Ours is a cosmopolitan country, made up of all sorts of people with various creeds. There should be room enough to allow each person to spend Sunday and every other day according to his own pleasure and his own profit. In spite of the Lord's Day Alliance and all other alliances, it is too late in the history of the world to bring back the Mosaic Sabbath. Regardless of their best endeavors it will probably never again be a crime punishable by death to work or play on what they are pleased to call the Lord's Day. Those ministers who have something to say that appeals to men and women will be able to make themselves heard without a law compelling people to go to church. If the Lord's Day Alliance can provide something equally attractive to compete with the Sunday newspapers, golf, baseball games, movies and the open air, they will get the trade. If they cannot provide such entertainment, then in spite of all their endeavors the churches will be vacant. It is time that those who believe in tolerance, and in freedom, should make themselves heard in no uncertain way. It is time that men should determine to defend their right to attend to their own affairs and live their own lives, regardless of the bigots who in all ages have menaced the welfare of the world and the liberty of man.

22
Why I Am An Unbeliever (1926)
Carl Van Doren

Let us be honest. There have always been men and women without the gift of faith. They lack it, do not desire it, and would not know what to do with it if they had it. They are apparently no less intelligent than the faithful, and apparently no less virtuous. How great the number of them is it would be difficult to say, but they exist in all communities and are most numerous where there is most enlightenment. As they have no organization and no creed, they can of course have no official spokesman. Nevertheless, any one of them who speaks out can be trusted to speak, in a way, for all of them. Like the mystics, the unbelievers, wherever found, are essentially of one spirit and one language. I cannot, however, pretend to represent more than a single complexion of unbelief.

The very terms which I am forced to use put me at the outset in a trying position. Belief, being first in the field, naturally took a positive term for itself and gave a negative term to unbelief. As an unbeliever, I am therefore obliged to seem merely to dissent from the believers, no matter how much more I may do. Actually I do more. What they call unbelief, I call belief. Doubtless I was born to it, but I have tested it with reading and speculation, and I hold it firmly. What I have referred to as the gift of faith I do not, to be exact, regard as a gift. I regard it, rather, as a survival from an earlier stage of thinking and feeling: in short, as a form of superstition. It, and not the thing I am forced to name unbelief, seems to me negative. It denies the reason. It denies the evidences in the case, in the sense that it insists upon introducing elements which come not from the facts as shown but from the imaginations and wishes of mortals. Unbelief does not deny the reason and it sticks as closely as it can to the evidences.

I shall have to be more explicit. When I say I am an unbeliever, I do not mean merely that I am no Mormon or no Methodist, or even that I am no Christian or no Buddhist. These seem to me relatively unimportant divisions and subdivisions of belief. I mean that I do not believe in any god that has ever been devised, in any doctrine that has ever claimed to be revealed, in any scheme of immortality that has ever been expounded.

As to gods, they have been, I find, countless, but even the names of most of them lie in the deep compost which is known as civilization, and the memories of few of them are green. There does not seem to me to be good reason for holding that some of them are false and some of them, or one of them, true. Each was created by the imaginations and wishes of men who could not account for the behavior of the universe in any other satisfactory way. But no god has satisfied his worshipers forever. Sooner or later they have realized that the attributes once ascribed to him, such as selfishness or lustfulness or vengefulness, are unworthy of the moral systems which men have evolved among themselves. Thereupon follows the gradual doom of the god, however long certain of the faithful may cling to his cult. In the case of the god who still survives in the loyalty of men after centuries of scrutiny, it can always be noted that little besides his name has endured. His attributes will have been so revised that he is really another god. Nor is this objection met by the argument that the concept of the god has been purified while the essence of him survived. In the concept alone can he be studied; the essence eludes the grasp of the human mind. I may prefer among the various gods that god who seems to me most thoroughly purged of what I regard as undivine elements, but I make my choice, obviously, upon principles which come from observation of the conduct of men. Whether a god has been created in the image of gross desires or of pure desires does not greatly matter. The difference proves merely that different men have desired gods and have furnished themselves with the gods they were able to conceive. Behind all their conceptions still lies the abyss of ignorance. There is no trustworthy evidence as to a god's absolute existence.

Nor does the thing called revelation, as I see it, carry the proof further. All the prophets swear that a god speaks through them, and yet they prophesy contradictions. Once more, men must choose in accordance with their own principles. That a revelation was announced long ago makes it difficult to examine, but does not otherwise attest its soundness. That some revealed doctrine has lasted for ages and has met the needs of many generations proves that it is the kind of doctrine which endures and satisfies, but not that it is divine. Secular doctrines which turned out to be perfectly false have also endured and satisfied. If belief in a god has to proceed from the assumption that he exists, belief in revelation has first to proceed from the assumption that a god exists and then to go further to the assumption that he communicates his will to certain men. But both are mere assumptions. Neither is, in the present state of knowledge, at all capable of proof. Suppose a god did exist, and suppose he did communicate his will to any of his creatures. What man among them could comprehend that language? What man could take that dictation? And what man could overwhelmingly persuade his fellows that he had been selected and that they must accept him as authentic? The best they could do would be to have faith in two assumptions and to test the revealed will by its correspondence to their imaginations and wishes. At this point it may be contended that revelation must be real because it arouses so much response in so many human bosoms. This does not follow without a leap of the reason into the realm of hypothesis. Nothing is proved by this general response except that men are everywhere very much alike. They have the same members, the same organs, the same glands, in varying degrees of activity. Being so much alike, they tend to agree upon a few primary desires. Fortunate the religion by which those desires appear to be gratified.

One desire by which the human mind is often teased is the desire to live after death. It is not difficult to explain. Men live so briefly that their plans far outrun their ability to execute them. They see themselves cut off before their will to live is exhausted. Naturally enough, they wish to survive, and, being men, believe in their chances for survival. But their wishes afford no possible proof. Life covers the earth with wishes, as it covers the earth with plants and animals. No wish, however, is evidence of anything beyond itself. Let millions hold it, and it is still only a wish. Let each separate race exhibit it, and it is still only a wish. Let the wisest hold it as strongly as the foolishest, and it is still only a wish. Whoever says he knows that immortality is a fact is merely hoping that it is. And whoever argues, as men often do, that life would be meaningless without immortality because it alone brings justice into human fate, must first argue, as no man has ever quite convincingly done, that life has an unmistakable meaning and that it is just. I, at least, am convinced on neither of these two points. Though I am, I believe, familiar with all the arguments, I do not find any of them notably better than the others. All I see is that the wish for immortality is wide-spread, that certain schemes of immortality imagined from it have here or there proved more agreeable than rival schemes, and that they have been more generally accepted. The religions which provide these successful schemes I can credit with keener insight into human wishes than other religions have had, but I cannot credit them with greater authority as regards the truth. They are all guesswork.

That I think thus about gods, revelation, and immortality ought to be sufficient answer to the question why I am an unbeliever. It would be if the question were always reasonably asked, but it is not. There is also an emotional aspect to be considered. Many believers, I am told, have the same doubts, and yet have the knack of putting their doubts to sleep and entering ardently into the communion of the faithful. The process is incomprehensible to me. So far as I understand it, such believers are moved by their desires to the extent of letting them rule not only their conduct but their thoughts. An unbeliever's desires have, apparently, less power over his reason. Perhaps this is only another way of saying that his strongest desire is to be as reasonable as he can. However the condition be interpreted, the consequence is the same. An honest unbeliever can no more make himself believe against his reason than he can make himself free of the pull of gravitation. For myself, I feel no obligation whatever to believe. I might once have felt it prudent to keep silence, for I perceive that the race of men, while sheep in credulity, are wolves for conformity; but just now, happily, in this breathing-spell of toleration, there are so many varieties of belief that even an unbeliever may speak out.

In so doing, I must answer certain secondary questions which unbelievers are often asked. Does it not persuade me, one question runs, to realize that many learned men have pondered upon supernatural matters and have been won over to belief? I answer, not in the least. With respect to the gods, revelation, and immortality no man is enough more learned than his fellows to have the right to insist that they follow him into the regions about which all men are ignorant. I am not a particle more impressed by some good old man's conviction that he is in the confidence of the gods than I am by any boy's conviction that there are fish in the horse-pond from which no fish has ever been taken. Does it not impress me to see some good old woman serene in the faith of a blessed immortality? No more than it impresses me to see a little girl full of trust in the universal munificence of a Christmas saint. Am I not moved by the spectacle of a great tradition of worship which has broadened out over continents and which brings all its worshipers punctually together in the observance of noble and dignified rites? Yes, but I am moved precisely by that as I am moved by the spectacle of men everywhere putting their seed seasonably in the ground, tending its increase, and patiently gathering in their harvests.

Finally, do I never suspect in myself some moral obliquity, or do I not at least regret the bleak outlook of unbelief? On these points I am, in my own mind, as secure as I know how to be. There is no moral obligation to believe what is unbelievable, any more than there is a moral obligation to do what is undoable. Even in religion, honesty is a virtue. Obliquity, I should say, shows itself rather in prudent pretense or in voluntary self-delusion. Furthermore, the unbelievers have, as I read history, done less harm to the world than the believers. They have not filled it with savage wars or snarled casuistries, with crusades or persecutions, with complacency or ignorance. They have, instead, done what they could to fill it with knowledge and beauty, with temperance and justice, with manners and laughter. They have numbered among themselves some of the most distinguished specimens of mankind. And when they have been undistinguished, they have surely not been inferior to the believers in the fine art of minding their own affairs and so of enlarging the territories of peace.

Nor is the outlook of unbelief, to my way of thinking, a bleak one. It is merely rooted in courage and not in fear. Belief is still in the plight of those ancient races who out of a lack of knowledge peopled the forest with satyrs and the sea with ominous monsters and the ends of the earth with misshapen anthropophagi. So the pessimists among believers have peopled the void with witches and devils, and the optimists among them have peopled it with angels and gods. Both alike have been afraid to furnish the house of life simply. They have cluttered it with the furniture of faith. Much of this furniture, the most reasonable unbeliever would never think of denying, is very beautiful. There are breathing myths, there are comforting legends, there are consoling hopes. But they have, as the unbeliever sees them, no authority beyond that of poetry. That is, they may captivate if they can, but they have no right to insist upon conquering. Beliefs, like tastes, may differ. The unbeliever's taste and belief are austere. In the wilderness of worlds he does not yield to the temptation to belittle the others by magnifying his own. Among the dangers of chance he does not look for safety to any watchful providence whose special concern he imagines he is. Though he knows that knowledge is imperfect, he trusts it alone. If he takes, therefore, the less delight in metaphysics, he takes the more in physics. Each discovery of a new truth brings him a vivid joy. He builds himself up, so far as he can, upon truth, and barricades himself with it. Thus doing, he never sags into superstition, but grows steadily more robust and blithe in his courage. However many fears he may prove unable to escape, he does not multiply them in his imagination and then combat them with his wishes. Austerity may be simplicity and not bleakness.

Does the unbeliever lack certain of the gentler virtues of the believer, the quiet confidence, the unquestioning obedience? He may, yet it must always be remembered that the greatest believers are the greatest tyrants. If the freedom rather than the tyranny of faith is to better the world, then the betterment lies in the hands, I think, of the unbelievers. At any rate, I take my stand with them.

23
Is There A God? (1952)
Bertrand Russell

The question whether there is a God is one which is decided on very different grounds by different communities and different individuals. The immense majority of mankind accept the prevailing opinion of their own community. In the earliest times of which we have definite history everybody believed in many gods. It was the Jews who first believed in only one. The first commandment, when it was new, was very difficult to obey because the Jews had believed that Baal and Ashtaroth and Dagon and Moloch and the rest were real gods but were wicked because they helped the enemies of the Jews. The step from a belief that these gods were wicked to the belief that they did not exist was a difficult one. There was a time, namely that of Antiochus IV, when a vigorous attempt was made to Hellenize the Jews. Antiochus decreed that they should eat pork, abandon circumcision, and take baths. Most of the Jews in Jerusalem submitted, but in country places resistance was more stubborn and under the leadership of the Maccabees the Jews at last established their right to their peculiar tenets and customs. Monotheism, which at the beginning of the Antiochan persecution had been the creed of only part of one very small nation, was adopted by Christianity and later by Islam, and so became dominant throughout the whole of the world west of India. From India eastward, it had no success: Hinduism had many gods; Buddhism in its primitive form had none; and Confucianism had none from the eleventh century onward. But, if the truth of a religion is to be judged by its worldly success, the argument in favor of monotheism is a very strong one, since it possessed the largest armies, the largest navies, and the greatest accumulation of wealth. In our own day this argument is growing less decisive. It is true that the un-Christian menace of Japan was defeated. But the Christian is now faced with the menace of atheistic Muscovite hordes, and it is not so certain as one could wish that atomic bombs will provide a conclusive argument on the side of theism.

But let us abandon this political and geographical way of considering religions, which has been increasingly rejected by thinking people ever since the time of the ancient Greeks. Ever since that time there have been men who were not content to accept passively the religious opinions of philosophy might have to say about the matter. In the commercial cities of Ionia, where philosophy was invented, there were free-thinkers in the sixth century B.C. Compared to modern free-thinkers they had an easy task, because the Olympian gods, however charming to poetic fancy, were hardly such as could be defended by the metaphysical use of the unaided reason. They were met popularly by Orphism (to which Christianity owes much) and, philosophically, by Plato, from whom the Greeks derived a philosophical monotheism very different from the political and nationalistic monotheism of the Jews. When the Greek world became converted to Christianity it combined the new creed with Platonic metaphysics and so gave birth to theology. Catholic theologians, from the time of Saint Augustine to the present day, have believed that the existence of one God could be proved by the unaided reason. Their arguments were put into final form by Saint Thomas Aquinas in the thirteenth century.

When modern philosophy began in the seventeenth century, Descartes and Leibniz took over the old arguments somewhat polished up, and, owing largely to their efforts, piety remained intellectually respectable. But Locke, although himself a completely convinced Christian, undermined the theoretical basis of the old arguments, and many of his followers, especially in France, became Atheists. I will not attempt to set forth in all their subtlety the philosophical arguments for the existence of God. There is, I think, only one of them which still has weight with philosophers, that is the argument of the First Cause. This argument maintains that, since everything that happens has a cause, there must be a First Cause from which the whole series starts. The argument suffers, however, from the same defect as that of the elephant and the tortoise. It is said (I do not know with what truth) that a certain Hindu thinker believed the earth to rest upon an elephant. When asked what the elephant rested upon, he replied that it rested upon a tortoise. When asked what the tortoise rested upon, he said, "I am tired of this. Suppose we change the subject." This illustrates the unsatisfactory character of the First-Cause argument. Nevertheless, you will find it in some ultra-modern treatises on physics, which contend that physical processes, traced backward in time, show that there must have been a sudden beginning and infer that this was due to divine Creation. They carefully abstain from attempts to show that this hypothesis makes matters more intelligible.

The scholastic arguments for the existence of a Supreme Being are now rejected by most Protestant theologians in favor of new arguments which to my mind are by no means an improvement. The scholastic arguments were genuine efforts of thought and, if their reasoning had been sound, they would have demonstrated the truth of their conclusion. The new arguments, which Modernists prefer, are vague; and the Modernists reject with contempt every effort to make them precise. There is an appeal to the heart as opposed to the intellect. It is not maintained that those who reject the new arguments are illogical, but that they are destitute of deep feeling or of moral sense. Let us nevertheless examine the modern arguments and see whether there is anything that they really prove.

One of the favourite arguments is from evolution. The world was once lifeless, and when life began it was a poor sort of life consisting of green slime and other uninteresting things. Gradually by the course of evolution, it developed into animals and plants and at last into MAN. Man, so the theologians assure us, is so splendid a Being that he may well be regarded as the culmination to which the long ages of nebula and slime were a prelude. I think the theologians must have been fortunate in their human contacts. They do not seem to me to have given due weight to Hitler or the Beast of Belsen. If Omnipotence, with all time at its disposal, thought it worth while to lead up to these men through the many millions of years of evolution, I can only say that the moral and aesthetic taste involved is peculiar. However, the theologians no doubt hope that the future course of evolution will produce more men like themselves and fewer men like Hitler. Let us hope so. But, in cherishing this hope, we are abandoning the ground of experience and taking refuge in an optimism which history so far does not support.

There are other objections to this evolutionary optimism. There is every reason to believe that life on our planet will not continue forever so that any optimism based upon the course of terrestrial history must be temporary and limited in its purview. There may, of course, be life elsewhere but, if there is, we know nothing about it and have no reason to suppose that it bears more resemblance to the virtuous theologians than to Hitler. The earth is a very tiny corner of the universe. It is a little fragment of the solar system. The solar system is a little fragment of the Milky Way. And the Milky Way is a little fragment of the many millions of galaxies revealed by modern telescopes. In this little insignificant corner of the cosmos there is a brief interlude between two long lifeless epochs. In this brief interlude, there is a much briefer one containing man. If really man is the purpose of the universe the preface seems a little long. One is reminded of some prosy old gentleman who tells an interminable anecdote all quite uninteresting until the rather small point in which it ends. I do not think theologians show a suitable piety in making such a comparison possible.

It has been one of the defects of theologians at all times to over-estimate the importance of our planet. No doubt this was natural enough in the days before Copernicus when it was thought that the heavens revolve about the earth. But since Copernicus and still more since the modern exploration of distant regions, this preoccupation with the earth has become rather parochial. If the universe had a Creator, it is hardly reasonable to suppose that He was specially interested in our little corner. And, if He was not, His values must have been different from ours, since in the immense majority of regions life is impossible.

There is a moralistic argument for belief in God, which was popularized by William James. According to this argument, we ought to believe in God because, if we do not, we shall not behave well. The first and greatest objection to this argument is that, at its best, it cannot prove that there is a God but only that politicians and educators ought to try to make people think there is one. Whether this ought to be done or not is not a theological question but a political one. The arguments are of the same sort as those which urge that children should be taught respect for the flag. A man with any genuine religious feeling will not be content with the view that the belief in God is useful, because he will wish to know whether, in fact, there is a God. It is absurd to contend that the two questions are the same. In the nursery, belief in Father Christmas is useful, but grown-up people do not think that this proves Father Christmas to be real.

Since we are not concerned with politics we might consider this sufficient refutation of the moralistic argument, but it is perhaps worthwhile to pursue this a little further. It is, in the first place, very doubtful whether belief in God has all the beneficial moral effects that are attributed to it. Many of the best men known to history have been unbelievers. John Stuart Mill may serve as an instance. And many of the worst men known to history have been believers. Of this there are innumerable instances. Perhaps Henry VIII may serve as typical.

However that may be, it is always disastrous when governments set to work to uphold opinions for their utility rather than for their truth. As soon as this is done it becomes necessary to have a censorship to suppress adverse arguments, and it is thought wise to discourage thinking among the young for fear of encouraging "dangerous thoughts." When such malpractices are employed against religion as they are in Soviet Russia, the theologians can see that they are bad, but they are still bad when employed in defence of what the theologians think good. Freedom of thought and the habit of giving weight to evidence are matters of far greater moral import than the belief in this or that theological dogma. On all these grounds it cannot be maintained that theological beliefs should be upheld for their usefulness without regard to their truth.

There is a simpler and more naive form of the same argument, which appeals to many individuals. People will tell us that without the consolations of religion they would be intolerably unhappy. So far as this is true, it is a coward's argument. Nobody but a coward would consciously choose to live in a fool's paradise. When a man suspects his wife of infidelity, he is not thought the better of for shutting his eyes to the evidence. And I cannot see why ignoring evidence should be contemptible in one case and admirable in the other. Apart from this argument the importance of religion in contributing to individual happiness is very much exaggerated. Whether you are happy or unhappy depends upon a number of factors. Most people need good health and enough to eat. They need the good opinion of their social milieu and the affection of their intimates. They need not only physical health but mental health. Given all these things, most people will be happy whatever their theology. Without them, most people will be unhappy, whatever their theology. In thinking over the people I have known, I do not find that on the average those who had religious beliefs were happier than those who had not.

When I come to my own beliefs, I find myself quite unable to discern any purpose in the universe, and still more unable to wish to discern one. Those who imagine that the course of cosmic evolution is slowly leading up to some consummation pleasing to the Creator, are logically committed (though they usually fail to realize this) to the view that the Creator is not omnipotent or, if He were omnipotent, He could decree the end without troubling about means. I do not myself perceive any consummation toward which the universe is tending. According to the physicists, energy will be gradually more evenly distributed and as it becomes more evenly distributed it will become more useless. Gradually everything that we find interesting or pleasant, such as life and light, will disappear—so, at least, they assure us. The cosmos is like a theatre in which just once a play is performed, but, after the curtain falls, the theatre is left cold and empty until it sinks in ruins. I do not mean to assert with any positiveness that this is the case. That would be to assume more knowledge than we possess. I say only that it is what is probable on present evidence. I will not assert dogmatically that there is no cosmic purpose, but I will say that there is no shred of evidence in favor of there being one.

I will say further that, if there be a purpose and if this purpose is that of an Omnipotent Creator, then that Creator, so far from being loving and kind, as we are told, must be of a degree of wickedness scarcely conceivable. A man who commits a murder is considered to be a bad man. An Omnipotent Deity, if there be one, murders everybody. A man who willingly afflicted another with cancer would be considered a fiend. But the Creator, if He exists, afflicts many thousands every year with this dreadful disease. A man who, having the knowledge and power required to make his children good, chose instead to make them bad, would be viewed with execration. But God, if He exists, makes this choice in the case of very many of His children. The whole conception of an omnipotent God whom it is impious to criticize, could only have arisen under oriental despotisms where sovereigns, in spite of capricious cruelties, continued to enjoy the adulation of their slaves. It is the psychology appropriate to this outmoded political system which belatedly survives in orthodox theology.

There is, it is true, a Modernist form of theism, according to which God is not omnipotent, but is doing His best, in spite of great difficulties. This view, although it is new among Christians, is not new in the history of thought. It is, in fact, to be found in Plato. I do not think this view can be proved to be false. I think all that can be said is that there is no positive reason in its favour.

Many orthodox people speak as though it were the business of sceptics to disprove received dogmas rather than of dogmatists to prove them. This is, of course, a mistake. If I were to suggest that between the Earth and Mars there is a china teapot revolving about the sun in an elliptical orbit, nobody would be able to disprove my assertion provided I were careful to add that the teapot is too small to be revealed even by our most powerful telescopes. But if I were to go on to say that, since my assertion cannot be disproved, it is intolerable presumption on the part of human reason to doubt it, I should rightly be thought to be talking nonsense. If, however, the existence of such a teapot were affirmed in ancient books, taught as the sacred truth every Sunday, and instilled into the minds of children at school, hesitation to believe in its existence would become a mark of eccentricity and entitle the doubter to the attentions of the psychiatrist in an enlightened age or of the Inquisitor in an earlier time. It is customary to suppose that, if a belief is widespread, there must be something reasonable about it. I do not think this view can be held by anyone who has studied history. Practically all the beliefs of savages are absurd. In early civilizations there may be as much as one percent for which there is something to be said. In our own day. . . . But at this point I must be careful. We all know that there are absurd beliefs in Soviet Russia. If we are Protestants, we know that there are absurd beliefs among Catholics. If we are Catholics, we know that there are absurd beliefs among Protestants. If we are Conservatives, we are amazed by the superstitions to be found in the Labour Party. If we are Socialists, we are aghast at the credulity of Conservatives. I do not know, dear reader, what your beliefs may be, but whatever they may be, you must concede that nine-tenths of the beliefs of nine-tenths of mankind are totally irrational. The beliefs in question are, of course, those which you do not hold. I cannot, therefore, think it presumptuous to doubt something which has long been held to be true, especially when this opinion has only prevailed in certain geographical regions, as is the case with all theological opinions.

My conclusion is that there is no reason to believe any of the dogmas of traditional theology and, further, that there is no reason to wish that they were true. Man, in so far as he is not subject to natural forces, is free to work out his own destiny. The responsibility is his, and so is the opportunity.

24
The Claims Of Theology (1973)
A.J. Ayer

The Existence of God

In W.H. Mallock's satire *The New Republic*, which was first published in the eighteen seventies, at a time when the conflict between science and religion was at its height, a character representing Dr Jowett is made to admit that an atheist opponent can disprove the existence of God, as he would define him. "All atheists can do that." This does not, however, disturb the doctor's faith. "For," he says, "the world has at present no adequate definition of God; and I think we should be able to define a thing before we can satisfactorily disprove it.

I said this was a satire, but the words which are put into Jowett's mouth represent a point of view which is still not uncommon. People who try to justify their belief in the existence of God by saying that it rests on faith are sometimes maintaining no more than that the proposition that God exists is one which they have the right to accept, in default of sufficient evidence; but sometimes they look to faith for the assurance that the words "God exists" express some true proposition, though they do not know what this proposition is; it is one that surpasses human understanding. The first of these positions is discussable, though I think it misguided, but the second is merely disingenuous. Until we have an intelligible proposition before us, there is nothing for faith to get to work on. It can be an article of faith that beings of superhuman intelligence, if there are any, entertain propositions that we cannot grasp. This requires only that we can make sense of the expression "beings with superhuman intelligence." But if we really cannot grasp these propositions, if the sentences which purport to express them have no meaning for us, then the fact, if it were a fact, that they did have meaning for some other beings would be of little interest to us; for this meaning might be anything whatsoever. The truth is, however, that those who take this position do understand, or think they understand, something by the words "God exists." It is only when the account they give of what they understand appears unworthy of credence that they take refuge in saying that it falls short of what the words really mean. But words have no meaning beyond the meaning that is given them, and a proposition is not made the more credible by being treated as an approximation to something that we do not find intelligible. In fact, the world is not without descriptions of Gods, whether or not they severally or collectively count as adequate definitions. Until we are provided with a criterion of adequacy, this is a detail that need not detain us. Thus, those who believe in many Gods tend to ascribe properties to them which fit the human activities over which they are thought to preside. The God of War is martial, the God of Love amorous. In some, though not in all cases, these Gods are at least intermittently corporeal and they operate in space and time. Those who believe that there is just one God are in general agreement that he is an intelligent person, or something like one, that he feels emotions such as love or moral indignation, that he is incorporeal, except in the case of the Christian God, when, for a period of about thirty years, if one assumes the identity of the Son and the Father, he had what are ordinarily supposed to be the incompatible properties of being both corporeal and incorporeal, that, again with this exception, he is not located in space, though capable of acting in space, that he is either eternal or with the same exception not located in time, though capable of acting in time, that he created the world and continues to oversee it, that he is not subject to change, that he is all-powerful and all-knowing, that he is morally perfect and consequently supremely benevolent, and that he necessarily exists.

There may be some doubt whether the predicates that are ascribed to this one God are all of them meaningful or mutually consistent. For instance, we have found reason to think that if the notion of disembodied persons is intelligible at all, they must at least be located in time. Neither is it clear how a being that feels emotions can fail to be subject to change, unless we suppose that he feels the same emotions with the same intensity all the time, in which case there must be some danger of their sometimes lacking their appropriate objects. What is anyhow obvious is that these different predicates are for the most part not logically connected. We shall have to consider later on whether it is possible to make sense of the idea that the world was created. If this is a significant proposition, it may be taken to entail that the creator was intelligent. It may also be taken to entail that he was incorporeal, on the ground that the existence of a physical body could not precede the existence of the universe, though then it is not clear why the same should not apply to the existence of a mind. It surely does not entail that the creator is eternal; he might have come into existence at any time before he created the world or ceased to exist at any time after. Neither does it entail that he is all powerful. He might have wished but been unable to create a different world, and having created the world that he did, he might subsequently have found that it escaped wholly or partly from his control. It might also develop in ways that he was unable to foresee. Clearly also, there is no logical connection between having any degree of power, including the power to create the universe, and being morally good. Indeed, if one thought of the world's history as having been planned by its creator, a strong case could be made for inferring that he was malevolent. Finally, even if the creator could consistently possess all these other properties it would not follow that he necessarily existed. If he was thought to be a God, his possession of them might be necessary, in the sense that they were ascribed to any God by definition, but this would not entail that it was not a contingent proposition that the definition was actually satisfied. ...

The Argument from Design

...The belief that the world affords sufficient evidence of an ulterior plan is responsible for the argument in favour of the existence of a God which is commonly known as the argument from design. The proponents of this argument do not take it to show that there necessarily is a God, but only that the assumption of his existence is a reasonable hypothesis. Their position is elegantly and fairly stated by one of the participants in Hume's *Dialogues Concerning Natural Religion.* "Look round the world: Contemplate the whole and every part of it: You will find it to be nothing but one great machine, subdivided into an infinite number of lesser machines, which again admit of subdivisions, to a degree beyond what human senses and faculties can trace and explain. All these various machines and even their most minute parts, are adjusted to each other with an accuracy, which ravishes into admiration all men, who have ever contemplated them. The curious adapting of means to ends, throughout all nature, resembles exactly, though it much exceeds, the productions of human contrivance; of human design, thought, wisdom, and intelligence. Since therefore the effects resemble each other, we are led to infer, by all the rules of analogy, that the causes also resemble: and that the Author of nature is somewhat similar to the mind of man: though possessed of much larger faculties, proportioned to the grandeur of the work, which he has executed."

Before we try to evaluate this argument, let us take a closer look at the conclusion. What properties is the author of nature supposed to have, and how is he related to the world for which he is made responsible? In the first place, as one of the other participants in Hume's dialogue remarks, there is nothing in the analogy to favour the assumption of a single author, rather than a multiplicity. There is nothing to favour the assumption that the world as we find it is the fruit of his only attempt to make a world, rather than the outcome of previous experiments on his own part or on that of others; if anything the analogy would point the other way. There is nothing either to license the inference that he is eternal or indeed that he is incorporeal; since all the designers that we have actually observed have been mortal and embodied, the analogy, if it were to be pressed, would again point the other way. It would suggest that his faculties are larger than ours, but not that he is omnipotent, nor yet that he is benevolent. The ascription of benevolence to him would require us to find empirical evidence not merely that the world had an author but that it had an author who meant well by the creatures whom he had put into it.

What now of the designer's relation to the world? If one supposes there to have been an act of creation, I do not see how one can avoid the conclusion that it took place at some time. If one supposes this to be the first instant in time, one will find it difficult to say in what sense the author of nature existed antecedently to its creation. The idea that he existed outside time is one to which it is difficult to attach any meaning. It is true that abstract entities can be said to exist outside time, if they can be said to exist at all, but the activities which are attributed to the deity are hardly such as are consistent with his existing after the fashion of an abstract entity. A more intelligible theory would be that events in his history temporally preceded the act of creation. This would be, in a way, to include him in the universe, but on the assumption of his existence, he would anyhow have to be included, if the universe was taken to comprehend everything that there is. The creation of the world as we know it would then appear more as a transformation, a radical change in the total course of events, though not necessarily as a transformation of preexisting matter. It is, however, to be noted that the analogy with the makers of human artifacts is still further weakened if we suppose the material world to have been created out of nothing at all.

In view of these difficulties, the proponents of this argument might be better advised to lay more stress upon the metaphor of the *author* of nature. Instead of comparing the world to a machine, which needed to be designed and built, they could compare it to a play, which needed to be written and directed. Among other things, this accords better with the ordinary concept of creation. The author, who would also be spectator and critic, would exist in time, but the time in which he existed would be incommensurable with that of the incidents in the play, which would have its own spatio-temporal structure. The participants in the play would not be able to verify the existence of its author, except on the dubious assumption that when they had played their parts they were somehow translated into his world, but it might be maintained that they could attach sense to the hypothesis that he existed, as the fundamental principle of a secondary system which they could use to account for the proceedings on their stage.

But now the question arises whether the character of the world as we know it gives any support to these analogies. The fact that regularities are detectable in it is not sufficient, for we have seen that no describable world can fail to exhibit some regularity. Neither is it sufficient that some processes within it are goal-directed, for the fact that ends are pursued and sometimes attained within a system is not a proof that the system as a whole is directed towards any end. What needs to be shown is that the entire universe presents the appearance of a teleological system. If one prefers the dramatic analogy, the play has to have a moral or at least some discernible plot. Can this requirement be met? It does not seem that it can. None of those who have compared the world to a vast machine has ever made any serious attempt to say what the machine could be for. They have spoken of there being an overall purpose, but have not said what it was. Again it will not do to say that there is a plan, but one too intricate for us to fathom. This answer might pass muster if the existence of a deity had been independently established, but if the sole reason given for believing in his existence is that the book of nature must have had an author, then the grounds for taking this metaphor seriously have to be produced.

Insofar as theists have held any view at all about the purpose for which the world was created, they have generally assumed that it had something to do with the emergence of man. This is a view which it is perhaps natural for men to take but hardly one that would be supported by a dispassionate consideration of the scientific evidence. Not only did man make a very late appearance upon the scene in a very small corner of the universe, but it is not even probable that, having made his appearance, he is there to say. As Russell put it, "The second law of thermodynamics makes it scarcely possible to doubt that the universe is running down, and that ultimately nothing of the slightest interest will be possible anywhere. Of course, it is open to us to say that when that time comes God will wind up the machinery again: but if we say this, we can base our assertion only upon faith, not upon one shred of scientific evidence. So far as scientific evidence goes, the universe has crawled by slow degrees to a somewhat pitiful result on this earth, and is going to crawl by still more pitiful stages to a condition of universal death. If this is to be taken as evidence of purpose, I can only say that the purpose is one that does not appeal to me. I see no reason therefore to believe in any sort of God, however vague and however attenuated."[1] ...

Religion and Morality

Is there any support for religious belief in the fact that men have moral sentiments to which their actions sometimes answer? The view that there is has been quite widely held. The main arguments which have been advanced in its favor are, first, that only the agency of God can account for the existence of morality, and, secondly, that God's authority is needed to give our moral standards some objective validity.

The first of these arguments seems very weak. The assumption which underlies it is that it is natural for men to behave only in a purely selfish manner. Consequently, if they sometimes forgo their interests, or what they believe to be their interests, in order to serve others, or because they think that the action which promotes their interests is wrong, or that some other course of action is morally binding on them, the ability to behave in this unnatural way must have been given to them by a higher power. Even if the starting-point of this argument were true, the reasoning would not be cogent, since it ignores the possibility that moral behaviour can be adequately explained in terms of social conditioning, but in fact it is not true. Antecedently to any actual observations that are made of human behaviour, there is no reason to expect it either to be selfish or to be unselfish; there is no reason to expect it either to conform or not to conform to any particular moral code. If it seems to us more natural for men to pursue their individual interests, this is only because they most commonly do so, at any rate in our own form of society. I believe that there are, or have been, societies in which it is more common for men to pursue the interest of some group of which they are members, their family or clan or tribe. But even if the prevalent tendency in all societies were for men to behave selfishly, it would not follow that unselfish behaviour was unnatural, in the sense of being contrary to nature. Nothing that actually happens is contrary to nature, though there are some actions that we misleadingly call unnatural as a way of expressing our disapproval of them. In fact, I think that a good case can be made for saying that altruistic impulses are innate, though they may be initially weaker in small children than the self-regarding or aggressive impulses. If they are not innate, at least the evidence shows that we have the capacity to acquire them. But how did we obtain this capacity? This question is on a level with any other question about the causes of human behaviour. It is no more and no less difficult than the question how we obtain our capacity to injure one another. If there were any good reason to believe that men were the outcome of a God's creation, their creator would be equally responsible for all their characteristics, however much or little we esteem them. Conversely, if there is otherwise no good reason to believe that men were so created, the fact that they behave unselfishly as well as selfishly to each other does not provide one.

In dealing with the argument that a God is required to ensure the objectivity of moral standards, we need to distinguish carefully between the motives for morality and its possible grounds. There is no doubt that belief in a God has frequently been the source of moral incentives. Sometimes the motive has been the altruistic one of love for a deity or a saint whose wishes one believes oneself to be carrying out, or love for other human beings on the ground that they are equally the children of God. Perhaps more frequently it has been the prudential motive of fear of future punishment or hope of future reward. It was the belief that men were not generally capable of behaving decently without this prudential motive that led Voltaire to say that if God did not exist it would be necessary to invent him.[2] This is a good epigram, but like many good epigrams, it probably distorts the truth. I do not know that a scientific study has ever been made of this question, but if one were to be made I doubt if it would reveal any strong correlation either of morally admirable behaviour with religious belief or of morally reprehensible behaviour with its absence. Much good has been done in the name of religion but also very much evil. When the long history of religious intolerance and persecution is taken into account, together with the tendency of religious hierarchies to side with the oppressors rather than the oppressed, it is arguable that the evil has outweighed the good. Many bad men have indeed been irreligious, but many agnostics and atheists have led very decent lives. Neither do those who are sincerely religious always live up to their good principles. My own conjecture is that the factors which make for the observance or disregard of morality are mainly psychological and social, and that religious belief has had a smaller influence either way than is commonly supposed. However this may be, it is dear that to show that belief in God had had a predominantly good effect would not be to show that the belief was true, any more than showing that it had had a predominantly bad effect would be to show that it was false.

I suspect that the widespread assumption that religious belief is necessary for the maintenance of moral standards arises not so much from any assessment of the empirical evidence as from a tacit or explicit acceptance of the proposition that if there is no God there is no reason to be moral. What is meant is that there is then no justification for morality, but because of the ambiguity of the word "reason," the fallacious inference is drawn that there is neither any ground nor any motive. The conclusion sought is that since there is reason to be moral, there is a God. This is the obverse of the Nietzschean idea that since God is dead, everything is permitted.

Whichever way it is taken, this proposition contains two serious errors, apart from the fallacy of thinking that the absence of grounds for morality entails the absence of motives. The first error is to suppose that morality needs an ulterior justification. The second error is to suppose that a God could supply it. The fallacy which is involved in thinking that morals could be founded on divine authority has been exposed by many philosophers, but perhaps most clearly and succinctly by Russell. "Theologians have always taught that God's decrees are good, and that this is not a mere tautology: it follows that goodness is logically independent of God's decrees."[3]

The point is that moral standards can never be justified merely by an appeal to authority, whether the authority is taken to be human or divine. There has to be the additional premise that the person whose dictates we are to follow is good, or that what he commands is right, and this cannot be the mere tautology that he is what he is, or that he commands what he commands. This does not mean that we cannot look for guidance in conduct to those whom we judge to be better or wiser or more experienced than ourselves. To a greater or lesser extent, we can and do take our morals on trust but in so doing we are making a moral decision. We are at least implicitly judging that the rules which we have been brought up to respect, or the verdicts of our mentor, are morally right: and again this is not the mere tautology that these rules and verdicts just are what they are. ...

The Meaning of Life

... There are those who would say that in pursuing the question whether there is adequate evidence for a God's existence, we have been approaching the subject of religion in the wrong way. According to them, the question we should have been asking is not whether the proposition that God exists is true as a matter of fact, or acceptable as an explanatory hypothesis, but rather what function the belief in God fulfils in the lives of those who hold it. The justification for the belief may then be said to be that it makes the lives of those who hold it appear meaningful to them in a way they otherwise would not.

This is substantially the position taken by the pragmatist William James. Having spoken in one book of "the craving of our nature for an ultimate peace behind all tempests, a blue zenith above all clouds,"[4] he criticizes in another the attempts of what he calls "systematic theology" to define the attributes of God. "Wherein," he asks, "is such a definition really instructive? It means less than nothing in its pompous robe of adjectives. Pragmatism alone can read a positive meaning into it, and for that she turns her back upon the intellectualist point of view altogether. 'God's in his heaven; all's right with the world'. *That's* the real heart of your theology, and for that you need no rationalist definitions."[5] Similarly, in his Gifford lectures on *The Varieties of Religious Experience* he speaks of his wish to vindicate "the instinctive belief of mankind: God is real since he produces real effects,"[6] and what he takes these real effects to be is no more than the feelings of greater energy, security and satisfaction which he thinks are enjoyed by those who hold religious beliefs.

As a psychological hypothesis, this could be questioned. For instance, the thesis of eternal damnation which has been a prominent feature of much Christian teaching is not likely to produce a feeling of greater security. On the other hand, there is no doubt that many people derive solace from the idea of their having a spiritual father who watches over them, especially when it is allied to the hope that he will secure to them in a future life the happiness which they may not have found in this one. To infer from this, however, that there is such a father, one needs to accept James's pragmatic theory that, since it is not to be expected of a religious hypothesis that it will either accord or fail to accord with any observable fact, the criterion for its truth is just that the vague assurance which it gives that "all's right with the world" is a source of emotional satisfaction. This is in line with the view of some contemporary theists that the doctrine associated with the religious practices in which they engage is acceptable as a useful myth. This view is so modest that it is hard to take issue with it, unless one wants to argue that the myth is harmful, but it does appear open to the practical objection that the satisfaction which most believers derive from their acceptance of religious doctrine depends upon their not judging it as mythical. A myth which is generally seen to be a myth must be in some danger of losing its utility.

But without the help of such a myth, can life be seen as having any meaning? The simple answer is that it can have just as much meaning as one is able to put into it. There is, indeed, no ground for thinking that human life in general serves any ulterior purpose, but this is no bar to a man's finding satisfaction in many of the activities which make up his life, or to his attaching value to the ends which he pursues, including some that he himself will not live to see realized. One may deplore the fact that life is so short, but if it were not independently worth living there would be no good reason to wish it prolonged. Where the discarding of the Christian myth may have a cruel effect is in the denial to those whose lives have not been happy of any serious hope that they will survive to find the balance redressed.

Notes

1. Bertrand Russell, *Why I Am Not a Christian,* pp. 24-25.

2. Voltaire, *Epistles* XCVI.

3. Bertrand Russell, *Human Society in Ethics and Politics,* p. 48.

4. William James, *The Will to Believe,* p. 180.

5. William James, *Pragmatism,* pp. 121-22.

6. William James, *The Varieties of Religious Experience,* p. 517.

25
The Unbelievers And Christians (1960)
Albert Camus

Inasmuch as you have been so kind as to invite a man who does not share your convictions to come and answer the very general question that you are raising in these conversations, before telling you what I think unbelievers expect of Christians, I should like first to acknowledge your intellectual generosity by stating a few principles.

First, there is a lay pharisaism in which I shall strive not to indulge. To me a lay pharisee is the person who pretends to believe that Christianity is an easy thing and asks of the Christian, on the basis of an external view of Christianity, more than he asks of himself. I believe indeed that the Christian has many obligations but that it is not up to the man who rejects them himself to recall their existence to anyone who has already accepted them. If there is anyone who can ask anything of the Christian, it is the Christian himself. The conclusion is that if I allowed myself at the end of this statement to demand of you certain duties, these could only be duties that it is essential to ask of any man today, whether he is or is not a Christian.

Secondly, I wish to declare also that, not feeling that I possess any absolute truth or any message, I shall never start from the supposition that Christian truth is illusory, But merely from the fact that I could not accept it. As an illustration of this position, I am willing to confess this:[1]

Three years ago a controversy made me argue against one, among you, and not the least formidable. The fever of those years, the painful memory of two or three friends assassinated had given me the courage to do so. Yet I can assure you that, despite some excessive expressions on the part of Francois Mauriac, I have not ceased meditating on what he said. At the end of this reflection-and in this way I give you my opinion as to the usefulness of the dialogue between believer and unbeliever—I have come to admit to myself, and now to admit publicly here, that for the fundamentals and on the precise point of our controversy Francois Mauriac got the better of me.

Having said that, it will be easier for me to state my third and last principle. It is simple and obvious. I shall not try to change anything that I think or anything that you think (insofar as I can judge of it) in order to reach a reconciliation that would be agreeable to all. On the contrary, what I feel like telling you today is that the world needs real dialogue, that falsehood is just as much the opposite of dialogue as is silence, and that the only possible dialogue is the kind between people who remain what they are and speak their minds. This is tantamount to saying that the world of today needs Christians who remain Christians. The other day at the Sorbonne, speaking to a Marxist lecturer, a Catholic priest said in public that he too was anticlerical. Well, I don't like priests who are anticlerical any more than philosophies that are ashamed of themselves. Hence I shall not, as far as I am concerned, try to pass myself off as a Christian in your presence. I share with you the same revulsion from evil. But I do not share your hope, and I continue to struggle against this universe in which children suffer and die.

And why shouldn't I say here what I have written elsewhere? For a long time during those frightful years I waited for a great voice to speak up in Rome. I, an unbeliever? Precisely. For I knew that the spirit would be lost if it did not utter a cry of condemnation when faced with force. It seems that that voice did speak up. But I assure you that millions of men like me did not hear it and that at that time believers and unbelievers alike shared a solitude that continued to spread as the days went by and the executioners multiplied.

It has been explained to me since that the condemnation was indeed voiced. But that it was in the style of the encyclicals, which is not at all clear. The condemnation was voiced and it was not understood! Who could fail to feel where the true condemnation lies in this case and to see that this example by itself gives part of the reply, perhaps the whole reply, that you ask of me. What the world expects of Christians is that Christians should speak out, loud and clear, and that they should voice their condemnation in such a way that never a doubt, never the slightest doubt, could rise in the heart of the simplest man. That they should get away from abstraction and confront the blood-stained face history has taken on today. The grouping we need is a grouping of men resolved to speak out clearly and to pay up personally. When a Spanish bishop blesses political executions, he ceases to be a bishop or a Christian or even a man; he is a dog just like the one who, backed by an ideology, orders that execution without doing the dirty work himself. We are still waiting, and I am waiting, for a grouping of all those who refuse to be dogs and are resolved to pay the price that must be paid so that man can be something more than a dog.

And now, what can Christians do for us? To begin with, give up the empty quarrels, the first of which is the quarrel about pessimism. I believe, for instance, that M. Gabriel Marcel would be well advised to leave alone certain forms of thought that fascinate him and lead him astray. M. Marcel cannot call himself a democrat and at the same time ask for a prohibition of Sartre's play. This is a position that is tiresome for everyone. What M. Marcel wants is to defend absolute values, such as modesty and man's divine truth, when the things that should be defended are the few provisional values that will allow M. Marcel to continue fighting someday, and comfortably, for those absolute values. ...

By what right, moreover, could a Christian or a Marxist accuse me, for example, of pessimism? I was not the one to invent the misery of the human being or the terrifying formulas of divine malediction. I was not the one to shout *Nemo honus* or the damnation of unbaptized children. I was not the one who said that man was incapable of saving himself by his own means and that in the depths of his degradation his only hope was in the grace of God. And as for the famous Marxist optimism! No one has carried distrust of man further, and ultimately the economic fatalities of this universe seem more terrible than divine whims.

Christians and Communists will tell me that their optimism is based on a longer range, that it is superior to all the rest, and that God or history, according to the individual, is the satisfying end-product of their dialectic. I can indulge in the same reasoning. If Christianity is pessimistic as to man, it is optimistic as to human destiny. Well, I can say that, pessimistic as to human destiny, I am optimistic as to man. And not in the name of a humanism that always seemed to me to fall short, but in the name of an ignorance that tries to negate nothing. This means that the words "pessimism" and "optimism" need to be clearly defined and that, until we can do so, we must pay attention to what unites us rather than to what separates us.

That, I believe, is all I had to say. We are faced with evil. And, as for me, I feel rather as Augustine did before becoming a Christian when he said: "I tried to find the source of evil and I got nowhere." But it is also true that I, and a few others, know what must be done, if not to reduce evil, at least not to add to it. Perhaps we cannot prevent this world from being a world in which children are tortured. But we can reduce the number of tortured children. And if you don't help us, who else in the world can help us do this?

Between the forces of terror and the forces of dialogue, a great unequal battle has begun. I have nothing but reasonable illusions as to the outcome of that battle. But I believe it must be fought, and I know that certain men at least have resolved to do so. I merely fear that they will occasionally feel somewhat alone, that they are in fact alone, and that after an interval of two thousand years we may see the sacrifice of Socrates repeated several times. The program for the future is either a permanent dialogue or the solemn and significant putting to death of any who have experienced dialogue. After having contributed my reply, the question that I ask Christians is this: "Will Socrates still be alone and is there nothing in him and in your doctrine that urges you to join us?"

It may be, I am well aware, that Christianity will answer negatively. Oh, not by your mouths, I am convinced. But it may be, and this is even more probable, that Christianity will insist on maintaining a compromise or else on giving its condemnations the obscure form of the encyclical. Possibly it will insist on losing once and for all the virtue of revolt and indignation that belonged to it long ago. In that case Christians will live and Christianity will die. In that case the others will in fact pay for the sacrifice. In any case such a future is not within my province to decide, despite all the hope and anguish it awakens in me. I can speak only of what I know. And what I know—which sometimes creates a deep longing in me—is that if Christians made up their minds to it, millions of voices—millions, I say—throughout the world would be added to the appeal of a handful of isolated individuals who, without any sort of affiliation, today intercede almost everywhere and ceaselessly for children and for men.

Note
1. Fragments of a statement made at the Dominican Monastery of Latour-Maubourg in 1948.

26
Science And Religion (1940)
Albert Einstein

It would not be difficult to come to an agreement as to what we understand by science. Science is the century-old endeavor to bring together by means of systematic thought the perceptible phenomena of this world into as thoroughgoing an association as possible. To put it boldly, it is the attempt at the posterior reconstruction of existence by the process of conceptualization. But when asking myself what religion is I cannot think of the answer so easily. And even after finding an answer which may satisfy me at this particular moment, I still remain convinced that I can never under any circumstances bring together, even to a slight extent, the thoughts of all those who have given this question serious consideration.

At first, then, instead of asking what religion is I should prefer to ask what characterizes the aspirations of a person who gives me the impression of being religious: a person who is religiously enlightened appears to me to be one who has, to the best of his ability, liberated himself from the fetters of his selfish desires and is preoccupied with thoughts, feelings, and aspirations to which he clings because of their super-personal value. It seems to me that what is important is the force of this super-personal content and the depth of the conviction concerning its overpowering meaningfulness, regardless of whether any attempt is made to unite this content with a divine Being, for otherwise it would not be possible to count Buddha and Spinoza as religious personalities. Accordingly, a religious person is devout in the sense that he has no doubt of the significance and loftiness of those super-personal objects and goals which neither require nor are capable of rational foundation. They exist with the same necessity and matter-of-factness as he himself. In this sense religion is the age-old endeavor of mankind to become clearly and completely conscious of these values and goals and constantly to strengthen and extend their effect. If one conceives of religion and science according to these definitions then a conflict between them appears impossible. For science can only ascertain what is, but not what should be, and outside of its domain value judgments of all kinds remain necessary. Religion, on the other hand, deals only with evaluations of human thought and action: it cannot justifiably speak of facts and relationships between facts. According to this interpretation the well-known conflicts between religion and science in the past must all be ascribed to a misapprehension of the situation which has been described.

For example, a conflict arises when a religious community insists on the absolute truthfulness of all statements recorded in the Bible. This means an intervention on the part of religion into the sphere of science; this is where the struggle of the Church against the doctrines of Galileo and Darwin belongs. On the other hand, representatives of science have often made an attempt to arrive at fundamental judgments with respect to values and ends on the basis of scientific method, and in this way have set themselves in opposition to religion. These conflicts have all sprung from fatal errors.

Now, even though the realms of religion and science in themselves are clearly marked off from each other, nevertheless there exist between the two strong reciprocal relationships and dependencies. Though religion may be that which determines the goal, it has, nevertheless, learned from science, in the broadest sense, what means will contribute to the attainment of the goals it has set up. But science can only be created by those who are thoroughly imbued with the aspiration toward truth and understanding. This source of feeling, however, springs from the sphere of religion. To this there also belongs the faith in the possibility that the regulations valid for the world of existence are rational, that is, comprehensible to reason. I cannot conceive of a genuine scientist without that profound faith. The situation may be expressed by an image: science without religion is lame, religion without science is blind.

Though I have asserted above that in truth a legitimate conflict between religion and science cannot exist, I must nevertheless qualify this assertion once again on an essential point, with reference to the actual content of historical religions. This qualification has to do with the concept of God. During the youthful period of mankind's spiritual evolution human fantasy created gods in man's own image, who, by the operations of their will were supposed to determine, or at any rate to influence, the phenomenal world. Man sought to alter the disposition of these gods in his own favor by means of magic and prayer. The idea of God in the religions taught at present is a sublimation of that old concept of the gods. Its anthropomorphic character is shown, for instance, by the fact that men appeal to the Divine Being in prayers and plead for the fulfillment of their wishes.

Nobody, certainly, will deny that the idea of the existence of an omnipotent, just, and omni-beneficent personal God is able to accord man solace, help, and guidance; also, by virtue of its simplicity it is accessible to the most undeveloped mind. But, on the other hand, there are decisive weaknesses attached to this idea in itself, which have been painfully felt since the beginning of history. That is, if this being is omnipotent, then every occurrence, including every human action, every human thought, and every human feeling and aspiration is also His work; how is it possible to think of holding men responsible for their deeds and thoughts before such an almighty Being? In giving out punishment and rewards He would to a certain extent be passing judgment on Himself. How can this be combined with the goodness and righteousness ascribed to Him?

The main source of the present-day conflicts between the spheres of religion and of science lies in this concept of a personal God. It is the aim of science to establish general rules which determine the reciprocal connection of objects and events in time and space. For these rules, or laws of nature, absolutely general validity is required—not proven. It is mainly a program, and faith in the possibility of its accomplishment in principle is only founded on partial successes. But hardly anyone could be found who would deny these partial successes and ascribe them to human self-deception. The fact that on the basis of such laws we are able to predict the temporal behavior of phenomena in certain domains with great precision and certainty is deeply embedded in the consciousness of the modern man, even though he may have grasped very little of the contents of those laws. He need only consider that planetary courses within the solar system may be calculated in advance with great exactitude on the basis of a limited number of simple laws. In a similar way, though not with the same precision, it is possible to calculate in advance the mode of operation of an electric motor, a transmission system, or of a wireless apparatus, even when dealing with a novel development.

To be sure, when the number of factors coming into play in a phenomenological complex is too large, scientific method in most cases fails us. One need only think of the weather, in which case prediction even for a few days ahead is impossible. Nevertheless no one doubts that we are confronted with a causal connection whose causal components are in the main known to us. Occurrences in this domain are beyond the reach of exact prediction because of the variety of factors in operation, not because of any lack of order in nature.

We have penetrated far less deeply into the regularities obtaining within the realm of living things, but deeply enough nevertheless to sense at least the rule of fixed necessity. One need only think of the systematic order in heredity, and in the effect of poisons, as for instance alcohol, on the behavior of organic beings. What is still lacking here is a grasp of connections of profound generality, but not a knowledge of order in itself. The more a man is imbued with the ordered regularity of all events the firmer becomes his conviction that there is no room left by the side of this ordered regularity for causes of a different nature. For him neither the rule of human nor the rule of divine will exists as an independent cause of natural events. To be sure, the doctrine of a personal God interfering with natural events could never be refuted, by science, for this doctrine can always take refuge in those domains in which scientific knowledge has not yet set foot.

But I am persuaded that such behavior on the part of the representatives of religion would not only be unworthy but also fatal. For a doctrine which is able to maintain itself not in clear light but only in the dark, will of necessity lose its effect on mankind, with incalculable harm to human progress. In their struggle for the ethical good, teachers of religion must have the stature to give up the doctrine of a personal God, that is, give up that source of fear and hope which in the past placed such vast power in the hands of priests. In their labors they will have to avail themselves of those forces which are capable of cultivating the Good, the True, and the Beautiful in humanity itself. This is, to be sure, a more difficult but an incomparably more worthy task. (This thought is convincingly presented in Herbert Samuel's book, *Belief and Action*.) After religious teachers accomplish the refining process indicated they will surely recognize with joy that true religion has been ennobled and made more profound by scientific knowledge.

If it is one of the goals of religion to liberate mankind as far as possible from the bondage of egocentric cravings, desires, and fears, scientific reasoning can aid religion in yet another sense. Although it is true that it is the goal of science to discover rules which permit the association and foretelling of facts, this is not its only aim. It also seeks to reduce the connections discovered to the smallest possible number of mutually independent conceptual elements. It is in this striving after the rational unification of the manifold that it encounters its greatest successes, even though it is precisely this attempt which causes it to run the greatest risk of falling a prey to illusions. But whoever has undergone the intense experience of successful advances made in this domain is moved by profound reverence for the rationality made manifest in existence. By way of the understanding he achieves a far-reaching emancipation from the shackles of personal hopes and desires, and thereby attains that humble attitude of mind toward the grandeur of reason incarnate in existence, and which, in its profoundest depths, is inaccessible to man. This attitude appears to me to be religious, in the highest sense of the word. And so it seems to me that science not only purifies the religious impulse of the dross of its anthropomorphism but also contributes to a religious spiritualization of our understanding of life.

The further the spiritual evolution of mankind advances, the more certain it seems to me that the path to genuine religiosity does not lie through the fear of life, and the fear of death, and blind faith, but through striving after rational knowledge. In this sense I believe that the priest must become a teacher if he wishes to do justice to his lofty educational mission.

FROM THE LATER 20th CENTURY and 21st CENTURY

The church says the earth is flat, but I know that it is round, for I have seen the shadow on the moon, and I have more faith in a shadow than in the church.
—*Ferdinand Magellan, 16th century Portuguese maritime explorer*

If the concept of God has any validity or use, it can only be to make us larger, freer, and more loving. If God cannot do this, then it is time we got rid of Him.
—*James Baldwin, novelist, playwright, poet, essayist, and civil rights activist*

I can very well do without God both in my life and in my painting, but I cannot, suffering as I am, do without something which is greater than I am, which is my life, the power to create.
—*Vincent Willem van Gogh, Post-Impressionist artist*

Religion is regarded by the common people as true, by the wise as false, and by the rulers as useful.
—*Edward Gibbon, 18th century British historian*

The whole thing is so patently infantile, so foreign to reality, that to anyone with a friendly attitude to humanity it is painful to think that the great majority of mortals will never be able to rise above this view of life.
—*Sigmund Freud, Austrian physician, neurologist, and founder of psychoanalysis*

You were born without purpose, you live without meaning, living is its own meaning. When you die, you are extinguished. From being you will be transformed to non-being. A god does not necessarily dwell among our capricious atoms.
—*Ingmar Bergman, film and theater director*

I'm an atheist, and that's it. I believe there's nothing we can know except that we should be kind to each other and do what we can for each other.
—*Katharine Hepburn, actor*

The fundamentalist believer is mostly a weird intellectual who often lacks real faith altogether. As a self-appointed attorney for God, who is in no need of attorneys, he very easily turns out to be more godless than the agnostic and the unbeliever. At all events, he seems deaf to poetry.
—*Steve Allen, comedian, writer, musician, and television host*

To you I'm an atheist; to God, I'm the Loyal Opposition.
—*Woody Allen, director, actor, writer*

I'm sickened by all religions. Religion has divided people. I don't think there's any difference between the pope wearing a large hat and parading around with a smoking purse and an African painting his face white and praying to a rock.
—*Howard Stern, radio personality, author*

27
Monotheism And Its Discontents (1992)
Gore Vidal

The word "radical" derives from the Latin word for root. Therefore, if you want to get to the root of anything you must be radical. It is no accident that the word has now been totally demonized by our masters, and no one in politics dares even to use the word favorably, much less track any problem to its root. But then a ruling class that has been able to demonize the word "liberal" is a master at controlling—indeed stifling—any criticism of itself. "Liberal" comes from the Latin *liberalis,* which means pertaining to a free man. In politics, to be liberal is to want to extend democracy through change and reform. One can see why that word had to be erased from our political lexicon.

Meanwhile, the word "isolationist" has been revived to describe those who would like to put an end to the national security state that replaced our Republic a half-century ago while extending the American military empire far beyond our capacity to pay for it. The word was trotted out in the presidential election of 1992 to describe one Pat Buchanan, who was causing great distress to the managers of our national security state by saying that America must abandon the empire if we are ever to repair the mess at home. Also, as a neo-isolationist, Buchanan must be made to seem an anti-Semite. This is not hard to do. Buchanan is a classic Archie Bunker type, seething with irrational prejudices and resentments, whose origin I'll get to presently.

The country is now dividing, as it did a half-century ago, between those who think that America comes first versus those who favor empire and the continued exertion of force everywhere in the name of democracy, something not much on display here at home. In any case, as the whole world is, more or less, a single economic unit in which the United States is an ever smaller component, there are no isolationists today. But the word games go on and the deliberate reversals of meaning are always a sign that our corporate masters are worried that the people are beginning to question their arrangements. Many things are now coming into focus. The *New York Times* promptly dismissed Buchanan as a minor irritant, which was true, but it ignored his potentially major constituency—those who now believe that it was a mistake to have wasted, since 1950, most of the government's revenues on war.

Another candidate, Jerry Brown, alarmed the *Times* even more than Buchanan did. There was the possibility that he could be elected. More important, he might actually change our politics in the sense of who pays for whom. In a sudden frenzy, the *Times* compared him to Péron our Jerry?—a dangerous demagogue whose "sharp-edged anger...resonates among a variety of Americans." Plainly, the ownership of the country is frightened that the current hatred of politicians, in general, may soon be translated into a hatred of that corporate few who control the many through Opinion, as manufactured by the *Times,* among others.

Now to the root of the matter. The great unmentionable evil at the center of our culture is monotheism. From a barbaric Bronze Age text known as the Old Testament, three antihuman religions have evolved—Judaism, Christianity and Islam. These are sky-god religions. They are, literally, patriarchal—God is the omnipotent father—hence the loathing of women for 2,000 years in those countries afflicted by the sky-god and his earthly male delegates. The sky-god is a jealous god, of course. He requires total obedience from everyone on earth, as he is in place not just for one tribe but for all creation. Those who would reject him must be converted or killed for their own good. Ultimately, totalitarianism is the only sort of politics that can truly serve the sky-god's purpose. Any movement of a liberal nature endangers his authority and that of his delegates on earth. One God, one King, one Pope, one master in the factory, one father-leader in the family at home.

The founders of the United States were not enthusiasts of the sky-god. Many, like Jefferson, rejected him altogether and placed man at the center of the world. The young Lincoln wrote a pamphlet *against* Christianity, which friends persuaded him to burn. Needless to say, word got around about both Jefferson and Lincoln and each had to cover his tracks. Jefferson said that he was a deist, which could mean anything or nothing, while Lincoln, hand on heart and tongue in cheek, said he could not support for office anyone who "scoffed" at religion.

From the beginning, sky-godders have always exerted great pressure in our secular republic. Also, evangelical Christian groups have traditionally drawn strength from the suppressed. African slaves were allowed to organize heavenly sky-god churches, as a surrogate for earthly freedom. White churches were organized in order to make certain that the rights of property were respected and that the numerous religious taboos in the New and Old Testaments would be enforced, if necessary, by civil law. The ideal to which John Adams subscribed that we would be a nation of laws, not of men was quickly subverted when the churches forced upon everyone, through supposedly neutral and just laws, their innumerable taboos on sex, alcohol, gambling. We are now indeed a nation of laws, mostly bad and certainly antihuman.

Roman Catholic migrations in the last century further reinforced the Puritan sky-god. The Church has also put itself on a collision course with the Bill of Rights when it asserts, as it always has, that "error has no rights." The last correspondence between John Adams and Thomas Jefferson expressed their alarm that the Jesuits were to be allowed into the United States. Although the Jews were sky-god folk, they followed Book One, not Book Two, so they have no mission to convert others; rather the reverse. Also, as they have been systematically demonized by the Christian sky-godders, they tended to be liberal and so turned not to their temple but to the ACLU. Unfortunately, the recent discovery that the sky-god, in his capacity as realtor, had given them, in perpetuity, some parcels of unattractive land called Judea and Samaria has, to my mind, unhinged many of them. I hope this is temporary.

In the First Amendment to the Constitution the Founders made it clear that this was not to be a sky-god nation with a national religion like that of England, from whom we had just separated. It is curious how little understood this amendment is —yes, everyone has a right to worship any god he chooses but he does *not* have the right to impose his beliefs on others who do not happen to share in his superstitions and taboos. This separation was absolute in our original Republic. But the sky-godders do not give up easily. During the Civil War, they actually got the phrase "In God We Trust" onto the currency, in direct violation of the First Amendment, while "Under God" was added to the Oath of Allegiance under Eisenhower.

Although many of the Christian evangelists feel it necessary to convert everyone on earth to their primitive religion, they have been prevented—so far—from forcing others to worship as they do, but they *have* forced—most tyrannically and wickedly—their superstitions and hatreds upon all of us through the civil law and through general prohibitions. So it is upon that account that I now favor an all-out war on the monotheists.

Let us dwell upon the evils they have wrought. The hatred of blacks comes straight from their Bad Book. As descendants of Ham (according to Redneck divines), blacks are forever accursed, while Saint Paul tells the slaves to obey their masters. Racism is in the marrow of the bone of the true believer. For him, black is forever inferior to white and deserves whatever ill fortune may come his way. The fact that some monotheists can behave charitably means, often, that their prejudice is at so deep a level that they are not aware it is there at all. In the end, this makes any radical change of attitude impossible. Meanwhile, welfare has been the price the sky-godders were willing to pay to exclude blacks from their earthly political system. So we must live presumably forever—with a highly enervating race war, set in train by the One God and his many hatreds.

Patriarchal rage at the thought of Woman ever usurping Man's place at the helm, in either home or workplace, is almost as strong now as it ever was, while the ongoing psychopathic hatred of same-sexuality has made the United States the laughingstock of the civilized world. After all, in most of the First World, monotheism is weak. Where it is weak or nonexistent, private sexual behavior has nothing at all to do with those not involved, much less with the law. At least when the Emperor Justinian, a sky-god man, decided to outlaw sodomy, he had to come up with a good *practical* reason, which he did. It is well known, Justinian declared, that buggery is a principal cause of earthquakes, and so must be prohibited. But our sky-godders, always eager to hate, still quote Leviticus, as if that loony text had anything useful to say about anything except, perhaps, the inadvisability of eating shellfish in the Jerusalem area.

We are now, slowly, becoming alarmed at the state of the planet. For a century, we have been breeding like a virus under optimum conditions, and now the virus has begun to attack its host, the earth. The lower atmosphere is filled with dust, we have just been told from our satellites in space. Climate changes; earth and water are poisoned. Sensible people grow alarmed; sky-godders are serene, even smug. The planet is just a staging area for heaven. Why bother to clean it up? Did not the sky-god tell his slaves to "be fruitful and multiply, and replenish the earth, and subdue it, and have dominion… over every living thing that moveth upon the earth." Well, we did just like you told us, massa. We've used everything up. We're ready for heaven now. Or maybe Mars will do.

Ordinarily, as a descendant of the eighteenth-century Enlightenment, which shaped our Republic, I would say live and let live and I would try not to "scoff"—to use Lincoln's verb at the monotheists. But I am not allowed to ignore them. They won't let me. They are too busy. They have a divine mission to take away our rights as private citizens. We are forbidden abortion here, gambling there, same-sex almost everywhere, drugs, alcohol in a dry county. Our prisons are the most terrible and the most crowded in the First World. Our death-row executions are a source of deep disgust in civilized countries, where more and more we are regarded as a primitive, uneducated and dangerous people. Although we are not allowed, under law, to kill ourselves or to take drugs that the good folk think might be bad for us, we are allowed to buy a handgun and shoot as many people as we can get away with.

Of course, as poor Arthur (There Is This Pendulum) Schlesinger Jr. would say, these things come in cycles. Every twenty years liberal gives way to conservative, and back again. But I suggest that what is wrong now is not cyclic but systemic. And our system, like any system, is obeying the second law of thermodynamics. Everything is running down; and we are well advanced along the cold, dusty road to entropy. I don't think much of anything can be done to halt this progress under our present political-economic system. We lost poor Arthur's pendulum in 1950 when our original Constitution was secretly replaced with the apparatus of that national security state, which still wastes most of our tax money on war or war-related matters. Hence deteriorating schools, and so on.

Another of our agreed-upon fantasies is that we do not have a class system in the United States. The Few who control the Many through Opinion have simply made themselves invisible. They have convinced us that we are a classless society in which anyone can make it. Ninety percent of the stories in the pop press are about winners of lotteries or poor boys and girls who, despite adenoidal complaints, become overnight millionaire singers. So there is still hope, the press tells the folks, for the 99 percent who will never achieve wealth no matter how hard they work. We are also warned at birth that it is not polite to hurt people's feelings by criticizing their religion, even if that religion may be damaging everyone through the infiltration of our common laws.

Happily, the few cannot disguise the bad times through which we are all going. Word is spreading that America is now falling behind in the civilization sweepstakes. So isn't it time to discuss what we all really think and feel about our social and economic arrangements?

Although we may not discuss race other than to say that Jesus wants each and every one of us for a sunbeam, history is nothing more than the bloody record of the migration of tribes. When the white race broke out of Europe five hundred years ago, it did many astounding things all over the globe. Inspired by a raging sky-god, the whites were able to pretend that their conquests were in order to bring the One God to everyone, particularly those with older and subtler religions. Now the tribes are on the move again. Professor Pendulum is having a nervous breakdown because so many different tribes are now being drawn to this sweet land of liberty and, thus far, there is no indication that any of the new arrivals intends ever to read *The Age of Jackson*. I think the taking in of everyone can probably be overdone. There may not be enough jobs for very many more immigrants, though what prosperity we have ever enjoyed in the past was usually based on slave or near-slave labor.

On the other hand, I think Asians and Hispanics are a plus culturally, and their presence tends to refocus, somewhat, the relentless white versus black war. Where I *am* as one with friend Pendulum is that the newcomers must grasp certain principles as expressed in the Declaration of Independence and the Bill of Rights. Otherwise, we shall become a racially divided totalitarian state enjoying a Brazilian economy.

To revert to the unmentionable, religion. It should be noted that religion seemed to be losing its hold in the United States in the second quarter of this century. From the Scopes trial in 1925 to the repeal of Prohibition in 1933, the sky-godders were confined pretty much to the backwoods. Then television was invented and the electronic pulpit was soon occupied by a horde of Elmer Gantrys, who took advantage of the tax exemption for religion. Thus, out of greed, a religious revival has been set in motion and the results are predictably poisonous to the body politic.

It is usual, on the rare occasions when essential problems are addressed, to exhort everyone to be kinder, gentler. To bring us together, O Lord, in our common humanity. Well, we have heard these exhortations for a couple of hundred years and we are further apart than ever. So instead of coming together in order that the many might be one, I say let us separate so that each will know where he stands. From the *one, many,* and each of us free of the sky-god as secular lawgiver. I preach, to put it bluntly, confrontation.

Whether Brown and Buchanan knew it or not, they were revealing two basic, opposing political movements. Buchanan speaks for the party of God—the sky-god with his terrible hatred of women, blacks, gays, drugs, abortion, contraception, gambling—you name it, he hates it. Buchanan is a worthy peddler of hate. He is also in harmony not only with the prejudices and superstitions of a good part of the population but, to give him his due, he is a reactionary in the good sense—reacting against the empire in favor of the old Republic, which he mistakenly thinks was Christian.

Brown speaks for the party of man—feminists can find another noun if they like. Thomas Paine, when asked *his* religion, said he subscribed only to the religion of humanity. There now seems to be a polarizing of the country of a sort that has never happened before. The potential fault line has always been there, but whenever a politician got too close to the facts of our case, the famed genius of the system would eliminate him in favor of that mean which is truly golden for the ownership, and no one else. The party of man would like to re-establish a representative government firmly based upon the Bill of Rights. The party of God will have none of this. It wants to establish, through legal prohibitions and enforced taboos, a sky-god totalitarian state. The United States ultimately as prison, with mandatory blood, urine and lie-detector tests and with the sky-godders as the cops, answerable only to God.

For once, it's all out there, perfectly visible, perfectly plain for those who can see. For the first time in 140 years, we now have the outline of two parties. Each knows the nature of its opposite, and those who are wise will not try to accommodate or compromise the two but will let them, at last, confront each other.

Jefferson's famous tree of liberty is all that we have ever really had. Now, for want of nurture—the blood of tyrants and of patriots—it is dying before our eyes. Of course, the sky-god never liked it. But some of us did—and some of us do. So, perhaps, through facing who and what we are, we may achieve a nation not under God but under man—or should I say our common humanity?

28
How Is Atheism To Be Characterized? (1985)
Kai Nielson

I

Many, perhaps most, educated twentieth-century believers and nonbelievers alike
are perplexed about the concept of God and other central religious notions of the
Jewish-Christian-Islamic faiths. Key concepts of such religions—God, heaven, hell,
sin, the Last Judgment, a human being's chief end, being resurrected, and coming to
be a new man with a new body—are all to one degree or another problematic. Indeed, their very intelligibility or rational acceptability are not beyond reasonable
doubt. These concepts form a system. Indeed, a religious faith or a religion should be
seen as a system of salvation and we should recognize that we cannot properly understand these concepts in isolation or apart from understanding the rationale of the
form of life of which they are an integral part. But in the various cultures of the West,
if our socialization has been even remotely normal, we know how to play Jewish or
Christian language-games and in varying degrees, we even have some understanding
of those forms of life. Yet what I said initially still remains true: many of us—believers
and nonbelievers alike—remain perplexed by the fundamental concepts of the dominant religion in our culture. We know how to use these terms perfectly well and we
have a reasonable understanding of why they have remained in circulation, for we acknowledge many of the aspirations that religion answers to. Yet we remain thoroughly perplexed over whether these terms in their religious employments answer
to anything real or even to anything we can coherently conceive. ...

II

Here, I shall seek perspicuously to characterize atheism and to contrast it with agnosticism and with religious belief-systems. What it is to be an atheist is not as
unproblematic as it is frequently thought to be. I shall move from common but less

adequate characterizations to what I take to be the proper delineation of what it is to be an atheist. With that characterization before us, I shall in the first instance try to show some of the attractions of this position and then close by criticizing a brisk way of dismissing my whole project.[1]

A central common core of Judaism, Christianity, and Islam is the affirmation of the realitiy of one and only one God. Adherents to these religions believe that there is a God who created the universe out of nothing and who is taken to have absolute sovereignty over all His creation, including, of course, human beings—beings who are not only utterly dependent on this creative power but who are also sinful and who, according to the faithful, can only make adequate sense of their lives by accepting without question God's ordinances for them. The varieties of atheism are quite numerous but all atheists are united in rejecting such a set of beliefs, which are central to the religious systems of Western cultures.

However, atheism casts a wider net and rejects all belief in "spiritual beings," and to the extent that belief in spiritual beings is definitive of what it is for a belief-system to be religious, atheism rejects religion. Thus, it is not only a rejection of the central conceptions of Judeo-Christianity; it is, as well, a rejection of the religious beliefs of such African religions as those of the Dinka and the Nuer, the anthropomorphic gods of classical Greece and Rome, and the transcendental conceptions of Hinduism and Buddhism.[2] Sometimes atheism is viewed simplistically as a denial of "God" or of "the gods" and, if religion is to be defined in terms of the belief in "spiritual beings," then atheism is the rejection of all religious belief.

However, if any tolerably adequate understanding of atheism is to be achieved, it is necessary to give a careful reading to "rejection of religious belief" and to realize how frightfully inadequate it is to characterize atheism as the denial of God (or the gods) or of all spiritual beings.

To say that atheism is the denial of God (or the gods) and that it is the opposite of theism, a system of belief which affirms the reality of God and seeks to demonstrate His existence, is inadequate in several ways. First, not all theologians who regard themselves as defenders of the Christian faith or of Judaism or Islam regard themselves as defenders of theism. The influential twentieth-century Protestant theologian Paul Tillich, for example, regards the God of theism as an idol and refuses to construe God as a being, even a supreme being, among beings or as an infinite being above finite beings.[3] God, for him, is being-itself, the ground of being and meaning. The particulars of Tillich's view are in certain ways idiosyncratic as well as obscure and problematic; but they have had a considerable impact on our cultural life, and his rejection of theism while retaining a belief in God is not eccentric in contemporary theology, though it may very well be an affront to the plain believer.

Secondly, and more importantly, it is not the case that all theists seek to demonstrate or even in any way rationally to establish the existence of God. Many theists regard such a demonstration as impossible, and fideistic believers (e.g., Georg Hamann and Soren Kirkegaard) believe such a demonstration to be undesirable even if it were possible, for, in their view, it would undermine faith. If we could prove, i.e., come to know for certain, that God exists, then we would not be in a position to accept Him on faith as our Sovereign Lord with all the risks that faith entails. There are theologians who have argued that for genuine faith to be possible God must necessarily be a hidden God, the mysterious ultimate reality, whose existence and authority we must accept simply on faith. This fideistic view has not, of course, gone without challenge from inside these major faiths. But it is of sufficient importance to raise serious questions about the adequacy of the above theism.

It should also be noted that not all denials of God come to the same thing. Sometimes believers deny God while not being at all in a state of doubt that God exists. Many willfully reject what they take to be His authority by not acting in accordance with what they take to be His will, while others simply live their lives as if God did not exist. In this important way, they deny Him in practice while in a sense remaining believers. But neither of the above deniers are atheists (unless we wish, misleadingly, to call them "practical atheists"). They are not even agnostics. They would never question the existence of God, even though they deny Him in other ways.

To be atheists we need to deny the *existence* of God. It is frequently, but I shall argue mistakenly, thought that this entails that we need to believe that it is false that God exists or, alternatively, that we must believe that God's existence is a speculative hypothesis of an extremely low order of probability.[4] Such a characterization, I shall argue, is defective in a number of ways. For one it is too narrow. There are atheists (including this atheist) who believe that the very concept of God, at least in developed and less anthropomorphic forms of Judeo-Christianity, is so incoherent that certain central religious claims, such as "God is my creator to whom everything is owed," are not genuine truth-claims. That is to say, as claims they are neither true nor false. Yet, believers do indeed take such religious propositions to be true, and *some* atheists, unlike this atheist, believe they are false; and there are agnostics who cannot make up their minds whether the propositions (putative propositions) are true *or* false. (The latter consider religious claims to be one or the other but believe that we cannot determine which.) It will be the underlying burden of my argument to show that all three stances are mistaken, for such putative truth-claims are not suffi-ciently intelligible to be genuine truth-claims that are either true or false. In reality there is nothing here to be believed or disbelieved, though, for the believer, there re-mains a powerful and humanly comforting illusion that there is.

While the above considerations about atheism and intelligibility will, if well-taken, show that the second characterization of atheism is too narrow, it would also be accurate to say that, in a way, the characterization is too broad. There are fideistic believers who quite unequivocally believe it to be the case that, when looked at objectively, propositions about God's existence have a very low probability weight. They do not believe in God because it is probable that He exists—they think it is more probable that He doesn't—but because such a belief is thought by them to be necessary to make sense of human life. The short of it is that such a characteriza-tion of atheism would not distinguish a fideistic believer (e.g., Blaise Pascal or Soren Kierkegaard) or an agnostic (e.g., T.H. Huxley or Leslie Stephen) from an atheist such as Baron Holbach or Thomas Paine. They all believe that propositions of the form "There is a God" and "God protects humankind," however emotionally important they may be, are, when viewed objectively, nothing more than speculative hypothe-ses of an extremely low order of probability. But this, since it does not distinguish be-lievers from nonbelievers, and does not distinguish agnostics from atheists, cannot be an adequate characterization of atheism.

It may be retorted that if *a priorism* and dogmatic atheism are to be avoided we must regard the existence of God as a hypothesis. There are no ontological (purely *a priori)* proofs or *disproofs* of God's existence. Without such a proof or disproof it is not reasonable (or at least ill-advised) to rule in advance that to say "God exists" makes no sense. It has often been argued—and not unreasonably—that all the atheist can reasonably claim is that there is no evidence that there is a God and that without such evidence he is justified in asserting that there is no God. Some opponents of this view have insisted that it is simply dogmatic for an atheist to assert that no possible evi-dence could ever provide grounds for a belief in God. Instead, it is argued, atheists should justify their unbelief by supporting (if they can) the assertion that no evidence currently warrants a belief in God. If atheism is justified, the advocate will have shown that in fact there is no evidence that God exists. But, the argument goes, it should not be part of his task to try to show that there couldn't be *any* evidence for the existence of God. If the atheist could somehow survive the death of his present body (assuming for the nonce that such talk makes sense) and came, much to his sur-prise, to stand in the presence of God, his answer should be "Oh! Lord you didn't give me enough evidence!" His belief that there is no God would have turned out to have been mistaken all along and now he realizes that he had believed something to be false that in fact was true. Given what he had come to experience in this transformed state, he now sees that he was mistaken in his judgment that there is no God. Still, he was not unjustified, in the light of the evidence available to him during his "earthly life," in believing that God did not exist. That judgment, given what he knew at the time, is not rendered unreasonable in the light of evidence that only could become available to him later. The reasonableness of our judgments should be assessed in the light of the evidence available to us at a given time. Not having any such post-mortem experiences of the presence of God (assuming for the occasion that he could have them), as things stand, and in the face of the evidence he actually has, and is likely to be able to get, he should say that it is false that God exists. When we legitimately assert that a proposition is false we need not be certain that it is false. "Knowing with certainty" is not a pleonasm. The claim is that this tentative posture is the reasonable position for the atheist to take.

An atheist who argues in this manner may also make a distinctive burden-of-proof argument. Given that God (if there is one) is by definition a very *recherché* reality, a reality that must be transcendent to the world, the burden of proof is not on the atheist to give grounds for believing that there is no reality of that order. Rather, the burden of proof is on the believer to give us evidence for God's existence, i.e., something to show that there is such a reality. Given what God must be, if there is a God, the believer needs to present the evidence for such a very strange reality. He needs to show that there is more in the world than is disclosed by our common experience. The scientific method, broadly conceived as a resolutely empirical method, and the scientific method alone, such an atheist asserts, affords a reliable method for establishing what is in fact the case. The believer will in turn assert that in addition to the varieties of empirical facts there are also "spiritual facts" or "transcendent facts," i.e., the fact that there is a supernatural, self-existent eternal power. To this the atheist can, and should, retort that such "facts" have not been shown to us. The believer has done nothing to deliver the goods here. No such facts have been presented. Atheists of the "we-don't-have-enough-evidence" variety will argue, against what they take to be dogmatic *a prioristic* atheists, that the atheist should be a fallibilist and remain open-minded about what the future may bring. After all, they argue, there may be such "transcendent facts," such *recherché* metaphysical realities.

It is not that such a fallibilistic atheist is really an agnostic who believes that he is not justified in either asserting that God exists or denying that He exists, and that to be maximally reasonable over this issue, what he must do is suspend belief. On the contrary, such an atheist believes he has very good grounds indeed, as things stand, for denying the existence of God. But what he will not deny is that things could be otherwise and, if they were, that he would not be justified in asserting that it is false that there is a God. Using reliable empirical techniques—proven methods for establishing matters of fact—he has found nothing in the universe that would make a belief in God's existence justifiable or even, everything considered, the most rational of the available options. He therefore draws the atheistic conclusion (also keeping in mind his burden-of-proof argument) that God does not exist. But his denial of God's existence is not set forth dogmatically in a high *a priori* fashion. The atheist remains a thorough and consistent fallibilist.

III

Such a form of atheism (the atheism of those pragmatists who are also naturalistic humanists) is not adequate. This can be seen if we take careful note of the concept of God in our forms of life. Unlike Zeus or Wotan, in developed forms of Judaism, Christianity, and Islam, God is not, like Zeus or Wotan, construed in a relatively plain anthropomorphic way.[5] Nothing that could count as "God" in such religions could possibly be observed, literally encountered, or detected in the universe. God, on such a conception, is transcendent to the world; He is conceived of as "pure spirit," an infinite individual who created the universe out of nothing and who is distinct from it, though, for Christians, God, in the form of Christ, is said to have walked the earth. Thus, somehow, for Christians—and only for Christians—God is said to be both transcendent and immanent. He is "pure spirit" *and* a person with a material embodiment. God is said to be an eternal transcendent reality but he is also said to be immanent. This appears at least to be incoherent, but, incoherent or not, Christians whose beliefs are at all close to established orthodoxy will not abandon their claim that God is transcendent to the world. Such a "transcendent reality"—a reality understood to be an ultimate mystery— can not be identified in the same way that objects or processes in the universe are identified. There can be no pointing at God, no ostensive teaching of "God," to show what "God" means. The word "God" can only be taught intra-linguistically. Someone who does not understand what the word "God" means can be taught by using descriptions such as "the maker of the universe," "the eternal, utterly independent being upon whom all other beings depend," "the first cause," "the sole ultimate reality," "a self-caused being," and the like. For someone who does not understand such descriptions (putative descriptions), there can be no understanding of the concept of God. Yet there is a very good reason for saying that we do not understand such "descriptions": they do not give us an empirical foundation for *what we* are talking about when we speak of God. The key terms employed in these "descriptions" are themselves no more capable of ostensive definition (i.e., capable of having their referents pointed out) than is "God." Unlike the referent for the term "Zeus," what is allegedly referred to by the term "God" is not construed anthropomorphically. (That does not mean that anyone has actually pointed to Zeus or observed Zeus but it does mean that we know roughly what it would be like to do so. We know, that is, roughly what would constitute pointing to Zeus.)

In coming to understand what is meant by "God," in such religious discourses, we must come to understand that God, whatever else He is, is a being that could not possibly be observed in any way. He could not be anything that is empirically detectable (again a pleonasm). Moreover, God is said by believers to be an intractable, ultimate mystery. A nonmysterious God would not be the God of Judaism, Christianity, and Islam.

The relevance of the preceding to our second characterization of atheism is that, if "God" is taken to be a transcendent mystery, we should then come to see that it is a mistake to claim that His existence can rightly be treated as a hypothesis and that it is also a mistake to claim that we, by the use of the experimental method or some determinate empirical method, can come to confirm or disconfirm God's existence as we could if He were an empirical reality. Such a proposed way of coming to know, or failing to come to know, God makes no sense for anyone who understands what kind of reality God is supposed to be. Anything whose existence could be so verified would not be the God of developed Judeo-Christianity. God could not be a reality whose presence is even faintly adumbrated in experience, for anything that could count as the God of Judeo-Christianity must be transcendent to the world. Anything that could actually be encountered or experienced could not be an eternal transcendent reality. This is indeed a conceptual argument, but it is an argument that has been made, and should be made, as indeed any argument should be made, in a thoroughly fallibilistic spirit. It is a putatively *a priori* claim, but whether it is a valid claim, whether it is genuinely *a priori* (analytically true or in some weaker way conceptually true) as its defenders claim, is in turn a thoroughly fallible belief. There need be, and indeed should be, nothing dogmatic about such a defense of atheism.

So at the very heart of a religion such as Christianity there is a cosmological belief—a thoroughly metaphysical belief—in a reality that is alleged to transcend the "empirical world." It is the metaphysical belief that there is an eternal, ever-present creative source and sustainer of the universe. The problem is how we could come to know or reasonably believe that such a strange reality exists or come to understand what such talk is about.

It is not that God is like a theoretical entity, such as a proton or neutrino in physics. Such theoretical entities, where they are construed as realities rather than as heuristically useful conceptual fictions, are thought to be part of the actual furniture of the universe. They are not said to be transcendent to the universe. Rather, they are invisible entities logically on a par with specks of dust and grains of sand only much much smaller. Theoretical entities are not a different kind of reality; it is only the case that they, as a matter of fact, cannot be seen. Indeed, we have no understanding of what it would be like to see a proton or a neutrino—in *that way* they are like God—and no provision is made in physical theory for seeing them. Still, there is no *logical* ban on our seeing them as there is on seeing God. We cannot correctly say that it is *logically* impossible that they could be seen.

Though invisible, theoretical entities are among the things in the universe and thus they can be postulated as causes of the things we do see. Since this is so, it becomes at least logically possible indirectly to verify by empirical methods the existence of such realities. It is also the case that there is no *logical* ban on establishing what is necessary to ascertain a causal connection, namely a constant conjunction of two discrete empirical realities. However, for the nonanthropomorphic conceptions of God of developed forms of Judeo-Christianity, no such constant conjunction can be established or even intelligibly asserted between God and the universe; thus the existence of God is not even indirectly confirmable or disconfirmable. God is not a discrete empirical thing or being and the universe is not some gigantic thing or process over and above the various particular things and processes in the universe of which it makes sense to say it has or had a cause. A particular thing in the universe could cause another particular thing. It is one discrete thing making another discrete thing happen. It is between things of this type that we can establish a constant conjunction. But neither "God" nor "the universe" are words standing for realities of which we have any idea at all what it would be like for them to stand in constant conjunction. Indeed, such talk has no intelligible home here. We have no basis for saying one is the cause of the other. But then there is no way, directly or indirectly, that we could empirically establish even the probability that there is a God since we have already disposed of the claim that God could be directly observed.

IV

There is the gnostic reply that God's existence can be established or made probable in some nonempirical way. There are, that is (or so the claim goes), truths about the nature of the cosmos that are neither capable of nor standing in need of verification.

There is, gnostics claim against empiricists, knowledge of the world that transcends experience and comprehends the sorry scheme of things entire.

Since the thorough probings of such epistemological foundations by David Hume and Immanuel Kant, skepticism about how, and indeed even that, such knowledge is possible has become very strong indeed.[6] With respect to knowledge of God in particular both Hume and Kant provide powerful critiques of the various traditional attempts to prove in any way His existence. (Kant set forth such an analysis of prevailing doctrine even though he remained a steadfast Christian.) While some of the *details* of their arguments have been rejected and refinements rooted in their argumentative procedures have been developed, there remains a very considerable consensus among contemporary philosophers and theologians that arguments like those developed by Hume and Kant show that no proof (*a priori* or empirical) of God's existence is possible.[7] And, alternatively, to speak of "intuitive knowledge" (an intuitive grasp of being, or of an intuition of the reality of the divine being) as gnostics do is to appeal to something that lacks sufficient clarity to be of any value in establishing or even understanding anything.

There is another turn that should be considered in this initial laying out of the problems with which I shall wrestle. Prior to the rise of anthropology and the scientific study of religion, an appeal to revelation and authority as a substitute for knowledge or warranted belief might have been thought to possess considerable force. But with a knowledge of other religions and their associated appeals to "Revealed Truth," such arguments are without probative force. Claimed (alleged) revelations are numerous, diverse, and not infrequently conflicting; we cannot claim by simply appealing to a given putative revelation, at least not without going in a very small and vicious circle, that it is the "true revelation" or the "genuine revelation" and that other so-called revelations are actually mistaken or, where nonconflicting, they are mere approximations of the truth. Similar things need to be said for religious authority. Moreover, it is at best problematic whether faith could sanction our speaking of testing the genuineness of revelation or of the acceptability of religious authority. Indeed, if something is a "genuine revelation," we cannot use our reason to assess it. But our predicament is that, as a matter of anthropological fact, we have this diverse and sometimes conflicting field of alleged revelations with no way of deciding or even having a reasonable hunch which, if any, of the candidate revelations is the genuine article. But even if we allow for the necessity of some tests for the genuineness of revelation, we still have a claim that clearly will not do, for such a procedure would make an appeal to revelation or authority supererogatory. Where such tests are allowed, it is not revelation or authority that can warrant the most fundamental religious truths on which the rest depend. It is something else, namely, that which establishes the genuineness of the revelation or authority. It is that which guarantees these religious truths (if such there be) including the proposition that God exists. But then the question surfaces again as to what that fundamental guarantee is or could be. Perhaps such a belief is nothing more than a cultural myth? There is, as we have seen, neither empirical knowledge nor *a priori* knowledge of God, and talk of "intuitive knowledge" is without logical force.[8]

If the above considerations are near to the mark, it is unclear what it would mean to say, as some agnostics and even some atheists have, that they are "skeptical God-seekers" who simply have not found, after a careful examination, enough evidence to make belief in God warranted or even reasonable. That is so because it is very unclear what it would be like to have or, for that matter, to fail to have evidence for the existence of God. It isn't that the "God-seeker" has to be able to give the evidence, for if that were so no search would be necessary; but he, or at least somebody, must at least be able to conceive what *would count* as evidence if he had it so that he, and we, would have some idea of what to look for. We need at least to have some idea of what evidence would look like here. But it appears that it is just this that we do not have.[9]

The response might be given that it is enough for the God-seeker not to accept any *logical* ban on the possibility of there being evidence. He need not understand what it would be like to have evidence in this domain. I would, in turn, retort that when we consider what kind of transcendent reality God is said to be, it appears at least, as I remarked earlier, that there is an implicit *logical* ban on the presence of empirical evidence (a pleonasm) for His existence.

Someone seeking to resist this conclusion might try to give empirical anchorage to talk of God by utilizing the following fanciful hypothetical case. It is important not to forget, however, that things even remotely like what I shall now describe do not happen. The fanciful case is this: suppose thousands of us were standing out under the starry skies and we all saw a set of stars rearrange themselves to spell out "God." We would be utterly astonished and indeed rightly think we had gone mad. Even if we could somehow assure ourselves that this was not some form of mass hallucination, though how we could do this is not evident, such an experience would still not constitute evidence for the existence of God, for we still would be without a clue as to what could be *meant* by speaking of an infinite individual transcendent to the world. Such an observation (i.e., the stars rearranging themselves), no matter how well confirmed, would not ostensively fix the reference range of "God." Talk of such an infinite individual would still remain incomprehensible and it would also have the same appearance of being incoherent. We do not know what we are talking about in speaking of such a transcendent reality. All we would know is that something very strange indeed had happened—something we would not know what to make of.[10]

The doubt arises (or at least it should arise) as to whether believers or indeed anyone else, in terms acceptable to believers, can give an intelligible account of the concept of God or of what belief in God comes to once the concept is thoroughly de-anthropomorphized. It is completely unclear how we could give such a term any empirical foundation. We do not know what it would be like to specify the denotation (the referent) of a nonanthropomorphic God.

V

Reflection on the above cluster of claims should lead us to a more adequate statement of what atheism is and indeed as well to what an agnostic or religious response to atheism should be. Instead of saying that an atheist is someone who believes that it is false or probably false that there is a God, a more adequate characterization of atheism, consists in the more complex claim that an atheist is someone who rejects belief in God for at least one of the following reasons (the specific reason will likely depend on how God is being conceived): (1) if an anthropomorphic God is proposed, the atheist rejects belief in God because it is false or probably false that there is such a God; (2) if it be a nonanthropomorphic God (i.e., the God of Luther and Calvin, Aquinas and Maimonides), he rejects belief in God because the concept of such a God is either meaningless, unintelligible, contradictory, incomprehensible, or incoherent; (3) the atheist rejects belief in God (here we speak of the God portrayed by some modern or contemporary theologians or philosophers) because the concept of God in question is such that it merely masks an atheistic substance, e.g., "God" is just another name for love or simply a symbolic term for moral ideals.[11]

Such a ramified conception of atheism, as well as its more reflective opposition, is much more complex than the simpler conceptions of atheism we initially considered. From what has been said about the concept of God in developed forms of Judeo-Christianity, it should be evident that the more crucial form of atheist rejection is not the one asserting that it is false that there is a God but instead the form of atheism that rejects belief in God based on the contention that the concept of God does not make sense: it is in some important sense incoherent or unintelligible. (Note: I do not say that it is unintelligible or meaningless full stop.)

Such a broader conception of atheism, of course, includes everyone who is an atheist in the narrower sense, i.e., the sense in which atheism is identified with the claim that "God exists" is false; but the converse plainly does not obtain. Moreover, this broad conception of atheism does not have to say that religious claims are in all aspects meaningless. The more typical, less paradoxical, and less tendentious claim is that utterances such as "There is an infinite, eternal creator of the universe" are incoherent and the conception of God reflected therein is in a crucial respect unintelligible and, because of that, in an important sense inconceivable and incredible: incapable of being a rational object of belief for a philosophically and scientifically sophisticated person touched by modernity.[12] This is a central belief of many contemporary atheists. And it is just such an atheism that I shall defend in this volume (Editor's note: This essay is taken from the book *Atheism and Philosophy*, Kai Nielsen, 2005). I shall argue that there (a) are good *empirical* grounds for believing that there are no Zeus-like spiritual beings and (b) that there are also sound grounds for believing that the non-anthropomorphic or at least radically less anthropomorphic conceptions of God are incoherent or unintelligible. (Remember that both of these conceptions admit of degree.) If these two claims can be justified, the atheist, to understate it, has very strong grounds for rejecting belief in God.

Atheism, as we have seen, is a critique and a denial of the central metaphysical belief-systems of salvation involving a belief in God or spiritual beings; however, a sophisticated atheist will not simply contend that all such cosmological claims are false but will take it that some are so problematic that, while purporting to be factual, they actually do not succeed in making coherent factual claims. In an important respect they do not make sense, and while believers are under the illusion that something intelligible is there in which to believe, in reality this is not the case. These seemingly grand cosmological claims are in reality best understood as myths or ideological claims reflecting a humanly understandable confusion on the part of the people who make them.[13]

It is not a well-taken rejoinder to atheistic critiques to say, as some contemporary Protestant and Jewish theologians have, that belief in God is the worst form of atheism and idolatry, for the language of Christian and Jewish belief, including such sentences as "God exists" and "God created the world," is not to be taken literally but rather as symbol or metaphor. Christianity, as Reinhold Niebuhr (a theologian who defends such views) once put it, is "true myth." On such an account, the claims of religion are not to be understood as metaphysical claims trying to convey some extraordinary facts but as metaphorical and analogical claims that are not understandable in any other terms. But this claim is incoherent: if something is a metaphor, it must at least in principle be possible to say what it is a metaphor of.[14] Thus metaphors cannot be understandable *only* in metaphorical terms. All metaphors and symbolic expressions must be capable of paraphrase, though, what is something else again, a user of such expressions may not be able on demand to supply that paraphrase. Moreover, and more simply and less controversially, if the language of religion becomes little more than the language of myth, and religious beliefs are viewed simply as powerful and often humanly compelling myths, then we have conceptions that actually possess an atheistic substance.[15] The believer is making no cosmological claim; he is making no claim that the atheist should feel obliged to deny. It is just that the believer's talk, including his unelucidated talk of "true myths," is language that has a more powerful emotive force for many people. But if the believer follows these theologians or Christian philosophers down this path, he will have abandoned his effort to make truth claims that are different from those made by the atheist.

VI

Many skeptics would prefer to think of themselves as agnostics rather than atheists because it seems less dogmatic. ...

Agnosticism has a parallel development to that of atheism. An agnostic, like an atheist, asserts that we can neither know nor have sound reasons for believing that God exists; but, unlike the atheist, the agnostic does not think we are justified in saying that God does not exist or, stronger still, that God cannot exist. Similarly, while some contemporary atheists will say that the concept of God in developed theism does not make sense and thus Jewish, Christian, and Islamic beliefs must be rejected, many contemporary agnostics will believe that, though the concept of God is radically problematic, we are not in a position to be able rationally to decide whether, on the one hand, the terms and concepts of such religions are so problematic that such religious beliefs do not make sense or whether, on the other, they still have just enough coherence to make a belief in an ultimate mystery a live option for a reflective and informed human being, even though the talk of such belief is indeed radically paradoxical and in many ways incomprehensible.

Such an agnostic recognizes that our puzzles about God cut deeper than perplexities concerning whether it is possible to attain adequate evidence for God's existence. Rather, he sees clearly the need to exhibit an adequate nonanthropomorphic, extra-linguistic referent for "God." (This need not commit him to the belief that there is any theory- independent acquisition of data.) Believers think that even though God is a mystery such a referent has been secured, though what it is still remains obscure. Atheists, by contrast, believe, as we have seen, that it has not been secured, and indeed some of them believe that it cannot be secured. To speak of mystery here, they maintain, is just an evasive way of talking about what we do not understand. Instead of being candid about their total incomprehension, believers use the evasive language of mystery. Contemporary agnostics (those agnostics who parallel the atheists characterized above) remain in doubt about whether our talk of God in this halting fashion just barely secures such reference or whether it fails after all and "God" refers to nothing religiously acceptable.

Intense religious commitment, as the history of fideism makes evident, has sometimes combined with deep skepticism concerning man's capacity to know God. It is agreed by almost all parties to the dispute between belief and unbelief that religious claims are paradoxical, and if there is a God, He is indeed a very mysterious reality. Furthermore, criteria for what is or is not meaningless and what is or is not intelligible are deeply contested; at least there seem to be no generally accepted criteria here.

Keeping these diverse considerations in mind, in the arguments between belief, agnosticism, and atheism, it is crucial to ask whether we have any good reason at all to believe that there is a personal creative reality that exists beyond the bounds of space and time and that transcends the world. Do we even have a sufficient understanding of such talk so that the reality to which it refers can be the object of religious commitment? We cannot have faith in or accept on faith that which we do not at all understand. We must at least in some way understand what it is we are to have faith in if we are actually to have faith in it. If someone asks me to trust *Irglig,* I cannot do so no matter how strongly I want to take that something-I-know-not-what simply on trust.[16]

What appears at least to be the case is that it is just a brute fact that there is that indefinitely immense collection of finite and contingent masses or conglomerations of things and processes we use the phrase "the universe" to refer to. There is no logical or rational necessity that there are any of these things or anything at all. It just manifestly is so. That we can in certain moods come to feel wonder, awe, and puzzlement that there is a world at all does not license the claim that there is a noncontingent reality on which the world (the sorry collection of such things entire) depends. It is not even clear that such a sense of contingency gives us an understanding of what a "noncontingent thing" could be. Some atheists (including this atheist) think that the reference range of "God" is so indeterminate and the concept so problematic that it is impossible for someone to be fully aware of this fact and, if the person is being nonevasive, to believe in God. Believers, by contrast, think that neither the reference range of "God" is so indeterminate nor the concept of God so problematic as to make belief in God irrational or incoherent.[17] We do know, they claim, that talk of God is problematic, but we do not know, and we cannot know, whether it is so problematic as to be without a religiously appropriate sense. After all, God is supposed to be an ultimate mystery. Agnostics, in turn, say that- there is no reasonable decision procedure here that would enable us to resolve the issue. We do not know and cannot ascertain whether "God" secures a religiously adequate referent. In reflecting on this issue, we should strive to ascertain whether (1) a "contingent thing" is a pleonasm, (2) an "infinite individual" is without sense and (3) whether when we go beyond anthropomorphism (or try to go beyond it), we have a sufficient understanding of *what* is referred to by "God" to make faith a coherent possibility. I shall argue that "a contingent thing" is pleonastic, that "infinite individual" is without sense, and that the last question should be answered in the negative. The agnostic, by contrast, is not led to faith, but he does believe that such questions cannot be answered.

I argue that it will not do to take a Pascalian or Dostoyevskian turn and claim that, intellectual absurdity or not, religious belief is, humanly speaking, necessary, for without belief in God, morality does not make sense and life is meaningless.[18] That claim is false; for even if there is no God and no purpose *to* life there are purposes *in* life.[19] There are things we care about and want to do that can remain perfectly intact even in a Godless world. God or no God, immortality or no immortality, it is vile to torture people just for the fun of it; and friendship, solidarity, love, and the attainment of self-respect are human goods even in an utterly Godless world. There are intellectual puzzles about how we know these things are good but that is doubly true for the distinctive claims of a religious ethic. With them, we have the standard perplexities concerning how we can know some things to be good and other things to be bad, as well as the additional perplexities concerning how we can come to understand, let alone assess, the truth of the distinctively religious claims embedded in these systems of belief. But that latter perplexity is one that the atheist can put to the side. However, with the moral beliefs just mentioned, the point is that these things are acknowledged to be desirable by believer and nonbeliever alike. How we can know they are desirable provides a philosophical puzzle for both believer and skeptic. But whether these things are desirable or not has nothing to do with whether God exists. When we reflect carefully on the fact that certain purposes remain intact even in a Godless world, we will, as a corollary, come to see that life can have a point even in a world without God.

VII

The kind of religious response I shall primarily be concerned with and will attempt to criticize, with what I hope is sensitivity and understanding, is a tortured religiosity that is well aware of the problematic nature of religious concepts and the questionable coherence of religious beliefs, yet still seeks to make sense of these beliefs and continues the attempt to bring to the fore their vital human import in the teeth of their paradoxical nature and their apparent incoherence. Such Jews, Moslems, and Christians seem to me to have taken to heart the problems posed by modernity.

There is, however, a growing movement in popular religion, with some representation in intellectual circles as well, that seeks to turn its back on these problems with what seems to be an obtuseness that is both peculiar and disheartening. Religious discourse does not seem to them paradoxical, and religious concepts, including the concept of God, do not seem to them problematic. "We know well enough what we are talking about when we talk about or to God," so they tell us. Christian revelation, they aver, is perfectly intact and the moral vision of that religion, viewed along orthodox lines, provides a firm and evident foundation for the moral life. There is no reason to follow a Kierkegaard, to say nothing of a Nietzsche, regarding any of these things. We can be quite confident of the coherence of God-talk and of the integrity of the Christian faith. The central philosophical task, such traditional Christian philosophers believe, is to provide a sound proof for the existence of God. Of course, they also aver, even without proof, we still have the certainty of revelation; but with proof as well, we have a philosophical basis for a foundationalist account in philosophical theology that would rationalize belief.

This view is the counterpart of both the simpler view of atheism, which regards the key theistic beliefs as simply false, and of a simple agnosticism, which believes that we understand the beliefs well enough but just do not have enough evidence to make a responsible judgment about their truth. Such an agnostic believes that theistic beliefs are plainly either true or false, but whether they are true *or* false is something he believes cannot be established. By contrast, as the previous sections of this chapter have brought to the fore, my atheism and its parallels in religious belief and agnosticism, is principally taken up, in reflecting on religious belief, with the logically prior questions of the coherence of God-talk. Our concern is with whether we have anything sufficiently unproblematic in the religious discourse of developed Judeo-Christianity such that something could really count there as religious truth. Such a view is very distant from Neo-Conservative Christianity.

Alvin Plantinga, a representative (indeed a well-known philosophical representative) of this fundamentalist Christian faith, has tried in short order to set aside those philosophical perplexities as unreal pseudo-problems.[20] In bringing this essay to a close, I want to note his line of argumentation—a line that is common enough in some circles—and succinctly to set out my response.

What is common ground between us is that we both take "God" to be some sort of referring expression. My skeptical questions, in light of this, can be put in the following terms. Where "God" is not employed purely anthropomorphically to refer to a kind of cosmic mickeymouse, to whom or to what does "God" refer? Is it a proper name, an abbreviated definite description, a special kind of descriptive predictable, or what? How could we be acquainted with, or otherwise come to know, what "God" stands for or characterizes? How do we—or do we—identify or individuate God? What are we talking about when we speak of God? What or who is this God we pray to, love, make sense of our lives in terms of, and the like?

We know, since we know how to use God-talk, that in talking about God, we are talking about a being of infinite love, mercy, power, and understanding. But such talk does not relieve our puzzlement. What literally are we talking about when we speak of this being? Of what kind of reality, if indeed it is of any kind of reality at all, do we speak when we use such awesome words? Do we really understand what we are talking about here? There is a challenge here to faith that has bothered many a believer and nonbeliever alike. It is a challenge that can perhaps be met, but it is puzzling and, to some, a disturbing challenge all the same.[21]

Plantinga remarks to the question "Who or what is God?" that the "question is the sort to which a definite description provides the appropriate answer."[22] The appropriate definite descriptions, Plantinga confidently remarks, are "the creator of the Universe," "the omnipotent, omniscient, and wholly good person," "the Father of Our Lord and Savior Jesus Christ." There is no more problem with "Who or what is God?," he incautiously proclaims, than there is with the definite descriptions supplied by way of an answer to the question "Who is Sylvia?," namely, such things as "the first person to climb the North Ridge of Mount Blanc" or "the local news announcer."

It is very difficult not to believe that Plantinga is being thoroughly disingenuous here. He knows full well that there are puzzles about the very understanding of the alleged definite descriptions answering to "God" in a way that there is no puzzle about the definite descriptions specifying for us who Sylvia is. He insinuates that it is as silly to be perplexed about who is God as it is, after some straightforward definite descriptions have been given, to be perplexed about who is Sylvia. But he *must* know that there are perplexities about "creator of the universe," "omnipotent, omniscient, and wholly good person," or "Our Savior Jesus Christ" that are just as considerable as our perplexities about "God." As Ronald Hepburn[23] pointed out years ago, Jesus Christ in Christian theology is taken to be the Son of God, and if we are puzzled about what we are talking about in speaking of God, we are going to be no less puzzled about what we are talking about in speaking of "the Son of God." And the phrases "the creator of the universe" or "the omnipotent, omniscient, and wholly good person" are, as the history of their discussion makes evident, thoroughly puzzling phrases. Many theologians (sincere and believing Christians), troubled by what, if any, appropriate sense could be given to them, have, as we have remarked, sought analogical or symbolic readings of these phrases. Plantinga writes with what at least appears to be an arrogant unconcern for years and years of our intellectual history. When he remarks that these definite descriptions are entirely appropriate "since God is a person—a living being who believes and knows, speaks and acts, approves and disapproves," he is either being evasively disingenuous or almost unbelievably naive. For people who do not construe God as a kind of cosmic Mickey Mouse, it has been a key task to demythologize such talk so that it can be seen to be something that a nonsuperstitious person might possibly accept. There can be no taking it as unproblematical in the way Plantinga attempts to.[24]

This is an extreme case of what I call "being bloody minded about God." It is a blind and stubborn refusal to face up to problems where there are indeed problems or where at least there certainly appear to be woblems for religious belief and understanding. Perhaps, just perhaps, some subtle Wittgensteinian technique could show us that there are, after all, no problems here, or perhaps we can find a way to meet these problems, but the kind of footstamping that Plantinga engages in is not even a beginning. It is a kind of misplaced Mooreanism, buttressed by some jargon taken from modal logic, where no such appeal to common sense is possible. What we need to recognize is that the concept of God is very problematic indeed. What is crucially at issue is to ascertain, if we can, whether sufficient sense can be made of religious conceptions to make faith a live option for a reflective and concerned human being possessing a reasonable scientific and philosophical understanding of the world he lives in, or whether some form of atheism or agnosticism is the most nonevasive option for such a person.

Notes

1. Kai Nielsen, *Ethics Without God* (Prometheus Books: Buffalo, New York, 1973); Kai Nielsen, "Linguistic Philosophy and 'the Meaning of Life,' " in E. D. Klemke (ed.) *The Meaning of Life* (New York: Oxford University Press, 1981, pp. 177-204; Kai Nielsen, "An Examination of the Thomistic Theory of Natural Law," *Natural Law Forum*, 4 (1959); and Kai Nielsen, "The Myth of Natural Law," in Sidney Hook (ed.) *Law and Philosophy* (New York University Press: New York, 1964).

2. For a clear statement of what anthropomorphism is see John Skorupski, *Symbol and Theory* (London: Cambridge University Press, 1976), p. 65.

3. Paul Tillich's massive *Systematic Theology* is very hard going indeed. The writing is cumbersome and obscure beyond any rational excuse. However, in his more popular writings, what he wants to say, at least on a superficial level, attains some measure of clarity. His *The Courage To Be,* (New Haven: Yale University Press, 1952) in most places has this quality, but most clearly and most revealingly of all a scattered group of his popular essays captures, I believe, what made Tillich important to a number of people touched deeply by modernity who were not philosophers or theologians. He spoke to people who had a need to believe but could not swallow the old supernaturalistic framework. Braithwaite and Hare also tried to answer to such needs but their gruel was too thin for people with such religious aspirations. But Tillich and his popularizing disciple Bishop Robinson filled the bill. See the following short essays, all by Tillich: "Religion," *Perspectives* 15 (Spring, 1956): 43-48; "The God above God," *The Listener* (August 3, 1961); "The Lost Dimension in Religion" in *Adventures of the Mind,* Richard Thruelson and John Kebler (eds.), (New York: Vintage Books, 1960); "The Idea of God as Affected by Modern Knowledge" in *In Search of God and Immortality,* (Boston: Beacon Press, 1961), no editor; "The Relationship Today Between Science and Religion" in *The Student Seeks An Answer* (Waterville, Maine: Colby College Press, 1960), pp. 297-306. For important critiques of Tillich see the essays on Tillich in Sidney Hook (ed.), *Religious Experience and Truth* (New York: New York University Press, 1961); Paul Edwards, "Professor Tillich's Confusions," *Mind* 74 (1965); and Alistair M. MacLeod, *Tillich* (London: George Allen & Unwin Ltd., 1973). For more sympathetic elucidations and examinations of Tillich (examinations that attend to some of the above criticisms of Tillich), see Malcolm L. Diamond, *Contemporary Philosophy and Religious Thought* (New York: McGraw-Hill Book Company, 1974), pp. 301-389; and William L. Rowe, *Religious Symbols and God* (Chicago: The University of Chicago Press, 1968).

4. In the sorting out of this issue the exchange between Sidney Hook and myself is, I believe, instructive. See Kai Nielsen, "Religion and Naturalistic Humanism: Some Remarks on Hook's Critique of Religion" in Paul Kurtz (ed.) *Sidney Hook and the Contemporary World* (New York: John Day Company, 1968), pp. 257-279; Kai Nielsen, "Secularism and Theology: Remarks on a Form of Naturalistic Humanism," *The Southern Journal of Philosophy* XIII (Spring, 1975): 109-126; Sidney Hook, "For An Open-Minded Naturalism," *The Southern Journal of Philosophy* XIII (Spring, 1975): 127-136; and his *The Quest For Being* (New York: St. Martin's Press, 1960), particularly pp. 115-135, 145-195.

5. John Skorupski gives us a good sense of such an anthropomorphism in the following passage: "A very common feature of traditional religious cosmologies is the belief that there are procedures which, if followed, will *give a* man the ability to see the spirits around him. Or people often be-

lieve that there are certain places such as streams or glades in which gods may be encountered—not simply in the sense that their presence is felt but in the sense that one might get a glimpse of them." John Skorupski, op.cit., p. 65.

6. This can survive a very thorough rejection of the methodological and epistemological programmes of both Hume and Kant and the traditions they have spawned in contemporary philosophy. This is shown clearly in the work of Richard Rorty, whose *Philosophy and the Mirror of Nature* (Princeton, New Jersey: Princeton University Press, 1979) is one such rejection—indeed a very persuasive rejection. Yet, for all his historicism, Rorty remarks, without any ambivalence at all, "that the preservation of the values of the Enlightenment is our best hope," pp. 335-6. And, for all his distance from positivism, Rorty also declares "the positivists were absolutely right in thinking it imperative to extirpate metaphysics, when 'metaphysics' means the attempt to give knowledge of what science cannot know," p. 384.

7. There has, of course, been some dissent, principally from neo-scholastic philosophers and, as well, from two modal-logic-with-God philosophers, Charles Hartshorne and Alvin Plantinga. But these are backward looking, rear-guard operations of little cultural or intellectual significance.

8. There is often an attempt at such a point to make an appeal to faith. In addition to "The Primacy of Philosophical Theology," reprinted here, I have tried critically to examine such moves in my "Can Faith Validate God- talk?" *Theology Today* XX (July, 1963); "Faith and Authority," *The Southern Journal of Philosophy* 3 (Winter, 1965); and "Religious Perplexity and Faith," *Crane Review* VIII (Fall, 1965).

9. This is one of the central things at issue in my exchange with Sidney Hook. See the references in footnote 4.

10. I have tried to defend this in my "On the Rationality of Radical Theological Neo-Naturalism," *Religious Studies* (1978): 193-204; in my "Radical Theological Non-Naturalism," *Sophia* XVIII (July, 1978): 1-6; and in my essays reprinted in *The Logic of God: Theology and Verification*, Malcolm L. Diamond and Thomas V. Litzenburg (Indianapolis, IN: The Bobbs-Merrill Company, 1975).

11. Richard B. Braithwaite, "An Empiricist's View of the Nature of Religious Belief" in *The Logic of God*, pp. 127-149 and R. M. Hare, "The Simple Believer" in *Religion and Morality*, Gene Outka and John Reeder, Jr. (Garden City, NY: Anchor Books, 1973), pp. 393-427.

12. See my penultimate essay in this volume, my "Principles of Rationality," *Philosophical Papers* III (October, 1974): 55-89 and my "Christian Empiricism," *The Journal of Religion* 61 (April, 1981): 146-167. The latter contains a critique of Braithwaite's and Hare's "Christian empiricism."

13. This claim is most extensively developed in my "On Speaking of God," *Theoria* XXVII (1962): 110-137. This essay is reprinted, together with a number of my other essays, in *Analytical Philosophy of Religion in Canada*, Mostafa Foghfowry (ed.), (Ottawa, ON: The University of Ottawa Press, 1982).

14. See here William P. Alston, "Tillich's Conception of a Religious Symbol" in *Religious Experience and Truth*, pp. 12-26 and chapter 7 of Paul Henle (ed.), *Language, Thought and Culture* (Ann Arbor, MI: The University of Michigan Press, 1958).

15. Sidney Hook, "The Atheism of Paul Tillich," in *Religious Experience and Truth*, pp. 59-63 and his *The Quest For Being*, pp. 145-171.

16. For the argument for this, see my "Can Faith Validate God-talk?" *Theology Today* XX (July, 1963).

17. Kai Nielsen, "On Fixing the Reference Range of 'God,' " in The Logic of God, pp. 330-340.

18. See Kurt Baier's essay and my essay in E. D. Klemke's (ed.) *The Meaning of Life*, pp. 1-117 and 177-204 and my *Ethics Without God*, pp. 48-64.

19. See Baier's essay cited above.

20. The citations in the text come from Plantinga's response to my "Religion and Groundless Believing," Frederick Crosson (ed.) *The Autonomy of Religious Belief* (Notre Dame, IN: The University of Notre Dame Press, 1981). The exchange took place at the conference on "Religion and Forms of Life" at the University of Notre Dame in 1979. See, as well, Plantinga's "Analytic Philosophy and Christianity," *Christianity Today* (October 25, 1963): 75-78 and his "Verificationism" in *The Logic of God,* pp. 446-455, and my response to it in my *Contemporary Critiques of Religion* (New York: Herder and Herder, 1971), pp. 55-71.

21. The challenge is powerfully put from the side of religious belief by Michael Durrant, *The Logical Status of 'God'* (New York: Macmillan, 1973) and his *Theology and Intelligibility* (Boston: Routledge and Kegan Paul, 1973).

22. In his response to my "Religion and Groundless Believing."

23. Ronald Hepburn, *Christianity and Paradox* (London: Watts, 1958), chapter 5. But also see, to tease the matter out a little more, John Hick's response in his "A Philosopher Criticizes Theology," *The Modern Quarterly* 31 (1962): 103-110.

24. Plantinga, op. Cit.

29
Atheism (2006)
Christine Overall

This piece is a revised transcript of an interview given by Christine Overall to Julian Samuels for his 2006 documentary, Atheism.

The absence of a belief in god is one form of atheism, which could be called 'negative' atheism. Yet, I believe a more important form of atheism is what some call 'positive' atheism—that is, having the belief that there is no god of any kind. Now, an agnostic is rather different, and agnosticism takes many forms.

An agnostic, simply, is one who *does not know* whether or not there is a god. However, one who identifies as an agnostic may do so for a number of different reasons, all of which I believe can be safely characterized as agnostic. For example, one might identify as an agnostic because he or she thinks that there is no way to decide whether or not god exists. Or, one might identify as an agnostic because he or she thinks that the evidence *for* the existence of god is about equal to the evidence *against* the existence of god, with the result that one must suspend belief.

There are many reasons to be an agnostic, or even an atheist. As the story says, Jesus performed a miracle. He was assembled with a group of his followers, when one of his disciples approached him in a panic: with only a few loaves and a few fishes, they certainly did not have enough food to feed the hungry masses before them. Jesus told them not to worry, and he miraculously multiplied the loaves and the fishes, so that there was enough to feed all of the assembled multitudes.

To religious believers, miracles are at the very heart of faith. Consider Christianity, a religion built upon miracles: a virgin gives birth to a child; this child becomes a divine prophet, who regularly converts the masses with his incredible feats; and finally this young man is unjustly killed, yet is brought back to life shortly after through the benevolence of his holy father. Is this not a religion that places miracles at its core?

Therefore, if religious believers renounce too many of their miracles, they begin, effectively, to renounce their belief as a whole. The vast majority of those who believe in god on this planet are firmly committed to the notion of miracles in the sense of events that contradict the laws of nature. Science, it is said, has had an influence within the academy; it has persuaded some theologians, and, perhaps, many philosophers, that the miracles of which we read in religious texts did not occur. Nonetheless, the belief in these miracles as literal events is alive and well, not only among religious believers, but within the academy—where one would think reason and the progress of science would have had the strongest effect.

Nonetheless, even if miracles are interpreted symbolically, they remain morally suspect, because miracles appear to reflect a certain favouritism on God's part. For, as we know, miracles happen to some people, and not others—what kind of symbolic interpretation can we make of this fact? Do religious believers really want to construe God as partial? Is this compatible with the idea of a Christian God, said to be the God of all people? I would wonder about that.

The point of morality is to help us live well. And by us, I mean all of us; all human beings, and I would add, all living beings, human or not. If this is the purpose of morality, we do not need a religious system to structure our morals.

I don't think there's any evidence that atheists or agnostics are any less moral than religious believers; and, of course, it's all too easy to point to examples of religious believers who have been utterly immoral. Now, it is true that religious belief has tended to be a fairly efficient way of inculcating certain moral systems. But, the fact that it is efficient does not mean that it is the best way. In particular, some religious systems have inculcated beliefs such as the inferiority of women, or the inferiority of certain races, or the inferiority of certain ethnicities. Religious belief, then, has put forward systems that are sometimes absolutely *immoral*.

Given this, I would ask: is there anything else that is lost if we relinquish belief in god? Certainly, there is a wonderful and global history of beautiful, religiously inspired architecture, art, and music. But we still have this history regardless of whether or not we believe in a god *now*. I can still travel to other countries and appreciate the greatness of religious art, despite the fact that I don't share the beliefs of its makers. The capacity to make art is a human gift. We can go on creating this great culture without suffering the illusion of religious belief.

Often it is argued, 'Everything in the universe looks so beautifully designed, it has such wonderful patterns; it must have been caused by a cosmic designer." Human beings, along with all of animal life, did not, in fact, simultaneously materialize six thousand years ago. Rather, there is a vast history of the evolution of all living beings, from tiny, single-celled organisms, to the complex entities we human beings are today. Science has been very effective in dispelling the idea of spontaneous, complete creation. It has discredited the very literal religious believers who have held their account of creation to be factual and accurate. As a result, many believers have revised their notion of god, conceding that 'god created the universe, but he created it by means of the big bang, from which everything then unfolded, including the processes of evolution that gradually produced human beings.'

What caused god? Need we make god the cause of the universe, or does this only defer the problem? If it is legitimate to ask 'what caused the universe?' it is also legitimate to ask, 'what caused god?' If the answer is that nothing caused god, because he is self-causing, why can't we simply say that *nothing caused the universe.*

My loss of religious belief was not coerced—it was a loss that evolved out of the process of my own rational thinking. It was a loss not only of a system of beliefs, but also feelings, rituals, and so on; it was a loss of an entire framework for understanding the universe, the world, and my place in it. I believe it is this loss, the loss of a framework for understanding, that makes the disappearance of religious faith painful.

Feuerbach, the nineteenth-century philosopher, sought to account for the ubiquity of religious belief. In effect, he concluded that human beings *are* god—that, in a sense, we make god. According to Feuerbach, to believe in god is to project our greatest hopes and our most important ideals into the heavens. For example, we claim mercy to be good; thus, there must be a god that is merciful. Or, we desire to be powerful, we desire to know; thus, there must be a being that is supremely powerful and supremely all-knowing. Feuerbach maintained that this habit of projection could explain the ubiquity of religious belief—why humanity has clung to its religious belief, generation after generation.

Marx, of course, maintained that religion's function is to keep people quiescent. Religion is one of the best systems to prevent people from rebelling against their limitations. Particularly, if you are a peasant, a serf, or a member of the working class, exploited by a corporation or an agricultural boss, an ideal way to keep you quiet, to keep you working—to ensure your acquiescence to exploitation—is to be told that 'god wants it this way, you were made by god to do this work. And some day, after your death, your grand reward awaits.'

If someone were to come along and present me with a fabulously strong and convincing argument to demonstrate that all my reasoning has been heretofore wrong, I wouldn't be disappointed. I don't think this is ever going to happen. But if it were to, I'd be pleased! I would be happy to know I was wrong, although I don't think I am. In other words, I'm open to the possibility.

I did not seek to lose my belief. I did not say to myself: I hate religion, I hate the church, I need to escape from them. The world was opened up to me by philosophers, and the path of rational thinking took me to atheism.

30

An Atheist Manifesto (2005)

Sam Harris

Somewhere in the world a man has abducted a little girl. Soon he will rape, torture and kill her. If an atrocity of this kind is not occurring at precisely this moment, it will happen in a few hours, or days at most. Such is the confidence we can draw from the statistical laws that govern the lives of 6 billion human beings. The same statistics also suggest that this girl's parents believe at this very moment that an all-powerful and all-loving God is watching over them and their family. Are they right to believe this? Is it good that they believe this?

No.

The entirety of atheism is contained in this response. Atheism is not a philosophy; it is not even a view of the world; it is simply a refusal to deny the obvious. Unfortunately, we live in a world in which the obvious is overlooked as a matter of principle. The obvious must be observed and re-observed and argued for. This is a thankless job. It carries with it an aura of petulance and insensitivity. It is, moreover, a job that the atheist does not want.

It is worth noting that no one ever needs to identify himself as a non-astrologer or a non-alchemist. Consequently, we do not have words for people who deny the validity of these pseudo-disciplines. Likewise, atheism is a term that should not even exist. Atheism is nothing more than the noises reasonable people make when in the presence of religious dogma. The atheist is merely a person who believes that the 260 million Americans (87% of the population) who claim to never doubt the existence of God should be obliged to present evidence for his existence and, indeed, for his benevolence, given the relentless destruction of innocent human beings we witness in the world each day. Only the atheist appreciates just how uncanny our situation is: Most of us believe in a God that is every bit as specious as the gods of Mount Olympus; no person, whatever his or her qualifications, can seek public office in the

United States without pretending to be certain that such a God exists; and much of what passes for public policy in our country conforms to religious taboos and superstitions appropriate to a medieval theocracy. Our circumstance is abject, indefensible and terrifying. It would be hilarious if the stakes were not so high.

We live in a world where all things, good and bad, are finally destroyed by change. Parents lose their children and children their parents. Husbands and wives are separated in an instant, never to meet again. Friends part company in haste, without knowing that it will be for the last time. This life, when surveyed with a broad glance, presents little more than a vast spectacle of loss. Most people in this world, however, imagine that there is a cure for this. If we live rightly—not necessarily ethically, but within the framework of certain ancient beliefs and stereotyped behaviors—we will get everything we want after we die. When our bodies finally fail us, we just shed our corporeal ballast and travel to a land where we are reunited with everyone we loved while alive. Of course, overly rational people and other rabble will be kept out of this happy place, and those who suspended their disbelief while alive will be free to enjoy themselves for all eternity.

We live in a world of unimaginable surprises—from the fusion energy that lights the sun to the genetic and evolutionary consequences of these lights dancing for eons upon the Earth—and yet Paradise conforms to our most superficial concerns with all the fidelity of a Caribbean cruise. This is wondrously strange. If one didn't know better, one would think that man, in his fear of losing all that he loves, had created heaven, along with its gatekeeper God, in his own image.

Consider the destruction that Hurricane Katrina leveled on New Orleans. More than a thousand people died, tens of thousands lost all their earthly possessions, and nearly a million were displaced. It is safe to say that almost every person living in New Orleans at the moment Katrina struck believed in an omnipotent, omniscient and compassionate God. But what was God doing while a hurricane laid waste to their city? Surely he heard the prayers of those elderly men and women who fled the rising waters for the safety of their attics, only to be slowly drowned there. These were people of faith. These were good men and women who had prayed throughout their lives. Only the atheist has the courage to admit the obvious: These poor people died talking to an imaginary friend.

Of course, there had been ample warning that a storm of biblical proportions would strike New Orleans, and the human response to the ensuing disaster was tragically inept. But it was inept only by the light of science. Advance warning of Katrina's path was wrested from mute Nature by meteorological calculations and satellite imagery. God told no one of his plans. Had the residents of New Orleans been content to rely on the beneficence of the Lord, they wouldn't have known that a killer hurricane was bearing down upon them until they felt the first gusts of wind on their faces. Nevertheless, a poll conducted by *The Washington Post* found that 80% of Katrina's survivors claim that the event has only strengthened their faith in God.

As Hurricane Katrina was devouring New Orleans, nearly a thousand Shiite pilgrims were trampled to death on a bridge in Iraq. There can be no doubt that these pilgrims believed mightily in the God of the Koran: Their lives were organized around the indisputable fact of his existence; their women walked veiled before him; their men regularly murdered one another over rival interpretations of his word. It would be remarkable if a single survivor of this tragedy lost his faith. More likely, the survivors imagine that they were spared through God's grace.

Only the atheist recognizes the boundless narcissism and self-deceit of the saved. Only the atheist realizes how morally objectionable it is for survivors of a catastrophe to believe themselves spared by a loving God while this same God drowned infants in their cribs. Because he refuses to cloak the reality of the world's suffering in a cloying fantasy of eternal life, the atheist feels in his bones just how precious life is—and, indeed, how unfortunate it is that millions of human beings suffer the most harrowing abridgements of their happiness for no good reason at all.

One wonders just how vast and gratuitous a catastrophe would have to be to shake the world's faith. The Holocaust did not do it. Neither did the genocide in Rwanda, even with machete-wielding priests among the perpetrators. Five hundred million people died of smallpox in the 20th Century, many of them infants. God's ways are, indeed, inscrutable. It seems that any fact, no matter how infelicitous, can be rendered compatible with religious faith. In matters of faith, we have kicked ourselves loose of the Earth.

Of course, people of faith regularly assure one another that God is not responsible for human suffering. But how else can we understand the claim that God is both omniscient and omnipotent? There is no other way, and it is time for sane human beings to own up to this. This is the age-old problem of theodicy, of course, and we should consider it solved. If God exists, either he can do nothing to stop the most egregious calamities or he does not care to. God, therefore, is either impotent or evil. Pious readers will now execute the following pirouette: God cannot be judged by merely human standards of morality. But, of course, human standards of morality are precisely what the faithful use to establish God's goodness in the first place. And any God who could concern himself with something as trivial as gay marriage, or the name by which he is addressed in prayer, is not as inscrutable as all that. If he exists, the God of Abraham is not merely unworthy of the immensity of creation; he is unworthy even of man.

There is another possibility, of course, and it is both the most reasonable and least odious: te biblical God is a fiction. As Richard Dawkins has observed, we are all atheists with respect to Zeus and Thor. Only the atheist has realized that the biblical god is no different. Consequently, only the atheist is compassionate enough to take the profundity of the world's suffering at face value. It is terrible that we all die and lose everything we love; it is doubly terrible that so many human beings suffer needlessly while alive. That so much of this suffering can be directly attributed to religion—to religious hatreds, religious wars, religious delusions and religious diversions of scarce resources—is what makes atheism a moral and intellectual necessity. It is a necessity, however, that places the atheist at the margins of society. The atheist, by merely being in touch with reality, appears shamefully out of touch with the fantasy life of his neighbors.

The Nature of Belief

According to several recent polls, 22% of Americans are certain that Jesus will return to Earth sometime in the next 50 years. Another 22% believe that he will probably do so. This is likely the same 44% who go to church once a week or more, who believe that God literally promised the land of Israel to the Jews and who want to stop teaching our children about the biological fact of evolution. As President Bush is well aware, believers of this sort constitute the most cohesive and motivated segment of the American electorate. Consequently, their views and prejudices now influence almost every decision of national importance. Political liberals seem to have drawn the wrong lesson from these developments and are now thumbing Scripture, wondering how best to ingratiate themselves to the legions of men and women in our country who vote largely on the basis of religious dogma. More than 50% of Americans have a "negative" or "highly negative" view of people who do not believe in God; 70% think it important for presidential candidates to be "strongly religious." Unreason is now ascendant in the United States—in our schools, in our courts and in each branch of the federal government. Only 28% of Americans believe in evolution; 68% believe in Satan. Ignorance in this degree, concentrated in both the head and belly of a lumbering superpower, is now a problem for the entire world.

Although it is easy enough for smart people to criticize religious fundamentalism, something called "religious moderation" still enjoys immense prestige in our society, even in the ivory tower. This is ironic, as fundamentalists tend to make a more principled use of their brains than "moderates" do. While fundamentalists justify their religious beliefs with extraordinarily poor evidence and arguments, at least they make an attempt at rational justification. Moderates, on the other hand, generally do nothing more than cite the good consequences of religious belief. Rather than say that they believe in God because certain biblical prophecies have come true, moderates will say that they believe in God because this belief "gives their lives meaning." When a tsunami killed a few hundred thousand people on the day after Christmas, fundamentalists readily interpreted this cataclysm as evidence of God's wrath. As it turns out, God was sending humanity another oblique message about the evils of abortion, idolatry and homosexuality. While morally obscene, this interpretation of events is actually reasonable, given certain (ludicrous) assumptions. Moderates, on the other hand, refuse to draw any conclusions whatsoever about God from his works. God remains a perfect mystery, a mere source of consolation that is compatible with the most desolating evil. In the face of disasters like the Asian tsunami, liberal piety is apt to produce the most unctuous and stupefying nonsense imaginable. And yet, men and women of goodwill naturally prefer such vacuities to the odious moralizing and prophesizing of true believers. Between catastrophes, it is surely a virtue of liberal theology that it emphasizes mercy over wrath. It is worth noting, however, that it is human mercy on display—not God's—when the bloated bodies of the dead are pulled from the sea. On days when thousands of children are simultaneously torn from their mothers' arms and casually drowned, liberal theology must stand revealed for what it is—the sheerest of mortal pretenses. Even the theology of wrath has more intellectual merit. If God exists, his will is not inscrutable. The only thing inscrutable in these terrible events is that so many neurologically healthy men and women can believe the unbelievable and think this the height of moral wisdom.

It is perfectly absurd for religious moderates to suggest that a rational human being can believe in God simply because this belief makes him happy, relieves his fear of death or gives his life meaning. The absurdity becomes obvious the moment we swap the notion of God for some other consoling proposition: Imagine, for instance, that a man wants to believe that there is a diamond buried somewhere in his yard that is the size of a refrigerator. No doubt it would feel uncommonly good to believe this. Just imagine what would happen if he then followed the example of religious moderates and maintained this belief along pragmatic lines: When asked why he thinks that there is a diamond in his yard that is thousands of times larger than any yet discovered, he says things like, "This belief gives my life meaning," or "My family and I enjoy digging for it on Sundays," or "I wouldn't want to live in a universe where there wasn't a diamond buried in my backyard that is the size of a refrigerator." Clearly these responses are inadequate. But they are worse than that. They are the responses of a madman or an idiot.

Here we can see why Pascal's wager, Kierkegaard's leap of faith and other epistemological Ponzi schemes won't do. To believe that God exists is to believe that one stands in some relation to his existence such that his existence is itself the reason for one's belief. There must be some causal connection, or an appearance thereof, between the fact in question and a person's acceptance of it. In this way, we can see that religious beliefs, to be beliefs about the way the world is, must be as evidentiary in spirit as any other. For all their sins against reason, religious fundamentalists understand this; moderates—almost by definition—do not.

The incompatibility of reason and faith has been a self-evident feature of human cognition and public discourse for centuries. Either a person has good reasons for what he strongly believes or he does not. People of all creeds naturally recognize the primacy of reasons and resort to reasoning and evidence wherever they possibly can. When rational inquiry supports the creed it is always championed; when it poses a threat, it is derided; sometimes in the same sentence. Only when the evidence for a religious doctrine is thin or nonexistent, or there is compelling evidence against it, do its adherents invoke "faith." Otherwise, they simply cite the reasons for their beliefs (e.g. "the New Testament confirms Old Testament prophecy," "I saw the face of Jesus in a window," "We prayed, and our daughter's cancer went into remission"). Such reasons are generally inadequate, but they are better than no reasons at all. Faith is nothing more than the license religious people give themselves to keep believing when reason fail. In a world that has been shattered by mutually incompatible religious beliefs, in a nation that is growing increasingly beholden to Iron Age conceptions of God, the end of history and the immortality of the soul, this lazy partitioning of our discourse into matters of reason and matters of faith is now unconscionable.

Faith and the Good Society

People of faith regularly claim that atheism is responsible for some of the most appalling crimes of the 20th century. Although it is true that the regimes of Hitler, Stalin, Mao and Pol Pot were irreligious to varying degrees, they were not especially rational. In fact, their public pronouncements were little more than litanies of delusion—delusions about race, economics, national identity, the march of history or the moral dangers of intellectualism. In many respects, religion was directly culpable even here. Consider the Holocaust: The anti-Semitism that built the Nazi crematoria brick by brick was a direct inheritance from medieval Christianity. For centuries, religious Germans had viewed the Jews as the worst species of heretics and attributed every societal ill to their continued presence among the faithful. While the hatred of Jews in Germany expressed itself in a predominately secular way, the religious demonization of the Jews of Europe continued. (The Vatican itself perpetuated the blood libel in its newspapers as late as 1914.)

Auschwitz, the gulag and the killing fields are not examples of what happens when people become too critical of unjustified beliefs; to the contrary, these horrors testify to the dangers of not thinking critically enough about specific secular ideologies. Needless to say, a rational argument against religious faith is not an argument for the blind embrace of atheism as a dogma. The problem that the atheist exposes is none other than the problem of dogma itself—of which every religion has more than its fair share. There is no society in recorded history that ever suffered because its people became too reasonable.

While most Americans believe that getting rid of religion is an impossible goal, much of the developed world has already accomplished it. Any account of a "god gene" that causes the majority of Americans to helplessly organize their lives around ancient works of religious fiction must explain why so many inhabitants of other First World societies apparently lack such a gene. The level of atheism throughout the rest of the developed world refutes any argument that religion is somehow a moral necessity. Countries like Norway, Iceland, Australia, Canada, Sweden, Switzerland, Belgium, Japan, the Netherlands, Denmark and the United Kingdom are among the least religious societies on Earth. According to the United Nations' Human Development Report (2005) they are also the healthiest, as indicated by measures of life expectancy, adult literacy, per capita income, educational attainment, gender equality, homicide rate and infant mortality. Conversely, the 50 nations now ranked lowest in terms of human development are unwaveringly religious. Other analyses paint the same picture: the United States is unique among wealthy democracies in its level of religious literalism and opposition to evolutionary theory; it is also uniquely beleaguered by high rates of homicide, abortion, teen pregnancy, STD infection and infant mortality. The same comparison holds true within the United States itself: Southern and Midwestern states, characterized by the highest levels of religious superstition and hostility to evolutionary theory, are especially plagued by the above indicators of societal dysfunction, while the comparatively secular states of the Northeast conform to European norms. Of course, correlational data of this sort do not resolve questions of causality—belief in God may lead to societal dysfunction; societal dysfunction may foster a belief in God; each factor may enable the other; or both may spring from some deeper source of mischief. Leaving aside the issue of cause and effect, these facts prove that atheism is perfectly compatible with the basic aspirations of a civil society; they also prove, conclusively, that religious faith does nothing to ensure a society's health.

Countries with high levels of atheism also are the most charitable in terms of giving foreign aid to the developing world. The dubious link between Christian literalism and Christian values is also belied by other indices of charity. Consider the ratio in salaries between top-tier CEOs and their average employee: in Britain it is 24 to 1; France 15 to 1; Sweden 13 to 1; in the United States, where 83% of the population believes that Jesus literally rose from the dead, it is 475 to 1. Many a camel, it would seem, expects to squeeze easily through the eye of a needle.

Religion as a Source of Violence

One of the greatest challenges facing civilization in the 21st century is for human beings to learn to speak about their deepest personal concerns—about ethics, spiritual experience and the inevitability of human suffering—in ways that are not flagrantly irrational. Nothing stands in the way of this project more than the respect we accord religious faith. Incompatible religious doctrines have balkanized our world into separate moral communities—Christians, Muslims, Jews, Hindus, etc.—and these divisions have become a continuous source of human conflict. Indeed, religion is as much a living spring of violence today as it was at any time in the past. The recent conflicts in Palestine (Jews versus Muslims), the Balkans (Orthodox Serbians versus Catholic Croatians; Orthodox Serbians versus Bosnian and Albanian Muslims), Northern Ireland (Protestants versus Catholics), Kashmir (Muslims versus Hindus), Sudan (Muslims versus Christians and animists), Nigeria (Muslims versus Christians), Ethiopia and Eritrea (Muslims versus Christians), Sri Lanka (Sinhalese Buddhists versus Tamil Hindus), Indonesia (Muslims versus Timorese Christians), Iran and Iraq (Shiite versus Sunni Muslims), and the Caucasus (Orthodox Russians versus Chechen Muslims; Muslim Azerbaijanis versus Catholic and Orthodox Armenians) are merely a few cases in point. In these places religion has been the explicit cause of literally millions of deaths in the last 10 years.

In a world riven by ignorance, only the atheist refuses to deny the obvious: Religious faith promotes human violence to an astonishing degree. Religion inspires violence in at least two senses: (1) People often kill other human beings because they believe that the creator of the universe wants them to do it (the inevitable psychopathic corollary being that the act will ensure them an eternity of happiness after death). Examples of this sort of behavior are practically innumerable, jihadist suicide bombing being the most prominent. (2) Larger numbers of people are inclined toward religious conflict simply because their religion constitutes the core of their moral identities. One of the enduring pathologies of human culture is the tendency to raise children to fear and demonize other human beings on the basis of religion. Many religious conflicts that seem driven by terrestrial concerns, therefore, are religious in origin. (Just ask the Irish.)

These facts notwithstanding, religious moderates tend to imagine that human conflict is always reducible to a lack of education, to poverty or to political grievances. This is one of the many delusions of liberal piety. To dispel it, we need only reflect on the fact that the Sept. 11 hijackers were college educated and middle class and had no discernable history of political oppression. They did, however, spend an inordinate amount of time at their local mosque talking about the depravity of infidels and about the pleasures that await martyrs in Paradise. How many more architects and mechanical engineers must hit the wall at 400 miles an hour before we admit to ourselves that jihadist violence is not a matter of education, poverty or politics? The truth, astonishingly enough, is this: a person can be so well educated that he can build a nuclear bomb while still believing that he will get 72 virgins in Paradise. Such is the ease with which the human mind can be partitioned by faith, and such is the degree to which our intellectual discourse still patiently accommodates religious delusion. Only the atheist has observed what should now be obvious to every thinking human being: If we want to uproot the causes of religious violence we must uproot the false certainties of religion.

Why is religion such a potent source of human violence?

Our religions are intrinsically incompatible with one another. Either Jesus rose from the dead and will be returning to Earth like a superhero or not; either the Koran is the infallible word of God or it isn't. Every religion makes explicit claims about the way the world is, and the sheer profusion of these incompatible claims creates an enduring basis for conflict.

There is no other sphere of discourse in which human beings so fully articulate their differences from one another, or cast these differences in terms of everlasting rewards and punishments. Religion is the one endeavor in which us-them thinking achieves a transcendent significance. If a person really believes that calling God by the right name can spell the difference between eternal happiness and eternal suffering, then it becomes quite reasonable to treat heretics and unbelievers rather badly.

It may even be reasonable to kill them. If a person thinks there is something that another person can say to his children that could put their souls in jeopardy for all eternity, then the heretic next door is actually far more dangerous than the child molester. The stakes of our religious differences are immeasurably higher than those born of mere tribalism, racism or politics.

Religious faith is a conversation-stopper. Religion is only area of our discourse in which people are systematically protected from the demand to give evidence in defense of their strongly held beliefs. And yet these beliefs often determine what they live for, what they will die for, and—all too often—what they will kill for. This is a problem, because when the stakes are high, human beings have a simple choice between conversation and violence. Only a fundamental willingness to be reasonable—to have our beliefs about the world revised by new evidence and new arguments—can guarantee that we will keep talking to one another. Certainty without evidence is necessarily divisive and dehumanizing. While there is no guarantee that rational people will always agree, the irrational are certain to be divided by their dogmas.

It seems profoundly unlikely that we will heal the divisions in our world simply by multiplying the opportunities for interfaith dialogue. The endgame for civilization cannot be mutual tolerance of patent irrationality. While all parties to liberal religious discourse have agreed to tread lightly over those points where their worldviews would otherwise collide, these very points remain perpetual sources of conflict for their coreligionists. Political correctness, therefore, does not offer an enduring basis for human cooperation. If religious war is ever to become unthinkable for us, in the way that slavery and cannibalism seem poised to, it will be a matter of our having dispensed with the dogma of faith.

When we have reasons for what we believe, we have no need of faith; when we have no reasons, or bad ones, we have lost our connection to the world and to one another. Atheism is nothing more than a commitment to the most basic standard of intellectual honesty: one's convictions should be proportional to one's evidence. Pretending to be certain when one isn't—indeed, pretending to be certain about propositions for which no evidence is even conceivable—is both an intellectual and a moral failing. Only the atheist has realized this. The atheist is simply a person who has perceived the lies of religion and refused to make them his own.

31
Why There Almost Certainly Is No God (2006)
Richard Dawkins

> The priests of the different religious sects…dread the advance of science as witches do the approach of daylight, and scowl on the fatal harbinger announcing the subdivision of the duperies on which they live. —Thomas Jefferson

The Ultimate Boeing 747

The argument from improbability is the big one. In the traditional guise of the argument from design, it is easily today's most popular argument offered in favour of the existence of God and it is seen, by an amazingly large number of theists, as completely and utterly convincing. It is indeed a very strong and, I suspect, unanswerable argument—but in precisely the opposite direction from the theist's intention. The argument from improbability, properly deployed, comes close to proving that God does *not* exist. My name for the statistical demonstration that God almost certainly does not exist is the Ultimate Boeing 747 gambit.

The name comes from Fred Hoyle's amusing image of the Boeing 747 and the scrapyard. I am not sure whether Hoyle ever wrote it down himself, but it was attributed to him by his close colleague Chandra Wickramasinghe and is presumably authentic.[1] Hoyle said that the probability of life originating on Earth is no greater than the chance that a hurricane, sweeping through a scrapyard, would have the luck to assemble a Boeing 747. Others have borrowed the metaphor to refer to the later evolution of complex living bodies, where it has a spurious plausibility. The odds against assembling a fully functioning horse, beetle or ostrich by randomly shuffling its parts are up there in 747 territory. This, in a nutshell, is the creationist's favourite argument—an argument that could be made only by somebody who doesn't understand the first thing about natural selection: somebody who thinks natural selection is a theory of chance whereas—in the relevant sense of chance—it is the opposite.

The creationist misappropriation of the argument from improbability always takes the same general form, and it doesn't make any difference if the creationist chooses to masquerade in the politically expedient fancy dress of 'intelligent design' (ID).[2] Some observed phenomenon—often a living creature or one of its more complex organs, but it could be anything from a molecule up to the universe itself—is correctly extolled as statistically improbable. Sometimes the language of information theory is used: the Darwinian is challenged to explain the source of all the information in living matter, in the technical sense of information content as a measure of improbability or 'surprise value.' Or the argument may invoke the economist's hackneyed motto: there's no such thing as a free lunch—and Darwinism is accused of trying to get something for nothing. In fact, as I shall show in this chapter, Darwinian natural selection is the only known solution to the otherwise unanswerable riddle of where the information comes from. It turns out to be the God Hypothesis that tries to get something for nothing. God tries to have his free lunch and be it too. However statistically improbable the entity you seek to explain by invoking a designer, the designer himself has got to be at least as improbable. God is the Ultimate Boeing 747.

The argument from improbability states that complex things could not have come about by chance. But many people define "come about by chance" as a synonym for "come about in the absence of deliberate design." Not surprisingly, therefore, they think improbability is evidence of design. Darwinian natural selection shows how wrong this is with respect to biological improbability. And although Darwinism may not be directly relevant to the inanimate world—cosmology, for example—it raises our consciousness in areas outside its original territory of biology.

A deep understanding of Darwinism teaches us to be wary of the easy assumption that design is the only alternative to chance, and teaches us to seek out graded ramps of slowly increasing complexity. Before Darwin, philosophers such as Hume understood that the improbability of life did not mean it had to be designed, but they couldn't imagine the alternative. After Darwin, we all should feel, deep in our bones, suspicious of the very idea of design. The illusion of design is a trap that has caught us before, and Darwin should have immunized us by raising our consciousness. Would that he had succeeded with all of us.

Natural Selection as a Consciousness-Raiser

In a science fiction starship, the astronauts were homesick: "Just to think that it's springtime back on Earth!" You may not immediately see what's wrong with this, so deeply ingrained is the unconscious northern hemisphere chauvinism in those of us who live there, and even some who don't. 'Unconscious' is exactly right. That is where consciousness-raising comes in. It is for a deeper reason than gimmicky fun that, in Australia and New Zealand, you can buy maps of the world with the South Pole on top. What splendid consciousness-raisers those maps would be, pinned to the walls of our northern hemisphere classrooms. Day after day, the children would be reminded that 'north' is an arbitrary polarity which has no monopoly on 'up.' The map would intrigue them as well as raise their consciousness. They'd go home and tell their parents—and, by the way, giving children something with which to surprise their parents is one of the greatest gifts a teacher can bestow.

It was the feminists who raised my consciousness of the power of consciousness-raising. 'Herstory' is obviously ridiculous, if only because the 'his' in 'history' has no etymological connection with the masculine pronoun. It is as etymologically silly as the sacking, in 1999, of a Washington official whose use of 'niggardly' was held to give racial offence. But even daft examples like 'niggardly' or 'herstory' succeed in raising consciousness. Once we have smoothed our philological hackles and stopped laughing, herstory shows us history from a different point of view. Gendered pronouns notoriously are the front line of such consciousness-raising. He or she must ask himself or herself whether his or her sense of style could ever allow himself or herself to write like this. But if we can just get over the clunking infelicity of the language, it raises our consciousness to the sensitivities of half the human race. Man, mankind, the Rights of Man, all men are created equal, one man one vote—English too often seems to exclude woman.[3] When I was young, it never occurred to me that women might feel slighted by a phrase like 'the future of man.' During the intervening decades, we have all had our consciousness raised. Even those who still use 'man' instead of 'human' do so with an air of self-conscious apology—or truculence, taking a stand for traditional language, even deliberately to rile feminists. All participants in the *Zeitgeist* have had their consciousness raised, even those who choose to respond negatively by digging in their heels and redoubling the offence.

Feminism shows us the power of consciousness-raising, and I want to borrow the technique for natural selection. Natural selection not only explains the whole of life; it also raises our consciousness to the power of science to explain how organized complexity can emerge from simple beginnings without any deliberate guidance. A full understanding of natural selection encourages us to move boldly into other fields. It arouses our suspicion, in those other fields, of the kind of false alternatives that once, in pre-Darwinian days, beguiled biology. Who, before Darwin, could have guessed that something so apparently *designed* as a dragonfly's wing or an eagle's eye was really the end product of a long sequence of non-random but purely natural causes?

Douglas Adams's moving and funny account of his own conversion to radical atheism—he insisted on the 'radical' in case anybody should mistake him for an agnostic—is testimony to the power of Darwinism as a consciousness-raiser. I hope I shall be forgiven the self-indulgence that will become apparent in the following quotation. My excuse is that Douglas's conversion by my earlier books—which did not set out to convert anyone—inspired me to dedicate to his memory this book—which does! In an interview, reprinted posthumously in *The Salmon of Doubt,* he was asked by a journalist how he became an atheist. He began his reply by explaining how he became an agnostic, and then proceeded:

> And I thought and thought and thought. But I just didn't have enough to go on, so I didn't really come to any resolution. I was extremely doubtful about the idea of god, but I just didn't know enough about anything to have a good working model of any other explanation for, well, life, the universe, and everything to put in its place. But I kept at it, and I kept reading and I kept thinking. Sometime around my early thirties I stumbled upon evolutionary biology, particularly in the form of Richard Dawkins's books *The Selfish Gene* and then *The Blind Watchmaker,* and suddenly (on, I think the second reading of *The Selfish Gene)* it all fell into place. It was a concept of such stunning simplicity, but it gave rise, naturally, to all of the infinite and baffling complexity of life. The awe it inspired in me made the awe that people talk about in respect of religious experience seem, frankly, silly beside it. I'd take the awe of understanding over the awe of ignorance any day.[4]

The concept of stunning simplicity that he was talking about was, of course, nothing to do with me. It was Darwin's theory of evolution by natural selection—the ultimate scientific consciousness-raiser. Douglas, I miss you. You are my cleverest, funniest, most open-minded, wittiest, tallest, and possibly only convert. I hope this book might have made you laugh—though not as much as you made me.

That scientifically savvy philosopher Daniel Dennett pointed out that evolution counters one of the oldest ideas we have: "The idea that it takes a big fancy smart thing to make a lesser thing. I call that the trickle-down theory of creation. You'll never see a spear making a spear maker. You'll never see a horse shoe making a blacksmith. You'll never see a pot making a potter."[5] Darwin's discovery of a workable process that does that very counterintuitive thing is what makes his contribution to human thought so revolutionary, and so loaded with the power to raise consciousness.

It is surprising how necessary such consciousness-raising is, even in the minds of excellent scientists in fields other than biology. Fred Hoyle was a brilliant physicist and cosmologist, but his Boeing 747 misunderstanding, and other mistakes in biology such as his attempt to dismiss the fossil *Archaeopteryx* as a hoax, suggest that he needed to have his consciousness raised by some good exposure to the world of natural selection. At an intellectual level, I suppose he understood natural selection. But perhaps you need to be steeped in natural selection, immersed in it, swim about in it, before you can truly appreciate its power.

Other sciences raise our consciousness in different ways. Fred Hoyle's own science of astronomy puts us in our place, metaphorically as well as literally, scaling down our vanity to fit the tiny stage on which we play out our lives—our speck of debris from the cosmic explosion. Geology reminds us of our brief existence both as individuals and as a species. It raised John Ruskin's consciousness and provoked his memorable heart cry of 1851: "If only the Geologists would let me alone, I could do very well, but those dreadful hammers! I hear the clink of them at the end of every cadence of the Bible verses." Evolution does the same thing for our sense of time—not surprisingly, since it works on the geological timescale. But Darwinian evolution, specifically natural selection, does something more. It shatters the illusion of design within the domain of biology, and teaches us to be suspicious of any kind of design hypothesis in physics and cosmology as well. I think the physicist Leonard Susskind had this in mind when he wrote, "I'm not an historian but I'll venture an opinion: Modern cosmology really began with Darwin and Wallace. Unlike anyone before them, they provided explanations of our existence that completely rejected supernatural agents ... Darwin and Wallace set a standard not only for the life sciences but for cosmology as well."[6] Other physical scientists who are far above needing any such consciousness-raising are Victor Stenger, whose book *Has Science Found God?* (the answer is no) I strongly recommend, and Peter Atkins, whose *Creation Revisited* is my favourite work of scientific prose poetry.

I am continually astonished by those theists who, far from having their consciousness raised in the way that I propose, seem to rejoice in natural selection as "God's way of achieving his creation." They note that evolution by natural selection would be a very easy and neat way to achieve a world full of life. God wouldn't need to do anything at all! Peter Atkins, in the book just mentioned, takes this line of thought to a sensibly godless conclusion when he postulates a hypothetically lazy God who tries to get away with as little as possible in order to make a universe containing life. Atkins's lazy God is even lazier than the deist God of the eighteenth-century Enlightenment: *deus otiosus*—literally

God at leisure, unoccupied, unemployed, superfluous, useless. Step by step, Atkins succeeds in reducing the amount of work the lazy God has to do until he finally ends up doing nothing at all: he might as well not bother to exist. My memory vividly hears Woody Allen's perceptive whine: "If it turns out that there is a God, I don't think that he's evil. But the worst that you can say about him is that basically he's an underachiever."

Irreducible Complexity

It is impossible to exaggerate the magnitude of the problem that Darwin and Wallace solved. I could mention the anatomy, cellular structure, biochemistry and behaviour of literally any living organism by example. But the most striking feats of apparent design are those picked out—for obvious reasons—by creationist authors, and it is with gentle irony that I derive mine from a creationist book. *Life—How Did It Get Here?*, with no named author but published by the Watchtower Bible and Tract Society in sixteen languages and eleven million copies, is obviously a firm favourite because no fewer than six of those eleven million copies have been sent to me as unsolicited gifts by well-wishers from around the world.

Picking a page at random from this anonymous and lavishly distributed work, we find the sponge known as Venus' Flower Basket *(Euplectella)*, accompanied by a quotation from Sir David Attenborough, no less: "When you look at a complex sponge skeleton such as that made of silica spicules which is known as Venus' Flower Basket, the imagination is baffled. How could quasi-independent microscopic cells collaborate to secrete a million glassy splinters and construct such an intricate and beautiful lattice? We do not know." The Watchtower authors lose no time in adding their own punchline: "But one thing we do know: Chance is not the likely designer." No indeed, chance is not the likely designer. That is one thing on which we can all agree. The statistical improbability of phenomena such as *Euplectella's* skeleton is the central problem that any theory of life must solve. The greater the statistical improbability, the less plausible is chance as a solution: that is what improbable means. But the candidate solutions to the riddle of improbability are not, as is falsely implied, design and chance. They are design and natural selection. Chance is not a solution, given the high levels of improbability we see in living organisms, and no sane biologist ever suggested that it was. Design is not a real solution either, as we shall see later; but for the moment I want to continue demonstrating the problem that any theory of life must solve: the problem of how to escape from chance.

Turning Watchtower's page, we find the wonderful plant known as Dutchman's Pipe *(Aristolochia trilobata)*, all of whose parts seem elegantly designed to trap insects, cover them with pollen and send them on their way to another Dutchman's Pipe. The intricate elegance of the flower moves Watchtower to ask: "Did all of this happen by chance? Or did it happen by intelligent design?" Once again, no of *course* it didn't happen by chance. Once again, intelligent design is not the proper alternative to chance. Natural selection is not only a parsimonious, plausible and elegant solution; it is the only workable alternative to chance that has ever been suggested. Intelligent design suffers from exactly the same objection as chance. It is simply not a plausible solution to the riddle of statistical improbability. And the higher the improbability, the more implausible intelligent design becomes. Seen clearly, intelligent design will turn out to be a redoubling of the problem. Once again, this is because the designer himself (/herself/itself) immediately raises the bigger problem of his own origin. Any entity capable of intelligently designing something as improbable as a Dutchman's Pipe (or a universe) would have to be even more improbable than a Dutchman's Pipe. Far from terminating the vicious regress, God aggravates it with a vengeance.

Turn another Watchtower page for an eloquent account of the giant redwood *(Sequoiadendron giganteum),* a tree for which I have a special affection because I have one in my garden—a mere baby, scarcely more than a century old, but still the tallest tree in the neighbourhood. "A puny man, standing at a sequoia's base, can only gaze upward in silent awe at its massive grandeur. Does it make sense to believe that the shaping of this majestic giant and of the tiny seed that packages it was not by design?" Yet again, if you think the only alternative to design is chance then, no, it does not make sense. But again the authors omit all mention of the real alternative, natural selection, either because they genuinely don't understand it or because they don't want to.

The process by which plants, whether tiny pimpernels or massive wellingtonias, acquire the energy to build themselves is photosynthesis. Watchtower again: "There are about seventy separate chemical reactions involved in photosynthesis," one biologist said. "It is truly a miraculous event." Green plants have been called nature's "factories"—beautiful, quiet, nonpolluting, producing oxygen, recycling water and feeding the world. Did they just happen by chance? Is that truly believable?' No, it is not believable; but the repetition of example after example gets us nowhere. Creationist 'logic' is always the same. Some natural phenomenon is too statistically improbable, too complex, too beautiful, too awe-inspiring to have come into existence by chance. Design is the only alternative to chance that the authors can imagine. Therefore a designer must have done it. And science's answer to this faulty logic is also always the same. Design is not the only alternative to chance. Natural selection is a better alternative. Indeed, design is not a real alternative at all because it raises an even bigger problem than it solves: who designed the designer? Chance and design both fail as solutions to the problem of statistical improbability, because one of them is the problem, and the other one regresses to it. Natural selection is a real solution. It is the only workable solution that has ever been suggested. And it is not only a workable solution, it is a solution of stunning elegance and power.

What is it that makes natural selection succeed as a solution to the problem of improbability, where chance and design both fail at the starting gate? The answer is that natural selection is a cumulative process, which breaks the problem of improbability up into small pieces. Each of the small pieces is slightly improbable, but not prohibitively so. When large numbers of these slightly improbable events are stacked up in series, the end product of the accumulation is very very improbable indeed, improbable enough to be far beyond the reach of chance. It is these end products that form the subjects of the creationist's wearisomely recycled argument. The creationist completely misses the point, because he (women should for once not mind being excluded by the pronoun) insists on treating the genesis of statistical improbability as a single, one-off event. He doesn't understand the power of *accumulation.*

In *Climbing Mount Improbable*, I expressed the point in a parable. One side of the mountain is a sheer cliff, impossible to climb, but on the other side is a gentle slope to the summit. On the summit sits a complex device such as an eye or a bacterial flagellar motor. The absurd notion that such complexity could spontaneously self-assemble is symbolized by leaping from the foot of the cliff to the top in one bound. Evolution, by contrast, goes around the back of the mountain and creeps up the gentle slope to the summit: easy! The principle of climbing the gentle slope as opposed to leaping up the precipice is so simple, one is tempted to marvel that it took so long for a Darwin to arrive on the scene and discover it. By the time he did, nearly three centuries had elapsed since Newton's *annus mirabilis,* although his achievement seems, on the face of it, harder than Darwin's.

Another favourite metaphor for extreme improbability is the combination lock on a bank vault. Theoretically, a bank robber could get lucky and hit upon the right combination of numbers by chance. In practice, the bank's combination lock is designed with enough improbability to make this tantamount to impossible—almost as unlikely as Fred Hoyle's Boeing 747. But imagine a badly designed combination lock that gave out little hints progressively—the equivalent of the 'getting warmer' of children playing Hunt the Slipper. Suppose that when each one of the dials approaches its correct setting, the vault door opens another chink, and a dribble of money trickles out. The burglar would home in on the jackpot in no time.

Creationists who attempt to deploy the argument from improbability in their favour always assume that biological adaptation is a question of the jackpot or nothing. Another name for the 'jackpot or nothing' fallacy is 'irreducible complexity' (IC). Either the eye sees or it doesn't. Either the wing flies or it doesn't. There are assumed to be no useful intermediates. But this is simply wrong. Such intermediates abound in practice—which is exactly what we should expect in theory. The combination lock of life is a "getting warmer, getting cooler, getting warmer" Hunt the Slipper device. Real life seeks the gentle slopes at the back of Mount Improbable, while creationists are blind to all but the daunting precipice at the front.

Darwin devoted an entire chapter of the *Origin of Species* to "Difficulties on the theory of descent with modification," and it is fair to say that this brief chapter anticipated and disposed of every single one of the alleged difficulties that have since been proposed, right up to the present day. The most formidable difficulties are Darwin's 'organs of extreme perfection and complication,' sometimes erroneously described as 'irreducibly complex.' Darwin singled out the eye as posing a particularly challenging problem: "To suppose that the eye with all its inimitable contrivances for adjusting the focus to different distances, for admitting different amounts of light, and for the correction of spherical and chromatic aberration, could have been formed by natural selection, seems, I freely confess, absurd in the highest degree." Creationists gleefully quote this sentence again and again. Needless to say, they never quote what follows. Darwin's fulsomely free confession turned out to be a rhetorical device. He was drawing his opponents towards him so that his punch, when it came, struck the harder. The punch, of course, was Darwin's effortless explanation of exactly how the eye evolved by gradual degrees. Darwin may not have used the phrase 'irreducible complexity,' or 'the smooth gradient up Mount Improbable,' but he clearly understood the principle of both.

"What is the use of half an eye?" and "What is the use of half a wing?" are both instances of the argument from 'irreducible complexity.' A functioning unit is said to be irreducibly complex if the removal of one of its parts causes the whole to cease functioning. This has been assumed to be self-evident for both eyes and wings. But as soon as we give these assumptions a moment's thought, we immediately see the fallacy. A cataract patient with the lens of her eye surgically removed can't see clear images without glasses, but can see enough not to bump into a tree or fall over a cliff. Half a wing is indeed not as good as a whole wing, but it is certainly better than no wing at all. Half a wing could save your life by easing your fall from a tree of a certain height. And 51 per cent of a wing could save you if you fall from a slightly taller tree.

Whatever fraction of a wing you have, there is a fall from which it will save your life where a slightly smaller winglet would not. The thought experiment of trees of different height, from which one might fall, is just one way to see, in theory, that there must be a smooth gradient of advantage all the way from 1 per cent of a wing to 100 per cent. The forests are replete with gliding or parachuting animals illustrating, in practice, every step of the way up that particular slope of Mount Improbable.

By analogy with the trees of different height, it is easy to imagine situations in which half an eye would save the life of an animal where 49 per cent of an eye would not. Smooth gradients are provided by variations in lighting conditions, variations in the distance at which you catch sight of your prey—or your predators. And, as with wings and flight surfaces, plausible intermediates are not only easy to imagine: they are abundant all around the animal kingdom. A flatworm has an eye that, by any sensible measure, is less than half a human eye. *Nautilus* (and perhaps its extinct ammonite cousins who dominated Paleozoic and Mesozoic seas) has an eye that is intermediate in quality between flatworm and human. Unlike the flatworm eye, which can detect light and shade but see no image, the *Nautilus* 'pinhole camera' eye makes a real image; but it is a blurred and dim image compared to ours. It would be spurious precision to put numbers on the improvement, but nobody could sanely deny that these invertebrate eyes, and many others, are all better than no eye at all, and all lie on a continuous and shallow slope up Mount Improbable, with our eyes near a peak—not the highest peak but a high one. In *Climbing Mount Improbable,* I devoted a whole chapter each to the eye and the wing, demonstrating how easy it was for them to evolve by slow (or even, maybe, not all that slow) gradual degrees, and I will leave the subject here.

So, we have seen that eyes and wings are certainly not irreducibly complex; but what is more interesting than these particular examples is the general lesson we should draw. The fact that so many people have been dead wrong over these obvious cases should serve to warn us of other examples that are less obvious, such as the cellular and biochemical cases now being touted by those creationists who shelter under the politically expedient euphemism of 'intelligent design theorists.'

We have a cautionary tale here, and it is telling us this: do not just declare things to be irreducibly complex; the chances are that you haven't looked carefully enough at the details, or thought carefully enough about them. On the other hand, we on the science side must not be too dogmatically confident. Maybe there is something out there in nature that really does preclude, by its *genuinely* irreducible complexity, the smooth gradient of Mount Improbable. The creationists are right that, if genuinely irreducible complexity could be properly demonstrated, it would wreck Darwin's theory. Darwin himself said as much: "If it could be demonstrated that any complex organ existed which could not possibly have been formed by numerous, successive, slight modifications, my theory would absolutely break down. But I can find no such case." Darwin could find no such case, and nor has anybody since Darwin's time, despite strenuous, indeed desperate, efforts. Many candidates for this holy grail of creationism have been proposed. None has stood up to analysis.

In any case, even though genuinely irreducible complexity would wreck Darwin's theory if it were ever found, who is to say that it wouldn't wreck the intelligent design theory as well? Indeed, it already *has* wrecked the intelligent design theory, for, as I keep saying and will say again, however little we know about God, the one thing we can be sure of is that he would have to be very very complex and presumably irreducibly so!

The Worship of Gaps

Searching for particular examples of irreducible complexity is a fundamentally unscientific way to proceed: a special case of arguing from present ignorance. It appeals to the same faulty logic as "the God of the Gaps" strategy condemned by the theologian Dietrich Bonhoeffer. Creationists eagerly seek a gap in present-day knowledge or understanding. If an apparent gap is found, it is *assumed* that God, by default, must fill it. What worries thoughtful theologians such as Bonhoeffer is that gaps shrink as science advances, and God is threatened with eventually having nothing to do and nowhere to hide. What worries scientists is something else. It is an essential part of the scientific enterprise to admit ignorance, even to exult in ignorance as a challenge to future conquests. As my friend Matt Ridley has written, "Most scientists are bored by what they have already discovered. It is ignorance that drives them on." Mystics exult in mystery and want it to stay mysterious. Scientists exult in mystery for a different reason: it gives them something to do. More generally, as I shall repeat in Chapter 8, one of the truly bad effects of religion is that it teaches us that it is a virtue to be satisfied with not understanding.

Admissions of ignorance and temporary mystification are vital to good science. It is therefore unfortunate, to say the least, that the main strategy of creation propagandists is the negative one of seeking out gaps in scientific knowledge and claiming to fill them with 'intelligent design' by default. The following is hypothetical but entirely typical. A creationist speaking: "The elbow joint of the lesser spotted weasel frog is irreducibly complex. No part of it would do any good at all until the whole was assembled. Bet you can't think of a way in which the weasel frog's elbow could have evolved by slow gradual degrees." If the scientist fails to give an immediate and comprehensive answer, the creationist draws a *default* conclusion: "Right then, the alternative theory, 'intelligent design,' wins by default." Notice the biased logic: if theory A fails in some particular, theory B must be right. Needless to say, the argument is not applied the other way around. We are encouraged to leap to the default theory without even looking to see whether it fails in the very same particular as the theory it is alleged to replace. Intelligent design—ID—is granted a Get Out Of Jail Free card, a charmed immunity to the rigorous demands made of evolution.

But my present point is that the creationist ploy undermines the scientist's natural —indeed necessary—rejoicing in (temporary) uncertainty. For purely political reasons, today's scientist might hesitate before saying: "Tim, interesting point. I wonder how the weasel frog's ancestors *did* evolve their elbow joint. I'm not a specialist in weasel frogs, I'll have to go to the University Library and take a look. Might make an interesting project for a graduate student." The moment a scientist said something like that—and long before the student began the project—the default conclusion would become a headline in a creationist pamphlet: "Weasel frog could only have been designed by God."

There is, then, an unfortunate hook-up between science's methodological need to seek out areas of ignorance in order to target research, and ID's need to seek out areas of ignorance in order to claim victory by default. It is precisely the fact that ID has no evidence of its own, but thrives like a weed in gaps left by scientific knowledge, that sits uneasily with science's need to identify and proclaim the very same gaps as a prelude to researching them. In this respect, science finds itself in alliance with sophisticated theologians like Bonhoeffer, united against the common enemies of naïve, populist theology and the gap theology of intelligent design.

The creationists' love affair with 'gaps' in the fossil record symbolizes their whole gap theology. I once introduced a chapter on the so-called Cambrian Explosion with the sentence, "It is as though the fossils were planted there without any evolutionary history." Again, this was a rhetorical overture, intended to whet the reader's appetite for the full explanation that was to follow. Sad hindsight tells me now how predictable it was that my patient explanation would be excised and my overture itself gleefully quoted out of context. Creationists adore 'gaps' in the fossil record, just as they adore gaps generally.

Many evolutionary transitions are elegantly documented by more or less continuous series of gradually changing intermediate fossils. Some are not, and these are the famous 'gaps.' Michael Shermer has wittily pointed out that if a new fossil discovery neatly bisects a 'gap,' the creationist will declare that there are now twice as many gaps! But in any case, note yet again the unwarranted use of a default. If there are no fossils to document a postulated evolutionary transition, the default assumption is that there was no evolutionary transition, therefore God must have intervened.

It is utterly illogical to demand complete documentation of every step of any narrative, whether in evolution or any other science. You might as well demand, before convicting somebody of murder, a complete cinematic record of the murderer's every step leading up to the crime, with no missing frames. Only a tiny fraction of corpses fossilize, and we are lucky to have as many intermediate fossils as we do. We could easily have had no fossils at all, and still the evidence for evolution from other sources, such as molecular genetics and geographical distribution, would be overwhelmingly strong. On the other hand, evolution makes the strong prediction that if a *single* fossil turned up in the *wrong* geological stratum, the theory would be blown out of the water. When challenged by a zealous Popperian to say how evolution could ever be falsified, J.B.S. Haldane famously growled: "Fossil rabbits in the Precambrian." No such anachronistic fossils have ever been authentically found, despite discredited creationist legends of human skulls in the Coal Measures and human footprints interspersed with dinosaurs.

Gaps, by default in the mind of the creationist, are filled by God. The same applies to all apparent precipices on the massif of Mount Improbable, where the graded slope is not immediately obvious or is otherwise overlooked. Areas where there is a lack of data, or a lack of understanding, are automatically assumed to belong, by default, to God. The speedy resort to a dramatic proclamation of 'irreducible complexity' represents a failure of the imagination. Some biological organ, if not an eye then a bacterial flagellar motor or a biochemical pathway, is *decreed* without further argument to be irreducibly complex. No attempt is made to *demonstrate* irreducible complexity. Notwithstanding the cautionary tales of eyes, wings and many other things, each new candidate for the dubious accolade is assumed to be transparently, self-evidently irreducibly complex, its status asserted by fiat. But think about it. Since irreducible complexity is being deployed as an argument for design, it should no more be asserted by fiat than design itself. You might as well simply assert that the weasel frog (bombardier beetle, etc.) demonstrates design, without further argument or justification. That is no way to do science.

The logic turns out to be no more convincing than this: "I [insert own name] am personally unable to think of any way in which [insert biological phenomenon] could have been built up step by step. Therefore it is irreducibly complex. That means it is designed." Put it like that, and you immediately see that it is vulnerable to some scientist coming along and finding an intermediate; or at least imagining a plausible intermediate. Even if no scientists do come up with an explanation, it is plain bad logic to assume that 'design' will fare any better. The reasoning that underlies 'intelligent design' theory is lazy and defeatist—classic "God of the Gaps" reasoning. I have previously dubbed it the Argument from Personal Incredulity.

Imagine that you are watching a really great magic trick. The celebrated conjuring duo Penn and Teller have a routine in which they simultaneously appear to shoot each other with pistols, and each appears to catch the bullet in his teeth. Elaborate precautions are taken to scratch identifying marks on the bullets before they are put in the guns, the whole procedure is witnessed at close range by volunteers from the audience who have experience of firearms, and apparently all possibilities for trickery are eliminated. Teller's marked bullet ends up in Penn's mouth and Penn's marked bullet ends up in Teller's. I [Richard Dawkins] am utterly unable to think of any way in which this could be a trick. The Argument from Personal Incredulity screams from the depths of my prescientific brain centres, and almost compels me to say, "It must be a miracle. There is no scientific explanation. It's got to be supernatural." But the still small voice of scientific education speaks a different message. Penn and Teller are world-class illusionists. There is a perfectly good explanation. It is just that I am too naïve, or too unobservant, or too unimaginative, to think of it. That is the proper response to a conjuring trick. It is also the proper response to a biological phenomenon that appears to be irreducibly complex. Those people who leap from personal bafflement at a natural phenomenon straight to a hasty invocation of the supernatural are no better than the fools who see a conjuror bending a spoon and leap to the conclusion that it is 'paranormal.'

In his book *Seven Clues to the Origin of Life,* the Scottish chemist A. G. Cairns-Smith makes an additional point, using the analogy of an arch. A free-standing arch of rough-hewn stones and no mortar can be a stable structure, but it is irreducibly complex: it collapses if any one stone is removed. How, then, was it built in the first place? One way is to pile a solid heap of stones, then carefully remove stones one by one. More generally, there are many structures that are irreducible in the sense that they cannot survive the subtraction of any part, but which were built with the aid of scaffolding that was subsequently subtracted and is no longer visible. Once the structure is completed, the scaffolding can be removed safely and the structure remains standing. In evolution, too, the organ or structure you are looking at may have had scaffolding in an ancestor which has since been removed.

'Irreducible complexity' is not a new idea, but the phrase itself was invented by the creationist Michael Behe in 1996.[7] He is credited (if credited is the word) with moving creationism into a new area of biology: biochemistry and cell biology, which he saw as perhaps a happier hunting ground for gaps than eyes or wings. His best approach to a good example (still a bad one) was the bacterial flagellar motor.

The flagellar motor of bacteria is a prodigy of nature. It drives the only known example, outside human technology, of a freely rotating axle. Wheels for big animals would, I suspect, be genuine examples of irreducible complexity, and this is probably why they don't exist. How would the nerves and blood vessels get across the bearing?[8] The flagellum is a thread-like propeller, with which the bacterium burrows its way through the water. I say 'burrows' rather than 'swims' because, on the bacterial scale of existence, a liquid such as water would not feel as a liquid feels to us. It would feel more like treacle, or jelly, or even sand, and the bacterium would seem to burrow or screw its way through the water rather than swim. Unlike the so-called flagellum of larger organisms like protozoans, the bacterial flagellum doesn't just wave about like a whip, or row like an oar. It has a true, freely rotating axle which turns continuously inside a bearing, driven by a remarkable little molecular motor. At the molecular level, the motor uses essentially the same principle as muscle, but in free rotation rather than in intermittent contraction.[9] It has been happily described as a tiny outboard motor (although by engineering standards—and unusually for a biological mechanism—it is a spectacularly inefficient one).

Without a word of justification, explanation or amplification, Behe simply *proclaims* the bacterial flagellar motor to be irreducibly complex. Since he offers no argument in favour of his assertion, we may begin by suspecting a failure of his imagination. He further alleges that specialist biological literature has ignored the problem. The falsehood of this allegation was massively and (to Behe) embarrassingly documented in the court of Judge John E. Jones in Pennsylvania in 2005, where Behe was testifying as an expert witness on behalf of a group of creationists who had tried to impose 'intelligent design' creationism on the science curriculum of a local public school—a move of 'breathtaking inanity,' to quote Judge Jones (phrase and man surely destined for lasting fame). This wasn't the only embarrassment Behe suffered at the hearing, as we shall see.

The key to demonstrating irreducible complexity is to show that none of the parts could have been useful on its own. They all needed to be in place before any of them could do any good (Behe's favourite analogy is a mousetrap). In fact, molecular biologists have no difficulty in finding parts functioning outside the whole, both for the flagellar motor and for Behe's other alleged examples of irreducible complexity. The point is well put by Kenneth Miller of Brown University, for my money the most persuasive nemesis of 'intelligent design,' not least because he is a devout Christian. I frequently recommend Miller's book, *Finding Darwin's God,* to religious people who write to me having been bamboozled by Behe.

In the case of the bacterial rotary engine, Miller calls our attention to a mechanism called the Type Three Secretory System or TTSS.[10] The TTSS is not used for rotatory movement. It is one of several systems used by parasitic bacteria for pumping toxic substances through their cell walls to poison their host organism. On our human scale, we might think of pouring or squirting a liquid through a hole; but, once again, on the bacterial scale things look different. Each molecule of secreted substance is a large protein with a definite, three-dimensional structure on the same scale as the TTSS's own: more like a solid sculpture than a liquid. Each molecule is individually propelled through a carefully shaped mechanism, like an automated slot machine dispensing, say, toys or bottles, rather than a simple hole through which a substance might 'flow.' The goods-dispenser itself is made of a rather small number of protein molecules, each one comparable in size and complexity to the molecules being dispensed through it. Interestingly, these bacterial slot machines are often similar across bacteria that are not closely related. The genes for making them have probably been 'copied and pasted' from other bacteria: something that bacteria are remarkably adept at doing, and a fascinating topic in its own right, but I must press on.

The protein molecules that form the structure of the TTSS are very similar to components of the flagellar motor. To the evolutionist it is clear that TTSS components were commandeered for a new, but not wholly unrelated, function when the flagellar motor evolved. Given that the TTSS is tugging molecules through itself, it is not surprising that it uses a rudimentary version of the principle used by the flagellar motor, which tugs the molecules of the axle round and round. Evidently, crucial components of the flagellar motor were already in place and working before the flagellar motor evolved. Commandeering existing mechanisms is an obvious way in which an apparently irreducibly complex piece of apparatus could climb Mount Improbable.

A lot more work needs to be done, of course, and I'm sure it will be. Such work would never be done if scientists were satisfied with a lazy default such as 'intelligent design theory' would encourage. Here is the message that an imaginary 'intelligent design theorist' might broadcast to scientists: "If you don't understand how something works, never mind: just give up and say God did it. You don't know how the nerve impulse works? Good! You don't understand how memories are laid down in the brain? Excellent! Is photosynthesis a bafflingly complex process? Wonderful! Please don't go to work on the problem, just give up, and appeal to God. Dear scientist, don't *work* on your mysteries. Bring us your mysteries, for we can use them. Don't squander precious ignorance by researching it away. We need those glorious gaps as a last refuge for God." St Augustine said it quite openly: "There is another form of temptation, even more fraught with danger. This is the disease of curiosity. It is this which drives us to try and discover the secrets of nature, those secrets which are beyond our understanding, which can avail us nothing and which man should not wish to learn" (quoted in Freeman 2002).

Another of Behe's favourite alleged examples of 'irreducible complexity' is the immune system. Let Judge Jones himself take up the story:

> In fact, on cross-examination, Professor Behe was questioned concerning his 1996 claim that science would never find an evolutionary explanation for the immune system. He was presented with fifty-eight peer-reviewed publications, nine books, and several immunology textbook chapters about the evolution of the immune system; however, he simply insisted that this was still not sufficient evidence of evolution, and that it was not 'good enough.'

Behe, under cross-examination by Eric Rothschild, chief counsel for the plaintiffs, was forced to admit that he hadn't read most of those fifty-eight peer-reviewed papers. Hardly surprising, for immunology is hard work. Less forgivable is that Behe dismissed such research as 'unfruitful.' It certainly is unfruitful if your aim is to make propaganda among gullible laypeople and politicians, rather than to discover important truths about the real world. After listening to Behe, Rothschild eloquently summed up what every honest person in that courtroom must have felt:

> Thankfully, there are scientists who do search for answers to the question of the origin of the immune system . . . It's our defense against debilitating and fatal diseases. The scientists who wrote those books and articles toil in obscurity, without book royalties or speaking engagements. Their efforts help us combat and cure serious medical conditions. By contrast, Professor Behe and the entire intelligent design movement are doing nothing to advance scientific or medical knowledge and are telling future generations of scientists, don't bother.[11]

As the American geneticist Jerry Coyne put it in his review of Behe's book: "If the history of science shows us anything, it is that we get nowhere by labelling our ignorance 'God.'" Or, in the words of an eloquent blogger, commenting on an article on intelligent design in the *Guardian* by Coyne and me,

> Why is God considered an explanation for anything? It's not—it's a failure to explain, a shrug of the shoulders, an 'I dunno' dressed up in spirituality and ritual. If someone credits something to God, generally what it means is that they haven't a clue, so they're attributing it to an unreachable, unknowable sky-fairy. Ask for an explanation of where that bloke came from, and odds are you'll get a vague, pseudo-philosophical reply about having always existed, or being outside nature. Which, of course, explains nothing.[12]

Darwinism raises our consciousness in other ways. Evolved organs, elegant and efficient as they often are, also demonstrate revealing flaws—exactly as you'd expect if they have an evolutionary history, and exactly as you would not expect if they were designed. I have discussed examples in other books: the recurrent laryngeal nerve, for one, which betrays its evolutionary history in a massive and wasteful detour on its way to its destination. Many of our human ailments, from lower back pain to hernias, prolapsed uteruses and our susceptibility to sinus infections, result directly from the fact that we now walk upright with a body that was shaped over hundreds of millions of years to walk on all fours. Our consciousness is also raised by the cruelty and wastefulness of natural selection. Predators seem beautifully 'designed' to catch prey animals, while the prey animals seem equally beautifully 'designed' to escape them. Whose side is God on?[13]

The Anthropic Principle: Planetary Version

Gap theologians who may have given up on eyes and wings, flagellar motors and immune systems, often pin their remaining hopes on the origin of life. The root of evolution in non-biological chemistry somehow seems to present a bigger gap than any particular transition during subsequent evolution. And in one sense it is a bigger gap. That one sense is quite specific, and it offers no comfort to the religious apologist. The origin of life only had to happen once. We therefore can allow it to have been an extremely improbable event, many orders of magnitude more improbable than most people realize, as I shall show. Subsequent evolutionary steps are duplicated, in more or less similar ways, throughout millions and millions of species independently, and continually and repeatedly throughout geological time. Therefore, to explain the evolution of complex life, we cannot resort to the same kind of statistical reasoning as we are able to apply to the origin of life. The events that constitute run-of-the-mill evolution, as distinct from its singular origin (and perhaps a few special cases), cannot have been very improbable.

This distinction may seem puzzling, and I must explain it further, using the so-called anthropic principle. The anthropic principle was named by the British mathematician Brandon Carter in 1974 and expanded by the physicists John Barrow and Frank Tipler in their book on the subject.[14] The anthropic argument is usually applied to the cosmos, and I'll come to that. But I'll introduce the idea on a smaller, planetary scale. We exist here on Earth. Therefore Earth must be the kind of planet that is capable of generating and supporting us, however unusual, even unique, that kind of planet might be. For example, our kind of life cannot survive without liquid water. Indeed, exobiologists searching for evidence of extraterrestrial life are scanning the heavens, in practice, for signs of water. Around a typical star like our sun, there is a so-called Goldilocks zone—not too hot and not too cold, but just right—for planets with liquid water. A thin band of orbits lies between those that are too far from the star, where water freezes, and too close, where it boils.

Presumably, too, a life-friendly orbit has to be nearly circular. A fiercely elliptical orbit, like that of the newly discovered tenth planet informally known as Xena, would at best allow the planet to whizz briefly through the Goldilocks zone once every few (Earth) decades or centuries. Xena itself doesn't get into the Goldilocks zone at all, even at its closest approach to the sun, which it reaches once every 560 Earth years. The temperature of Halley's Comet varies between about 47°C at perihelion and minus 270°C at aphelion. Earth's orbit, like those of all the planets, is technically an ellipse (it is closest to the sun in January and furthest away in July[15]); but a circle is a special case of an ellipse, and Earth's orbit is so close to circular that it never strays out of the Goldilocks zone. Earth's situation in the solar system is propitious in other ways that singled it out for the evolution of life. The massive gravitational vacuum cleaner of Jupiter is well placed to intercept asteroids that might otherwise threaten us with lethal collision. Earth's single relatively large moon serves to stabilize our axis of rotation,[16] and helps to foster life in various other ways. Our sun is unusual in not being a binary, locked in mutual orbit with a companion star. It is possible for binary stars to have planets, but their orbits are likely to be too chaotically variable to encourage the evolution of life.

Two main explanations have been offered for our planet's peculiar friendliness to life. The design theory says that God made the world, placed it in the Goldilocks zone, and deliberately set up all the details for our benefit. The anthropic approach is very different, and it has a faintly Darwinian feel. The great majority of planets in the universe are not in the Goldilocks zones of their respective stars, and not suitable for life. None of that majority has life. However small the minority of planets with just the right conditions for life may be, we necessarily have to be on one of that minority, because here we are thinking about it.

It is a strange fact, incidentally, that religious apologists love the anthropic principle. For some reason that makes no sense at all, they think it supports their case. Precisely the opposite is true. The anthropic principle, like natural selection, is an *alternative* to the design hypothesis. It provides a rational, design-free explanation for the fact that we find ourselves in a situation propitious to our existence. I think the confusion arises in the religious mind because the anthropic principle is only ever mentioned in the context of the problem that it solves, namely the fact that we live in a life-friendly place. What the religious mind then fails to grasp is that two candidate solutions are offered to the problem. God is one. The anthropic principle is the other. They are *alternatives.*

Liquid water is a necessary condition for life as we know it, but it is far from sufficient. Life still has to originate in the water, and the origin of life may have been a highly improbable occurrence. Darwinian evolution proceeds merrily once life has originated. But how does life get started? The origin of life was the chemical event, or series of events, whereby the vital conditions for natural selection first came about. The major ingredient was heredity, either DNA or (more probably) something that copies like DNA but less accurately, perhaps the related molecule RNA. Once the vital ingredient—some kind of genetic molecule—is in place, true Darwinian natural selection can follow, and complex life emerges as the eventual consequence. But the spontaneous arising by chance of the first hereditary molecule strikes many as improbable. Maybe it is—very very improbable, and I shall dwell on this, for it is central to this section of the book.

The origin of life is a flourishing, if speculative, subject for research. The expertise required for it is chemistry and it is not mine. I watch from the sidelines with engaged curiosity, and I shall not be surprised if, within the next few years, chemists report that they have successfully midwifed a new origin of life in the laboratory. Nevertheless it hasn't happened yet, and it is still possible to maintain that the probability of its happening is, and always was, exceedingly low—although it did happen once!

Just as we did with the Goldilocks orbits, we can make the point that, however improbable the origin of life might be, we know it happened on Earth because we are here. Again as with temperature, there are two hypotheses to explain what happened—the design hypothesis and the scientific or 'anthropic' hypothesis. The design approach postulates a God who wrought a deliberate miracle, struck the prebiotic soup with divine fire and launched DNA, or something equivalent, on its momentous career.

Again, as with Goldilocks, the anthropic alternative to the design hypothesis is statistical. Scientists invoke the magic of large numbers. It has been estimated that there are between 1 billion and 30 billion planets in our galaxy, and about 100 billion galaxies in the universe. Knocking a few noughts off for reasons of ordinary prudence, a billion billion is a conservative estimate of the number of available planets in the universe. Now, suppose the origin of life, the spontaneous arising of something equivalent to DNA, really was a quite staggeringly improbable event. Suppose it was so improbable as to occur on only one in a billion planets. A grant-giving body would laugh at any chemist who admitted that the chance of his proposed research succeeding was only one in a hundred. But here we are talking about odds of one in a billion. And yet...even with such absurdly long odds, life will still have arisen on a billion planets—of which Earth, of course, is one.[17]

This conclusion is so surprising, I'll say it again. If the odds of life originating spontaneously on a planet were a billion to one against, nevertheless that stupefyingly improbable event would still happen on a billion planets. The chance of finding any one of those billion life-bearing planets recalls the proverbial needle in a haystack. But we don't have to go out of our way to find a needle because (back to the anthropic principle) any beings capable of looking must necessarily be sitting on one of those prodigiously rare needles before they even start the search.

Any probability statement is made in the context of a certain level of ignorance. If we know nothing about a planet, we may postulate the odds of life's arising on it as, say, one in a billion. But if we now import some new assumptions into our estimate, things change. A particular planet may have some peculiar properties, perhaps a special profile of element abundances in its rocks, which shift the odds in favour of life's emerging. Some planets, in other words, are more 'Earth-like' than others. Earth itself, of course, is especially Earth-like! This should give encouragement to our chemists trying to recreate the event in the lab, for it could shorten the odds against their success. But my earlier calculation demonstrated that even a chemical model with odds of success as low as one in a billion would *still* predict that life would arise on a billion planets in the universe. And the beauty of the anthropic principle is that it tells us, against all intuition, that a chemical model need only predict that life will arise on *one* planet in a billion billion to give us a good and entirely satisfying explanation for the presence of life here. I do not for a moment believe the origin of life was anywhere near so improbable in practice. I think it is definitely worth spending money on trying to duplicate the event in the lab and—by the same token, on SETI, because I think it is likely that there is intelligent life elsewhere.

Even accepting the most pessimistic estimate of the probability that life might spontaneously originate, this statistical argument completely demolishes any suggestion that we should postulate design to fill the gap. Of all the apparent gaps in the evolutionary story, the origin of life gap can seem unbridgeable to brains calibrated to assess likelihood and risk on an everyday scale: the scale on which grant-giving bodies assess research proposals submitted by chemists. Yet even so big a gap as this is easily filled by statistically informed science, while the very same statistical science rules out a divine creator on the "Ultimate 747" grounds we met earlier.

But now, to return to the interesting point that launched this section. Suppose somebody tried to explain the general phenomenon of biological adaptation along the same lines as we have just applied to the origin of life: appealing to an immense number of available planets. The observed fact is that every species, and every organ that has ever been looked at within every species, is good at what it does. The wings of birds, bees and bats are good at flying. Eyes are good at seeing. Leaves are good at photosynthesizing. We live on a planet where we are surrounded by perhaps ten million species, each one of which independently displays a powerful illusion of apparent design. Each species is well fitted to its particular way of life. Could we get away with the "huge numbers of planets" argument to explain all these separate illusions of design? No, we could not, repeat *not*. Don't even think about it. This is important, for it goes to the heart of the most serious misunderstanding of Darwinism.

It doesn't matter how many planets we have to play with, lucky chance could never be enough to explain the lush diversity of living complexity on Earth in the same way as we used it to explain the existence of life here in the first place. The evolution of life is a completely different case from the origin of life because, to repeat, the origin of life was (or could have been) a unique event which had to happen only once. The adaptive fit of species to their separate environments, on the other hand, is millionfold, and ongoing.

It is clear that here on Earth we are dealing with a generalized process for optimizing biological species, a process that works all over the planet, on all continents and islands, and at all times. We can safely predict that, if we wait another ten million years, a whole new set of species will be as well adapted to their ways of life as today's species are to theirs. This is a recurrent, predictable, multiple phenomenon, not a piece of statistical luck recognized with hindsight. And, thanks to Darwin, we know how it is brought about: by natural selection.

The anthropic principle is impotent to explain the multifarious details of living creatures. We really need Darwin's powerful crane to account for the diversity of life on Earth, and especially the persuasive illusion of design. The origin of life, by contrast, lies outside the reach of that crane, because natural selection cannot proceed without it. Here the anthropic principle comes into its own. We can deal with the unique origin of life by postulating a very large number of planetary opportunities. Once that initial stroke of luck has been granted—and the anthropic principle most decisively grants it to us—natural selection takes over: and natural selection is emphatically not a matter of luck.

Nevertheless, it may be that the origin of life is not the only major gap in the evolutionary story that is bridged by sheer luck, anthropically justified. For example, my colleague Mark Ridley in *Mendel's Demon* (gratuitously and confusingly retitled *The Cooperative Gene* by his American publishers) has suggested that the origin of the eucaryotic cell (our kind of cell, with a nucleus and various other complicated features such as mitochondria, which are not present in bacteria) was an even more momentous, difficult and statistically improbable step than the origin of life. The origin of consciousness might be another major gap whose bridging was of the same order of improbability. One-off events like this might be explained by the anthropic principle, along the following lines. There are billions of planets that have developed life at the level of bacteria, but only a fraction of these life forms ever made it across the gap to something like the eucaryotic cell. And of these, a yet smaller fraction managed to cross the later Rubicon to consciousness. If both of these are one-off events, we are not dealing with a ubiquitous and all-pervading *process,* as we are with ordinary, run-of-the- mill biological adaptation. The anthropic principle states that, since we are alive, eucaryotic and conscious, our planet has to be one of the intensely rare planets that has bridged all three gaps.

Natural selection works because it is a cumulative one-way street to improvement. It needs some luck to get started, and the " billions of planets' anthropic principle grants it that luck. Maybe a few later gaps in the evolutionary story also need major infusions of luck, with anthropic justification. But whatever else we may say, *design* certainly does not work as an explanation for life, because design is ultimately not cumulative and it therefore raises bigger questions than it answers—it takes us straight back along the Ultimate 747 infinite regress.

We live on a planet that is friendly to our kind of life, and we have seen two reasons why this is so. One is that life has evolved to flourish in the conditions provided by the planet. This is because of natural selection. The other reason is the anthropic one. There are billions of planets in the universe, and, however small the minority of evolution-friendly planets may be, our planet necessarily has to be one of them. Now it is time to take the anthropic principle back to an earlier stage, from biology back to cosmology.

The Anthropic Principle: Cosmological Version

We live not only on a friendly planet but also in a friendly universe. It follows from the fact of our existence that the laws of physics must be friendly enough to allow life to arise. It is no accident that when we look at the night sky we see stars, for stars are a necessary prerequisite for the existence of most of the chemical elements, and without chemistry there could be no life. Physicists have calculated that, if the laws and constants of physics had been even slightly different, the universe would have developed in such a way that life would have been impossible. Different physicists put it in different ways, but the conclusion is always much the same. Martin Rees, in *Just Six Numbers,* lists six fundamental constants, which are believed to hold all around the universe. Each of these six numbers is finely tuned in the sense that, if it were slightly different, the universe would be comprehensively different and presumably unfriendly to life.[18]

An example of Rees's six numbers is the magnitude of the so-called 'strong' force, the force that binds the components of an atomic nucleus: the nuclear force that has to be overcome when one " splits' the atom. It is measured as E, the proportion of the mass of a hydrogen nucleus that is converted to energy when hydrogen fuses to form helium. The value of this number in our universe is 0.007, and it looks as though it had to be very close to this value in order for any chemistry (which is a prerequisite for life) to exist. Chemistry as we know it consists of the combination and recombination of the ninety or so naturally occurring elements of the periodic table. Hydrogen is the simplest and commonest of the elements. All the other elements in the universe are made ultimately from hydrogen by nuclear fusion. Nuclear fusion is a difficult process which occurs in the intensely hot conditions of the interiors of stars (and in hydrogen bombs). Relatively small stars, such as our sun, can make only light elements such as helium, the second lightest in the periodic table after hydrogen. It takes larger and hotter stars to develop the high temperatures needed to forge most of the heavier elements, in a cascade of nuclear fusion processes whose details were worked out by Fred Hoyle and two colleagues (an achievement for which, mysteriously, Hoyle was not given a share of the Nobel Prize received by the others). These big stars may explode as supernovas, scattering their materials, including the elements of the periodic table, in dust clouds. These dust clouds eventually condense to form new stars and planets, including our own. This is why Earth is rich in elements over and above the ubiquitous hydrogen: elements without which chemistry, and life, would be impossible.

The relevant point here is that the value of the strong force crucially determines how far up the periodic table the nuclear fusion cascade goes. If the strong force were too small, say 0.006 instead of 0.007, the universe would contain nothing but hydrogen, and no interesting chemistry could result. If it were too large, say 0.008, all the hydrogen would have fused to make heavier elements. A chemistry without hydrogen could not generate life as we know it. For one thing, there would be no water. The Goldilocks value—0.007—is just right for yielding the richness of elements that we need for an interesting and life-supporting chemistry.

I won't go through the rest of Rees's six numbers. The bottom line for each of them is the same. The actual number sits in a Goldilocks band of values outside which life would not have been possible. How should we respond to this? Yet again, we have the theist's answer on the one hand, and the anthropic answer on the other. The theist says that God, when setting up the universe, tuned the fundamental constants of the universe so that each one lay in its Goldilocks zone for the production of life. It is as though God had six knobs that he could twiddle, and he carefully tuned each knob to its Goldilocks value. As ever, the theist's answer is deeply unsatisfying, because it leaves the existence of God unexplained. A God capable of calculating the Goldilocks values for the six numbers would have to be at least as improbable as the finely tuned combination of numbers itself, and that's very improbable indeed—which is indeed the premise of the whole discussion we are having. It follows that the theist's answer has utterly failed to make any headway towards solving the problem at hand. I see no alternative but to dismiss it, while at the same time marvelling at the number of people who can't see the problem and seem genuinely satisfied by the "Divine Knob-Twiddler" argument.

Maybe the psychological reason for this amazing blindness has something to do with the fact that many people have not had their consciousness raised, as biologists have, by natural selection and its power to tame improbability. J. Anderson Thomson, from his perspective as an evolutionary psychiatrist, points me to an additional reason, the psychological bias that we all have towards personifying inanimate objects as agents. As Thomson says, we are more inclined to mistake a shadow for a burglar than a burglar for a shadow. A false positive might be a waste of time. A false negative could be fatal. In a letter to me, he suggested that, in our ancestral past, our greatest challenge in our environment came from each other. "The legacy of that is the default assumption, often fear, of human intention. We have a great deal of difficulty seeing anything other than *human* causation." We naturally generalized that to divine intention.

Biologists, with their raised consciousness of the power of natural selection to explain the rise of improbable things, are unlikely to be satisfied with any theory that evades the problem of improbability altogether. And the theistic response to the riddle of improbability is an evasion of stupendous proportions. It is more than a restatement of the problem, it is a grotesque amplification of it. Let's turn, then, to the anthropic alternative. The anthropic answer, in its most general form, is that we could only be discussing the question in the kind of universe that was capable of producing us. Our existence therefore determines that the fundamental constants of physics had to be in their respective Goldilocks zones. Different physicists espouse different kinds of anthropic solutions to the riddle of our existence.

Hard-nosed physicists say that the six knobs were never free to vary in the first place. When we finally reach the long-hoped-for Theory of Everything, we shall see that the six key numbers depend upon each other, or on something else as yet unknown, in ways that we today cannot imagine. The six numbers may turn out to be no freer to vary than is the ratio of a circle's circumference to its diameter. It will turn out that there is only one way for a universe to be. Far from God being needed to twiddle six knobs, there are no knobs to twiddle.

Other physicists (Martin Rees himself would be an example) find this unsatisfying, and I think I agree with them. It is indeed perfectly plausible that there is only one way for a universe to be. But why did that one way have to be such a set-up for our eventual evolution? Why did it have to be the kind of universe which seems almost as if, in the words of the theoretical physicist Freeman Dyson, it "must have known we were coming?" The philosopher John Leslie uses the analogy of a man sentenced to death by firing squad. It is just possible that all ten men of the firing squad will miss their victim. With hindsight, the survivor who finds himself in a position to reflect upon his luck can cheerfully say, "Well, obviously they all missed, or I wouldn't be here thinking about it." But he could still, forgivably, wonder why they all missed, and toy with the hypothesis that they were bribed, or drunk.

This objection can be answered by the suggestion, which Martin Rees himself supports, that there are many universes, co-existing like bubbles of foam, in a "multiverse" (or "megaverse," as Leonard Susskind prefers to call it).[19] The laws and constants of any one universe, such as our observable universe, are by-laws. The multi-verse as a whole has a plethora of alternative sets of by-laws. The anthropic principle kicks in to explain that we have to be in one of those universes (presumably a minority) whose by-laws happened to be propitious to our eventual evolution and hence contemplation of the problem.

An intriguing version of the multiverse theory arises out of considerations of the ultimate fate of our universe. Depending upon the values of numbers such as Martin Rees's six constants, our universe may be destined to expand indefinitely, or it may stabilize at an equilibrium, or the expansion may reverse itself and go into contraction, culminating in the so-called 'big crunch.' Some big crunch models have the universe then bouncing back into expansion, and so on indefinitely with, say, a 20-billion-year cycle time. The standard model of our universe says that time itself began in the big bang, along with space, some 13 billion years ago. The serial big crunch model would amend that statement: our time and space did indeed begin in our big bang, but this was just the latest in a long series of big bangs, each one initiated by the big crunch that terminated the previous universe in the series. Nobody understands what goes on in singularities such as the big bang, so it is conceivable that the laws and constants are reset to new values, each time. If bang—expansion—contraction—crunch cycles have been going on for ever like a cosmic accordion, we have a serial, rather than a parallel, version of the multiverse. Once again, the anthropic principle does its explanatory duty. Of all the universes in the series, only a minority have their 'dials' tuned to biogenic conditions. And, of course, the present universe has to be one of that minority, because we are in it. As it turns out, this serial version of the multiverse must now be judged less likely than it once was, because recent evidence is starting to steer us away from the big crunch model. It now looks as though our own universe is destined to expand for ever.

Another theoretical physicist, Lee Smolin, has developed a tantalizingly Darwinian variant on the multiverse theory, including both serial and parallel elements. Smolin's idea, expounded in *The Life of the Cosmos*, hinges on the theory that daughter universes are born of parent universes, not in a fully fledged big crunch but more locally in black holes. Smolin adds a form of heredity: the fundamental constants of a daughter universe are slightly 'mutated' versions of the constants of its parent. Heredity is the essential ingredient of Darwinian natural selection, and the rest of Smolin's theory follows naturally. Those universes that have what it takes to 'survive' and 'reproduce' come to predominate in the multiverse. 'What it takes' includes lasting long enough to 'reproduce.' Because the act of reproduction takes place in black holes, successful universes must have what it takes to make black holes. This ability entails various other properties. For example, the tendency for matter to condense into clouds and then stars is a prerequisite to making black holes. Stars also, as we have seen, are the precursors to the development of interesting chemistry, and hence life. So, Smolin suggests, there has been a Darwinian natural selection of universes in the multiverse, directly favouring the evolution of black hole fecundity and indirectly favouring the production of life. Not all physicists are enthusiastic about Smolin's idea, although the Nobel Prize-winning physicist Murray Gell-Mann is quoted as saying: " Smolin? Is he that young guy with those crazy ideas? He may not be wrong.[20] A mischievous biologist might wonder whether some other physicists are in need of Darwinian consciousness-raising.

It is tempting to think (and many have succumbed) that to postulate a plethora of universes is a profligate luxury which should not be allowed. If we are going to permit the extravagance of a multiverse, so the argument runs, we might as well be hung for a sheep as a lamb and allow a God. Aren't they both equally unparsimonious ad hoc hypotheses, and equally unsatisfactory? People who think that have not had their consciousness raised by natural selection. The key difference between the genuinely extravagant God hypothesis and the apparently extravagant multi-verse hypothesis is one of statistical improbability. The multiverse, for all that it is extravagant, is simple. God, or any intelligent, decision-taking, calculating agent, would have to be highly improbable in the very same statistical sense as the entities he is supposed to explain. The multiverse may seem extravagant in sheer *number* of universes. But if each one of those universes is simple in its fundamental laws, we are still not postulating anything highly improbable. The very opposite has to be said of any kind of intelligence.

Some physicists are known to be religious (Russell Stannard and the Reverend John Polkinghorne are the two British examples I have mentioned). Predictably, they seize upon the improbability of the physical constants all being tuned in their more or less narrow Goldilocks zones, and suggest that there must be a cosmic intelligence who deliberately did the tuning. I have already dismissed all such suggestions as raising bigger problems than they solve. But what attempts have theists made to reply? How do they cope with the argument that any God capable of designing a universe, carefully and foresightfully tuned to lead to our evolution, must be a supremely complex and improbable entity who needs an even bigger explanation than the one he is supposed to provide?

The theologian Richard Swinburne, as we have learned to expect, thinks he has an answer to this problem, and he expounds it in his book *Is There a God?*. He begins by showing that his heart is in the right place by convincingly demonstrating why we should always prefer the simplest hypothesis that fits the facts. Science explains complex things in terms of the interactions of simpler things, ultimately the interactions of fundamental particles. I (and I dare say you) think it a beautifully simple idea that all things are made of fundamental particles which, although exceedingly numerous, are drawn from a small, finite set of *types* of particle. If we are sceptical, it is likely to be because we think the idea too simple. But for Swinburne it is not simple at all, quite the reverse.

Given that the number of particles of any one type, say electrons, is large, Swinburne thinks it too much of a coincidence that so many should have the same properties. One electron, he could stomach. But billions and billions of electrons, *all with the same properties*, that is what really excites his incredulity. For him it would be simpler, more natural, less demanding of explanation, if all electrons were different from each other. Worse, no one electron should naturally retain its properties for more than an instant at a time; each should change capriciously, haphazardly and fleetingly from moment to moment. That is Swinburne's view of the simple, native state of affairs. Anything more uniform (what you or I would call more simple) requires a special explanation. "It is only because electrons and bits of copper and all other material objects have the same powers in the twentieth century as they did in the nineteenth century that things are as they are now."

Enter God. God comes to the rescue by deliberately and continuously sustaining the properties of all those billions of electrons and bits of copper, and neutralizing their otherwise ingrained inclination to wild and erratic fluctuation. That is why when you've seen one electron you've seen them all; that is why bits of copper all behave like bits of copper, and that is why each electron and each bit of copper stays the same as itself from microsecond to microsecond and from century to century. It is because God constantly keeps a finger on each and every particle, curbing its reckless excesses and whipping it into line with its colleagues to keep them all the same.

But how can Swinburne possibly maintain that this hypothesis of God simultaneously keeping a gazillion fingers on wayward electrons is a *simple* hypothesis? It is, of course, precisely the opposite of simple. Swinburne pulls off the trick to his own satisfaction by a breathtaking piece of intellectual *chutzpah*. He asserts, without justification, that God is only a *single* substance. What brilliant economy of explanatory causes, compared with all those gigazillions of independent electrons all just happening to be the same!

Theism claims that every other object which exists is caused to exist and kept in existence by just one substance, God. And it claims that every property which every substance has is due to God causing or permitting it to exist. It is a hallmark of a simple explanation to postulate few causes. There could in this respect be no simpler explanation than one which postulated only one cause. Theism is simpler than polytheism. And theism postulates for its one cause, a person [with] infinite power (God can do anything logically possible), infinite knowledge (God knows everything logically possible to know), and infinite freedom.

Swinburne generously concedes that God cannot accomplish feats that are *logically* impossible, and one feels grateful for this forbearance. Having said that, there is no limit to the explanatory purposes to which God's infinite power is put. Is science having a little difficulty explaining X? No problem. Don't give X another glance. God's infinite power is effortlessly wheeled in to explain X (along with everything else), and it is always a supremely *simple* explanation because, after all, there is only one God. What could be simpler than that?

Well, actually, almost everything. A God capable of continuously monitoring and controlling the individual status of every particle in the universe *cannot* be simple. His existence is going to need a mammoth explanation in its own right. Worse (from the point of view of simplicity), other corners of God's giant consciousness are simultaneously preoccupied with the doings and emotions and prayers of every single human being—and whatever intelligent aliens there might be on other planets in this and 100 billion other galaxies. He even, according to Swinburne, has to decide continuously *not* to intervene miraculously to save us when we get cancer. That would never do, for, "If God answered most prayers for a relative to recover from cancer, then cancer would no longer be a problem for humans to solve." And *then* what would we find to do with our time?

Not all theologians go as far as Swinburne. Nevertheless, the remarkable suggestion that the God Hypothesis is *simple* can be found in other modern theological writings. Keith Ward, then Regius Professor of Divinity at Oxford, was very clear on the matter in his 1996 book *God, Chance and Necessity*:

> As a matter of fact, the theist would claim that God is a very elegant, economical and fruitful explanation for the existence of the universe. It is economical because it attributes the existence and nature of absolutely everything in the universe to just one being, an ultimate cause which assigns a reason for the existence of everything, including itself. It is elegant because from one key idea—the idea of the most perfect possible being—the whole nature of God and the existence of the universe can be intelligibly explicated.

Like Swinburne, Ward mistakes what it means to explain something, and he also seems not to understand what it means to say of something that it is simple. I am not clear whether Ward really thinks God is simple, or whether the above passage represented a temporary 'for the sake of argument' exercise. Sir John Polkinghorne, in *Science and Christian Belief*, quotes Ward's earlier criticism of the thought of Thomas Aquinas: "Its basic error is in supposing that God is logically simple—simple not just in the sense that his being is indivisible, but in the much stronger sense that what is true of any part of God is true of the whole. It is quite coherent, however, to suppose that God, while indivisible, is internally complex." Ward gets it right here. Indeed, the biologist Julian Huxley, in 1912, defined complexity in terms of "heterogeneity of parts," by which he meant a particular kind of functional indivisibility.[21]

Elsewhere, Ward gives evidence of the difficulty the theological mind has in grasping where the complexity of life comes from. He quotes another theologian-scientist, the biochemist Arthur Peacocke (the third member of my trio of British religious scientists), as postulating the existence in living matter of a "propensity for increased complexity." Ward characterizes this as "some inherent weighting of evolutionary change which favours complexity." He goes on to suggest that such a bias "might be some weighting of the mutational process, to ensure that more complex mutations occurred." Ward is sceptical of this, as well he should be. The evolutionary drive towards complexity comes, in those lineages where it comes at all, not from any inherent propensity for increased complexity, and not from biased mutation. It comes from natural selection: the process which, as far as we know, is the only process ultimately capable of generating complexity out of simplicity. The theory of natural selection is genuinely simple. So is the origin from which it starts. That which it explains, on the other hand, is complex almost beyond telling: more complex than anything we can imagine, save a God capable of designing it.

An Interlude at Cambridge

At a recent Cambridge conference on science and religion, where I put forward the argument I am here calling the Ultimate 747 argument, I encountered what, to say the least, was a cordial failure to achieve a meeting of minds on the question of God's simplicity. The experience was a revealing one, and I'd like to share it.

First I should confess (that is probably the right word) that the conference was sponsored by the Templeton Foundation. The audience was a small number of hand-picked science journalists from Britain and America. I was the token atheist among the eighteen invited speakers. One of the journalists, John Horgan, reported that they had each been paid the handsome sum of $15,000 to attend the conference, on top of all expenses. This surprised me. My long experience of academic conferences included no instances where the audience (as opposed to the speakers) was paid to attend. If I had known, my suspicions would immediately have been aroused. Was Templeton using his money to suborn science journalists and subvert their scientific integrity? John Horgan later wondered the same thing and wrote an article about his whole experience.[22] In it he revealed, to my chagrin, that my advertised involvement as a speaker had helped him and others to overcome their doubts:

> The British biologist Richard Dawkins, whose participation in the meeting helped convince me and other fellows of its legitimacy, was the only speaker who denounced religious beliefs as incompatible with science, irrational, and harmful. The other speakers—three agnostics, one Jew, a deist, and 12 Christians (a Muslim philosopher canceled at the last minute)—offered a perspective clearly skewed in favor of religion and Christianity.

Horgan's article is itself endearingly ambivalent. Despite his misgivings, there were aspects of the experience that he clearly valued (and so did I, as will become apparent below). Horgan wrote:

> My conversations with the faithful deepened my appreciation of why some intelligent, well-educated people embrace religion. One reporter discussed the experience of speaking in tongues, and another described having an intimate relationship with Jesus. My convictions did not change, but others' did. At least one fellow said that his faith was wavering as a result of Dawkins's dissection of religion. And if the Templeton Foundation can help bring about even such a tiny step toward my vision of a world without religion, how bad can it be?

Horgan's article was given a second airing by the literary agent John Brockman on his 'Edge' website (often described as an on-line scientific *salon)* where it elicited varying responses, including one from the theoretical physicist Freeman Dyson. I responded to Dyson, quoting from his acceptance speech when he won the Templeton Prize. Whether he liked it or not, by accepting the Templeton Prize Dyson had sent a powerful signal to the world. It would be taken as an endorsement of religion by one of the world's most distinguished physicists.

> I am content to be one of the multitude of Christians who do not care much about the doctrine of the Trinity or the historical truth of the gospels.

But isn't that exactly what any atheistic scientist *would* say, if he wanted to sound Christian? I gave further quotations from Dyson's acceptance speech, satirically interspersing them with imagined questions (in italics) to a Templeton official:

> *Oh, you want something a bit more profound, as well? How about . . .*

"I do not make any clear distinction between mind and God. God is what mind becomes when it has passed beyond the scale of our comprehension."

Have I said enough yet, and can I get back to doing physics now? Oh, not enough yet? OK then, how about this:

"Even in the gruesome history of the twentieth century, I see some evidence of progress in religion. The two individuals who epitomized the evils of our century, Adolf Hitler and Joseph Stalin, were both avowed atheists."[23]

Can I go now?

Dyson could easily refute the implication of these quotations from his Templeton acceptance speech, if only he would explain clearly what evidence he finds to believe in God, in something more than just the Einsteinian sense which we can all trivially subscribe to. If I understand Horgan's point, it is that Templeton's money corrupts science. I am sure Freeman Dyson is way above being corrupted. But his acceptance speech is still unfortunate if it seems to set an example to others. The Templeton Prize is two orders of magnitude larger than the inducements offered to the journalists at Cambridge, having been explicitly set up to be larger than the Nobel Prize. In Faustian vein, my friend the philosopher Daniel Dennett once joked to me, " Richard, if ever you fall on hard times... ."

For better or worse, I attended two days at the Cambridge conference, giving a talk of my own and taking part in the discussion of several other talks. I challenged the theologians to answer the point that a God capable of designing a universe, or anything else, would have to be complex and statistically improbable. The strongest response I heard was that I was brutally foisting a scientific epistemology upon an unwilling theology.[24] Theologians had always defined God as simple. Who was I, a scientist, to dictate to theologians that their God had to be complex? Scientific arguments, such as those I was accustomed to deploying in my own field, were inappropriate since theologians had always maintained that God lay outside science.

I did not gain the impression that the theologians who mounted this evasive defence were being wilfully dishonest. I think they were sincere. Nevertheless, I was irresistibly reminded of Peter Medawar's comment on Father Teilhard de Chardin's *The Phenomenon of Man,* in the course of what is possibly the greatest negative book review of all time: "Its author can be excused of dishonesty only on the grounds that before deceiving others he has taken great pains to deceive himself."[25] The theologians of my Cambridge encounter were *defining* themselves into an epistemological Safe Zone where rational argument could not reach them because they had *declared by fiat* that it could not. Who was I to say that rational argument was the only admissible kind of argument? There are other ways of knowing besides the scientific, and it is one of these other ways of knowing that must be deployed to know God.

The most important of these other ways of knowing turned out to be personal, subjective experience of God. Several discussants at Cambridge claimed that God spoke to them, inside their heads, just as vividly and as personally as another human might. At the Cambridge conference I add two points. First, that if God really did communicate with humans that fact would emphatically not lie outside science. God comes bursting through from whatever other-worldly domain is his natural abode, crashing through into our world where his messages can be intercepted by human brains—and that phenomenon has nothing to do with science? Second, a God who is capable of sending intelligible signals to millions of people simultaneously, and of receiving messages from all of them simultaneously, cannot be, whatever else he might be, simple. Such bandwidth! God may not have a brain made of neurones, or a CPU made of silicon, but if he has the powers attributed to him he must have something far more elaborately and non-randomly constructed than the largest brain or the largest computer we know.

Time and again, my theologian friends returned to the point that there had to be a reason why there is something rather than nothing. There must have been a first cause of everything, and we might as well give it the name God. Yes, I said, but it must have been simple and therefore, whatever else we call it, God is not an appropriate name (unless we very explicitly divest it of all the baggage that the word 'God' carries in the minds of most religious believers). The first cause that we seek must have been the simple basis for a self-bootstrapping crane which eventually raised the world as we know it into its present complex existence. To suggest that the original prime mover was complicated enough to indulge in intelligent design, to say nothing of mindreading millions of humans simultaneously, is tantamount to dealing yourself a perfect hand at bridge. Look around at the world of life, at the Amazon rainforest with its rich interlacement of lianas, bromeliads, roots and flying buttresses; its army ants and its jaguars, its tapirs and peccaries, treefrogs and parrots. What you are looking at is the statistical equivalent of a perfect hand of cards (think of all the other ways you could permute the parts, none of which would work)—except that we know how it came about: by the gradualistic crane of natural selection. It is not just scientists who revolt at mute acceptance of such improbability arising spontaneously; common sense balks too. To suggest that the first cause, the great unknown which is responsible for something existing rather than nothing, is a being capable of designing the universe and of talking to a million people simultaneously, is a total abdication of the responsibility to find an explanation. It is a dreadful exhibition of self-indulgent, thought-denying skyhookery.

I am not advocating some sort of narrowly scientistic way of thinking. But the very least that any honest quest for truth must have in setting out to explain such monstrosities of improbability as a rainforest, a coral reef, or a universe is a crane and not a skyhook. The crane doesn't have to be natural selection. Admittedly, nobody has ever thought of a better one. But there could be others yet to be discovered. Maybe the 'inflation' that physicists postulate as occupying some fraction of the first yoctosecond of the universe's existence will turn out, when it is better understood, to be a cosmological crane to stand alongside Darwin's biological one. Or maybe the elusive crane that cosmologists seek will be a version of Darwin's idea itself: either Smolin's model or something similar. Or maybe it will be the multiverse plus anthropic principle espoused by Martin Rees and others. It may even be a superhuman designer—but, if so, it will most certainly *not* be a designer who just popped into existence, or who always existed. If (which I don't believe for a moment) our universe was designed, and *a fortiori* if the designer reads our thoughts and hands out omniscient advice, forgiveness and redemption, the designer himself must be the end product of some kind of cumulative escalator or crane, perhaps a version of Darwinism in another universe.

The last-ditch defence by my critics in Cambridge was attack. My whole world-view was condemned as 'nineteenth-century.' This is such a bad argument that I almost omitted to mention it. But regrettably I encounter it rather frequently. Needless to say, to call an argument nineteenth-century is not the same as explaining what is wrong with it. Some nineteenth-century ideas were very good ideas, not least Darwin's own dangerous idea. In any case, this particular piece of namecalling seemed a bit rich coming, as it did, from an individual (a distinguished Cambridge geologist, surely well advanced along the Faustian road to a future Templeton Prize) who justified his own Christian belief by invoking what he called the historicity of the New Testament. It was precisely in the nineteenth century that theologians, especially in Germany, called into grave doubt that alleged historicity, using the evidence-based methods of history to do so. This was, indeed, swiftly pointed out by the theologians at the Cambridge conference.

In any case, I know the 'nineteenth-century' taunt of old. It goes with the 'village atheist' gibe. It goes with "Contrary to what you seem to think Ha Ha Ha we don't believe in an old man with a long white beard any more Ha Ha Ha." All three jokes are code for something else, just as, when I lived in America in the late 1960s, 'law and order' was politicians' code for anti-black prejudice.[26] What, then, is the coded meaning of 'You are so nineteenth-century' in the context of an argument about religion? It is code for: "You are so crude and unsubtle, how could you be so insensitive and ill-mannered as to ask me a direct, point-blank question like 'Do you believe in miracles?' or 'Do you believe Jesus was born of a virgin?' Don't you know that in polite society we don't ask such questions? That sort of question went out in the nineteenth century." But think about why it is impolite to ask such direct, factual questions of religious people today. It is because it is embarrassing! But it is the answer that is embarrassing, if it is yes.

The nineteenth-century connection is now clear. The nineteenth century is the last time when it was possible for an educated person to admit to believing in miracles like the virgin birth without embarrassment. When pressed, many educated Christians today are too loyal to deny the virgin birth and the resurrection. But it embarrasses them because their rational minds know it is absurd, so they would much rather not be asked. Hence, if somebody like me insists on asking the question, it is I who am accused of being 'nineteenth-century.' It is really quite funny, when you think about it.

I left the conference stimulated and invigorated, and reinforced in my conviction that the argument from improbability—the "Ultimate 747" gambit—is a very serious argument against the existence of God, and one to which I have yet to hear a theologian give a convincing answer despite numerous opportunities and invitations to do so. Dan Dennett rightly describes it as "an unrebuttable refutation, as devastating today as when Philo used it to trounce Cleanthes in Hume's *Dialogues* two centuries earlier. A sky-hook would at best simply postpone the solution to the problem, but Hume couldn't think of any cranes, so he caved in."[27] Darwin, of course, supplied the vital crane. How Hume would have loved it.

At the risk of sounding repetitive, I shall summarize it as a series of six numbered points.

1 One of the greatest challenges to the human intellect, over the centuries, has been to explain how the complex, improbable appearance of design in the universe arises.

2 The natural temptation is to attribute the appearance of design to actual design itself. In the case of a man-made artefact such as a watch, the designer really was an intelligent engineer. It is tempting to apply the same logic to an eye or a wing, a spider or a person.

3 The temptation is a false one, because the designer hypothesis immediately raises the larger problem of who designed the designer. The whole problem we started out with was the problem of explaining statistical improbability. It is obviously no solution to postulate something even more improbable. We need a 'crane,' not a 'skyhook,' for only a crane can do the business of working up gradually and plausibly from simplicity to otherwise improbable complexity.

4 The most ingenious and powerful crane so far discovered is Darwinian evolution by natural selection. Darwin and his successors have shown how living creatures, with their spectacular statistical improbability and appearance of design, have evolved by slow, gradual degrees from simple beginnings. We can now safely say that the illusion of design in living creatures is just that—an illusion.

5 We don't yet have an equivalent crane for physics. Some kind of multiverse theory could in principle do for physics the same explanatory work as Darwinism does for biology. This kind of explanation is superficially less satisfying than the biological version of Darwinism, because it makes heavier demands on luck. But the anthropic principle entitles us to postulate far more luck than our limited human intuition is comfortable with.

6 We should not give up hope of a better crane arising in physics, something as powerful as Darwinism is for biology. But even in the absence of a strongly satisfying crane to match the biological one, the relatively weak cranes we have at present are, when abetted by the anthropic principle, self-evidently better than the self-defeating skyhook hypothesis of an intelligent designer.

If the argument of this chapter is accepted, the factual premise of religion—the God Hypothesis—is untenable. God almost certainly does not exist. ...

Notes

1. An exhaustive review of the provenance, usages and quotations of this analogy is given, from a creationist point of view, by Gert Korthof, at http://home.wxs.nl/-gkorthof/kortho46a.htm.

2. Intelligent design has been unkindly described as creationism in a cheap tuxedo.

3. Classical Latin and Greek were better equipped. Latin *homo* (Greek *anthropo-*) means human, as opposed to *vir* (*andro-*) which means man, and *femina* (*gyne-*) which means woman. Thus anthropology pertains to all humanity, where andrology and gynecology are sexually exclusive branches of medicine.

4. Adams (2002), p. 99. My "Lament for Douglas," written the day after his death, is reprinted as the Epilogue to *The Salmon of Doubt*, and also in *A Devil's Chaplain*, which also has my eulogy at his memorial meeting in the church of St. Martin-in-the-Fields.

5. Interview in *Der Spiegel*, 26 Dec. 2005.

6. Susskind (2006: 17).

7. Behe (1996).

8. There is an example in fiction. The children's writer Philip Pullman, in *His Dark Materials,* imagines a species of animals, the 'mulefa,' that co-exist with trees that produce perfectly round seedpods with a hole in the centre. These pods the mulefa adopt as wheels. The wheels, not being part of the body, have no nerves or blood vessels to get twisted around the 'axle' (a strong claw of horn or bone). Pullman perceptively notes an additional point: the system works only because the planet is paved with natural basalt ribbons, which serve as 'roads.' Wheels are no good over rough country.

9. Fascinatingly, the muscle principle is deployed in yet a third mode in some insects such as flies, bees and bugs, in which the flight muscle is intrinsically oscillatory, like a reciprocating engine. Whereas other insects such as locusts send nervous instructions for each wing stroke (as a bird does), bees send an instruction to switch on (or switch off) the oscillatory motor. Bacteria have a mechanism which is neither a simple contractor (like a bird's flight muscle) nor a reciprocator (like a bee's flight muscle), but a true rotator: in that respect it is like an electric motor or a Wankel engine.

10. http://www.millerandlevine.com/km/evol/design2/article.html.

11. This account of the Dover trial, including the quotations, is from A. Bottaro, M.A. Inlay and N.J. Matzke, "Immunology in the Spotlight at the Dover 'Intelligent Design' Trial," *Nature Immunology* 7, 2006, 433-5.

12. J. Coyle, "God in the details: the biochemical challenge to evolution," *Nature* 383, 1996, 227-8. The article by Coyle and me, "One side can be wrong," was published in the *Guardian*, 1 Sept. 2005: http://www.guardian.co.uk/life/feature/story/0,13026,1559742,00.htm. The quotation from the "eloquent blogger" is at http://www.religionisbullshit.net/blog/2005_09_01_archive.php.

13. Dawkins (1995).

14. Carter admitted later that a better name for the overall principle would be "cognizability principle": B. Carter, "The anthropic principle and its implications for biological evolution," *Philosophical Transactions of the Royal Society of London A*, 310, 1983, 347-63. For a book-length discussion of the anthropic principle, see Barrow and Tipler (1998).

15. If you find that surprising, you may be suffering from northern hemisphere chauvinism, as described on page 114-15.

16. Comins (1993).

17. I spelled this argument out more fully in *The Blind Watchmaker* (Dawkins 1986).

18. I say 'presumably,' partly because we don't know how different alien forms of life might be, and partly because it is possible that we make a mistake if we consider only the consequences of changing one constant at a time. Could there be other *combinations* of values of the six numbers which would turn out to be friendly to life, in ways that we do not discover if we consider them only one at a time? Nevertheless, I shall proceed, for simplicity, as though we really do have a big problem to explain in the apparent fine-tuning of the fundamental constants.

19. Susskind (2006) gives a splendid advocacy of the anthropic principle in the megaverse. He says the idea is hated by most physicists. I can't understand why. I think it is beautiful—perhaps because my consciousness has been raised by Darwin.

20. Murray Gell-Mann, quoted by John Brockman on the "Edge" website http://www.edge.org/3rd _culture/bios/smolin.html.

21. Ward (1996: 99); Polkinghorne (1994: 55).

22. J. Horgan, "The Templeton Foundation: a skeptic's take," *Chronicle of Higher Education*, 7 April 2006. See also http://www.edge.org/3rd_culture/horgan06/horgan06_index.html.

23. This calumny is dealt with in Chapter 7.

24. This accusation is reminiscent of 'NOMA,' whose overblown claims I dealt with in Chapter 2.

25. P.B. Medawar, review of *The Phenomenon of Man*, repr. In Medawar (1982: 242).

26. In Britain 'inner cities' had the equivalent coded meaning, prompting Auberon Waugh's wickedly hilarious reference to 'inner cities of both sexes.'

27. Dennett (1995: 153).

32
Religion As An Original Sin (2007)
Christopher Hitchens

There are, indeed, several ways in which religion is not just amoral, but positively immoral. And these faults and crimes are not to be found in the behavior of its adherents (which can sometimes be exemplary) but in its original precepts. These include:

- Presenting a false picture of the world to the innocent and the credulous
- The doctrine of blood sacrifice
- The doctrine of atonement
- The doctrine of eternal reward and/or punishment
- The imposition of impossible tasks and rules

All the creation myths of all peoples have long been known to be false, and have fairly recently been replaced by infinitely superior and more magnificent explanations. To its list of apologies, religion should simply add an apology for foisting man-made parchments and folk myths upon the unsuspecting, and for taking so long to concede that this had been done. One senses a reluctance to make this admission, since it might tend to explode the whole religious worldview, but the longer it is delayed the more heinous the denial will become.

Blood Sacrifice

Before monotheism arose, the altars of primitive society reeked of blood, much of it human and some of it infant. The thirst for this, at least in animal form, is still with us. Pious Jews are at this moment trying to breed the spotlessly pure "red heifer" mentioned in the book of Numbers, chapter 19, which if slaughtered again according to the exact and meticulous ritual will bring about the return of animal sacrifices in the Third Temple, and hasten the end of time and the coming of the Messiah. This may appear merely absurd, but a team of like-minded Christian maniac farmers are attempting as I write to help their co-fundamentalists by employing special breeding techniques (borrowed or stolen from modern science) to produce a perfect "Red Angus" beast in Nebraska. Meanwhile in Israel, the Jewish biblical fanatics are also trying to raise a human child, in a pure "bubble" free from contamination, who will at the attainment of the right age be privileged to cut that heifer's throat. Ideally, this should be done on the Temple Mount, awkwardly the site of the Muslim holy places but nonetheless the very spot where Abraham is alleged to have drawn the knife over the live body of his own child. Other sacramental guttings and throat-cuttings, particularly of lambs, occur every year in the Christian and Muslim world, either to celebrate Easter or the feast of Eid.

The latter, which honors Abraham's willingness to make a human sacrifice of his son, is common to all three monotheisms, and descends from their primitive ancestors. There is no softening the plain meaning of this frightful story. The prelude involves a series of vilenesses and delusions, from the seduction of Lot by both his daughters to the marriage of Abraham to his stepsister, the birth of Isaac to Sarah when Abraham was a hundred years old, and many other credible and incredible rustic crimes and misdemeanors. Perhaps afflicted by a poor conscience, but at any rate believing himself commanded by god, Abraham agreed to murder his son. He prepared the kindling, laid the tied-up boy upon it (thus showing that he knew the procedure), and took up the knife in order to kill the child like an animal. At the last available moment his hand was stayed, not by god as it happens, but by an angel, and he was praised from the clouds for showing his sturdy willingness to murder an innocent in expiation of his own crimes. As a reward for his fealty, he was promised a long and large posterity.

Not long after this (though the Genesis narrative is not very well illustrated in point of time) his wife Sarah expired at the age of one hundred and twenty-seven, and her dutiful husband found her a place of burial in a cave in the town of Hebron. Having outlived her by attaining the fine old age of one hundred and seventy-five, and having fathered six more children meanwhile, Abraham was eventually buried in the same cave. To this day, religious people kill each other and kill each other's children for the right to exclusive property in this unidentifiable and unlocatable hole in a hill.

There was a terrible massacre of Jewish residents of Hebron during the Arab revolt of 1929, when sixty-seven Jews were slaughtered.

Many of these were Lubavitchers, who regard all non-Jews as racially inferior and who had moved to Heron because they believed the Genesis myth, but this does not excuse the pogrom. Remaining outside the border of Israel until 1967, the town was captured that year with much fanfare by Israeli forces and became part of the occupied West Bank. Jewish settlers began to "return," under the leadership of a particularly violent and obnoxious rabbi named Moshe Levinger, and to build an armed settlement named Kiryat Arba above the town, as well as some smaller settlements within it. The Muslims among the mainly Arab inhabitants continued to claim that the praiseworthy Abraham indeed had been willing to murder his son, but only for *their* religion and not for the Jews. This is what "submission" means. When I visited the place I found that the supposed "Cave of the Patriarchs," or "Cave of Machpela," had separate entrances and separate places of worship for the two warring claimants to the right to celebrate this atrocity in their own names.

A short while before I arrived, another atrocity had occurred. An Israeli zealot named Dr. Baruch Goldstein had come to the cave and, unslinging the automatic weapon that he was allowed to carry, discharged it into the Muslim congregation. He killed twenty-seven worshippers and injured countless others before being overwhelmed and beaten to death. It turned out that many people already knew that Dr. Goldstein was dangerous. While serving as a physician in the Israeli army he had announced that he would not treat non-Jewish patients, such as Israeli Arabs, especially on the Sabbath. As it happens, he was obeying rabbinic law in declining to do this, as many Israeli religious courts have confirmed, so an easy way to spot an inhumane killer was to notice that he was guided by a sincere and literal observance of the divine instruction. Shrines in his name have been set up by the more doggedly observant Jews ever since, and of those rabbis who condemned his action, not all did so in unequivocal terms. The curse of Abraham continues to poison Hebron, but the religious warrant for blood sacrifice poisons our entire civilization.

Atonement

Previous sacrifices of humans, such as the Aztec and other ceremonies from which we recoil, were common in the ancient world and took the form of propitiatory murder. An offering of a virgin or an infant or a prisoner was assumed to appease the gods: once again, not a very good advertisement for the moral properties of religion. "Martyrdom," or a deliberate sacrifice of oneself, can be viewed in a slightly different light, though when practiced by the Hindus in the form of suttee, it the strongly suggested "suicide" of widows, it was put down by the British in India for imperial as much as for Christian reasons. Those "martyrs" who wish to kill others as well as themselves, in an act of religious exaltation, are viewed more differently still: Islam is ostensibly opposed to suicide *per se* but cannot seem to decide whether to condemn or recommend the act of such a bold *Shahid*.

However, the idea of a *vicarious* atonement, of the sort that so much troubled even C. S. Lewis, is a further refinement of the ancient superstition. Once again we have a father demonstrating love by subjecting a son to death by torture, but this time the father is not trying to impress god. He *is* god, and he is trying to impress humans. Ask yourself the question: how moral is the following? I am told of a human sacrifice that took place two thousand years ago, without my wishing it and in circumstances so ghastly that, had I been present and in possession of any influence, I would have been duty-bound to try and stop it. In consequence of this murder, my own manifold sins are forgiven me, and I may hope to enjoy everlasting life.

Let us just for now overlook all the contradictions between the tellers of the original story and assume that it is basically true. What are the further implications? They are not as reassuring as they look at first sight. For a start, and in order to gain the benefit of this wondrous offer, I have to accept that I am *responsible* for the flogging and mocking and crucifixion, in which I had no say and no part, and agree that every time I decline this responsibility, or that I sin in word or deed, I am intensifying the agony of it. Furthermore, I am required to believe that the agony was *necessary* in order to compensate for an earlier crime in which I also had no part, the sin of Adam. It is useless to object that Adam seems to have been created with insatiable discontent and curiosity and then forbidden to slake it: all this was settled long before even Jesus himself was born. Thus my own guilt in the matter is deemed "original" and inescapable. However, I am still granted free will with which to reject the offer of vicarious redemption. Should I exercise this choice, however, I face an eternity of torture much more awful than anything endured at Calvary, or anything threatened to those who first heard the Ten Commandments.

The tale is made no easier to follow by the necessary realization that Jesus both wished and needed to die and came to Jerusalem at Passover in order to do so, and that all who took part in his murder were unknowingly doing god's will, and fulfilling ancient prophecies. (Absent the gnostic version, this makes it hopelessly odd that Judas, who allegedly performed the strangely redundant act of identifying a very well-known preacher to those who had been hunting for him, should suffer such opprobrium. Without him, there could have been no "Good Friday," as the Christians naively call it even when they are not in a vengeful mood.)

There is a charge (found in only one of the four Gospels) that the Jews who condemned Jesus asked for his blood to be "on their heads" for future generations. This is not a problem that concerns only the Jews, or those Catholics who are worried by the history of Christian anti-Semitism. Suppose that the Jewish Sanhedrin *had* in fact made such a call, as Maimonides thought they had, and should have. How could that call possibly be binding upon successor generations? Remember that the Vatican did not assert that it was *some Jews who* had killed Christ. It asserted that it was *the Jews* who had ordered his death, and that the *Jewish people* as a whole were *the* bearers of a collective responsibility. It seems bizarre that the church could not bring itself to drop the charge of generalized Jewish "deicide" until very recently. But the key to its reluctance is easy to find. If you once admit that the descendants of Jews are not implicated, it becomes very hard to argue that anyone else not there present was implicated, either. One rent in the fabric, as usual, threatens to tear the whole thing apart (or to make it into something simply man-made and woven, like the discredited Shroud of Turin). The collectivization of guilt, in short, is immoral in itself, as religion has been occasionally compelled to admit.

Eternal Punishment and Impossible Tasks

The Gospel story of the Garden of Gethsemane used to absorb me very much as a child, because its "break" in the action and its human whimper made me wonder if some of the fantastic scenario might after all be true. Jesus asks, in effect, "Do I *have* to go through with this?" It is an impressive and unforgettable question, and I long ago decided that I would cheerfully wager my own soul on the belief that the only right answer to it is "no." We cannot, like fear-ridden peasants of antiquity, hope to load all our crimes onto a goat and then drive the hapless animal into the desert. Our everyday idiom is quite sound in regarding "scapegoating" with contempt. And religion is scapegoating writ large. I can pay your debt, my love, if you have been imprudent, and if I were a hero like Sidney Carton in *A Tale of Two Cities* I could even serve your term in prison or take your place on the scaffold. Greater love hath no man. But I cannot absolve you of your responsibilities. It would be immoral of me to offer, and immoral of you to accept. And if the same offer is made from another time and another world, through the mediation of middlemen and accompanied by inducements, it loses all its grandeur and becomes debased into wish-thinking or, worse, a combination of blackmailing with bribery.

The ultimate degeneration of all this into a mere bargain was made unpleasantly obvious by Blaise Pascal, whose theology is not far short of sordid. His celebrated "wager" puts it in hucksterish form: what have you got to lose? If you believe in god and there is a god, you win. If you believe in him and you are wrong—so what? I once wrote a response to this cunning piece of bet-covering, which took two forms.

The first was a version of Bertrand Russell's hypothetical reply to the hypothetical question: what will you say if you die and are confronted with your Maker? His response? "I should say, Oh God, you did not give us enough evidence." My own reply: Imponderable Sir, I presume from some if not all of your many reputations that you might prefer honest and convinced unbelief to the hypocritical and self-interested affectation of faith or the smoking tributes of bloody altars. But I would not count on it.

Pascal reminds me of the hypocrites and frauds who abound in Talmudic Jewish rationalization. Don't do any work on the Sabbath yourself, but pay someone else to do it. You obeyed the letter of the law: who's counting? The Dalai Lama tells us that you can visit a prostitute as long as someone else pays her. Shia Muslims offer "temporary marriage," selling men the permission to take a wife for an hour or two with the usual vows and then divorce her when they are done. Half of the splendid buildings in Rome would never have been raised if the sale of indulgences had not been so profitable: St. Peter's itself was financed by a special one-time offer of that kind. The newest pope, the former Joseph Ratzinger, recently attracted Catholic youths to a festival by offering a certain "remission of sin" to those who attended.

This pathetic moral spectacle would not be necessary if the original rules were ones that it would be possible to obey. But to the totalitarian edicts that begin with revelation from absolute authority, and that are enforced by fear, and based on a sin that had been committed long ago, are added regulations that are often immoral and impossible at the same time. The essential principle of totalitarianism is to make laws that are *impossible to obey.* The resulting tyranny is even more impressive if it can be enforced by a privileged caste or party which is highly zealous in the detection of error. Most of humanity, throughout its history, has dwelt under a form of this stupefying dictatorship, and a large portion of it still does. Allow me to give a few examples of the rules that must, yet cannot, be followed.

The commandment at Sinai which forbade people even to *think* about coveting goods is the first clue. It is echoed in the New Testament by the injunction which says that a man who looks upon a woman in the wrong way has actually committed adultery already. And it is almost equaled by the current Muslim and former Christian prohibition against lending out money at interest. All of these, in their different fashion, attempt to place impossible restrains on human initiative. They can only be met in one of two ways. The first is by a continual scourging and mortification of the flesh, accompanied by incessant wrestling with "impure" thoughts which become actual as soon as they are named, or even imagined. From this come hysterical confessions of guilt, false promises of improvement, and loud, violent denunciations of other backsliders and sinners: a spiritual police state. The second solution is organized hypocrisy, where forbidden foods are rebaptized as something else, or where a donation to the religious authorities will purchase some wiggle-room, or where ostentatious orthodoxy will buy some time, or where money can be paid into one account and then paid back—with perhaps a slight percentage added in a non-usurious manner—into another. This we might term the spiritual banana republic. Many theocracies, from medieval Rome to modern Wahhabi Saudi Arabia, have managed to be spiritual police states *and* spiritual banana republics at the same time.

This objection applies even to some of the noblest and some of the basest rules. The order to "love thy neighbor" is mild and yet stern: a reminder of one's duty to others. The order to "love thy neighbor *as thyself*" is too extreme and too strenuous to be obeyed, as is the hard to interpret instruction to love others "as I have loved you." Humans are not so constituted as to care for others as much as themselves: the thing simply cannot be done (as any intelligent "creator" would well understand from studying his own design). Urging humans to be superhumans, on pain of death and torture, is the urging of terrible self-abasement at their repeated and inevitable failure to keep the rules. What a grin, meanwhile, on the face of those who accept the cash donations that are made in lieu! The so-called Golden Rule, sometimes needlessly identified with a folktale about the Babylonian Rabbi Hillel, simply enjoins us to treat others as one would wish to be treated by them. This sober and rational precept, which one can teach to any child with its innate sense of fairness (and which predates all Jesus's "beatitudes" and parables), is well within the compass of any atheist and does not require masochism and hysteria, or sadism and hysteria, when it is breached. It is gradually learned, as part of the painfully slow evolution of the species, and once grasped is never forgotten. Ordinary conscience will do, without any heavenly wrath behind it.

As to the basest rules, one need only consult the argument from design once more. People wish to enrich and better themselves, and though they may well lend or even give money to a friend or relative in need and ask for nothing but its eventual return or its grateful acknowledgment, they will not advance money to perfect strangers without expecting interest. By a nice chance, cupidity and avarice are the spur to economic development. No student of the subject from David Ricardo to Karl Marx to Adam Smith has been unaware of this fact. It is "not from the benevolence" of the baker, observed Smith in his shrewd Scots manner, that we expect our daily bread, but from his self-interest in baking and selling it. In any case, one may choose to be altruistic, whatever that may mean, but by definition one may not be *compelled* into altruism. Perhaps we would be better mammals if we were not "made" this way, but surely nothing could be sillier than having a "maker" who then forbade the very same instinct he instilled.

"Free will," reply the casuists. You do not have to obey the laws against murder or theft either. Well, one may be genetically programmed for a certain amount of aggression and hatred and greed, and yet also evolved enough to beware of following every prompting. If we gave in to our every base instinct every time, civilization would have been impossible and there would be no writing in which to continue this argument. However, there can be no question that a human being, whether standing up or lying down, finds his or her hand resting just next to the genitalia. Useful no doubt in warding off primeval aggressors once our ancestors decided to take the risk of going erect and exposing the viscera, this is both a privilege and a provocation denied to most quadrupeds (some of whom can compensate by getting their mouths to the same point that we can reach with our fingers and palms). Now: who devised the rule that this easy apposition between the manual and the genital be forbidden, even as a thought? To put it more plainly, who ordered that you *must* touch (for other reasons having nothing to do with sex or reproduction) but that you also *must not*? There does not even seem to be any true scriptural authority here, yet almost all religions have made the prohibition a near-absolute one.

One could write an entire book that was devoted only to the grotesque history of religion and sex, and to holy dread of the procreative act and its associated impulses and necessities, from the emission of semen to the effusion of menstrual blood. But a convenient way of condensing the whole fascinating story may be to ask one single provocative question.

33
In The Service Of The Death Fixation
Michel Onfray

Selective bones of contention. The ability to select at will from all three monotheist books could have yielded the best of results. It would have sufficed to choose Deuteronomy's injunction against killing, transforming it into a universal absolute allowing not a single exception; to stress the evangelists' theme of brotherly love (excluding everything that contradicted that categorical imperative); to give unequivocal support to the Koranic sura which holds that killing one man means killing all of humankind...Then the three religions of the book might have appeared to us as respectable, pleasurable, desirable.

If rabbis insisted that one could not be Jewish and at the same time slaughter, colonize, and deport whole populations in the name of their religion...if priests condemned everyone who did away with his neighbor...if the pope, first among Christians, always took the side of the victims, the weak, the poor, the lowly, the descendants of the humble folk who were Christ's first followers...if caliphs, imams, ayatollahs, mullahs, and other Muslim dignitaries pilloried the wielders of swords, the Jew-killers, the murderers of Christians, the impalers of the unfaithful...If all these representatives of their one God on earth chose peace, love, and tolerance, we would first and foremost have known of it and witnessed it, and next we would have been able to support the three religions on the basis of their principles. And finally we could have condemned the exploitation of those principles by the bad, the wicked. Instead of all this, these representatives of their one God do the opposite. They select the worst options, and, save for extremely rare, intermittent, particular, and personal exceptions, they have historically supported war leaders, saber-rattlers, soldiers, warriors, rapists, pillagers, war criminals, torturers, promoters of genocide, dictators (except for Communist ones)—the very dregs of the earth.

For monotheism is fatally fixated on death. It loves death, cherishes death; it exults in death, is fascinated by death. It gives death, doles it out in massive doses; it threatens death and moves from threat to action: from the bloody sword of the Israelites killing off the Canaanites to the use of airliners as flying bombs in New York, stopping off on the way to release an atomic cargo over Hiroshima and Nagasaki. Everything is done in the name of God, blessed by him, but blessed most of all by those claiming to act in his name.

Today, the Grand Rabbinate of Jerusalem castigates the bomb-clad Palestinian terrorist in the streets of Jaffa but remains silent when Tsahal missiles kill the inhabitants of a West Bank neighborhood. The pope thunders out against the pill, responsible for "the greatest genocide of all time," but actively defends the massacre of hundreds of thousands of Tutsi by the Catholic Hutu of Rwanda. The most exalted spheres of world Islam denounce the crimes of colonialism, the humiliation and exploitation visited on Muslims by the Western world, but rejoice in a worldwide jihad carried out under the auspices of Al-Qaeda. Fascination with the deaths of people, miscreants, and infidels—all three of them additionally convinced that atheism is their single common enemy!

Monotheist indignation is selective, with esprit de corps working full blast. The Jews have their Covenant, the Christians their church, the Muslims their ummah. Three brotherhoods operating outside the law and enjoying an ontological and metaphysical extraterritoriality. Among members of the same community everything is permissible and justifiable. A Jew—Ariel Sharon—may order the killing of a Palestinian—the hard to-defend Sheikh Ahmad Yassin—without offending Yahweh, for the murder is committed in his name. A Christian—Pius XII—has the right to justify an exterminator of Jews—Eichmann, exfiltrated from postwar Europe with the Vatican's help—without offending his Lord, for the Nazi genocide avenges the decide attributed to the Jewish people. A Muslim—the Mullah Omar—may order the hanging of women accused of adultery, thus gratifying Allah in whose name the gallows are erected…Behind all these abominations stand verses from the Torah, passages from the Gospels, and suras from the Koran, legitimizing, justifying, blessing.

As soon as religion triggers public and political results, it substantially increases its power to harm. When we point to a phrase culled from one or another of the three books in order to explain the rightness and legitimacy of a crime, we automatically render the crime immune to attack, for how can we attack the revealed word, the utterance of God, the divine urging? God does not speak—except to the Jewish people and the handful of visionaries, virgins for example, to whom he occasionally sends messages—but the clergy has him talk his head off. When a man of the church gives his opinion, quoting pieces from his book, opposing him becomes the equivalent of telling God no in person. Who possesses the moral strength and conviction to refuse the word of (a man of) God? Every theocracy is a denial of democracy. Even better: the smallest hint of theocracy neutralizes the very essence of democracy.

The Jewish invention of holy war. Let us give credit where it is due. The Jews invented monotheism and everything that went with it. First divine right and its mandatory correlative: the chosen people exalted, other peoples discounted; a logical enough sequence. Then, more importantly, came the divine strength needed to buttress this heaven-sent right, because the sword arm is what guarantees its realization here below. God utters, speaks, and his prophets, messiahs, and other emissaries translate his otherwise not very intelligible speech. The clergy transforms that speech into orders upheld by iron-plated, caparisoned, determined troops, armed to the teeth. Hence the three founding pillars of all civilizations: the prince representing God on earth, the priest providing the prince with ideas, and the soldier guaranteeing the priest's brute strength. And the people, of course, *always* pay the costs of theocratic perfidy.

The Jews invented the temporal dimension of monotheist spirituality. Well before them, the priest acted in concert with the king: the association was primitive, prehistoric, antediluvian. But the chosen people adapted this skillful and very practical logic for their own purposes: the earth had to be organized in the same way as heaven. Theological schemas had to be reproduced on the terrain of history. Immanence had to demarcate the rules of transcendence. The Torah tells the story without beating about the bush.

Yahweh blessed war and those who waged it. He sanctified combat, led it, supervised it, although admittedly not in person—ectoplasm has trouble wielding a sword—but by inspiring his people. He sanctioned crimes, murders, assassination, gave his blessing to the liquidation of innocents, killed animals like men and men like animals. He could be humane (unless he was dealing with Canaanites). He proposed an alternative to battle, offering slavery—a token of goodness and love—in its place. To the indigenous population of Palestine, already living there when the Hebrews arrived, he promised total destruction—*holy war,* to use the terrifying and ultramodern expression of Joshua (6:21).

For two thousand five hundred years, no leading figure descended from the chosen people has declared that these pages are rooted in fable, in prehistoric and highly dangerous—because criminal—fictions and nonsense. Quite the contrary. There exist on this planet a considerable number of people who live, think, act, and conceive of the world on the basis of these texts that call for generalized butchery. And there isn't the slightest danger that they will be denied the right to publish on the grounds that they encourage murder, racism, and other incitements to breaches of the peace. Yeshiva students memorize these passages, no more inclined to change a single comma than to touch a single one of Yahweh's hairs. The Torah offers the first Western version of the many arts of war published in the course of the centuries.

Christian anti-Semitism. It is hard for a Christian to love his neighbor, particularly if the neighbor is a Jew... Saul-become-Paul channeled all his passion into dismantling Judaism—the same passion that (before the road to Damascus) he brought to persecuting Christians, helping mistreat them, and even hastening their encounter with the beyond. To sell the sect he had newly embraced, he had to persuade his listeners that Jesus was the Messiah foretold in the Old Testament, and that Christ had abolished Judaism by fulfilling the prophecy. Since Yahweh's faithful did not buy the nonsense about a Son of God who died on the cross to save humankind, Jews emerged as fundamental adversaries. Then, very quickly, they became the enemy.

It is said that the Wandering Jew was afflicted with his curse because the first of them refused to slake Christ's thirst on the path to Golgotha. For this failure to help the Crucified One, the curse fell upon him—not very charitable of Jesus—but also and above all on his kind, his descendants, his people. This was all the more portentous because the Christian version of Jesus's death assumes that the Jews were responsible—not the Romans... And Pontius Pilate? Neither responsible nor guilty. Paul affirmed it when speaking of the Jews who "killed the Lord Jesus" (1 Thessalonians 2:15). The Gospels abound in openly anti-Semitic passages. Daniel Goldhagen lists forty or so in Mark, eighty in Matthew, one hundred and thirty in John, one hundred and forty in the Acts of the Apostles... Jesus himself, gentle Jesus, described the Jews as being "of your father, the devil" (John 8:44). In such circumstances, loving one's neighbor was difficult.

From the first Christian transformation of the Jews into a people of God-killers to the long-delayed recognition of the state of Israel by John Paul II at the end of 1993 (and taking into account the church's long love affair with every manifestation of anti-Semitism in history, including most significantly the twelve years of German National Socialism), the picture is clear. The extreme expression of this hatred was the active collaboration between the Vatican and Nazism. And then—which is less widely known—that of Nazism with the Vatican. For Pius XII and Adolf Hitler shared a certain number of points of view, in particular the loathing of Jews in all their guises.

The Vatican admired Adolf Hitler. The love-marriage between the Catholic Church and Nazism cannot be denied. Instances—and they are not minor ones—abound. Their complicity did not reside in unspoken approval, explicit omissions, or calculations made on the basis of partisan positions. The facts are clear to anyone who approaches the issue by interrogating history: it was not a marriage of reason, determined by concern for the survival of the church, but a shared loathing of the same implacable enemies: Jews and Communists—most often packaged together in the same grab bag labeled Judeo Bolshevism.

From the birth of National Socialism to the extrusion of the Third Reich's war criminals after the regime's collapse to the church's silence on these questions ever since, the domain of Christ's heir Saint Peter was also that of Adolf Hitler and his henchmen, German Nazis and French fascists, collaborators of the Nazis, Vichyites, fascist militias, and other war criminals. Even today, it is still impossible to consult the Vatican's archives on the subject.

The facts, then. The Catholic Church approved the rearmament of Germany in the 1930s, which was of course contrary to the spirit of the Versailles Treaty but also to a part of Jesus's teachings, particularly those celebrating peace, mildness, love of one's neighbor. The Catholic Church signed a concordat with Adolf Hitler as soon as the chancellor took office in 1933. The Catholic Church held its tongue over the boycott of Jewish businesses, remained silent over the proclamation of the Nuremberg racial laws in 1935, and was equally silent over Kristallnacht in 1938. The Catholic Church provided the Nazis with its genealogical records, which told them who in Germany was Christian, and therefore non-Jewish. (On the other hand, the Catholic Church did invoke the principle of "pastoral secrecy" in order not to communicate the names of Jews converted to Christ's religion or married to Christians.) The Catholic Church supported, defended, and aided the pro-Nazi Ustachi regime of Ante Pavelic in Croatia. The Catholic Church gave its absolution to France's collaborationist Vichy regime in 1940. The Catholic Church, although fully aware of the policy of extermination set in motion in 1.942, did not condemn it in private or in public, and never ordered any priest or bishop to condemn the criminal regime in the hearing of his flock.

The Allied armies liberated Europe, reached Berchtesgaden, discovered Auschwitz. What did the Vatican do? It continued to support the defeated regime. The Catholic Church, in the person of Cardinal Bertram, ordered a requiem Mass in memory of Adolf Hitler. The Catholic Church was mute and showed no disapproval at the discovery of the mass graves, the gas chambers, and the death camps. Even better, the Catholic Church did for the Nazis (shorn of their Führer) what it had never done for a single Jew or victim of National Socialism: it set up a network designed to smuggle war criminals out of Europe. The Catholic Church used the Vatican, delivered papers stamped with its visas to fugitive Nazis, established a chain of European monasteries that served as hiding places for dignitaries of the ruined Reich. The Catholic Church promoted into its hierarchy people who had performed important tasks for the Hitler regime. And the Catholic Church will never apologize for any of these things, particularly since it has acknowledged none of them.

If there is ever to be repentance, we shall probably have to wait four centuries for it, the time it took for a pope to acknowledge the church's error in the Galileo affair. Chiefly because the doctrine of papal infallibility proclaimed at the first Vatican Council in 1869-70 *(Pastor Aeternas)* forbids challenging the church—for when the supreme pontiff speaks or makes a decision he does so not as a man capable of being wrong but as the representative of God on earth, constantly inspired by the Holy Spirit—the famous doctrine of "saving grace." Are we to conclude from all this that the Holy Spirit is fundamentally Nazi?

While the church remained silent on the Nazi question during and after the war, it missed no chance to act against Communists. Where Marxism is concerned, the Vatican has given proof of a commitment, a militancy, and a vigor better expended in fighting and discrediting the Nazi Reich. Faithful to church tradition (which, through the grace of Pius IX and Pius X, condemned human rights as contrary to the teachings of the church), Pius XII, the pope so famously well-disposed toward National Socialism, excommunicated the Communists of the whole world en masse in 1949. He asserted collusion between the Jews and Bolshevism as one of the reasons for his decision.

To recapitulate: no run-of-the-mill National Socialist, no Nazi of elevated rank or member of the Reich's staff was ever excommunicated. No group was ever excluded from the church for preaching and practicing racism or anti-Semitism or operating gas chambers. Adolf Hitler was not excommunicated, and *Mein Kampf* was never put on the *Index*. We should not forget that after 1924, the date Hitler's book appeared, the famous *Index Librorum Prohibitorium* added to its list—alongside Pierre Larousse, guilty of the *Grand Dictionnaire Universel* (!)—Henri Bergson, André Gide, Simone de Beauvoir, and Jean-Paul Sartre. Adolf Hitler never appeared on it.

Hitler admired the Vatican. A widely held notion that fails to stand up to the most rudimentary analysis, still less to a reading of the texts, represents Hitler as a pagan fascinated by Nordic cults a lover of Wagnerian horned helmets, of Valhalla and of generous-breasted Valkyrie, an antichrist, the very antithesis of Christian. Apart from evoking the difficulty of being at once atheist and pagan—denying the existence of God or gods while at the same time believing in them—to believe this means that we must ignore Hitler's writings *(Mein Kampf)* , his political action (the Reich's failure to persecute the Catholic, Apostolic, and Roman Church, as opposed, for example, to its treatment of Jehovah's Witnesses), and the Führer's private confidences (his published conversations with Albert Speer), in which he consistently and unambiguously expressed his admiration for Christianity.

Was it an atheist Führer who decided to stamp the words *Gott mit uns* on the belt buckles of the Reich's soldiers? Do people know that the slogan comes from the scriptures? Notably from Deuteronomy, one of the books of the Torah, which says, "For the Lord thy God is he that goeth with you" (Deuteronomy 20:4). These words were lifted from the speech Yahweh addressed to the Jews leaving to fight their enemies, the Egyptians, to whom God held out the promise of unspecified extermination (Deuteronomy 2:13).

Was it an atheist Führer who ordered all schoolchildren in the National Socialist Reich to begin their day with a prayer to Jesus? Not to God, which might have made a deist of Hitler, but to Jesus, which explicitly labels him a Christian. The same supposedly atheist Führer asked Goering and Goebbels, in the presence of Albert Speer who recorded the conversation, to remain within the bosom of the Catholic Church, as he himself would until his dying day.

Christianity and National Socialism: points in common. The understanding between Hitler and Pius XII went far beyond personal compatibility. The two doctrines shared more than one point of convergence. The infallibility of the pope, who we should remember was also a head of state, could not have been displeasing to a Führer also convinced of his infallibility. The possibility of building an empire, a civilization, a culture with a supreme guide invested with full powers—like Constantine and several Christian emperors who succeeded him—was something that fascinated Hitler during the writing of his book. The Christian eradication of everything redolent of paganism? The destruction of altars and temples? The book burnings (remember that Paul recommended them)? The persecution of all who opposed the new faith? All excellent things, Hitler concluded.

The Führer admired the theocratic evolution of Christianity. He wrote (*Mein Kampf*, volume 2, chapter 5, page 454) that it was only by virtue of "passionate intolerance" for pagan altars that an "apodictic faith" could grow up—Hitler's term for "unshakable faith:' He marveled at the church's determination to give up nothing, even and especially in the face of science when it contradicted certain of its positions or took its dogma to task (page 459); the flexibility of the church, for which Hitler predicted a future well beyond what people might imagine (page 459); the permanence of the venerable institution (volume 1, chapter 3, page 115) despite the occasionally deplorable behavior of clergy (which did nothing to affect overall church policy). In all this, Hitler asked his readers to "take lessons from the Catholic Church" (page 459, but also pages 114-20).

What is the "true Christianity" Hitler mentions in *Mein Kampf* (volume 1, chapter 11, page 307)? That of the "great founder of the new doctrine": Jesus, the same Jesus to whom children in the schools of the Third Reich prayed. But which Jesus? Not the one who turned the other cheek, no, but the angry Jesus who ejected the moneylenders from the Temple with a whip. Hitler specifically mentioned this passage from John in his argument. Also, let us not forget what sort of people this most Christian whip served to drive out: unbelievers, non-Christians, vendors, merchants, money-changers—in short, Jews, the unspoken key word in this complicity between Reich and Vatican. John's Gospel (2:14) does not invalidate Hitler's philo-Christian and anti-Semitic reading; indeed, it makes it possible. Particularly if we take note of the many passages in the New Testament consigning the Jews to hellfire. The Jews were a race of deicides. Here lies the key to this fatal partnership: they use religion, said Hitler, in order to do business; they are, he adds, the enemies of any kind of humanity; he goes on to specify that it was the Jews who created Bolshevism. Let everyone make up his own mind. But to Hitler himself things were clear: "to the political leader, the religious ideas and institutions of his people must remain inviolable" (page 116). So the gas chambers could be operated in the name of Saint John.

Wars, fascisms, and other pursuits. The partnership of Christianity and Nazism is not an accident of history, a regrettable and isolated mistake along the wayside, but the fulfillment of a two-thousand-year-old logic. From Paul of Tarsus, who justified fire and the sword in turning a private sect into a religion contaminating the empire and the world, to the Vatican's twentieth-century justification of the nuclear deterrent, the line has endured. Thou shalt not kill...except from time to time...and when the church tells you to.

Augustine, a saint by trade, dedicated all his talent to justifying the worst in the church: slavery, war, capital punishment, etc. Blessed are the meek? The peacemakers? Augustine is no more enthusiastic than Hitler about this side of Christianity, too soft, not virile or warlike enough, squeamish about bloodshed—the feminine face of religion. He offered the church the concepts it lacked to justify punitive expeditions and massacres. These things the Jews had practiced to acquire their land, on a limited geographical scale, but the Christians drew from that local action inspiration for action across the face of the glob, for their goal was converting the world itself. The chosen people generated catastrophes that were *first of all* local. Universal Christianity created *universal* upheavals. Once it triumphed, every continent became a battlefield.

With the church's blessing, Augustine, bishop of Hippo, sanctioned *just persecution* in a letter (185).A choice formulation, which he presents in contrast to *unjust persecution!* What differentiates the good corpse from the bad? Flaying of victims—when is it defensible and when is it indefensible? All persecution by the church was good, because motivated by love; while persecution directed against the church was indefensible, because inspired by cruelty. We should relish the rhetoric and talent for sophistry of Saint Augustine, who preferred his Jesus to brandish the whip and not to suffer it at the hands of the Roman soldiery.

Which brings us to the concept *of just war,* itself formulated by the saine church father, a man who decidedly never shrank from brutality, vice, or perversion. As the heir of the ancient pagan fable—Greek as it happened—Christianity recycled trial by ordeal. In a war, the victor was designated by God; so too, therefore, was the vanquished. By deciding in the conflict between winners and losers, God designates the true and the false, good and bad, legitimate and illegitimate. Magical thinking, to say the least.

Jesus at Hiroshima. Jesus and his scourge, Paul and his belief in power emanating from God, and Augustine with his just war together constitute a Trinitarian assault group capable of justifying every operation committed in the name of God over the last two millennia. They gave us the Crusades against the Saracens, the Inquisition against supposed heretics, the so-called holy wars against unbelievers—what glory! Saint Bernard of Clairvaux confiding in a letter (363): "the best solution is to kill them," or again, "a pagan's death is a Christian's glory"—the most Christian campaigns of extermination against peoples called primitive, colonial wars to evangelize every continent, the fascisms of the twentieth century, including of course Nazism, all of them furiously unleashed against the Jews.

Little wonder, then, that official Christianity in the era of postmodern war opted for the nuclear deterrent, defended it, and excused it. John Paul II accepted its principle on June 11, 1982, via a truly extraordinary logical fallacy: the atom bomb, he said, opened the road to peace! France's bishops followed close behind, armed with their own reasons, which included the need to struggle against "the domineering and aggressive nature of Marxist-Leninist ideology." Sweet Jesus! What power of decision, what lucidly stated positions! How we would have welcomed an equally clear and straightforward condemnation of Nazism during its twelve-year reign. We would even have been grateful for a similar moral assertion *after* the death camps were liberated.

When the Berlin Wall fell and the Bolshevik threat could at least be said to have diminished, the church upheld its position. In part III, section II, chapter 2, article 5, item 2315 of its latest *Catechism*, the Vatican expresses "strong moral reservations" about the arms race. Note the understatement! The accumulation of nuclear weapons is not an effective deterrent to war, but the Vatican condemns it not at all. In the same document, under the article heading "You shall not kill"—long live logic and coherence!—item 2267 states, "The traditional teaching of the Church does not exclude recourse to the death penalty" Ix is scarcely surprising that the index has no listing for "capital punishment," "death sentence," or "punishment." On the other hand, euthanasia, abortion, suicide, issues addressed in the same chapter, are fully referenced.

As we know, the crew of the *Enola Gay* dropped an atomic bomb on Hiroshima on August 6, 1945. In a few seconds the nuclear explosion caused the death of more than a hundred thousand people, women, the old, children, the sick, innocents whose only crime was being Japanese. The crew returned safely to base: the Christian God had protected these new Crusaders. We should add that Father George Zabelka had solemnly blessed the crew before its deadly mission! Three days later, a second atomic bomb struck Nagasaki and killed eighty thousand people.

Colonialism, genocide, ethnocide. The logical sequence to justification of slavery was colonialism, which entailed exporting one's religion to the four corners of the world and the use of force, of physical, mental, spiritual, psychic, and of course armed constraint to achieve those ends. Exporting slavery and extending it to every continent was the work first of Christianity and then of Islam. As for the Jewish people, they have sought to establish their dominion over *only one* territory, their territory, without ever seeking further. Zionism is neither expansionist nor internationalist. On the contrary, the dream brought to fruition by Theodor Herzl implies nationalism, a centrifugal movement, the desire of a closed society existing for oneself alone—and not a desire for mastery of the whole planet, a desire shared by Christianity and Islam.

The Catholic, Apostolic, and Roman Church excels in the destruction of civilizations. It invented ethnocide, the spiritual rather than the physical extinction of cultures. The year 1492 does not merely spell the discovery of the New World but the destruction of other worlds. Christian Europe laid waste a considerable number of Amerindian civilizations. Soldiers, accompanied by the scum of society—jailbirds, petty criminals, strong-arm men, mercenaries—disembarked from the caravels. Once the ensuing ethnic cleansing was over, the priests followed at a safe distance in solemn procession, with crucifixes, ciboria, Hosts, and portable altars, all most useful in preaching brotherly love, forgiveness of sins, the sweetness of the angelic virtues, and other tokens of biblical joy—original sin, hatred of women, of the body and of sexuality, guilt. Meanwhile, Christendom gave the peoples it called savages its housewarming gifts of syphilis and other transmissible diseases.

The partnership of the church and Nazism likewise aimed at extermination of a race reconfigured for the purposes of the cause into a people of God-killers. Six million dead. To which we must add complicity in the deportation and murder of gypsies, homosexuals, Communists, Freemasons, left-wingers, laymen, Jehovah's Witnesses, antifascists, and other people guilty of not being very Christian.

The Christian passion for mass extermination is old and enduring. A recent example was the genocide of Tutsis by the Hutu of Rwanda, supported, defended, and covered up by the Catholic establishment on the spot and by the supreme pontiff himself. The pope was much quicker to ensure that priestly genocide-bent war criminals, monks, nuns, and other members of the Catholic community might escape the firing squads than to offer one word of compassion to the Tutsi community.

For in Rwanda, a country with an overwhelmingly Christian population, the church even *before* the genocide had practiced racial discrimination in accepting candidates for seminaries, in training, in the administration of Catholic schools, in ordination or promotion in the ecclesiastical hierarchy. *During* the genocide some members of the clergy played an active part: purchase and delivery of machetes by members of the Catholic establishment, sniffing out the victims' hiding places, actively participating in orgies of brutality—people locked into churches, the churches burned down, their remains obliterated by bulldozers—denunciations, sermons to fire up the masses, exploitation of racial language.

After the massacres, the Catholic Church stayed on course. Convents were taken over to hide guilty Christians from justice, networks galvanized to help smuggle this or that criminal out to European countries, air tickets provided by Christian humanitarian organizations. Guilty priests were farmed out to provincial Belgian and French parishes, bishops implicated in the genocide were whisked from view. And the church resorted to public attitudes of denial—insisting, for example, on referring to "fratricidal war" in preference to "genocide."

Silent on the preparations, silent during the massacres—nearly one million dead in three months (between April and June 1994)—silent after the scope of the disaster (carried out with the blessings of French president François Mitterrand) was revealed, John Paul II emerged from his silence to write a letter to the president of Rwanda on April 23, 1998. Its contents? Did he deplore? Did he express compassion? Did he repent? Regret? Blame his clergy? Wash his hands of their actions? No, not at all: he requested a stay of execution for Hutus found guilty of genocide. Not a single word for the victims.

Repressions and the death fixation. The fixation of the three monotheisms on the death instinct can be explained. How can we escape the domination of that instinct after so effectively killing off the life urge both within and outside ourselves? Fear of death, of the void, horror at the idea of the emptiness that follows death, all help generate consoling fables, fictions that incite us to deny use of our full powers. The real is not. Fiction, on the other hand, is. This false world, which forces us to live in the here and now buttressed by hopes of a tinsel afterlife, leads to denial, contempt, or hatred of the here and now.

Hence countless opportunities for seeing this hatred at work: on the body, desires, passions, drives, on the flesh, women, love, sex, on life in all its forms, on matter, on the things that enhance our existence in this world, in other words, on reason, intelligence, books, science, culture. This suppression of everything living forces on us the celebration of everything that dies—bloodshed and war—of whatever kills, of those who kill. Whereas intelligent reading from the three books would let us select whatever confers maximum power on the life force, religion seeks out the death force in all its forms. Suppression of the living engenders love of death. And generally speaking, all contempt for women—we prefer virgins, mothers, and wives—goes hand in hand with a cult of death.

Civilizations are not founded on the death drive. Sacrificial blood, the scapegoat, laying the foundations of a society through an act of ritual murder—these are sinister social constants. The Jewish extermination of the Canaanites, the Christian crucifixion of the Messiah, the Muslim jihad of the Prophet all shed the blood that blesses and sanctifies the monotheist cause. Primitive, magical aspersion, disemboweling of the propitiatory victims—who happen to be men, women, and children. The primitive survives in the postmodern, the animal survives in man, the beast still dwells in *Homo sapiens.*

34
Thank Goodness! (2006)
Daniel C. Dennett

There are no atheists in foxholes, according to an old but dubious saying, and there is at least a little anecdotal evidence in favor of it in the notorious cases of famous atheists who have emerged from near-death experiences to announce to the world that they have changed their minds. The British philosopher Sir A.J. Ayer, who died in 1989, is a fairly recent example. Here is another anecdote to ponder.

Two weeks ago, I was rushed by ambulance to a hospital where it was determined by CT scan that I had a "dissection of the aorta"—the lining of the main output vessel carrying blood from my heart had been torn up, creating a two—channel pipe where there should only be one. Fortunately for me, the fact that I'd had a coronary artery bypass graft seven years ago probably saved my life, since the tangle of scar tissue that had grown like ivy around my heart in the intervening years reinforced the aorta, preventing catastrophic leakage from the tear in the aorta itself. After a nine-hour surgery, in which my heart was stopped entirely and my body and brain were chilled down to about 45 degrees to prevent brain damage from lack of oxygen until they could get the heart-lung machine pumping, I am now the proud possessor of a new aorta and aortic arch, made of strong Dacron fabric tubing sewn into shape on the spot by the surgeon, attached to my heart by a carbon-fiber valve that makes a reassuring little click every time my heart beats.

As I now enter a gentle period of recuperation, I have much to reflect on, about the harrowing experience itself and even more about the flood of supporting messages I've received since word got out about my latest adventure. Friends were anxious to learn if I had had a near-death experience, and if so, what effect it had had on my longstanding public atheism. Had I had an epiphany? Was I going to follow in the footsteps of Ayer (who recovered his aplomb and insisted a few days later "what I should have said is that my experiences have weakened, not my belief that there is no life after death, but my inflexible attitude towards that belief"), or was my atheism still intact and unchanged?

Yes, I did have an epiphany. I saw with greater clarity than ever before in my life that when I say "Thank goodness!" this is not merely a euphemism for "Thank God!" (We atheists don't believe that there is any God to thank.) I really do mean thank goodness! There is a lot of goodness in this world, and more goodness every day, and this fantastic human-made fabric of excellence is genuinely responsible for the fact that I am alive today. It is a worthy recipient of the gratitude I feel today, and I want to celebrate that fact here and now.

To whom, then, do I owe a debt of gratitude? To the cardiologist who has kept me alive and ticking for years, and who swiftly and confidently rejected the original diagnosis of nothing worse than pneumonia. To the surgeons, neurologists, anesthesiologists, and the perfusionist, who kept my systems going for many hours under daunting circumstances. To the dozen or so physician assistants, and to nurses and physical therapists and x-ray technicians and a small army of phlebotomists so deft that you hardly know they are drawing your blood, and the people who brought the meals, kept my room clean, did the mountains of laundry generated by such a messy case, wheel-chaired me to x-ray, and so forth. These people came from Uganda, Kenya, Liberia, Haiti, the Philippines, Croatia, Russia, China, Korea, India—and the United States, of course—and I have never seen more impressive mutual respect, as they helped each other out and checked each other's work. But for all their teamwork, this local gang could not have done their jobs without the huge background of contributions from others. I remember with gratitude my late friend and Tufts colleague, physicist Allan Cormack, who shared the Nobel Prize for his invention of the CT scanner. Allan—you have posthumously saved yet another life, but who's counting? The world is better for the work you did. Thank goodness. Then there is the whole system of medicine, both the science and the technology, without which the best-intentioned efforts of individuals would be roughly useless. So I am grateful to the editorial boards and referees, past and present, of Science, Nature, Journal of the American Medical Association, Lancet, and all the other institutions of science and medicine that keep churning out improvements, detecting and correcting flaws.

Do I worship modern medicine? Is science my religion? Not at all; there is no aspect of modern medicine or science that I would exempt from the most rigorous scrutiny, and I can readily identify a host of serious problems that still need to be fixed. That's easy to do, of course, because the worlds of medicine and science are already engaged in the most obsessive, intensive, and humble self-assessments yet known to human institutions, and they regularly make public the results of their self-examinations. Moreover, this open-ended rational criticism, imperfect as it is, is the secret of the astounding success of these human enterprises. There are measurable improvements every day. Had I had my blasted aorta a decade ago, there would have been no prayer of saving me. It's hardly routine today, but the odds of my survival were actually not so bad (these days, roughly 33 percent of aortic dissection patients die in the first twenty-four hours after onset without treatment, and the odds get worse by the hour thereafter).

One thing in particular struck me when I compared the medical world on which my life now depended with the religious institutions I have been studying so intensively in recent years. One of the gentler, more supportive themes to be found in every religion (so far as I know) is the idea that what really matters is what is in your heart: if you have good intentions, and are trying to do what (God says) is right, that is all anyone can ask. Not so in medicine! If you are wrong—especially if you should have known better—your good intentions count for almost nothing. And whereas taking a leap of faith and acting without further scrutiny of one's options is often celebrated by religions, it is considered a grave sin in medicine. A doctor whose devout faith in his personal revelations about how to treat aortic aneurysm led him to engage in untested trials with human patients would be severely reprimanded if not driven out of medicine altogether. There are exceptions, of course. A few swashbuckling, risk-taking pioneers are tolerated and (if they prove to be right) eventually honored, but they can exist only as rare exceptions to the ideal of the methodical investigator who scrupulously rules out alternative theories before putting his own into practice. Good intentions and inspiration are simply not enough.

In other words, whereas religions may serve a benign purpose by letting many people feel comfortable with the level of morality they themselves can attain, no religion holds its members to the high standards of moral responsibility that the secular world of science and medicine does! And I'm not just talking about the standards 'at the top'—among the surgeons and doctors who make life or death decisions every day. I'm talking about the standards of conscientiousness endorsed by the lab technicians and meal preparers, too. This tradition puts its faith in the unlimited application of reason and empirical inquiry, checking and re-checking, and getting in the habit of asking "What if I'm wrong?" Appeals to faith or membership are never tolerated. Imagine the reception a scientist would get if he tried to suggest that others couldn't replicate his results because they just didn't share the faith of the people in his lab! And, to return to my main point, it is the goodness of this tradition of reason and open inquiry that I thank for my being alive today.

What, though, do I say to those of my religious friends (and yes, I have quite a few religious friends) who have had the courage and honesty to tell me that they have been praying for me? I have gladly forgiven them, for there are few circumstances more frustrating than not being able to help a loved one in any more direct way. I confess to regretting that I could not pray (sincerely) for my friends and family in time of need, so I appreciate the urge, however clearly I recognize its futility. I translate my religious friends' remarks readily enough into one version or another of what my fellow brights have been telling me: "I've been thinking about you, and wishing with all my heart [another ineffective but irresistible self-indulgence] that you come through this OK." The fact that these dear friends have been thinking of me in this way, and have taken an effort to let me know, is in itself, without any need for a supernatural supplement, a wonderful tonic. These messages from my family and from friends around the world have been literally heart-warming in my case, and I am grateful for the boost in morale (to truly manic heights, I fear!) that it has produced in me. But I am not joking when I say that I have had to forgive my friends who said that they were praying for me. I have resisted the temptation to respond "Thanks, I appreciate it, but did you also sacrifice a goat?" I feel about this the same way I would feel if one of them said "I just paid a voodoo doctor to cast a spell for your health." What a gullible waste of money that could have been spent on more important projects! Don't expect me to be grateful, or even indifferent. I do appreciate the affection and generosity of spirit that motivated you, but wish you had found a more reasonable way of expressing it.

But isn't this awfully harsh? Surely it does the world no harm if those who can honestly do so pray for me! No, I'm not at all sure about that. For one thing, if they really wanted to do something useful, they could devote their prayer time and energy to some pressing project that they can do something about. For another, we now have quite solid grounds (e.g., the recently released Benson study at Harvard) for believing that intercessory prayer simply doesn't work. Anybody whose practice shrugs off that research is subtly undermining respect for the very goodness I am thanking. If you insist on keeping the myth of the effectiveness of prayer alive, you owe the rest of us a justification in the face of the evidence. Pending such a justification, I will excuse you for indulging in your tradition; I know how comforting tradition can be. But I want you to recognize that what you are doing is morally problematic at best. If you would even consider filing a malpractice suit against a doctor who made a mistake in treating you, or suing a pharmaceutical company that didn't conduct all the proper control tests before selling you a drug that harmed you, you must acknowledge your tacit appreciation of the high standards of rational inquiry to which the medical world holds itself, and yet you continue to indulge in a practice for which there is no known rational justification at all, and take yourself to be actually making a contribution. (Try to imagine your outrage if a pharmaceutical company responded to your suit by blithely replying "But we prayed good and hard for the success of the drug! What more do you want?")

The best thing about saying thank goodness in place of thank God is that there really are lots of ways of repaying your debt to goodness—by setting out to create more of it, for the benefit of those to come. Goodness comes in many forms, not just medicine and science. Thank goodness for the music of, say, Randy Newman, which could not exist without all those wonderful pianos and recording studios, to say nothing of the musical contributions of every great composer from Bach through Wagner to Scott Joplin and the Beatles. Thank goodness for fresh drinking water in the tap, and food on our table. Thank goodness for fair elections and truthful journalism. If you want to express your gratitude to goodness, you can plant a tree, feed an orphan, buy books for schoolgirls in the Islamic world, or contribute in thousands of other ways to the manifest improvement of life on this planet now and in the near future.

Or you can thank God—but the very idea of repaying God is ludicrous. What could an omniscient, omnipotent Being (the Man Who has Everything?) do with any paltry repayments from you? (And besides, according to the Christian tradition God has already redeemed the debt for all time, by sacrificing his own son. Try to repay that loan!) Yes, I know, those themes are not to be understood literally; they are symbolic. I grant it, but then the idea that by thanking God you are actually doing some good has got to be understood to be just symbolic, too. I prefer real good to symbolic good.

Still, I excuse those who pray for me. I see them as like tenacious scientists who resist the evidence for theories they don't like long after a graceful concession would have been the appropriate response. I applaud you for your loyalty to your own position—but remember: loyalty to tradition is not enough. You've got to keep asking yourself: What if I'm wrong? In the long run, I think religious people can be asked to live up to the same moral standards as secular people in science and medicine.

35
For The Love Of Reason (2007)
Louise M. Antony

I always had trouble with Limbo. Limbo, I was taught, is a place where good but unbaptized people go when they die. We are all born carrying the stain of original sin on our souls, and unless the stain is washed away through baptism, we are unfit to be in the presence of God.[1]

There was no part of this doctrine that made any sense to me. For starters, there was the whole idea of "original" sin. The *original* original sin, of course, was the one committed by Adam when he disobeyed God's commandment not to eat from the tree of knowledge of good and evil.[2] Adam himself was punished—fair enough—but then somehow, this sin that Adam committed got "passed down," besmirching the soul of every one of Adam's descendants. I found it repugnant, the idea that a crime committed by one of my ancestors could sully my personal soul. It was an idea quite at odds with the liberal, meritocratic principles to which my parents seemed otherwise to subscribe.

This concept of original sin was often presented to me in terms of natural law-like gravity, it's just the way things are. But the analogy seemed inapt; gravity had nothing to do with what you deserved. And anyway, I'd protest, didn't God make the laws? If so, why did He choose to make things so that you inherited your parents' guilt? Why make the laws of spiritual heredity Lamarckian rather than Darwinian?[3]

I was also troubled by the idea of a soul's being "unfit" to be in the presence of God, irrespective of the rectitude of its owner. It made sense to me that the souls of unrepentant sinners would be unfit, but the people in Limbo could have been as saintly as Gandhi—could even be Gandhi—and God still wouldn't have them. This "fitness" sounded almost aesthetic—as if the unbaptized righteous had body odor, or weren't dressed properly. Maybe God was allergic...? At the very least, if something made baptism a condition of entrance into heaven, why didn't He see to it that the sacrament was a little more widely available?

Now my mother felt the force of this consideration, and as a consequence was a great supporter of the Maryknoll missionaries. (This was long before they became associated with radical liberation theology.) She would write them a small check every month and encourage me to make a contribution as well. She impressed upon me the cosmic importance of bringing the Word of God and, crucially, the sacrament of baptism to the innocents of the Mexican jungles. "This is the work that God wants us to do for Him," she'd explain. But wait a minute, I thought. Now you're telling me that the eternal fate of some poor child in Africa depends on what I do? This was a heavy burden to bear for a youngster with twenty-five cents in her pocket and a new issue of *Action Comics* beckoning from the news rack. It would only be much later that I'd come to realize that the setup presumed by my mother's creed, whereby the spiritual fates of millions of others is made precarious in order to provide me with opportunities to practice virtue, was at least as repugnant as the original injustice.

But there was something that bothered me almost as much as Limbo itself: the way grownups reacted to my questions about it. First they'd offer a perfunctory, stock, and utterly impertinent response. "The souls in Limbo don't suffer," they'd all say. Huh? Maybe they're not in actual pain, like the souls in Hell, and or even the ones in Purgatory, but these poor souls are being deprived of the Beatific Vision, an experience of which, it was emphasized in other contexts, is the final purpose and goal of human existence!

So the next move would be "but they don't know they're being deprived of anything." Double huh. It's OK not to share your chocolate with your sister as long as she never finds out you have it? This "ignorance is bliss" reasoning seemed specious to me even as a small child. And it was, once again, inconsistent with the messages I got in every other, non-religious context. My father, for example, was an elementary school administrator, and he was passionate in his support for public education. He would go on and on about the need to cultivate in children—to inculcate in children—the "desire to learn." He would have been incensed had anyone suggested that as long as an illiterate child had no conception of the pleasures of reading, it was fine to leave well enough alone.

Not many adults were willing to go on to round three. They would grow impatient. "Louise," my mother would say, "you just think too much." Sometimes they'd get positively angry. What was the matter with me? Why did I have to argue about everything? Didn't I realize that some things just had to be taken on faith? In general, I was informed, I should concentrate more on loving my neighbor and less on being a smarty-pants.

None of the nuns or priests from whom I received religious instruction were of any help on the matter of Limbo, nor, for that matter, on any of the other issues that troubled me. There was also the Trinity: how could there be "three persons in one God"? I remember trying to wrap my childish head around this "holy mystery" in the classes preparatory to my receiving my First Communion. For several months running, I would go home from religious education one week, think hard about the whole thing, then return the next week with a new idea to offer Sister. It was always wrong. Maybe God was like a family, I suggested. There was, after all, a Father, a Son, and (remember, now, I was only six-and-a-half, and He was usually depicted as a bird) the family pet, Holy Ghost. No, said Sister, God is not like a family. OK—maybe God is like a three-leafed clover (I had just been taught that this was how St. Patrick explained the Trinity to the heathen Celts in Ireland)—the Father is one leaf, the Son is another, the Holy Ghost is a third, and they're all parts of God. No, said Sister, God is not like a three-leafed clover, St. Patrick notwithstanding. Well, maybe each person is like a different mood of God—God the Father is the angry mood, God the Son is the loving mood, and the Holy Ghost is some other kind of mood. No, said Sister, not moods, either. Finally Sister, clearly exhausted, told me that I'd never understand the Trinity because it was a *mystery of faith.* Mysteries of faith are, by their nature, incomprehensible. We must simply believe them. But how can I believe something I don't understand, I asked? "Just memorize your Catechism," was Sister's reply. "Belief will come."

Now it wasn't just religion. Limbo wasn't the only mystery with which I was preoccupied. I also had problems with Santa Claus. I had no trouble with flying reindeer—remember that my world was amply stocked with miraculous violations of physical law. The difficulty again was moral. Barbara Perkins, my friend who lived at the top of the hill near the bus stop, always got loads of presents "from Santa Claus" at Christmas time. We're talking play kitchens, bicycles, puppies, Barbie dolls with Dream Houses—major loot. I, on the other hand, generally received one present from Santa, carefully selected and duly solicited from one of Santa's department store "helpers" (I had asked about the baffling proliferation of Santas early on, and had received and accepted the standard answer), and this one present was never very grand.

Now this was curious, I thought. I understood that there were well-off families in the world, and not-so-well-off families, and I understood that mine was one of the not-so-well-off ones. But why did Santa Claus respect these distinctions? Why did he bring more toys to the rich kids than to the poor ones? Apparently, in the cases of really indigent kids, he planned to bring nothing at all—why else the "toys for tots" drives at our church every Christmas? If anything, you'd think that Santa would try to rectify economic inequities—that he'd give that play kitchen to the little girl whose parents couldn't afford to buy her anything. Was Santa Claus a supply-sider?

I made the enormous social blunder of bringing this up with other kids, indeed, with Barbara Perkins herself. I'm pretty sure I suggested that she could do a little to bring moral order to the universe by giving me her play kitchen.) They were not interested—reasonably enough: one's not a kid forever, and there are cartoons to be watched. But adults didn't appreciate my questions, either. I'd get a little patronizing approval for asking "such a serious question!" but once they saw that I really meant to know what was going on, they'd get irritated. I don't know how I described their reactions to myself at the time, but as I remember them now, it seems clear that they, no less than their kids, thought I was being a colossal drag.

What I got from all of this was that thinking was fine and good, but only in its place. A little learning might be a dangerous thing, but a lot of thinking was worse. Today I am a parent, and I know firsthand the tedium and frustration of dealing with a child who won't stop asking "why." I also know that the questions of an inquiring child may be more motivated by the hope of delaying bedtime than by the love of knowledge. And finally, I know there are children who relish making their superiors squirm; I surely was one of them. But with all that said, I still, to this day, resent the way I was made to feel as a child—that my questioning was inherently bad, that there was something wrong with me for wanting things to make sense.

As I've said, the reactions of grownups to my questions about religion were doubly distressing to me because of their dissonance with the principles adults were explicitly promoting in other contexts. In school, a broadly libertarian and individualistic ethos prevailed. We were always being exhorted to "think for ourselves." In reading, we were urged to "sound out the words instead of just asking," and in arithmetic to figure out the problems on our own. Science teachers and science books agreed heartily that curiosity is a marvelous thing, the engine of all scientific achievement. One must not take things for granted; one must always ask "why." The best scientists, it was stressed, are the ones who see mystery in the everyday, who press for deeper and deeper understanding. In the biographies of Marie Curie I devoured, she was praised for seeing questions no one else did and for persisting in her work until she got her answers. (My mother, by the way, got me these books. She was a secret feminist. She kept the secret even from herself.) In my elementary school citizenship classes, democracy was praised as the most perfect political form because it allowed every citizen to "follow his own conscience." My parents and teachers, counseling me about personal behavior, stressed the importance of doing what I knew was right, regardless of what other people thought. Why in religion was I supposed to dumbly accept whatever the authorities told me?

Somewhere along the line, I came to the conclusion that my inquisitiveness was sinful. It was not just that it was prideful—I'd been told that explicitly, and often enough. This new idea was that the questions had been put into my head by the devil, and that, indeed, the whole world had been mined with dangerous ideas, ideas that could threaten my faith if I indulged them. No one ever told me such a thing in so many words, but it seemed to me a good explanation for the taboo against thinking in religion, together with my apparent inability to respect it.

My little theory kept me in a pretty constant state of anxiety, lest I take seriously something that turned out to be incompatible with religious teachings. I was pretty interested in biology and genetics as a kid and read everything I could get my hands on. Before very long, I encountered the theory of evolution. It seemed really plausible to me, and ingenious. But I didn't see where in the theory souls were supposed to come in. It's not that I had ever been told that evolution was inconsistent with Catholicism—the Church in which I was raised was not fundamentalist, and condoned metaphorical readings of Scripture. The conflict was more of my own making. It seemed to me that if evolutionary theory was correct, then biological differences were matters of degree: apes just gradually became people. But that seemed parlously at odds with the religious picture: that human beings, in virtue of possessing immortal souls, were fundamentally different from everything else in nature. I decided that I should try not to believe in evolution.

I remember, too, being terrified by a particular cover on *Time* magazine that posed, in huge red letters against a black background, the shocking question: "Is God Dead?"[4] It's hard for me, to this day, to explain just what I found so profoundly unsettling about this question—I certainly wasn't simply shocked that anyone would think such a thing. It was rather the elemental uncanniness of the concept of God's dying—of the end of an eternal, all-powerful being. (Obviously, I never read the article—I might have been reassured to learn that the "death of God" was just a particularly provocative way of expressing disbelief.)

You might think, given all these complaints, that I resented my religion and wanted nothing more than to be free of it. But that's not the way it was. Despite my frustrations, I was passionately devout. I tried really hard to say my prayers mindfully, to pay attention at Mass, and to obey the Ten Commandments, especially the fourth, which apparently covered not teasing the cat. I failed regularly in these efforts, but made regular Confessions. I didn't particularly like candy, so I would make a point of giving up comic books for Lent. (Although I must admit this was sly of me, since Sundays were not part of Lent, and Sundays were when we went to the drug-store where comic books were sold.) I memorized prayers that no one else knew, and read unassigned books about saints. I took seriously all the rules of observance, never missing Mass on Sundays, and strictly following the more obscure require-ments of Lenten abstinence (I was told frequently that I took things too seriously). I respected and trusted my parents: if they told me all this stuff was true, then I was pretty sure it had to be true. I just couldn't figure out how it could be true.

I think I identified being religious with being good. Most of my charitable acts, such as they were, were carried out under church auspices, though probably not for the right reasons. I found the idea of martyrdom really exciting and prayed that I might someday give my life for Christ. (My mother's suggestion—that God's plan for me might have more to do with dusting and table setting than with famished lions or flaming stakes—was ill received.) But I also heard in the Sunday sermons, and in the Gospel readings, two consistent moral messages that moved me deeply—first, that every human being had an immortal soul of surpassing moral value, and second, that our overarching duty on Earth was to demonstrate our love of God through our acts of love for humankind. I would be martyred, I decided, while teaching deaf and blind leukemia victims in Mrica.

Because I was usually in the minority, being a Catholic made me feel special. In the Upstate New York suburb where I spent some of my childhood, and later in West-ern Massachusetts, nearly everyone I knew was some sort of Protestant (exception: my best friend in Vestal, New York, who attended the Polish American Catholic church. She's also now a philosopher—go figure). There was one Jew that I knew of in Vestal, and one who attended my high school in Sheffield, but all I knew about Jews or their religion was that they didn't believe in Jesus, and so did not celebrate Christ-mas. My mother assured me that they could, nonetheless, be Very Good People. (Swelling the population of Limbo, I thought.) Protestantism was very mysterious to me. I could tell anyone who wanted to know exactly what my theological beliefs were—they could have the short version, in the form of the Apostle's Creed, or the long—very long—version codified in the Baltimore Catechism, which I had memo-rized. But if I asked my Protestant friends what they believed, they seemed not to have a clue. In some cases, they were unclear even as to which denomination they be-longed. Several of my friends reported that they attended the church they did be-cause their parents liked the minister there. What with fasting Sunday mornings before Communion, abstaining from meat on Fridays, and giving up candy for Lent, I felt smugly superior to these Protestant friends, whose religions, it seemed to me, required very little of them.

My religion was with me every day. I said my prayers in the morning on waking, and again before I went to bed at night. I reminded myself that it was my religious duty to treat my elderly Great-Aunt Louise—an imperious and stentorian woman who had come to live with us upon the death of her husband with respect. (Not that I was very successful.) Minor medical discomforts, like my weekly gamma globulin shot, were offered up for the poor souls in Purgatory. (Purgatory is not the same as Limbo. The souls in Purgatory will eventually enter heaven, once they've done their time.) I made it a practice to receive Holy Communion every Sunday (unless I was ill, and excused from attending Mass).

Another daily reminder of my religion—not a pleasant one—was my almost continual sense of guilt. I have already mentioned my failures with respect to Aunt Louise. I was no better about teasing the cat, or about fighting with my sister. The worst attack of guilt I ever suffered, however, came one time when I yielded to the temptation to preserve my Communion record, and received the sacrament without being sure that it had really been sixty full minutes since I had eaten. I had been spending the night with friends who owned a small boat, and while my mother had extracted from them a promise to get me to mass as a condition *of* my being allowed to stay, they were themselves freethinkers and not terribly enthusiastic about the whole enterprise. The only Catholic church in the area was about a half-hour drive from the marina, and we needed to get to the earliest service—8:30 a.m.—in order to preserve a reasonable chunk *of* the day for boating. Despite the early hour, my friends insisted that I eat something before we left. I must not have had a watch; I remember calculating that if it took us half an hour to get to the church, then by the time the priest actually distributed Communion, it might possibly be an hour later than my last bite. I knew perfectly well that if I wasn't sure I had completed the required period of fast then I ought not to receive Communion. It was a mortal sin to take the sacrament if one was not "properly prepared"—a condition that also precluded being in a state of mortal sin. Nonetheless, I was fetishistic about my record, and persuaded myself—for the moment at least—that I was in the clear.

The second after I received the host, however, the scruples set in. By the middle of the brilliantly sunny and perfectly still afternoon, I was stricken with nausea and the shakes. I refused to go swimming, terrified that I might drown in a state of mortal sin and go straight to Hell. I told my hosts that I was seasick. They favored the more plausible diagnosis, given the circumstances, that I'd contracted some stomach virus, and cut short the day to get me home. Once there, I burst into tears, confessed the whole story to my mother, and demanded that she call the church and arrange for me to make a confession. Now, my mother, while very devout and scrupulously observant, was also a sensible and loving parent and tried her best to persuade me that no one as obviously sorry as I was (for an offense she was not even convinced I'd committed) was destined for Hell, and that I could just wait until the regularly scheduled confessions the next Saturday. Nothing for it—I was hysterical at the thought that I would have to carry the weight of my blackened soul all through the week. So she called the rectory and reached our young assistant pastor, who agreed to hear my confession over the phone.

This worked in the end, but the rescue was nearly derailed by the earnest young priest's attempts to convince me that I was too young (I was eleven) to have really, knowingly, and willingly committed a mortal sin. I was righteously insulted by this suggestion. I knew the definition *of* a mortal sin, I exclaimed, and every clause was fulfilled: 1) it was a grievous wrong, 2) I *knew* it was a grievous wrong, and 3) I wanted to do it anyway. (Now, at some level, I surprised myself. I had earlier argued to Sister that no one could possibly satisfy all these conditions at the same time—that you couldn't really, really want to do something that you, at the very same time, really, really believed was wrong. But now, suddenly, talking to Father, I saw that yes, you really, really could!)

Most of my youth, I did not look forward to Sunday mass. When I was a girl, it was still said in Latin, and though I'd follow along in my missal (once I learned how to read), I found most of the ritual pretty boring. There was no singing, unless it was a high mass, and then it was the priest who sang (so much the worse!). I did, for the most part, rather like the sermons, and the Gospel and Epistle readings. And I did find my religious education classes interesting (although, as I've been at pains to explain, often for the wrong reasons).

A great deal changed, though, once the Second Vatican Council reforms were implemented—mass in the vernacular, responses recited and hymns sung by the congregation—my concentration, and consequently my piety, were much improved. I loved the "folk mass." Like all good flower children, I knew two separate chord progressions on the guitar and was thus amply equipped to strum accompaniments to "Hear O Lord" and "Sons of God." (Accustomed as I was to staring at a bloodied body while I prayed, I was taken aback by a non-Catholic friend's horrified reaction to the cheerful exhortation to cannibalism in the chorus of the latter hymn: "Eat His body/Drink His blood/ Allelu-, allelu-, allelu-, allelu-u-ia…") I began attending a teen discussion group in a neighboring parish run by an inspiring young priest from the seminary up in Lenox, a student (I now surmise) of liberation theology. Doctrinal difficulties began to recede, and my religious practice began to resonate with the calls for justice and liberation sounding throughout U.S. society.

Thus I continued to consider myself a devout Catholic all during high school. (Leave aside the odd mortal sin. Many non-Catholics I talk to are certain that my loss of faith had to do with sex, but this just reflects their prejudice. Like many, many of my Catholic peers, I found it pretty easy to dismiss the Church's teachings about premarital sex and contraception as inessential, old-fashioned, and not to be taken seriously.) But while I carried my religious identity with me to college, I carried right along with it a still-unsated curiosity about matters theological and moral. The one was about to come crashing into conflict with the other.

I knew absolutely nothing about the subject when I sat down in my first philosophy class. I was taking it to fulfill a distribution requirement and was dimly apprehensive that the readings would be incomprehensible and would somehow require knowledge of ancient history. Imagine my delight, then, when I discovered that philosophy was all about arguing! Not only was my constant questioning tolerated; it was positively encouraged. Finally, finally—a place where reasons had to be given, a place where no one would tell you it was impertinent to ask. I could scarcely believe that I could earn credits just for doing what (to me) came naturally.

So the good news was that everything could be questioned; everything was up for debate. But that, it turned out, was also the bad news. It was one thing, I discovered, to raise my questions about the nature of the afterlife and the justice of the Creator from a background of religious commitment, and quite another to raise such questions in the context of a no-holds-barred debate. I began to realize that in all my childhood worrying, it had never occurred to me that my questions might just not have answers. I certainly had never really considered what it would mean for my own religious faith if that turned out to be the case. But now I found myself in the company of people who saw religious commitment itself as open to challenge, who were asking a question I had never, ever dared to even formulate: is there a God?

The first rumblings of distress arose with our survey of the traditional arguments for the existence of God. I fought tooth and nail to make one of them work, but I had to admit in the end that none of them seemed fully convincing. First came the *a priori* arguments, the arguments that were supposed to proceed from self-evident principles. Anselm's argument seemed like verbal sleight of hand. Each of Aquinas's five ways depended on premises that seemed far from self-evident to me. Descartes's argument involved the puzzling claim that an idea could contain no more "reality" than its source, but how do you measure "amounts" of reality? Much as I hated to admit it, these arguments seemed frivolous, more suited to *Alice in Wonderland* than the New Testament. The arguments that appealed to empirical evidency seemed more promising, at least initially. But William James's argument, based on his own religious experience, finally failed to convince. Far too many of my friends had had "religious experiences" of the chemical type (it was, after all, 1971) for me to trust any "insights" gleaned on that basis. The argument from design—wherein God is posited to explain the intricate orderliness of nature—seemed, despite its problems, the last hope.

But then came the day that literally changed my life—the day when I first heard the "argument from evil." The reasoning is easy to state: Suffering exists. If God can do anything, He must not want to prevent suffering; but if He does not want to prevent suffering, He cannot be perfectly good. Therefore, there is no all powerful, perfectly good Being. The argument has been known for centuries, and many replies have been attempted. For example, many theists point out that a great deal of the suffering in the world is the result of human beings' exercising their freedom. We must be free, they argue, if we are to be capable of virtuous actions, but free will carries with it, necessarily, the possibility for vicious action as well. Since God cannot intervene to prevent human actions that He knows will cause suffering without compromising the freedom of the actors, He must acquiesce. With respect to the rest of the world's suffering—that due to droughts and floods and earthquakes and disease—the most popular explanation is that it is simply the necessary consequence of God's enacting what is, in fact, the best of all possible systems of natural law.

I was not satisfied with the proffered explanations of natural evil. I saw no particular reason to believe, other than the mere desire to do so, that an *omnipotent* God could not devise a better way of organizing the world than the plan currently in evidence. (Voltaire, of course, satirizes the suggestion in the person of the ridiculous Dr. Pangloss.) The free will defense, on the other hand, I found not merely unpersuasive, but morally disturbing. It's fine and good that God should afford me the opportunity to practice virtue, but why should innocent others be allowed to suffer if I choose to practice vice instead? Also, is there no limit to the amount of suffering that must be permitted under this justification? The U.S. Constitution enshrines freedom as a societal value, but our civic institutions ensure that my freedom is consistent with equal freedom for everyone else. If I perform an act that infringes upon your rights, then I am subject to punishment and to restraint. Why, then, couldn't God have set things up similarly, with serious criminals being whisked away to Hell before they did too much harm? As things stand, there are apparently no limits on the nature and scope of atrocities that God will allow some human beings to perpetrate against others. Didn't Hitler show his true colors pretty decisively after—I don't know—the first million?

My childhood worries about Limbo returned with new significance, and new urgency. How could a just God design such a system, a system that doomed innocent people, before they were even born, to an eternity of deprivation? Hurricanes and plagues might come with an otherwise functional network of natural law. Murder might be the regrettable cost of giving human beings free will. But Limbo seemed to be utterly and profoundly *optional*. I could find no connection between it and any otherwise desirable purpose. The only possible response I could think of was the one I had spent all of my short life hitherto resisting: "It's a mystery."

By the middle of my first semester, I was experiencing a full-blown crisis of faith. I could not accept the possibility that my religious belief had no rational defense, especially not now after I'd fallen in love with a discipline devoted to rational defenses. But neither could I relinquish my belief. A world without God seemed literally unimaginable; everything would be changed. I was frightened, in contradictory ways: there is no God, and surely He'll punish me for thinking this. At the same time, I was angry: *why* were there no good answers? Why had God made it so difficult to make sense of His will? If He wanted us to believe, why had He made all the reason and evidence work against belief? Indeed, I achieved a few days' respite from my struggles when I considered that if God had given me the faculty of reason, He must have expected me to use it, and so couldn't reasonably fault me for giving up my belief. But this expedient didn't work for long. Limbo, after all, wasn't reasonable, either, but there it was.

In the end, it was more philosophy that saved me. My class had moved on from the existence of God (even if I hadn't, quite) and was studying the basis of moral value. One theory we considered was called "divine command theory," the view that it is God who puts moral value into the world, that what is morally good is whatever He wants to happen. Initially, I thought that this was the view that I did and ought to hold, indeed, that all religious people must hold. But an argument from Plato changed my mind. In his dialogue *Euthyphro*, Socrates asks the eponymous character to define "piety." Euthyphro responds that pious acts are those that are beloved by the gods. Fine, says Socrates—that tells us which acts are the pious ones, but it does not tell us what makes them pious: is it the gods' loving them that make them pious, or is it their being pious that accounts for the gods' loving them? In familiar terms: are acts of kindness, courage, and so forth good only because they are the kinds of things God happens to like? Or is it rather that God, being perfectly good, likes such acts because they are also good?

The first possibility struck me as morally repugnant: it made God's preferences morally arbitrary. God *happens* to dislike murder, but had He liked it, then it would have been morally OK. In contrast, on the second option, God dislikes murder because it is morally wrong: it doesn't become wrong only because He chooses to prohibit it. On this alternative view, His prescriptions and prohibitions do not *constitute* moral goodness; they are, rather, *manifestations* of it. The more I considered the matter, the more convinced I became that this second view was really the more religious—indeed the more pious. So the Euthyphro argument did not, in itself, aggravate the threat to my faith: had I discovered it before I acquired my doubts, it would not have occasioned any. In the context of my growing skepticism, however, the discovery of this argument liberated me from any felt need for faith. Once I realized that God was not necessary for there to be objective moral value, I also realized that religious belief was not necessary for anyone to be a good person. The objectivity of moral value is simply independent of God's existence. All that is lost, if there is no God, is a divine enforcer. In a world without God, there is no guarantee that the virtuous will ever be rewarded, nor that the vicious will ever be punished. We must do what is right simply because it is right.

At last I was ready to admit to myself that I no longer believed in God. I'll never forget the sudden upsurge of relief when I finally acknowledged that my faith was gone. I felt suddenly free—free of the obligation to avow propositions I didn't understand, free of the struggle to make sense of doctrines that couldn't be made sensible, and free of the need to square everything I learned with Catholic dogma. My only doxastic obligations henceforth would be to reason and evidence. "Now," I thought to myself, "all I have to believe is what I think is true."

OK, OK. I said that's where my *obligations* lay; I didn't say I always discharged them. As I pursued my philosophical interests, and as I began to take a more serious interest in politics, I came to realize that intellectual integrity is pretty hard to achieve. Time and again, I fell prey (and still do, of course) to non-rational influences. I wanted to sound smart, and I wanted to agree with my smart friends. I wanted to defend the views of favorite teachers, and I wanted people I didn't like to be wrong. Once I began committing my own philosophical views to paper, and eventually, to print, I found that I felt constrained by what I'd already said, whether or not I still believed it was right. So I can hardly claim that by giving up religious commitments I had freed myself of dogmatism and wishful thinking. Still, there was a big difference. The little voice inside my head that used to whisper warnings when I ventured onto doctrinally dangerous ground ("Catholics don't read that book") had now become reason's agent ("You don't really believe that," "You know she's right about that," 'What's your evidence?") While I earlier strove to reconcile disturbing facts with Catholic teachings—or indeed, to avoid encountering the disturbances in the first place—I now tried to keep my belief apportioned to the strength of the argument.

Equal in importance to what I now assigned as the having of reasons was my explicit commitment to the providing of reasons. I came to understand that my earlier frustrations had been as much with my teachers' and parents' refusal to engage in rational discussion as with my inability to discover what I wanted to know. And I saw clearly the nature of the conflict between the rhetoric of individual worth inherent in my childhood education and the grownups' retreat to dogmatism and authoritarianism in response to my questions: the refusal to give reasons is disrespectful to the person who asks for them. We will not all agree with each other, and given that, we cannot all be right. But if we are to treat each other properly as equals, we must be willing to explain ourselves. I owe it to someone with whom I disagree to show her the basis of my position, so that she can evaluate it for herself.

Simply announcing one's reasons is, of course, merely the beginning of rational engagement. "God (or Marx or George W. Bush) said it, I believe it, and that's the end of it" is not what I have in mind. Commitment to the practice of reason giving entails a willingness to continue the chain of reason giving until common ground is reached. Nowhere is this principle more important than in the political realm. Philosophy holds it to be an intellectual duty to provide arguments for one's positions, but when we are talking about the establishment and implementation of public policy, the duty becomes civic as well. My friend's reasons for opposing abortion may be religious in nature; it is certainly her right to be moved by her church's teachings, or by her reading of the books she regards as Holy Scripture. But if I am to acquiesce in a prohibition on the practice, I'm entitled to a reason that moves me.

Looking back on my development from devout Catholic girl to adamant atheist, I think that it was its bottom-line dogmatism that drove me away from the Church, and indeed, from the very possibility of religious faith. "Faith" presents a paradox: if a doctrine can be defended on rational grounds, then it needn't be taken on faith. But if it cannot be defended on rational grounds, why should you believe it?

I've often heard people quote approvingly the aphorism that "faith is believing where you cannot prove." The idea seems to be that since matters of great importance outstrip the human power to know, we must jump in and simply commit ourselves to certain ideas. The question, though, is which ones? There's very, very little that can literally be proven that is shown to be true without any possibility of doubt—only the propositions of logic and mathematics, and some philosophers will dispute even those! Nothing about the world of experience can be demonstrated with complete certainty. The evidence of our senses is partial, and we sometimes make mistakes. We must rely every day on memory and the testimony of others—both fallible—for a great deal of the information we need to make our way in the world. If we had to foreswear all these less-than-perfect sources, we'd know virtually nothing. But the aphorism, when taken as an endorsement of faith, suggests that, once we leave the realm of certainty, no distinctions can be made—that it's as rational to believe in unicorns as it is to believe in bacteria. The occurrence of the Holocaust cannot be proven, in this strict sense; must we therefore take deniers seriously? Lack of proof cannot entitle one to believe, or else anyone would be warranted in believing anything she wanted to.

Now, in truth, few people would explicitly endorse an inference of the form "there's no proof that *p;* therefore, I am entitled to believe that *p.*" But I've encountered many who accept a related, and equally fallacious, pattern of reasoning: "There's no proof that *p* is false; therefore it's not irrational to believe that *p* is true." So people will say, "Since no one can prove there is no God, I'm not irrational if I believe in Him." But once again, "proof" is a red herring. I cannot *prove* that aliens have never visited Earth, but given all the considerations against it, I'd be irrational not to reject the proposition. Reason makes demands in two directions.

Of course everyone has a moral and, at least in the United States, at least so far, a political right to believe whatever she wants. As a card-carrying member of the ACLU,[5] and insofar as I have the courage, I will defend this right to the death. But this gets us back to the point I was insisting on above. You are certainly entitled to believe whatever you like, if the matter affects you alone. But if what you believe is supposed to have bearing on what happens to someone else, then you had better have good grounds for your opinion. Majority rule is a kind of tyranny when people don't respect each other enough to form their opinions responsibly. More and more I hear people in my own country speaking about matters of social policy and foreign affairs with the same blithe fideism they evince when expressing their religious views. "Bush will keep us more secure." Really? What makes you say so? "Oh, it's just what I believe." And so thousands must die in Iraq.

Throughout contemporary U.S. society, reason is denigrated as cold, mechanical, and sterile, while irreason is celebrated. Inspirational posters cite the authority of Einstein in elevating supposedly irrational "creativity" over rational thought:

"Logic will get you from A to B; imagination will take you everywhere" or "'Imagination is more important than knowledge." Right—there's our problem: too much logic, not enough fantasy. Have you met my president?

The human interest stories in my local paper (on the front page of the "Faith" section—there is no "Reason" section) regularly honor the fidelity of people suffering the most appalling depredations: debilitating accidents, ruthless illnesses, spouses and children lost to senseless wars—all consistent, in the minds of these latter-day Jobs, with the limitless goodness of God. Likely as not, there will be featured, in the same edition, people who have prevailed against astonishing odds—the woman who survived the cancer that all the medical experts said would kill her, the husband who survived the landmine that killed all his buddies—all cheerfully attributing their own good fortune to God's great love for them. Never mind the quick paradox (He loved you enough to get you through chemotherapy, just not enough not to spare you the cancer in the first place)—what about the illogic of divine responsibility? God is to be thanked for the good things that happen but never blamed for the bad.

A college friend born and raised in a reformed Jewish household, never very religious, suddenly surprised all his childhood and college friends—not to mention his Jewish wife—by converting to messianic Judaism, becoming a "Jew for Jesus." One evening a few months after his conversion, my husband and I visited for dinner. My friend was recounting an incredible story from his hellion adolescence: he had failed to see a "road out" sign and driven his motorcycle over a fifteen-foot cliff, tumbling off the bike, and landing, "miraculously" unhurt, at the bottom of the ravine. At this point in the story, he suddenly stopped, looked off into the distance, and announced solemnly, "I see now that Christ was saving me for something." Oh, I thought to myself, so I guess He was just all finished with my father, who died suddenly of a heart attack at the age of fifty-three, leaving behind a homemaker wife, her elderly aunt, one daughter just starting graduate school, and another (me) only eleven years old.

After a deadly plane crash in North Carolina, I was contacted by a reporter at the local paper, who asked me to comment on a series of striking coincidences and tragic ironies. One young woman had been scheduled to fly into Charlotte aboard the doomed flight for a family reunion but became ill and canceled four hours before takeoff. A honeymooning couple had been awarded, by sentimental airline personnel, a complementary upgrade to first-class and were both killed. What did it all mean? the reporter wanted to know. Could I, as a philosopher, make sense of all this? Well, no, I couldn't "make sense of it," I said, which didn't stop me from blathering on for a good five minutes. My immortal words, quoted in full: "There are an infinite number of things that happen, and they all have causes. Some of the causes are evident and some are not. Some of the things are preventable; some are not. Some of them are things that we are happy happened. Some are not."[6] You'll not be surprised to hear that they didn't call me much after that.

More edifying, presumably, were the also-quoted remarks of a local rabbi, reflecting on the significance of the patterns of destruction wielded by Hurricane Fran. She saw the Hand of God in the fact that a large, expensive, and recently installed stained-glass window in the synagogue had been spared, despite a tree's having come down right next to the building. But then in the same breath, as it were, she cautioned the faithful not to yield to the temptation to blame God for damages they had suffered. God's plan is mysterious, she reminded everyone. (No kidding—stained glass windows are more important than people's lives!) Apparently, in her world, God gets the credit if the outcome is good, but need take no responsibility if it's bad. We expect our politicians to behave like that, but God?

I see the celebration of irrationality everywhere in popular culture. In movies and TV shows, reason and respect for science are almost invariably characteristic of arrogant and closed-minded villains; good guys have "imagination" and rely on "faith." Consider, just for starters, the 1947 "feel-good movie" *Miracle on 34th Street* (remade in 1994). The plot concerns Doris Walker, a no-nonsense single mother (played by Maureen O'Hara) working as a public relations executive at Macy's. She has raised her daughter, Susan (Natalie Wood), in accordance with her belief that "we should be realistic and completely truthful with our children, and not have them growing up believing in a lot of legends and myths… Like Santa Claus, for example."[7] Susan's preternatural gravity shows us that a childhood shaped by such principles is devoid of color and joy. Doris herself is all business and has no time for either Susan or romance. (Is it her ruthless realism that unsexes her, or her professional ambition? The movie manages to trash working moms and clear thinking in one fell swoop.)

Doris is finally redeemed—and Susan's childhood restored—when she is won over to the cause of Kris Kringle, the jolly old gent she hires to be the Macy's store Santa. Kind and generous (though awful in his rage against crass materialism), the man has one quirk: he believes he is the *real* Santa Claus. This is patently impossible, defying all fact and all logic, and is, for just that reason, the very thing that must be accepted by all sympathetic characters before the gratifying denouement. Doris is a hard nut to crack, but finally, conquered by the patient equanimity of the wise old Kris—not to mention the romantic attentions of his handsome lawyer—Doris finally abandons her "silly common sense."[8]

It's a little tricky to figure out what the real message of this film is supposed to be. It's not that we all should really believe in Santa Claus (although why not?). Rather, it's that we should believe *in something*. But why use the figure of Santa Claus to make this point? Is it that commitment to moral values is on a par, rationally speaking, with belief in fairies, that the one is no more rationally defensible than the other? What's going on, I think, is a linkage—one I'm eager to sever—between two kinds of rationality. One is the human capacity for logical reflection; the other is the construct of classical economics, the coldly calculating self-interest that eschews values and affection. It is this latter kind of "rationality" that has commercialized Christmas, not the former. We are supposed to read Doris's skepticism about Kris as cynicism about the possibility of disinterested virtue—Kris is just too good to be true. But why yoke idealism to credulity?

One needn't subscribe to the central dogma of Christianity to appreciate the moral value of charity. Nor must one be a theist to regret and resist the exploitation and commodification of every laudable impulse human beings possess. Indeed, if one judges by trends in the United States, the relationship between materialism and religiosity is precisely the reverse. Today's most enthusiastic cheerleaders for free market capitalism—that juggernaut of commercialization—are also the most vociferou sly "Christian." On the other hand, you'll find no more eloquent critic of commodification than the atheist Karl MaDe. I know that many people experienced a deep sense of loss when they left the religious communities in which they had been reared. I must say that, for me, the feeling of relief was paramount, eclipsing any glimmer of regret. If I have any regrets at all, they are ones that have emerged since I became a parent. I am sorry that I was not able to provide my children with the kind of structured moral community that churches and synagogues can offer. My husband and I have both been active in progressive movements, and we've made sure that our kids logged plenty of time at demonstrations and political meetings ("Yes, you have to come; this is 'church' for us," I'd explain.). But there simply are no secular institutions that can serve the myriad psychological, social, and moral purposes that religious institutions currently do. However, I see this fact as a challenge to secular moralists, not a reason to pretend to believe something I don't.

In fact, it hardly matters whether I have any regrets or not. The pragmatic argument for religion—"believe and all this can be yours"—is bound to fail, at least for me. I find it impossible to believe things that make no sense to me or that I have profound reasons for thinking are false. Given the number of times this pragmatic line has been urged upon me ("for your children's sake, if not for your own!"), I'm inclined to think that I'm anomalous in this regard. Or maybe not. Maybe many people don't actually believe the tenets of their religion but rather collectively agree—in some subtle and wholly implicit way—just to say they do.[9] I have good reason to think that many people don't actually know what tenets their denominational affiliation commits them to. I know for a fact that many Catholics simply ignore doctrines they find unpalatable and disregard injunctions they find inconvenient. But even if this kind of doublethink makes religion possible for some, it's not a strategy I could adopt. There would be no "doubleness" in my case; there would be only pretense.

Some people have told me that they feel safer in a universe watched over by a benevolent God, and suggested that I would, too, if I could just recover my faith. I beg to differ. The world of my childhood, a world in which the supernatural intruded regularly into daily life, was a frightening world, a world in which anything could happen: the sun could stop, the dead could rise, virgins could give birth. Angels were real, but so were demons, and demons could take over your soul. As a child, I had been morbidly fascinated by the story of St. Jean Vianney, the "Cure d'Ars," a humble parish priest who was said to have struggled for years with demonic possession, until finally cured by exorcism. (Or so I remember.) I had not thought about the Cure until many years later when I attended the London premiere of *The Exorcist*. Despite the fact that I had been, at that point, an atheist for two years—or maybe *because* of that—I found the film utterly terrifying. For months afterward, I was beset with unwanted memories of the demon-dominated child. I couldn't sleep in the dark and I couldn't remain in a room if the stupid theme music came on over the radio.[10]

In contrast, my children's world is governed by natural law, which is extremely strict. The sun does not stop (at least not in my lifetime) and the dead do not rise (without cardio-pulmonary resuscitation). It's true that this means one must abandon hope for miraculous interventions. After a car accident during my first year of graduate school, I remember looking in the rear view mirror at my horrifically bloodied face (broken nose—don't worry) and thinking with profound distress that my fate lay entirely in the hands of merely human doctors. But the upside of a thoroughly natural world is that you know what you're dealing with. You can have confidence, for example, that your newborn is not a demon in human form, come to prepare the way for a satanic invasion. (It's hard enough being a parent without having to worry about that.) And don't tell me that praying protects you from anything. The Jewish and Christian traditions are replete with stories of righteous and holy people, from Job to St. John Vianney, tempted and tortured by God, always for His own mysterious purposes.

My children, in fact, are pretty unflappable where ghosts and monsters are concerned. When my husband and I took them to the Museum of the Moving Image, it just so happened that the museum was featuring an exhibit on special effects in my old nemesis, *The Exorcist.* As I was trying to warn the children—then about seven and eleven—that the pictures might be too scary for them, they rushed past me to scrutinize a life-sized model of Linda Blair (the actress who portrayed the possessed child), fully demonic, levitated above her bed. They watched the out takes from the infamous head-spinning scene with clinical dispassion, and pored over the various devices and prostheses required for the magic of projectile vomit. The final verdict on this totemic film of my youth: OK for how old it was, but pretty clunky. I was incredulous (if relieved): didn't they find it *scary?* "Mom," said my son, rolling his eyes. "Stuff like that isn't real." Right on, son.

I have no trouble calling myself an atheist, but if I had to choose a designation, analogous to "Catholic" or "Christian," that might convey something about my positive commitments, I would choose "humanist." I would connect myself with thinkers like Aristotle, Descartes, Hume, Kant, and Marx, who were awed and inspired by human capacities: for thought, for creation, and for sympathy. As they appreciated, our value as persons does not depend upon and cannot be secured by the patronage of any external being. It emanates from within.

Human dignity is not, and should not be thought to be, hostage to any myth. Ironically, this may be the message of at least one story in a sacred text. Early in my career, I was asked to teach a course on theories of human nature; the syllabus began with the creation story in the second and third chapters of Genesis. I had never read the Hebrew Bible as a child and was familiar with the story of Adam and Eve only from retellings. I was fascinated to read the actual text (albeit in translation), which differed in many significant ways from the narrative I remembered. God; for example, appears more calculating than loving: He creates Adam for the express purpose of tending His garden (Gen. 2:15), and Eve for the express purpose of helping Adam in his work, no other beast being suitable for this task (Gen. 2:18–23). And He lies: He tells Adam that if he eats from the Tree of Knowledge of Good and Evil, "in the day that thou eatest, thou shalt surely die" (Gen. 2:17). The serpent (who is never identified as evil, only as "more subtle than any beast of the field"—Gen. 3:1) is the one who actually tells the truth: that they won't die if they eat from the tree and that the reason God has forbidden them from doing so is that He is afraid of their becoming "as gods, knowing good and evil" (Gen. 3:5). This is confirmed when God, in consultation with unidentified others, expels Adam and Eve from the garden—not, mind you, as part of their punishment, but to keep them away from the Tree of Life: "Behold, the man has become as one of us, to know good and evil, and now, lest he put forth his hand, and take also of the tree of life, and eat, and live for ever: Therefore the Lord God sent him forth from the garden of Eden" (Gen. 3:22–23).

I am no Bible scholar but note only that the story, taken at face value, renders a trope familiar from many ancient mythologies: the stealing of a divine prerogative by the presumptuous human. Always such thefts are punished: Prometheus is sentenced to eternal torment, Pandora releases pain and sadness into the world, and Adam and Eve, with all their descendants, must toil and suffer. What's the lesson? Well, it could be that it's prudent to do what powerful divinities tell you to do—in Adam and Eve's case, to remain in a state of childlike ignorance, devoid of conscience or principle, dependent but safe. Or one could extract a different, more noble message: that knowledge and reason, those godlike powers, are so valuable that having them is worth enduring the wrath of the most powerful being in the universe. On this reading, Adam and Eve did not "fall from grace," they ascended into moral responsibility. This is how I choose to read the story, and how I conceive our struggle as a species—to claim our rationality, to confront the harsh realities that constrain us, and to acknowledge our own responsibility, in spite of the cost therein to make ourselves "as gods."

Notes

My thanks to Judith Ferster and Joseph Levine fir their comments on an earlier draft of this essay.

1. As the *Catholic Encylopedia* certifies: "Limbus Infantium" is "the permanent place or state of those unbaptized children adn others who, dying without grievous personal sin, are excluded from the beatific vision on account of original sin alone." See *New Advent* (www.newadvent.org/cathen /09256a.htm). Apparently, the Church has recently revised its teachings, and eliminated Limbo.

2. Not Eve—*her* sin didn't count—but leave *that* alone for now.

3. Jean-Baptist Lamarck (1744-1829) was a naturalist, a predecessor of Darwin's . Like Darwin, he believed that species evolved, but unlike Darwin, he held that characteristics *acquired* by the organism during its lifetime could be passed on to future generations.

4. You can view it at www./time/covers/0,16641,1101660408,00.html.

5. The American Civil Liberties Union.

6. *Raleigh News and Observer*, July 7, 1994.

7. Valentine Davies, Screenplay, *Miracle on 34th Street* (transcribed).

8. Davies, *Miracle on 34th Street.*

9. Rey argues, in this volume that this is typically the case.

10. "Tubular Bells"—released, as irony will have it, on Virgin Records. Amazon.com will let you listen: www.amazon.com/gp/product/BooooooWG4/104-4076158-4010317?=glance&n=5174.

36

If God Is Dead, Is Everything Permitted? (2007)

Elizabeth Anderson

At the Institute for Creation Research Museum in Santee, California, visitors begin their tour by viewing a plaque displaying the "tree of evolutionism," which, it is said (following Matt. T18), "bears only corrupt fruits." The "evil tree" of evolution is a stock metaphor among proponents of the literal truth of the biblical story of creation. In different versions, it represents evolutionary theory as leading to abortion, suicide, homosexuality, the drug culture, hard rock, alcohol, "dirty books," sex education, alcoholism, crime, government regulation, inflation, racism, Nazism, communism, terrorism, socialism, moral relativism, secularism, feminism, and humanism, among other phenomena regarded as evil. The roots of the evil tree grow in the soil of "unbelief," which nourishes the tree with "sin." The base of its trunk represents "no God"—that is, atheism.

The evil tree vividly displays two important ideas. First, the fundamental religious objection to the theory of evolution is not scientific but moral. Evolutionary theory must be opposed because it leads to rampant immorality, on both the personal and political scales. Second, the basic cause of this immorality is atheism. Evolutionary theory bears corrupt fruit because it is rooted in denial of the existence of God.

Most forms of theism today are reconciled to the truth of evolutionary theory. But the idea of the evil tree still accurately depicts a core objection to atheism. Few people of religious faith object to atheism because they think the evidence for the existence of God is compelling to any rational inquirer. Most of the faithful haven't considered the evidence for the existence of God in a spirit of rational inquiry—that is, with openness to the possibility that the evidence goes against their faith. Rather, I believe that people object to atheism because they think that without God, morality is impossible. In the famous words (mis)attributed to Dostoyevsky, "If God is dead, then everything is permitted." Or, in the less famous words of Senator Joe Lieberman, we must not suppose "that morality can be maintained without religion."

Why think that religion is necessary for morality? It might be thought that people wouldn't know the difference between right and wrong if God did not reveal it to them. But that can't be right. Every society, whether or not it Was founded on theism, has acknowledged the basic principles of morality, excluding religious observance, which are laid down in the Ten Commandments. Every stable society punishes murder, theft, and bearing false witness; teaches children to honor their parents; and condemns envy of one's neighbor's possessions, at least when such envy leads one to treat one's neighbors badly.[1] People figured out these rules long before they were exposed to any of the major monotheistic religions. This fact suggests that moral knowledge springs not from revelation but from people's experiences in living together, in which they have learned that they must adjust their own conduct in light of others' claims.

Perhaps, then, the idea that religion is necessary for morality means that people wouldn't care about the difference between right and wrong if God did not promise salvation for good behavior and threaten damnation for bad behavior. On this view, people must be goaded into behaving morally through divine sanction. But this can't be right, either. People have many motives, such as love, a sense of honor, and respect for others, that motivate moral behavior. Pagan societies have not been noticeably more immoral than theistic ones. In any event, most theistic doctrines repudiate the divine sanction theory of the motive to be moral. Judaism places little emphasis on hell. Christianity today is dominated by two rival doctrines of salvation. One says that the belief that Jesus is one's savior is the one thing necessary for salvation. The other says that salvation is a free gift from God that cannot be earned by anything a person may do or believe. Both doctrines are inconsistent with the use of heaven and hell as incentives to morality.

A better interpretation of the claim that religion is necessary for morality is that *there wouldn't be a difference between right and wrong* if God did not make it so. Nothing would really be morally required or prohibited, so everything would be permitted. William Lane Craig, one of the leading popular defenders of Christianity, advances this view.[2] Think of it in terms of the authority of moral rules. Suppose a person or group proposes a moral rule—say, against murder. What would give this rule authority over those who disagree with it? Craig argues that, in the absence of God, nothing would. Without God, moral disputes reduce to mere disputes over subjective preferences. There would be no right or wrong answer. Since no individual has any inherent authority over another, each would be free to act on his or her own taste. To get authoritative moral rules, we need an authoritative commander. Only God fills that role. So, the moral rules get their authority, their capacity to obligate us, from the fact that God commands them.

Sophisticates will tell you that this moralistic reasoning against atheism is illogical. They say that whether God exists depends wholly on the factual evidence, not on the moral implications of God's existence. Do not believe them. We know the basic moral rules—that it is wrong to engage in murder, plunder, rape, and torture, to brutally punish people for the wrongs of others or for blameless error, to enslave others, to engage in ethnic cleansing and genocide—with greater confidence than we know any conclusions drawn from elaborate factual or logical reasoning. If you find a train of reasoning that leads to the conclusion that everything, or even just these things, is permitted, this is a good reason for you to reject it. Call this "the moralistic argument." So, if it is true that atheism entails that everything is permitted, this is a strong reason, to reject atheism.

While I accept the general form of the moralistic argument, I think it applies more forcefully to theism than to atheism. This objection is as old as philosophy. Plato, the first systematic philosopher, raised it against divine command theories of morality in the fifth century BCE.[3] He asked divine-command moralists: are actions right because God commands them, or does God command them because they are right? If the latter is true, then actions are right independent of whether God commands them, and God is not needed to underwrite the authority of morality. But if the former is true, then God could make any action right simply by willing it or by ordering others to do it. This establishes that, if the authority of morality depends on God's will, then, *in principle,* anything is permitted.

This argument is not decisive against theism, considered as a purely philosophical idea. Theists reply that because God is necessarily good, He would never do anything morally reprehensible Himself, nor command us to perform heinous acts. The argument is better applied to the purported evidence for theism. I shall argue that if we take the evidence for theism with utmost seriousness, we will find ourselves committed to the proposition that the most heinous acts are permitted. Since we know that these acts are not morally permitted, we must therefore doubt the evidence for theism.

Now "theism" is a pretty big idea, and the lines of evidence taken to support one or another form of it are various. So I need to say more about theism and the evidence for it. By "theism" I mean belief in the God of Scripture. This is the God of the Old and New Testaments and the Koran—the God of Judaism, Christianity, and Islam. It is also the God of any other religion that accepts one or more of these texts as containing divine revelation, such as the Mormon Church, the Unification Church, and Jehovah's Witnesses. God, as represented in Scripture, has plans for human beings and intervenes in history to realize those plans. God has a moral relationship to human beings and tells humans how to live. By focusing on theism in the Scriptural sense, I narrow my focus in two ways. First, my argument doesn't immediately address polytheism or paganism, as is found, for example, in the religions of Zeus and Baal, Hinduism, Wicca. (I'll argue later that, since the evidence for polytheism is on a par with the evidence for theism, any argument that undermines the latter undermines the former.) Second, my argument doesn't immediately address deism, the philosophical idea of God as a first cause of the universe, who lays down the laws of nature and then lets them run like clockwork, indifferent to the fate of the people subject to them.

What, then, is the evidence for theism? It is Scripture, plus any historical or contemporary evidence of the same kind as presented in Scripture: testimonies of miracles, revelations in dreams, or what people take to be direct encounters with God: experiences of divine presence, and prophecies that have been subject to test. Call these things "extraordinary evidence," for short. Other arguments for the existence of God offer cold comfort to theists. Purely theoretical arguments, such as for the necessity of a first cause of the universe, can at most support deism. They do nothing to show that the deity in question cares about human beings or has any moral significance. I would say the same about attempts to trace some intelligent design in the evolution of life. Let us suppose, contrary to the scientific evidence, that life is the product of design. Then the prevalence of predation, parasitism, disease, and imperfect human organs strongly supports the view that the designer is indifferent to us.

The core evidence for theism, then, is Scripture. What if we accept Scripture as offering evidence of a God who has a moral character and plans for human beings, who intervenes in history and tells us how to live? What conclusions should we draw from Scripture about God's moral character and about how we ought to behave? Let us begin with the position of the fundamentalist, of one who takes Scripture with utmost seriousness, as the inerrant source of knowledge about God and morality. If we accept biblical inerrancy, I'll argue, we must conclude that much of what we take to be morally evil is in fact morally permissible and even required. Consider first God's moral character, as revealed in the Bible.[4] He routinely punishes people for the sins of others. He punishes all mothers by condemning them to painful childbirth, for Eve's sin. He punishes all human beings by condemning them to labor, for Adam's sin (Gen. 3:16–18). He regrets His creation, and in a fit of pique, commits genocide and ecocide by flooding the earth (Gen. 6:7). He hardens Pharaoh's heart against freeing the Israelites (Ex. 7–3); so as to provide the occasion for visiting plagues upon the Egyptians, who, as helpless subjects of a tyrant, had no part in Pharaoh's decision. (So much for respecting free will, the standard justification for the existence of evil in the world.)

He kills all the firstborn sons, even of slave girls who had no part in oppressing the Is- raelites (Ex. n:s). He punishes the children, grandchildren, great-grandchildren, and great-great-grandchildren of those who worship any other god (Ex. 20:3–S). He sets a plague upon the Israelites, killing twenty-four thousand, because some of them had sex with the Baal-worshiping Midianites (Num. 2S:1–9). He lays a three-year famine on David's people for Saul's slaughter of the Gibeonites (2 Sam. 21:1). He orders Da- vid to take a census of his men, and then sends a plague on Israel, killing seventy thousand, for David's sin in taking the census (2 Sam. 24–:1, ra, IS). He sends two bears out of the woods to tear forty-two children to pieces, because they called the prophet Elisha a bald head (2 Kings 2:23–24). He condemns the Samarians, telling them that their children will be "dashed to the ground, their pregnant women ripped open" (Hosea 13:16).[5] This is but a sample of the evils celebrated in the Bible.

Can all this cruelty and injustice be excused on the ground that God may do what humans may not? Look, then, at what God commands humans to do. He com- mands us to put to death adulterers (Lev. 20:10), homosexuals (Lev. 20:13), and peo- ple who work on the Sabbath (Ex. 35:2). He commands us to cast into exile people who eat blood (Lev. 7:27), who have skin diseases (Lev. 13:46), and who have sex with their wives while they are menstruating (Lev. 20:18). Blasphemers must be stoned (Lev. 24:16), and prostitutes whose fathers are priests must be burned to death (Lev. 21:9). That's just the tip of the iceberg. God repeatedly directs the Israelites to com- mit ethnic cleansing (Ex. 34:11–14, Lev. 26:7–9) and genocide against numerous cit- ies and tribes: the city of Hormah (Num. 21:2–;3), the land of Bashan (Num. 21:33–35), the land of Heshbon (Deut. 2:26–35), the Canaanites, Hittites, Hivites, Perizzites, Girgashites, Amorites, and Jebusites (Josh. 1–12). He commands them to show their victims "no mercy" (Deut. 7:2), to "not leave alive anything that breathes" (Deut. 20:16). In order to ensure their complete extermination, he thwarts the free will of the victims by hardening their hearts (Deut. 2:30, Josh. 11:20) so that they do not sue for peace. These genocides are, of course, instrumental to the wholesale theft of their land (Josh. 1:1–6) and the rest of their property (Deut. 20:14, Josh. 11:14). He tells eleven tribes of Israel to nearly exterminate the twelfth tribe, the Benjamites, because a few of them raped and killed a Levite's concubine. The result- ing bloodbath takes the lives of 40,000 Israelites and 25,100 Benjamites (Judg. 20:21, 25, 35). He helps Abijiah kill half a million Israelites (2 Chron. 13:15–20) and helps Asa kill a million Cushites, so his men can plunder all their property (2 Chron. 14:8–13).

Consider also what the Bible *permits*. Slavery is allowed (Lev. 25:44–46, Eph. 6:5, Col. 3:22). Fathers may sell their daughters into slavery (Ex. 21:7). Slaves may be beaten, as long as they survive for two days after (Ex. 21:20–21, Luke 12:45– 48). Female captives from a foreign war may be raped or seized as wives (Deut. 21:10–14). Disobedient children should be beaten with rods (Prov. 13:24, 23:13). In the Old Testament, men may take as many wives and concubines as they like because adultery for men consists only in having sex with a woman who is married (Lev. 18:20) or engaged to someone else (Deut. 22:23). Prisoners of War may be tossed off a cliff (2 Chron. 24:12). Children may be sacrificed to God in return for His aid in battle (2 Kings 3:26–27, Judg. 11), or to persuade Him to end a famine (2 Sam. 21).

Christian apologists would observe that most of these transgressions occur in the Old Testament. Isn't the Old Testament God a stern and angry God, while Jesus of the New Testament is all-loving? We should examine the quality of the love that Jesus promises to bring to humans. It is not only Jehovah who is jealous. Jesus tells us his mission is to make family members hate one another, so that they shall love him more than their kin (Matt. 10:35–37). He promises salvation to those who abandon their wives and children for him (Matt. 19:29, Mark 10:29–30, Luke 18:29–30). Disciples must hate their parents, siblings, wives, and children (Luke 14:26). The rod is not enough for children who curse their parents; they must be killed (Matt. 15:4–7, Mark 7–9–10, following Lev. 20:9). These are Jesus' "family values." Peter and Paul add to these family values the despotic rule of husbands over their silenced wives, who must obey their husbands as gods (I Cor. n:3, 14:34–5; Eph. 5:22–24; Col. 3:18; I Tim. 2:U12; I Pet. 3:1).

To be sure, genocide, God-sent plagues, and torture do not occur in the times chronicled by the New Testament. But they are prophesied there, as they are repeatedly in the Old Testament (for instance, in Isaiah, Jeremiah, Ezekiel, Micah, and Zepheniah). At the second coming, any city that does not accept Jesus will be destroyed, and the people will suffer even more than they did when God destroyed Sodom and Gomorrah (Matt. 10:14–15, Luke 10:12). God will flood the Earth as in Noah's time (Matt. 24: 37). Or perhaps He will set the Earth on fire instead, to destroy the unbelievers (2 Pet. 3–7, 10). But not before God sends Death and Hell to kill one quarter of the Earth "by sword, famine and plague, and by the wild beasts" (Rev. 6:8). Apparently, it is not enough to kill people once; they have to be killed more than once to satisfy the genocidal mathematics of the New Testament. For we are also told that an angel will burn up one third of the Earth (8:7), another will poison a third of its water (8:10–n), four angels will kill another third of humanity by plagues of fire, smoke, and sulfur (9:13, 17–18), two of God's witnesses will visit plagues on the Earth as much as they like (n:6), and there will be assorted deaths by earthquakes (n:13, 16:18–19) and hailstones (16:21). Death is not bad enough for unbelievers, however;

they must be tortured first. Locusts will sting them like scorpions until they want to die, but they will be denied the relief of death (9:3–6). Seven angels will pour seven bowls of God's wrath, delivering plagues of painful sores, seas and rivers of blood, burns from solar flares, darkness and tongue-biting (16:2–10).

That's just what's in store for people while they inhabit the Earth. Eternal damnation awaits most people upon their deaths (Matt. 7:13–14). They will be cast into a fiery furnace (Matt. 13:42, 25:41), an unquenchable fire (Luke 3:17). For what reason? The New Testament is not consistent on this point. Paul preaches the doctrine of predestination, according to which salvation is granted as an arbitrary gift from God, wholly unaffected by any choice humans may make (Eph. I: 4–9). This implies that the rest are cast into the eternal torments of hell on God's whim. Sometimes salvation is promised to those who abandon their families to follow Christ (Matt. 19:27–30, Mark 10:28–30, Luke 9:59–62). This conditions salvation on a shocking indifference to family members. More often, the Synoptic Gospels promise salvation on the basis of good works, especially righteousness and helping the poor (for example, Matt. 16:27, 19:16–17; Mark 10:17–25; Luke 18:18–22, 19:8–(1). This at least has the form of justice, since it is based on considerations of desert. But it metes out rewards and punishments grossly disproportional to the deeds people commit in their lifetimes. Finite sins cannot justify eternal punishment. Since the Reformation, Christian thought has tended to favor either predestination or justification by faith. In the latter view, the saved are all and only those who believe that Jesus is their savior. Everyone else is damned. This is the view of the Gospel of John (John 3:15–16, 18, 36; 6:47; 11:25–26). It follows that infants and anyone who never had the opportunity to hear about Christ are damned, through no fault of their own. Moreover, it is not clear that even those who hear about Christ have a fair chance to assess the merits of the tales about him. God not only thwarts our free will so as to visit harsher punishments upon us than we would have received had we been free to choose, He also messes with our heads. He sends people "powerful delusions" so they will not believe what is needed for salvation, to make sure that they are condemned (2 Thess. 2:11–12). Faith itself may be a gift of God rather than a product of rational assessment under our control and for which we could be held responsible. If so, then justification by faith reduces to God's arbitrary whim, as Paul held (Eph. 2:8–1). This at least has the merit of acknowledging that the evidence offered in favor of Christianity is far from sufficient to rationally justify belief in it. Granting this fact, those who do not believe are blameless and cannot be justly punished, even if Jesus really did die for our sins.

And what are we to make of the thought that Jesus died for our sins (Rom. 5 :8 9, 15–18; I John 2:2; Rev. 1:5)? This core religious teaching of Christianity takes Jesus to be a scapegoat for humanity. The practice of scapegoating contradicts the whole moral principle of personal responsibility. It also contradicts any moral idea of God. If God is merciful and loving, why doesn't He forgive humanity for its sins straightaway, rather than demanding His 150 pounds of flesh, in the form of His own son? How could any loving father do that to his son?

I find it hard to resist the conclusion that the God of the Bible is cruel and unjust and commands and permits us to be cruel and unjust to others. Here are religious doctrines that on their face claim that it is all right to mercilessly punish people for the wrongs of others and for blameless error, that license or even command murder, plunder, rape, torture, slavery, ethnic cleansing, and genocide.

We know such actions are wrong. So we should reject the doctrines that represent them as right. Of course, thoughtful Christians and Jews have struggled with this difficulty for centuries. Nothing I have said would come as a surprise to any reflective person of faith. Nor are theists without options for dealing with these moral embarrassments. Let us consider them.

One option is to bite the bullet. This is the only option open to hard-core fundamentalists, who accept the inerrancy of the Bible. In this view, the fact that God performed, commanded, or permitted these actions demonstrates that they are morally right. This view concedes my objection to theism, that it promotes terrible acts of genocide, slavery, and so forth. But it denies the moral force of this objection. We know where this option has led: to holy war, the systematic extirpation of heretics, the Crusades, the Inquisition, the Thirty Years War, the English Civil War, witch-hunts, the cultural genocide of Mayan civilization, the brutal conquest of the Aztecs and the Inca, religious support for ethnic cleansing of Native Americans, slavery of Mexicans in the Americas, colonialist tyranny across the globe, confinement of the Jews to ghettos, and periodic pogroms against them, ultimately preparing the way for the Holocaust.[6] In other words, it has led to centuries steeped in bloodshed, cruelty, and hatred without limit across continents.

Since this is clearly reprehensible, one might try a stopgap measure. One could deny that the dangerous principles in the Bible have any application after biblical times. For example, one might hold that, while it is in principle perfectly all right to slaughter whoever God tells us to, in fact, God has stopped speaking to us. This argument runs into the difficulty that many people even today claim that God has spoken to them. It is hard to identify any reason to be comprehensively skeptical about current claims to have heard divine revelation that does not apply equally to the past.

But to apply such skepticism to the past is to toss out revelation and hence the core evidence for God.

Another option is to try to soften the moral implications of embarrassing biblical episodes by filling in unmentioned details that make them seem less bad. There is a tradition of thinking about "hard sayings" that tries to do this? It imagines some elaborate context in which, for instance, it would be all right for God to command Abraham to sacrifice his son, or for God to inflict unspeakable suffering on His blameless servant Job, and then insists that that was the context in which God actually acted. I have found such excuses for God's depravity to be invariably lame. To take a typical example, it is said of David's seemingly innocent census of his army that he sinned by counting what was not his, but God's. Even if we were to grant this, it still does not excuse God for slaughtering seventy thousand of David's men, rather than focusing His wrath on David alone. I also find such casuistic exercises to be morally dangerous. To devote one's moral reflections to constructing elaborate rationales for past genocides, human sacrifices, and the like is to invite applications of similar reasoning to future actions.

I conclude that there is no way to cabin off or soft-pedal the reprehensible moral implications of these biblical passages. They must be categorically rejected as false and depraved moral teachings. Morally decent theists have always done so in practice. Nevertheless, they insist that there is much worthy moral teaching that can be salvaged from the Bible. They would complain that the sample of biblical moral lessons I cited above is biased. I hasten to agree. There are many admirable moral teachings in the Bible, even beyond the obvious moral rules against murder, stealing, lying, and the like—that are acknowledged by all societies. "Love your neighbor as yourself" (Lev. 19:18, Matt. 22:39, Mark 12:31, Luke 10:27, James 2:8) concisely encapsulates the moral point of view. The Bible courageously extends this teaching to the downtrodden, demanding not just decency and charity to the poor and disabled (Ex. 23:6, 2]:11; Lev. 19:10, 23:22; Deut. 15:7–8, 24:14–15; Prov. 22:22; Eph. 4:28; James 2:15–16), but provisions in the structure of property rights to liberate people from landlessness and oppressive debts (Deut. 15, Lev. 25:10–28). Although the details of these provisions make little economic sense (for instance, canceling debts every seven years prevents people from taking out loans for a longer term), their general idea, that property rights should be structured so as to enable everyone to avoid oppression, is sound. Such teachings were not only morally advanced for their day but would dramatically improve the world if practiced today.

So, the Bible contains both good and evil teachings. This fact bears upon the standing of Scripture, both as a source of evidence for moral claims, and as a source of evidence for theism. Consider first the use of Scripture as a source of evidence for moral claims. We have seen that the Bible is morally inconsistent. If we try to draw moral lessons from a contradictory source, we must pick and choose which ones to accept. This requires that we use our own independent moral judgment, founded on some source other than revelation or the supposed authority of God, to decide which biblical passages to accept. In fact, once we recognize the moral inconsistencies in the Bible, it's clear that the hard-core fundamentalists who today preach hatred toward gay people and the subordination of women, and who at other times and places have, with biblical support, claimed God's authority for slavery, apartheid, and ethnic cleansing, have been picking and choosing all along. What distinguishes them from other believers is precisely their attraction to the cruel and despotic passages in the Bible. Far from being a truly independent guide to moral conduct, the Bible is more like a Rorschach test: which passages people choose to emphasize reflects as much as it shapes their moral character and interests.

Moral considerations, then, should draw theists inexorably away from fundamentalism and toward liberal theology—that is, toward forms of theism that deny the literal truth of the Bible and that attribute much of its content to ancient confusion, credulity, and cruelty. Only by moving toward liberal theology can theists avoid refutation at the hands of the moralistic argument that is thought to undermine atheism. Only in this way can theists affirm that the heinous acts supposedly committed or commanded by God and reported in the Bible are just plain morally wrong.

The great Enlightenment philosopher Immanuel Kant took this line of reasoning to its logical conclusion for morality. He considered the case of an inquisitor who claims divine 'authority for executing unbelievers. That the Bible commends such acts is undeniable (see Ex. 22:20, 2 Chron. 15:13, Luke 19:27, Acts 3:23). But how do we know that the Bible accurately records God's revealed word? Kant said: That it is wrong to deprive a man of his life because of his religious faith is certain, unless…a Divine Will, made known in extraordinary fashion, has ordered it otherwise. But that God has ever ordered this terrible injunction can be asserted only on the basis of historical documents and is never apodictically certain. After all, the revelation has reached the inquisitor only through men and has been interpreted by men, and even did it appear to have come from God Himself (like the command delivered to Abraham to slaughter his own son like a sheep) it is at least possible that in this instance a mistake has prevailed. But if this is so, the inquisitor would risk the danger of doing what would be wrong in the highest degree; and in this very act he is behaving unconscientiously.[8]

Kant advances a moral criterion for judging the authenticity of any supposed revelation. If you hear a voice or some testimony purportedly revealing God's word and it tells you to do something you know is wrong, don't believe that it's really God telling you to do these things. I believe that Kant correctly identified the maximum permissible moral limits of belief in extraordinary evidence concerning God. These limits require that we reject the literal truth of the Bible. My colleague Jamie Tappenden argues in this volume that such a liberal approach to faith is theologically incoherent. Perhaps it is. Still, given a choice between grave moral error and theological muddle, I recommend theological muddle every time.

But these are not our only alternatives. We must further ask whether we should accept any part of the Bible as offering evidence about the existence and nature of God. Once we have mustered enough doubt in the Bible to reject its inerrancy, is there any stable position short of rejecting altogether its claims to extraordinary evidence about God? And once we reject its claims, would this not undermine all the extra-biblical extraordinary evidence for God that is of the same kind alleged by believers in the Bible? Here we have a body of purported evidence for theism, consisting in what seem to be experiences of divine presence, revelation, and miracles, testimonies of the same, and prophecies. We have seen that such experiences, testimonies, and prophecies are at least as likely to assert grave moral errors as they are to assert moral truths. This shows that these sources of extraordinary evidence are deeply unreliable. *They can't be trusted.* So not only should we think that they offer no independent support for *moral* claims, but we should not think they offer independent support for theological claims.

Against this, defenders of liberal theology need to argue that the claims derived from these extraordinary sources fall into two radically distinct groups. In one group, there are the purported revelations that assert moral error, which should not be accepted as having come from God and offer no independent support for any claim about God. In the other group, there are the genuine revelations that assert moral truths or some morally neutral proposition (for example, claims about historical events and prophecies of the future), as well as testimonies of miracles and experiences of divine presence, which should be accepted as having come from God and do provide evidence for the existence and nature of God.

I think this fallback position should be rejected for two reasons. First, it does not explain why these extraordinary types of evidence should be thought to fall into two radically distinct groups. Why should they ever have generated grave moral errors? Second, it does not explain why all religions, whether monotheistic, polytheistic, or non-theistic, appear to have access to the same sources of evidence. Believers in anyone religion can offer no independent criteria for accepting their own revelations, miracles, and religious experiences while rejecting the revelations, miracles, and religious experiences that appear to support contradictory religious claims. I believe that the best explanation for both of these phenomena—that the extraordinary sources of evidence generate grave moral error as well as moral truth and that they offer equal support for contradictory religious claims—undermines the credibility of these extraordinary sources of evidence altogether.

So first, why were the ancient biblical peoples as ready to ascribe evil as good deeds, to God? Why did they think God was so angry that He chronically unleashed tides of brutal destruction on humanity? The answer is that they took it for granted that all events bearing on human well-being are willed by some agent for the purpose of affecting humans for good or ill. If no human was observed to have caused the event, or if the event was of a kind (e.g., a plague, drought, or good weather) that no human would have the power to cause, then they assumed that some unseen, more-powerful agent had to have willed it, precisely for its good or bad effects on humans. So, if the event was good for people, they assumed that God willed it out of love for them; if it was bad, they assumed that God willed it out of anger at them. This mode of explanation is universally observed among people who lack scientific understanding of natural events. It appears to be a deeply rooted cognitive bias of humans to reject the thought of meaningless suffering. If we are suffering, someone must be responsible for it!

Why did these representations of God as cruel and unjust not make God repugnant to the authors of Scripture and their followers? They were too busy trembling in their sandals to question what they took to be God's will. The seventeenth-century philosopher Thomas Hobbes observed that people honor raw power irrespective of its moral justification: Nor does it alter the case of honour, whether an action (so it be great and difficult, and consequently a sign of much power) be just or unjust: for honour consisteth only in the opinion of power. Therefore the ancient heathen did not think they dishonoured, but greatly honoured the Gods, when they introduced them in their poems, committing rapes, thefts, and other great, but unjust, or unclean acts: insomuch as nothing is so much celebrated in Jupiter, as his adulteries; nor in Mercury, as his frauds, and thefts: of whose praises, in a hymn of Homer, the greatest is this, that being born in the morning, he had invented music at noon, and before night, stolen away the cattle of Apollo, from his herdsmen.[9]

Hobbes's psychological explanation applies even more emphatically to the authors of Scripture, the ancient Hebrews and the early Christians, whose God commits deeds several orders of magnitude more terrible than anything the Greek gods did.

Ancient social conditions also made God's injustice less obvious to the early Jews and Christians. Norms of honor and revenge deeply structure the social order of tribal societies. These norms treat whole clans and tribes, rather than individuals, as the basic units of responsibility. A wrong committed by a member of a tribe could therefore be avenged by an injury inflicted on any other member of that tribe, including descendants of the wrongdoer. Given that people in these societies habitually visited the iniquities of the fathers on the sons, it did not strike the early Hebrews and Christians as strange that God would do so as well, although on a far grander scale.[10]

So the tendency, in the absence of scientific knowledge, to ascribe events having good and bad consequences for human beings to corresponding benevolent and malevolent intentions of unseen spirits, whether these be gods, angels, ancestors, demons, or human beings who deploy magical powers borrowed from some spirit world, explains the belief in a divine spirit as well as its (im)moral character. This explanatory tendency is pan-cultural. The spiritual world everywhere reflects the hopes and fears, loves and hatreds, aspirations and depravities of those who believe in it. This is just as we would expect if beliefs in the supernatural are, like Rorschach tests, projections of the mental states of believers, rather than based on independent evidence. The same cognitive bias that leads pagans to believe in witches and multiple gods leads theists to believe in God. Indeed, once the explanatory principle—to ascribe worldly events that bear on human well—being to the intentions and powers of unseen spirits, when no actual person is observed to have caused them—is admitted, it is hard to deny that the evidence for polytheism and spiritualism of all heretical varieties is exactly on a par with the evidence for theism.

Every year in my town, Ann Arbor, Michigan, there is a summer art fair. Not just artists, but political and religious groups, set up booths to promote their wares, be these artworks or ideas. Along one street one finds booths of Catholics, Baptists, Calvinists, Christian Orthodox, other denominational and nondenominational Christians of all sorts, Muslims, Hindus, Buddhists, Baha'i, Mormons, Christian Scientists, Jehovah's Witnesses, Jews for Jesus, Wiccans, Scientologists, New Age believers—representatives of nearly every religion that has a significant presence in the United States. The believers in each booth offer evidence of exactly the same kind to advance their religion. Every faith points to its own holy texts and oral traditions, its spiritual experiences, miracles and prophets, its testimonies on wayward lives turned around by conversion, rebirth of faith, or return to the church.

Each religion takes these experiences and reports them as conclusive evidence for its peculiar set of beliefs. Here we have purported sources of evidence for higher, unseen spirits or divinity, which systematically point to contradictory beliefs. Is there one God, or many? Was Jesus God, the son of God, God's prophet, or just a man? Was the last prophet Jesus, Muhammad, Joseph Smith, or the Rev. Sun Myung Moon?

Consider how this scene looks to someone like me, who was raised outside of any faith. My father is nominally Lutheran, in practice religiously indifferent. My mother is culturally Jewish but not practicing. Having been rejected by both the local Lutheran minister and the local rabbi (in both cases, for being in a mixed marriage), but thinking that some kind of religious, education would be good for their children, my parents helped found the local Unitarian church in the town where I grew up. Unitarianism is a church without a creed; there are no doctrinal requirements of membership. (Although Bertrand Russell once quipped that Unitarianism stands for the proposition that there is at most one God, these days pagans are as welcome as all others.) It was a pretty good fit for us, until New Age spiritualists started to take over the church. That was too loopy for my father's rationalistic outlook, so we left. Thus, religious doctrines never had a chance to insinuate themselves into my head as a child. So I have none by default or habit.

Surveying the religious booths every year at the Ann Arbor art fair, I am always struck by the fact that they are staffed by people who are convinced of their own revelations and miracles, while most so readily disparage the revelations and miracles of other faiths. To a mainstream Christian, Jew, or Muslim, nothing is more obvious than that founders and prophets of other religions, such as Joseph Smith, the Rev. Moon, Mary Baker Eddy, and L. Ron Hubbard, are either frauds or delusional, their purported miracles or cures tricks played upon a credulous audience (or worse, exercises of black magic), their prophecies false, their metaphysics absurd. To me, nothing is more obvious than that the evidence cited on behalf of Christianity, Judaism, and Islam is of exactly the same type and quality as that cited on behalf of such despised religions. Indeed, it is on a par with the evidence for Zeus, Baal, Thor, and other long-abandoned gods, who are now considered ridiculous by nearly everyone.

The perfect symmetry of evidence for all faiths persuades me that the types of extraordinary evidence to which they appeal are not credible. The sources of evidence for theism—revelations, miracles, religious experiences, and prophecies, nearly all known only by testimony transmitted through uncertain chains of long-lost original sources—systematically generate contradictory beliefs, many of which are known to be morally abhorrent or otherwise false. Of course, ordinary sources of evidence, such as eyewitness testimony of ordinary events, also often lead to conflicting beliefs. But in the latter case, we have independent ways to test the credibility of the evidence—for instance, by looking for corroborating physical evidence. In the former cases, the tests advanced by believers tend to be circular: don't believe that other religion's testimonies of miracles or revelations, since they come from those who teach a false religion (Deut. 1TI–5). It is equally useless to appeal to the certainty in one's heart of some experience of divine presence. For exactly the same certainty has been felt by those who think they've seen ghosts, been kidnaped by aliens, or been possessed by Dionysus or Apollo. Furthermore, where independent tests exist, they either disconfirm or fail to confirm the extraordinary evidence. There is no geological evidence of a worldwide flood, no archaeological evidence that Pharaoh's army drowned in the Red Sea after Moses parted it to enable the Israelites to escape. Jesus' central prophecy, that oppressive regimes would be destroyed in an apocalypse, and the Kingdom of God established on Earth, within the lifetime of those witnessing his preaching (Mark 8:389:1, 1T24–27, 30), did not come to pass.[11] If any instance of these extraordinary sources of evidence is what it purports to be, it is like the proverbial needle in the haystack—except that there is no way to tell the difference between it and the hay. I conclude that none of the evidence for theism—that is, for the God of Scripture—is credible. Since exactly the same types of evidence are the basis for belief in pagan Gods, I reject pagan religions too.

It follows that we cannot appeal to God to underwrite the authority of morality. How, then, can I answer the moralistic challenge to atheism, that without God moral rules lack any authority? I say: the authority of moral rules lies not with God, but with each of us. We each have moral authority with respect to one another. This authority is, of course, not absolute. No one has the authority to order anyone else to blind obedience. Rather, each of us has the authority to make claims on others, to call upon people to heed our interests and concerns.[12] Whenever we lodge a complaint, or otherwise lay a claim on others' attention and conduct, we presuppose our own authority to give others reasons for action that are not dependent on appealing to the desires and preferences they already have. But whatever grounds we have for assuming our own authority to make claims is equally well possessed by anyone who we expect to heed our own claims. For, in addressing others as people to whom our claims are justified, we acknowledge them as judges of claims, and hence as moral authorities. Moral rules spring from our practices of reciprocal claim making, in which we work out together the kinds of considerations that count as reasons that all of us must heed, and thereby devise rules for living together peacefully and cooperatively, on a basis of mutual accountability.

What of someone who refuses to accept such accountability? Doesn't this possibility vindicate Craig's worry, that without some kind of higher authority external to humans, moral claims amount to nothing more than assertions of personal preference, backed up by power? No. We deal with people who refuse accountability by restraining and deterring their objectionable behavior. Such people have no proper complaint against this treatment. For, in the very act of lodging a complaint, they address others as judges of their claims, and thereby step into the very system of moral adjudication that demands their accountability.

I am arguing that morality, understood as a system of reciprocal claim making, in which everyone is accountable to everyone else, does not need its authority underwritten by some higher, external authority. It is underwritten by the authority we all have to make claims on one another. Far from bolstering the authority of morality, appeals to divine authority can undermine it. For divine command theories of morality may make believers feel entitled to look only to their idea of God to determine what they are justified in doing. It is all too easy under such a system to ignore the complaints of those injured by one's actions, since they are not acknowledged as moral authorities in their own right. But to ignore the complaints of others is to deprive oneself of the main source of information one needs to improve one's conduct. Appealing to God rather than those affected by one's actions amounts to an attempt to escape accountability to one's fellow human beings.

This is not an indictment of the conduct of theists in general. Theistic moralities, like secular ones, have historically inspired both highly moral and highly immoral action. For every bloodthirsty holy warrior we can find an equally violent communist or fascist, enthusiastically butchering and enslaving others in the name of some dogmatically held ideal. Such observations are irrelevant to my argument. For my argument has not been about the causal consequences of belief for action. It has been about the logical implications of accepting or rejecting the core evidence for theism.

I have argued that if we take with utmost seriousness the core evidence for theism, which is the testimonies of revelations, miracles, religious experiences, and prophecies found in Scripture, then we are committed to the view that the most heinous acts are morally right, because Scripture tells us that God performs or commands them. Since we know that such acts are morally wrong, we cannot take at face value the extraordinary evidence for theism recorded in Scripture. We must at least reject that part of the evidence that supports morally repugnant actions. Once we have stepped this far toward liberal theological approaches to the evidence for God, however, we open ourselves up to two further challenges to this evidence. First, the best explanation of extraordinary evidence—the only explanation that accounts for its tendency to commend heinous acts as well as good acts—shows it to reflect either our own hopes and feelings, whether these be loving or hateful, just or merciless, or else the stubborn and systematically erroneous cognitive bias of representing all events of consequence to our welfare as intended by some agent who cares about us, for good or for ill. Extraordinary evidence, in other words, is a projection of our own wishes, fears, and fantasies onto an imaginary deity. Second, all religions claim the same sorts of extraordinary evidence on their behalf. The perfect symmetry of this type of evidence for completely contradictory theological systems, and the absence of any independent ordinary evidence that corroborates one system more than another, strongly supports the view that such types of evidence are not credible at all. And once we reject such evidence altogether, there is nothing left that supports theism (or polytheism either). The moralistic argument, far from threatening atheism, is a critical wedge that should open morally sensitive theists to the evidence against the existence of God.

Notes

I thank Ed Curley, Chris Dodsworth, David Jacobi, and Jamie Tappenden for helpful advice concerning this paper.

1. This agreement exists at the level of generality with which the moral rules are expressed in the Ten Commandments. It does not exist for more fine-grained descriptions of moral rules, where exceptions, justifications, and excuses for violations are articulated. All moral systems, including those found in Scripture, acknowledge exceptions to the basic moral rules. But societies vary dramatically in the exceptions they allow. For example, some permit killing in retaliation for insults; others permit killing for the greater glory of God; others permit suicide in the face of terminal illness. Societies also vary dramatically in their views of who is included within the scope of protection of the moral rules. Are only fellow tribe members included, or fellow nationals, or all people, without exception? Finally, the rules of sexual morality are even more variable than the rules against killing, theft, and lying. While most societies have condemned adultery, this is by no means universal, and adultery has often been defined much more permissively for men than for women. My point is simply that all societies agree that certain types of conduct are morally objectionable on their face and so require some kind of revelation or divine inspiration. Nor is recognition of the right exceptions based on divine sources. For as we shall see, societies founded on biblical morality are hardly superior to others in discerning the allowable exceptions.

2. William Lane Craig, "The Indispensability of Theological Meta-Ethical Foundations for Morality," *Foundations* 5 (1997): 9-12, www.leaderu.com/offices/billcraig/docs/meta-eth.html.

3. Plato, "Euthyphro," in *Collected Dialogues of Plato*, eds. Edith Hamilton and Huntington Cairnes (Princeton, NJ: Princeton University Press, 1961).

4. I here omit any parallel critique of the Koran, on the assumption that most readers of this essay are not Muslim. But the Koran does not differ fundamentally from the Old and New Testaments in characterizing God as committing, commanding, and permitting great evil. See Ibn Warraq, *Why I Am Not a Muslim* (New York: Prometheus Books, 1995).

5. All quotations are drawn from the *Holy Bible: New International Version* (NIV) (Grand Rapids, MI: Zondervan, 1978). This modern translation softens some of the harsh verses found in the King James Version (KJV) of the Bible, which tends to be favoured by fundamentalists. For example, in the KJV, David tortures his enemies with God's support, cutting them with saws, harrows, and axes (I Chron. 20:3). The same verse in the NIV represents David merely "consigning them to labor" with these tools.

6. This is not to say that the Holocaust was a specifically Christian enterprise. My point is rather that without centuries of Church-sponsored anti-Semitism in Eastern Europe, Hitler could not have recruited in these countries the legions of executioners, whose religiously inspired enthusiasm was needed to enable the Holocaust to proceed as far as it did. Christian anti-Semitism does, of course, have a textual grounding in the Gospels. For instance, John calls the Jews the children of the devil (8:44) and stresses their role in the death of Christ (18:35, 19:12-3). Matthew 27:25 has the Jews accepting responsibility for murdering Christ ("Let his blood be upon us and on our children!").

7. See, for example, Walter Kaiser et al., *Hard Sayings of the Bible* (Downers Grove, IL: InterVarsity Press, 1996).

8. Immanuel Kant, *Religion within the Limits of Reason Alone*, trans. And ed Theodore Greene and Hoyt Hudson (1793; repr., New York: Harper & Row, 1960), 175.

9. Thomas Hobbes, *Leviathan*, ed. Edwin Curley, (1651; repr., Indianapolis: Hackett, 1994), ch. 10, para. 48, p. 54.

10. Yet we should also not suppose that the ancient Hebrews lacked the moral concepts necessary to recognize God's injustice When God smites seventy thousand men for David's sinful census, David tells him, "I am the one who has sinned and done wrong. These are but sheep. What have they done? Let your hand fall upon me and my family" (2 Sam. 24:17).

11. That this was Jesus' central teaching is the dominant view among biblical scholars writing today. See Bart Ehrman, *Jesus: Apocalyptic Prophet of the New Millennium* (Oxford: Oxford University Press, 1999) for a compelling and accessible account of the evidence for this interpretation.

12. Stephen Darwall has developed this conception of morality as equal accountability in his book *The Second-Person Standpoint: Morality, Respect, and Accountability* (Harvard University Press, 2006).

37
An Atheist Childhood (2002)
Tariq Ali

I never really believed in God. Not even for a week, not even between the ages of six and ten, when I was an agnostic. This unbelief was instinctive. I was sure there was nothing else out there except space. It could have been my lack of imagination. During the sweet, jasmine-scented summer: nights, long before mosques were allowed to use loud-speakers, it was enough to savour the silence, look upwards at the exquisitely lit sky, count the shooting stars and fall asleep. The early morning call of the muezzin was like a pleasant-sounding alarm clock.

There were many advantages in being an unbeliever. Threatened with divine sanctions by family retainers, relations or cousins—'If you do this Allah will be angry' or 'If you don't do that Allah will punish you'—I was unmoved. Let him do his worst, I used to tell myself, but he never did, and I think it was this passivity on his part that strengthened my belief in his non-existence. An early case of scepticism as the spare rib of vulgar empiricism.

My parents, too, were non-believers. So were most of their close friends. Religion played a tiny part in our Lahore household. There were others, of course, who professed the faith, but even they did so sheepishly and without a fuss. In the second half of the last century a large proportion of educated Muslims had embraced modernity. They realised that organised religion was an anachronism. Old habits persisted, nonetheless: the would-be virtuous made their ablutions and sloped off sheepishly to Friday prayers. Sometimes they fasted for a few days each year, usually just before the new moon was sighted, marking the end of Ramadan. I doubt whether more than a quarter of the population in the cities fasted for a whole month. Café life continued unabated. Many more claimed that they had fasted so as to take advantage of the free food doled out at the end of each fasting day by the mosques or the kitchens of the wealthy. In the countryside the figure was slightly lower, since outdoor work was difficult without sustenance, and especially without water when Ramadan coincided with the summer months. Eid, however, was celebrated by all.

One day, I think in the autumn of 1956, when I was twelve, I was eavesdropping on an after-dinner conversation at home—children, like servants, were regarded as both deaf and invisible. This worked in our favour, since we amassed a great deal of information not intended for innocent ears. On this occasion my sister, assorted cousins and I had been asked nicely to occupy ourselves elsewhere. From an adjoining room, we began to giggle as we heard a particularly raucous, wooden-headed aunt and a bony uncle berating my parents in loud whispers: 'We know what you're like …we know you're unbelievers, but these children should be given a chance… They must be taught their religion.'

My giggles were premature. A few months later a tutor was hired to teach me the Koran and Islamic history. 'You live here,' said my father. 'You should study the texts. You should know our history. Later you may do as you wish. Even if you reject everything, it's always better to know what it is that one is rejecting.'

Sensible enough advice, but regarded by me at the time as hypocritical and a betrayal. How often in our house had I heard talk of superstitious idiots, often relatives, who hated a Satan they never knew and worshipped a God they didn't have the brains to doubt? Now I was being forced to study religion. I strongly resented the imposition and was determined to sabotage the process.

It didn't occur to me at the time that my father's decision might have had something to do with an episode from his own life. Perhaps he recalled the religious experience he was compelled to undergo at a similar age. In 1928, aged twelve, he had accompanied his mother and his old wet-nurse (my grandmother's most trusted and senior maid) on the pilgrimage to perform the hadj ceremony. Women, then as now, could only visit Mecca if accompanied by a male over twelve years old. The older men flatly refused. My father, as the youngest male in the family, was not given a choice in the matter. His oldest brother, the most religious member of the family, never let my father forget the pilgrimage. His letters addressed to my father always used to arrive with the prefix *al-Haj* (the Pilgrim) attached to his name, a cause for much merriment at teatime.

Decades later, when the pores of the Saudi elite were sweating petrodollars, my father would remember the poverty he had witnessed in the Hijaz and recall the woeful tales recounted by numerous non-Arab pilgrims who had been robbed on the road to Mecca. In the days before oil, the annual pilgrimage had been one of the main sources of income for the locals. Often they would augment their meagre earnings with well-organised raids on pilgrims' lodgings. The ceremony itself requires the pilgrim to come clothed in a simple white sheet and nothing else: all valuables have to be left behind. Local gangs were especially adept at stealing watches and gold. Soon the more experienced pilgrims realised that the 'pure souls' of Mecca weren't worth a damn. They began to take precautions and a war of wits ensued. Perhaps one day an Iranian film-maker will present us with an Eastern *hommage* to Buñuel.

The trip to the Holy Land had little impact on my father. Or perhaps it did, because several years later he became an orthodox communist and remained one for the rest of his life. Moscow became his Mecca. Perhaps he thought that immersing me in religion at a young age might also result in a similar transformation. I like to think that this was his real motive, rather than pandering to the more dim-witted members of our family, whose company he rarely sought and whose presence was always irksome. He always found it strange that these healthy young men and women could expend so much energy on trivia and did so unselfconsciously for the rest of their lives.

In later years, I came to admire my father for breaking away from what he would re-fer to as 'the emptiness of the feudal world.'[1] He had done so by developing an interest in political theory and a political party that made hin sensitive to and aware of the realities underlying both, an option that is nonexistent in the Islamic world today.

Since I did not read Arabic, the Koran could only be learnt by rote. This did strike my father as marginally distasteful, but his proposed solution enhanced the torture. He suggested that before I embark on a course of Koranic studies, I should learn the divine language. I refused point-blank, justifying my Philistinism by the fact that it *was* the di-vine language. This is something I have long regretted, but never remedied.

My tutor, Nizam Din, arrived on the appointed day and work commenced. Thanks to his heroic efforts, I can still recite the opening lines from the Koran in the divine language: *Akalam, mini* and then the crucial sentence...*This book is not to be doubted.* Nizam Din, to my great delight, was not deeply religious himself: From his late teens to his late twenties, he had sprouted a beard. In 1940 he went into top gear, shaved off his beard, deserted religion for the anti-imperialist cause and be-came a devotee of left-wing politics. Like many others he had served a spell in a colo-nial prison and been further radicalised. But he never forgot the Koran. As late as December 2000, he would say that truth was a very powerful concept in it, but had never been translated into practical life because the mullahs had destroyed Islam.

At an early stage Nizam Din realised that I was bored with learning Koranic verses, with the result that he did not even attempt to teach me Islamic history. A pity. He might have had an unusual interpretation or perhaps, what is more likely, he knew very little of the real history himself.

The allotted hour was usually spent discussing history: the nationalist struggle against British imperialism, the origins of terrorism in Bengal and the Punjab, the heroism of the Sikh terrorist Bhagat Singh, who had thrown a bomb in the Punjab Legislative Assembly to protest against repressive legislation and the massacre of Jallianwala Bagh (Amritsar) in 1919. Once imprisoned, he had refused to plead for mercy. In prison, he renounced terrorism as a tactic and moved close to a traditional Marxism. He was tried in secret and executed by the British in the Central Jail in Lahore, a fifteen- minute walk from where Nizam Din was telling me the story. 'If he had lived'; Nizam Din used to say, 'he would have become a leader the British really feared. And look at us now. Just because he was a Sikh, we have not even marked his martyrdom with a monument.'

He spoke of good times when all the villages in what was now Pakistan had been inhabited by Hindus and Sikhs and of their coexistence. Many of his non-Muslim friends had left for India. We would often discuss the politicians and the never-ending political crisis in Pakistan.

'They are pygmies,' Nizam Din would tell me in a slightly raised, high-pitched voice. 'Do you understand what I'm saying, Tariqji? Pygmies! Look at India. Observe the difference. Gandhi was a giant. Jawaharlal Nehru is a giant.' Over the years, I learnt far more about history, politics and everyday life from Nizam Din than I ever did at school. Much of it was a foundational knowledge, useful to this day. But his failure to interest me in religion had been noted.

A young maternal uncle, who had grown a beard at an early age and sought refuge in religion, volunteered to take on the task. His weekly unannounced visits to our house when I had just returned from school irritated me greatly. We would pace the garden while, in unctuous tones, he related a version of Islamic history which, like him, was unconvincing and dull. It comprised tales of endless heroism, with the Prophet raised to the stature of a divinity, and a punitive Allah. As he droned on, I would watch the paper kites flying and tangling with each other in the afternoon sky, mentally replay a lost game of marbles, or look forward to the first cricket match Pakistan was due to play against the Vilest Indies. Anything but religion. After a few weeks he too gave up, announcing that the unbeliever's gene in me was too strong to dislodge. Secretly the sly viper nourished the hope that something of what he had taught would stay. He was wrong. Nothing remained.

During the summer months when the heat in the plains became unbearable and the schools closed down for over two months, we would flee to the Himalayan foothills, to Nathiagali, then a tiny and isolated hill-resort perched on the ridge of a thick pine forest and overlooked by the Himalayan peaks. Nature dwarfed all else. Here I would make friends with Pashtun boys and girls from the Frontier towns of Peshawar and Marlon. Even the children from. Lahore whom I rarely saw in the winter months became summer friends.

Friendships indeed became intense. The atmosphere in the mountains was relaxed, social restrictions virtually non-existent. I acquired a taste for total freedom. We all had our favourite hiding places, which included mysterious cemeteries with English names. It always moved me that death had caught them so young. There was a deserted wooden Gothic church, which had been charred by lightning. It had one of the best views of the valley below and was occasionally used as a trysting place.

And then the burnt houses. How were they burned? I would ask the locals. Back would come a casual reply. 'They belonged to Hindus and Sikhs. Our fathers and uncles burnt them.' But why? 'So they could never come back, of course.' But why? 'Because we were now Pakistan. Their home was India.' But why, I persisted, when they had lived here for centuries, just like your families, spoken the same language, despite the different gods? The only reply was a sheepish grin and a shrugging of shoulders. It was strange to think that Hindus and Sikhs had been here, had been killed in the villages below. In these idyllic surroundings, the killings and burnings seemed strangely abstract to our young minds. We knew, but could not fully understand, and therefore did not dwell on these awful events till much later. The friends from Peshawar would speak of Hindu and Sikh Pashtuns who had migrated to India. In the tribal areas—the no-man's-land between Afghanistan and Pakistan—quite a few Hindus stayed on and were protected by the tribal codes. The same was true in Afghanistan itself (till the mujahidin and the Taliban arrived).

One of my favourite spots in Nathiagali was a space that lay between two giant oaks. From here one could watch the sun set on Nanga Parbat (number three in the pecking order after Everest and K2). The snow covering the peak would turn orange, then crimson. The cold nights could be even more dramatic. The sky and its offspring appeared much lower here than in the plains. When the full moon shone on the snow-covered peak of Nanga Parbat it bathed the entire valley in its light. Here we would breathe the air from China, look in the direction of Kashmir and marvel at the moon. Given all this, why would one need a multi-layered heaven that lay beyond, let alone the crucial seventh layer that belonged to us alone—the Islamic paradise? It must have been different in the desert.

These sights filled one's head with romantic fantasies, not religion. During the day our gang, male and female, would climb mountains, try and provoke the wild monkeys into a war of pine cones that we hurled at them. The locals always warned us against throwing stones at them. There was the legend of a British colonial officer of the nineteenth century, who had shot a monkey dead. One day, while he was out for a walk, the monkeys had ambushed and stoned him to death. The death had been real enough, but it was difficult to believe in the legend of the killer monkey. The women of this region were both attractive and unveiled, and it was much more likely that the Englishman had molested one of them and been punished somewhat severely by her male relatives. But this was always denied vigorously by the *paharis* (people of the mountains). 'You think we could kill a White man and survive?' It remained an unsolved mystery to be discussed the following summer.

We would return to our homes exhausted and ready for lunch. In the afternoons there was tennis and more walks and bridge and, yes, teenage romances. At night cheetahs and leopards prowled the forests in search of prey. What had religion to do with any of this?

One day, to my horror, my mother informed me that a local mullah from a neighbouring mountain village had been hired to make sure I completed the Koran. She had pre-empted all my objections. He would explain what each verse meant. This was torture. My summer was about to be wrecked. I moaned. I groaned. I protested, pleaded and tantrumed. To no avail. My friends were sympathetic but powerless. Most of them had undergone the same ritual.

Mullahs, especially the rural variety, were objects of ridicule, widely regarded as dishonest, hypocritical and lazy. It was widely believed that they had grown beards and chosen this path not because they were imbued with spiritual fervour, but in order to earn a crust. Unless attached to a mosque, they depended on voluntary contributions, tuition fees for teaching the Koran and free meals. The jokes that circulated at their expense, however, concerned their sexual appetites; in particular, a penchant for boys below a certain age. The fictional mullah of story-tellers or puppet-masters who travelled from village to village was a greedy and lustful arch-villain who used religion to pursue his desires and ambitions. He humiliated and cheated he poor peasant, while toadying to the local landlord or potentates. In all these tales virtue and purity became a natural cover for vice.

On the dreaded day, the mullah arrived and ate a hearty lunch. He was introduced to me by our old family retainer, Khuda Baksh (God Bless), who had served in my grandfather's household and often accompanied us to the mountains. Because of his status and age, he enjoyed a familiarity denied to other servants. God Bless was bearded, a staunch believer in the primacy of Islam; he said his prayers and fasted regularly but was deeply hostile to the mullahs, whom he regarded as pilferers, perverts and parasites. Nonetheless, he could not restrain a smile as the mullah, a man of medium height, in his late fifties, exchanged greetings with me. The sky was cloudless and the snowcapped peaks of the Himalayas clearly visible. We took our seats around a garden table placed to catch the warming sun. The afternoon chorus was in full flow. I breathed a delicious scent of sun-roasted pine needles and wild strawberries.

When the bearded man began to speak I noticed he was nearly toothless. The rhymed verse at once lost its magic. The few false teeth he had wobbled. I began to wonder if it would happen, and then it did: he became so excited with fake emotion that his false teeth dropped out on to the table. He smiled, picked them up and put them back in his mouth. At first I managed to restrain myself, but then I heard a suppressed giggle from the veranda and made the mistake of turning round. God Bless had stationed himself behind the large rhododendron to eavesdrop on the lesson and was choking with silent laughter. At this point I excused myself and rushed indoors. Thus ended the first lesson.

The following week God Bless, approaching his sixtieth birthday, dared me to ask the mullah a question before the lesson began. I did. 'Have your false teeth been supplied by the local butcher?' I inquired with an innocent expression, in an ultra-polite voice. The mullah asked me to leave: he wished to see my mother alone. A few minutes later he, too, left, never to return. Later that day he was sent an envelope full of money to pay for my insolence. God Bless and I celebrated his departure in the bazaar café with a delicious brew of mountain tea and home-made biscuits.

The attempt was never repeated. Henceforth my only religious duty was to substitute for my father once a year and accompany the male servants of our household to Eid prayers at the mosque, a painless enough task.

Some years later, when I came to Britain to study, the first group of people I met were hard-core rationalists. I might have missed the Humanist Group's stall at the Fresher's Fair had it not been for a young spotty Irishman, dressed in a faded maroon corduroy jacket, with a mop of untidy dark brown hair, standing on a table and in a melodious, slightly breathless voice shouting: 'Down with God!' When he saw me staring, he smiled and added 'and Allah' to the refrain. I joined on the spot and was immediately roped into becoming the Humanist rep at my college. Some time afterwards when I asked how he had known I was of Muslim origin rather than a Hindu or a Zoroastrian, he replied that his chant only affected Muslims and Catholics. Hindus, Sikhs, Jews and Protestants ignored him completely.

It wasn't only as a consequence of my new Humanist duties that my knowledge of Islamic history remained slender (though I noticed that those who studied it diligently and were awarded university degrees did not appear to know much more than I did). As the years progressed, Pakistan regressed. Islamiat—the study of Islam—was made compulsory in the late Seventies, and still the children gained only a very limited knowledge, a tiny sprinkling of history on a very large portion of fairy-tales and mythology.

My interest in Islam lay dormant till the Third Oil War (also known as the Gulf War) in 1990. The Second Oil War in 1967 had seen Israel, backed by the West, inflict a severe defeat on the combined might of Arab nationalism, from which it never really recovered. The 1990 war was accompanied by a wave of crude anti-Arab propaganda.. The level of ignorance displayed by most pundits and politicians was distressing. I began to ask myself questions which, till then, had barely seemed relevant.

Why had Islam not undergone a Reformation? Why had the Ottoman empire been left untouched by the Enlightenment? A reply necessitated long hours in the library. I began to study Islamic history quite obsessively, and later travelled to the regions where it had been made, concentrating on its clashes with Western Christendom. My study and travels, which helped greatly in writing the first three novels of my planned Quintet, are not yet over.[2]

Notes

1. Empty the feudal world may have been on several levels, but it always knew how to defend its class interests. My father's membership of the Communist Party of India did not ruffle as many feathers as he had imagined. He was approached by his father and cousins and offered a safe seat—safe in the sense that it, like several others in the region was controlled by our family—in the 1946 elections to the Punjab Legislative Assembly, which was to determine the make-up of the Constituent Assembly after the birth of Pakistan in 1947. My father took the offer to the Politburo of the CPI. The comrades thought long and hard. They were tempted by the thought of gaining easy representation, but finally decided to reject the offer as unprincipled. The person chosen to contest the seat for the CPI was a veteran working-class militant, Fazal Elahi Qurban, who picked up a few hundred votes as a result of some intensive canvassing by my parents. The actual victor was some obscure relation whose name I cannot recall.

2. It was travelling to Spain that inspired me to start writing the series of historical novels known as the 'Islam Quintet.' *Shadows of the Pomegranate Tree, The Book of Saladin* and *The Stone Woman* are completed. On 5 September 2001, I had begun to write *The Night of the Golden Butterfly*. It was proceeding well when one of the characters disrupted history. My punishment and his, when I return to that book, will be to remove him altogether. The banality of keeping him in would be unbearable.

A Rational Response[1]

Greydon Square

> Grand Unified Theory
> Rational Response Squad's Newest Member
> My name is…Greydon Square
> And I'm a always give it to you straight
> Check it. Yo Yo.

I'm like the Atheist spokesman
That why I come under fire and pressure attacks like Rex Grossman
Yea this game is intense
I been sayin' it since agnostics people been playin' the fence
They keep sayin' its the same in a sense
That evolution requires faith, that universe just came to exist
First of all, microevolution been proven
In the same way that sound waves let you listen to music
And macroevolution is the system of change
At or above the level of the species inflicted with change
That's microevolution on a grand scale we can't even word
because our life span's too short to observe
"But carbon dating is flawed"
"Its half life is 5730 years, and that supports our cause"
Now that'd be great if we used it to date
But since we don't then I'm a question that argument's weight
We use potassium argon to date to date the globe
Not carbon 12 or carbon 14 not none of those
So before you attack Grey go get ya facts straight
Because in the facts race, your God comes into last place

> Belief in Gods, we can fix that
> Irrational thoughts we get dispatched
> It may be hard be we'll get back
> In the position to just to end that

To battle me you need to reason clearly
Now I'm not sayin' fear me
But at least be versed in punctuated equilibrium theory
Grand unified fields, quantum mechanics and dark planets
With logic that's sharper than a blade of d'Artagnan's

(continued ⇨)

To destroy arguments of creationists who cant stand it
Then they try and hit me with the wager
Who? Pascal's wager. Who? Pascal's wager.
Now that's a fool's bet
And against the intelligent it's used less
Really? You bet
This ain't nothing new, they use it on kids
But for those who don't know it goes a little like this
Wouldn't you rather believe in God and be wrong
Then to not believe in God and be wrong
If you believe in God and your wrong you've lost nothing
But if you don't believe and you're wrong its all suffering
The problem is you can try it on anything
Switch the Gods around and apply it to anything
The Flyin' Spaghetti Monster, Zeus, Amin, Ra
Krishna, Odin, Baal and then Allah
Which one of em's our God?
None of 'em all false
And blame it on the Atheists its always our fault
Except it never is
So don't get mad at us we just showin' ya'll the evidence

> Belief in Gods, we can fix that
> Irrational thoughts we get dispatched
> It may be hard be we'll get back
> In the position to just to end that

Grand Unified Theory
Rational Response Squad
I'm a make the fundies hate me
They gon' need a new reason to shut down rap
But they wont shut down rap that degrades women though huh.
They wont shut down rap that talks about sellin' crack though huh
Hypocrites
Its all good…

Note

1. Written by hip hop artist and atheist Greydon Square, this song appears on his independent album *The Compton Effect*, released in 2007.

38
Humanism And The Territory Of Novelists (2007)
Salman Rushdie

In honour of its thirtieth anniversary, the Humanist Chaplaincy at Harvard University hosted The New Humanism conference April 20 – 22, 2007. The event kicked off Friday night in the Memorial Church at Harvard Yard with a literary reading by renowned novelist and humanist Salman Rushdie. Rushdie was presented the first Outstanding Lifetime Achievement Award in Cultural Humanism jointly by the chaplaincy and the American Humanist Association. What follows is an edited version of Rushdie's remarks in acceptance and excerpts of the question and answer period that followed his reading.

Most of my life I was brought up happily free from religion. I grew up in a community in Bombay, India, where there were, in our immediate neighbourhood, people of every conceivable religion and no religion. There were children of Christian, Hindu, Muslim, Buddhist, Sikh, Parsi, and a few, like my family, unbelieving households. And they somehow all cancelled each other out—except that we all decided we would celebrate each other's holidays as well as our own. And this led me later in life to wonder, where was the holiday for people who didn't believe in God?

Speaking specifically of humanism, I remember that when I was a university student, the most popular lecturer at Cambridge had nothing to do with my subject, which was history. He was an elderly, heavily Mittel-European accented professor of architecture, Nikolas Pevsner, who had written the classical study of the churches of England and Europe. His lectures, because he was a mesmeric speaker, would be packed every week, with people literally hanging from the rafters. You had to get there an hour early to get a place, which was not always the case in college lectures. I have always remembered his explanation, given with much flamboyant arm waving, of the difference between the Gothic and the Renaissance principles of architecture.

He said that in the Gothic cathedral, the eye is led forward towards the altar and upward toward God. But the Renaissance church was made in an X shape; it looks like a cross but, in fact, the only way one can experience the church is if a human being stands at the center. Instead of making a movement towards God, Pevsner said, it makes a movement towards the human. This works as a description not just of architecture but of a movement from the period of the Gothic into the period of the Renaissance, which is also a movement away from worshipping God to placing human beings at the center of the story. I thought it was an unforgettable explanation. And here I am forty years later repeating it, because it seems to have informed a lot of what I have subsequently thought. In the words of Alexander Pope:

> *Know then thyself, presume not God to scan.*
> *The proper study of mankind is man.*

For a novelist, of course, if you don't study mankind then you aren't doing anything.

The great thing about the novel as a form is that even the most abstract fiction can never entirely lose the human scale. If you do not have a thing the size of a human being at the center of a work of literature, around which everything else is woven, then you don't have literature, you have something else. So it almost follows in trying to be a novelist that you would find yourself involved with the ideas of humanism. For me it just comes with the territory.

And thank you for this honor, by which, really, I do feel slightly overwhelmed. People like being praised—but sort of in their absence. I just like to hope that people would say this kind of thing when I wasn't there. But I guess I'll never know.

Question from the audience: What is your favourite book?

Salman Rushdie: That's difficult. I mean it's easy to say what your favourite one hundred books are, but it's quite difficult to choose just one. And it also depends what day of the week it is and what you had for lunch. The question of the 'desert island book'—when I've been asked that before I tend to cheat and ask for the *Arabian Nights*, which is like having twelve books in one.

But I think the reason I say that is because a lot of the way I think about writing was shaped by growing up in the culture of the wonderful tale—in the culture in which you know that stories are not true, that stories are make believe. And that's why it's possible for carpets to fly. The truth of stories, the truth of literature, is another kind of truth; it's a felt emotional truth, not a sort of documentary, journalistic, reportage truth.

Question: Is God a good character, an interesting character?

Rushdie: No, I don't like him very much, actually. Speaking in purely fictional terms, I much prefer the polytheistic gods to the solo gods. Because the great thing about the pantheons, whether the Greek gods or the Roman gods or the Norse gods or the Hindu gods is that they don't behave well. They're kind of mean spirited and vengeful. And that's what's even better about them is that they don't ask you to do as they do. They don't set themselves up as moral exemplars. They're simply ourselves writ large.

Question: What advice would you give to an aspiring writer?

Rushdie: My real answer is, if you need the advice, don't do it. Because everybody I've ever known who was a writer had some real fire burning inside them that forced them to do it. They didn't have an option, they had to be a writer, they couldn't *not* be a writer.

Question: Thinking about the idea of defining ourselves by what we don't believe in versus defining ourselves by what we do believe in—I'm wondering if you could comment on the idea of calling ourselves atheists versus humanists or naturalists. I would also love it if you could comment on the values of the Enlightenment and whether you're optimistic about an enlightenment period within the Islamic world.

Rushdie: Well, in a way I think you're right that all these labels are in some way partial, but I do think that the question of origins and the question of ethics—which are the two big things which lead people to religion—are things which for me are not answered by religion. I don't believe in any of the religious stories of the origin of the universe and I don't look to priests for my moral answers. And so, in that sense, I suppose it is a bit of a definition against. Because it's also *not belief*, so it's difficult to define it as another kind of belief.

As for enlightenment in Islam, I think there is much enlightened thought in Islam, and there always has been, and there is now, which we don't hear about because we hear the loud angry voices. At the same time it's very important to recognize that those loud angry voices have all the momentum just now and that other, gentler ways of thinking have been in retreat in the Muslim world for the last twenty or thirty years. Can that change again? I hope so. But don't hold your breath.

39
Why My Dog Is Not A Humanist (1992)

Kurt Vonnegut

I was once a Boy Scout. The motto of the Boy Scouts, as you know, is "Be Prepared" So, several years ago I wrote a speech to be delivered in the event that I won the Nobel Prize for Literature. It was only eight words long. I think I had better use it here. "Use it or lose it:" as the saying goes.

This is it: "You have made me an old, old man."

I think I got this great honor because I've lasted so long. I dare to say of humanism what Lyndon Johnson said of politics. He said, "Politics ain't hard. You just hang around and go to funerals."

Forgive me if I am not solemn about my award tonight. I am here for your companionship and not any award. Nicholas Murray Butler, the late president of Columbia University, was said by H.L. Mencken to have received more honorary degrees and medals and citations and so on than anyone else then on the planet. Mencken declared that all that remained to be done for him was to wrap him in sheet gold and burnish him until he blinded the sun itself.

This is not the first time I have been accused of being a humanist. All of 25 years ago, when I was teaching at the University of Iowa, a student all of a sudden said to me, "I hear you're a humanist." I said, "Oh, yeah? What's a humanist?" He said, "That what I'm asking you. Aren't you getting paid to answer questions like that?"

I pointed out that my salary was a very modest one. I then gave him the names of several full professors who were making a heck of a lot more money than I was and who were doctors of philosophy besides—which I sure as heck wasn't, and which I am not now.

But his accusation stuck in my craw. And in the process of trying to cough it up so I could look at it, it occurred to me that a humanist, perhaps, was somebody who was crazy about human beings, who, like Will Rogers, had never met one he didn't like. That certainly did not describe me. It did describe my dog, though. His name was Sandy, although he wasn't a Scotsman. He was a puli—a Hungarian sheepdog with a face full of hair. I am a German, with a face full of hair.

I took Sandy to the little zoo in Iowa City. I expected him to enjoy the buffalo and the prairie dogs and the raccoons and the possums and the foxes and the wolves and so on, and especially their stinks, which in the case of the buffalo were absolutely overwhelming. But all Sandy paid any attention to was people, his tail wagging all the time. What a person looked like or smelled like didn't matter to Sandy. It could be a baby. It could be a drunk who hated dogs. It could be a young woman as voluptuous as Marilyn Monroe. It could have been Hitler. It could have been Eleanor Roosevelt. Whoever it was, Sandy would have wagged his tail. I disqualified him as a humanist, though, after reading in the *Encyclopedia Britannica* that humanists were inspired by ancient Greece and Rome at their most rational, and by the Renaissance. No dog, not even Rin Tin Tin or Lassie, has ever been that. Humanists, moreover, I learned, were strikingly secular in their interests and enthusiasms, did not try to factor God Almighty into their equations, so to speak, along with all that could be seen and heard and felt and smelled and tasted in the here and now. Sandy obviously worshiped not just me but simply any person as though he or she were the creator and manager of the universe.

He was simply too dumb to be a humanist.

Sir Isaac Newton, incidentally, did think that was a reasonable thing to do—to factor in a conventional God Almighty, along with whatever else might be going on. I don't believe Benjamin Franklin ever did. Charles Darwin pretended to do that, because of his place in polite society. But he was obviously very happy, after his visit to the Galapagos Islands, to give up that pretense. That was only 150 years ago.

As long as I've mentioned Franklin, let me digress a moment. He was a Freemason, as were Voltaire and Frederick the Great, and so were Washington and Jefferson and Madison. Most of us here, I guess, would be honored if it was said that such great human beings were our spiritual ancestors. So why isn't this a gathering of Freemasons? Can somebody here, after this speech, if you don't mind, tell me what went wrong with Freemasonry?

This much I think I understand: in Franklin's time—and in Voltaire's—Freemasonry was perceived as being anti-Catholic. To be a Freemason was cause for excommunication from the Roman Catholic Church.

As the Roman Catholic population of this country grew by leaps and bounds, to be anti-Catholic—in New York and Chicago and Boston, at least—was political suicide. It was also business suicide.

None of my real ancestors, blood ancestors, genetic ancestors in this country —every one of them of German decent—was a Freemason, so far as I know, and I am the fourth generation Vonnegut to be born here. Before World War I, though, a lot of them took part in the activities of a highly respectable but not impossibly serious organization much like this one, which they called "the Freethinkers."

There are a few Americans who call themselves that still—some of you in this room, no doubt. But the Freethinkers no longer exist as an organized presence of which communities are aware. This is because the movement was so overwhelmingly German-American, and most German-Americans found it prudent to abandon all activities that might make them seem apart from the general population when we entered World War I. Many Freethinkers, incidentally, were German-Jews.

My great grandfather Clemens Vonnegut, an immigrant merchant from Munster, became a Freethinker after reading Darwin. In Indianapolis, there is a public school named after him. He was head of the school board there for many years.

So the sort of humanism I represent, to which I am an heir, draws energy not from the Renaissance or from an idealized pre-Christian Greece and Rome but, rather, from very recent scientific discoveries and modes of seeking truth.

I myself at one time tried to become a biochemist—as did our darling, terribly missed brother Isaac Asimov. He actually became one. I didn't have a chance. He was smarter than me. We both knew that, incidentally. He is in heaven now.

My paternal grandfather and father were both architects, restructuring the reality of Indianapolis with meticulously measured quantities of materials whose presence—unlike that of a conventional God Almighty—could not be doubted: wood and steel, sand and lime and stone, copper, brass, bricks.

My only surviving sibling, Dr. Bernard Vonnegut, eight years my senior, is a physical chemist who thinks and thinks about the distribution of electrical charges in thunderstorms. But now my big brother, like Isaac Asimov near the end of his life, surely, and like most of us here, has to admit that the fruits of science so far, put into the hands of governments, have turned out to be cruelties and stupidities exceeding by far those of the Spanish Inquisition and Genghis Khan and Ivan the Terrible and most of the demented Roman emperors, not excepting Heliogabalus.

Heliogabalus had a hollow iron bull in his banquet hall that had a door in its side. Its mouth was a hole, so sound could get out. He would have a human being put inside the bull and then a fire built on a hearth under its belly, so that the guests at his banquets would be entertained by the noises the bull made.

We modern humans roast people alive, tear their arms and legs off, or whatever, using airplanes or missile launchers or ships or artillery batteries—and do not hear their screams.

When I was a little boy in Indianapolis, I used to be thankful that there were no longer torture chambers with iron maidens and racks and thumbscrews and Spanish boots and so on. But there may be more of them now than ever—not in this country but elsewhere, often in countries we call our friends. Ask the Human Rights Watch. Ask Amnesty International if this isn't so. Don't ask the U.S. State Department.

And the horrors of those torture chambers—their powers of persuasion—have been upgraded, like those of warfare, by applied science, by the domestication of electricity and the de tailed understanding of the human nervous system, and so on.

Napalm, incidentally, is a gift to civilization from the chemistry department of Harvard University.

So science is yet another human made God to which I, unless in a satirical mood, an ironical mood, a lampooning mood, need not genuflect.

Epilogue
A New Enlightenment: The Second Wave
Dimitrios Roussopoulos

Enlightenment is a term used to designate a period in history of great intellectual advancement in the cause of general education and culture, including the self-emancipation from prejudice, superstition and convention. This movement touched Germany from the 17th century; it had roots in England and spread into France and Italy. It is also a term applied to the period of the Greek Sophists and in the study of the Renaissance. The impact of the Enlightenment was considerable in the 18th century into the 20th. Its influence also became a target for criticism,

We attempt here to go beyond the current public debate in a number of ways. In doing so we acknowledge the courage and foresight of the first Enlightenment beginning in 1700 with the founding of the Berlin Academy of Sciences to its halt in1799 with the seizure of State power by Napoleon setting humanity back. Humanism, within which the distinctiveness of atheism is found, was a cornerstone of the Enlightenment with new values of democratic and, in the 20th century, ecological dimensions.

Many of the intellectual giants of the Enlightenment were unknown by the vast majority in the 18th century. It was a period of verbal cacophony and paradox. In Berlin it was called *Aufklarung,* in Paris *les Lumieres,* in Milano it was *illuminismo.* The ideas emerged in different cities over a number of decades. The common denominator was, however a perspective that embraced rational discourse and critique, invariably hostile to and distant from superstition, intolerance, and traditional religion. The first notions of human rights were articulated in opposition to torture which had been conducted and justified by the religiously inspired, in reaction to fears and insecurity of those in power as they observed the shifting world of beliefs among the populace.

From John Locke's *Essay Concerning Human Understanding* of 1690, to Voltaire's novella of 1758 *Candide,* Immanuel Kant's 1784 essay 'Was ist Aufklarung?' *Of Crimes and Punishments* by Cesare Beccaria, and then Jean Le Rond D'Alembert, Denis

Diderot, George-Louis Leclerc, Comte de Buffron, Guillaume-Thomas, the editors of the *Encyclopedie*, Baron d'Holbach, to J.J. Rousseau and others the Enlightenment developed. Critical literature accumulated, reading became a passion as did discussion. Consider the atmosphere of intellectual excitement on the one hand and the tremendous insecurity among the ruling class of Church and State on the other, as a flood of periodicals, pamphlets and books in various forms matched innovations in printing technology. The literature crossed borders in an unprecedented way, creating a century which broke from the past with the winds of change.

Don't Think! Believe!

The exploration of the self and personal identity also began with a number of new insights and philosophical steps for individual and social emancipation. It was Kant who defined the Enlightenment as "man's throwing off his self-imposed immaturity," meaning man's inability to exercise one's mind without a reference to some outside authority and so he adds "Dare to know! Have the courage to follow your understanding!" His definition recognizes obstacles which are ever present even today, human cowardice and laziness. He points to people who take little initiative even with their own lives, allowing others to do the thinking and acting for them. Indeed, leading a life of such passivity, they have no need to seriously think for themselves even though they may cover up their passivity by pretensions. With this severe judgment he continues, noting that there are only a few people who have been able to free themselves and recover the use of their reason. Kant recognizes that this is difficult since surrounding society clamors for conformity, (calling it "responsibility") from the military to the tax department to the clergyman..

Everywhere there are artificial limits imposed on freedom, yesteryear and today. Kant proposes what is needed for the individual and society to counter these restrictions: the public use of reason which brings into play the public and private dimensions of the Enlightenment. The public use of reason is exemplified by the learned person in relation to the world of readers (*Leserwealt*). Private reason refers to the exercise of an office or profession, according to Kant, and here freedom has to have certain limits. A soldier must obey his superiors, although he should have the freedom to publicly display his disagreements.

Kant asks a question which is the heart of his essay: is there an enlightened age ? No is the answer, although the Age of Enlightenment exists; the obstacles are becoming fewer but there is a long road ahead. The growth of intellectual freedom can have a destabilizing effect on the State and society, so he declares that only by assuming limitations can the space for freedom be truly fulfilled, and with this he steps aside from the other major figures of the Enlightenment. Freedom of thought must not be pursued to its final consequence otherwise it will damage the order of society, was his position. To should be noted that Kant was a relative moderate in comparison to the more engaging and politically developed Parisian radicals of the Enlightenment.

The reaction to the growing influence of the Enlightenment was sweeping, and still is. No other time in history has had as great an influence on the moral values of our present Western society, except for the classical period of ancient Greece and early Rome. The Enlightenment was a philosophical and social movement: a case in point, it doesn't bear the name of any one person or singular moment in history. It is a movement and an epoch which bears a clarity of ideas.

These ideas, however, were seen by some parts of society as causes of evil. The dangerous 'unfettered' use of critical reason was of great concern to the Jesuits, for its effect on both religious and political life. They analyzed the Enlightenment as a period leading to chaos and weakening the Church and the State. The whole epoch was deemed devastating to religion in that it promoted tolerance which consequently put all religions on an equal footing. Thus 'truth' or 'falsehoods' were relative, and therefore the ultimate moral source becomes, us: humans.

For Hegel, critic of the Enlightenment, it was a failed attempt to close the Protestant Reformation of the 16th century. He contended that it was a movement devoid of a set of beliefs because it positioned man as an end in himself, with an unfulfilled religious mission, an outcrop of the laws of nature, phenomena known only by humans. This line of thinking lay under the skin of the Enlightenment throughout its evolution into the 20th century, McGill university's Charles Taylor being its latest intellectual critic.

Others thought, from the mid-18th century on, that the Enlightenment was a conspiracy by philosophers who sought to attack religion and consequently was not historically grounded; instead it introduced thought that caused ruin and ultimately the French Revolution. The proclamation of the *Rights of Man and Citizen*, based on abstractions, was proclaimed by the revolution of 1789. Further, the revolution of 1792 abolished the monarchy, attacked the huge property holdings of the Church and created citizen assemblies in the Parisian sections that radicalized further the democratic definition of citizenship. This latter social revolution was just too shocking to the political order. Enter Napoleon who in 1799 took State power and who in 1803 attacked the philosophers of the Enlightenment for the use of "impious language that teaches the people to distain their fathers…teaches them to revolt against authority…a code of atheism…a code of immorality… ."

The Twists and Turns on the Road

There is an exciting sequence that runs through the Enlightenment. Two powerful currents flow through the French Revolutions of 1789 and 1792, and flow into the European revolts of the 1820s and 1830s, as well as the Revolution of 1848. One current was expressed by political theorist Alexis de Tocqueville who wrote down his worries about 1848 which, he predicted, would lead to an authoritarian turn and which was indeed, reflected in the ultimate seizure of State power by Napoleon III in 1852. The consequences and effects of the 18th century and the French Revolution, Tocqueville insisted, lay not so much with the philosophy of the Enlightenment but with the increased power of the centralized State, which grew unabated from the Ancien Regime into the resulting Revolution. This growth of the State, he argued, extinguished liberty. The political actors of the Enlightenment brought to power during 1789, having no practical experience in administration, quickly drifted into a vacuum responding not unlike many others before and since, by centralizing power and defending this turn through political terror. This Jacobin current was and is all too present in revolutions. Countering this current is that of a libertarian and democratic one which emerged in the Parisian sections of 1792, but at a time when exhaustion was everywhere, and when the prevailing contradictions did not allow enough time to develop strong new directly democratic institutions to be established which could have changed the fortunes of the Revolution and prevented the continuation of further dislocation ultimately opening the door to Napoleon.

The second current was reflected in the writings and political lives of Pierre-Joseph Proudhon and William Godwin with his companion Mary Wollstonecraft . Wollstonecraft who emerged from a humble background was able through her writings to overcome the limits of her education. She became a journalist, reporting on the French Revolution, and also learned from the ideas of the Enlightenment which allowed her to earn an independent living. While she was the wife of the anarchist philosopher Godwin, (tragically she died at the age of 38 in childbirth 1797), she wrote and published the celebrated *Vindication of the Rights of Women* in 1792 which caused a furor and is still considered a feminist and political classic. In this text, the author compares the two very different kinds of education available to women and men. She urged her gender to overcome the limitations imposed by the prevailing environment, and went on to denounce the legal, financial constraints which created a form of slavery of women in the sense of a complete dependence and lack of rights. Wollstonecraft embraced the Enlightenment and its idea of universal reason; while pointing out that in practice it attributed different characteristics to the genders, she also pointed out that it was founded on ideas such as reason and virtue which were said to be innate in all humans. Rationality was what was denied women by Rousseau, and virtue for women was defined in a sexual sense and not much beyond. Therefore Wollstonecraft pointed out that such thinking could only lead to a dangerous moral relativism which would retard progress as envisaged by the Enlightenment. Her intellectual contribution was thus a brilliant contribution in saving the Enlightenment from the gendered biased contradictions between theory and practice.

Proudhon ,Godwin and other early anti-authoritarians of the times described in some detail a society that could be based on a horizontal distribution of power in contrast to the vertical structure that existed before the Revolution and in most ways continued into the post-revolution period.

From the restraints of Kant, to the bold and imaginative advocacy of the radical Encyclopedists and the corrections made by Mary Wollstonecraft, the sweep of the Enlightenment laid the basis for the advances of science in the 19th century into the 20th in a number of crucial fields of human endeavor which substantially enhanced our understanding of ourselves, our society and the universe around us.

The 20th Century Critique

However, Europe especially, lapsed into a number of ugly, painful and cruel outbursts which undermined the progress of civilization in many ways. From the late 19th century into the 20th through World Wars I and II into the Cold War between nuclear armed super military empires we slipped into an unprecedented assault on Nature driven by an insatiable and predatory economy which eventually has caused us to question the basic premises of the modern era.

Small wonder German theorists like Max Horkheimer and Theodor Adorno in 1947 raised some difficult questions in their *Dialectic of Enlightenment* published in the aftermath of a devastating war and holocaust wherein they asked "why mankind, instead of entering into a truly human condition, is sinking into a new kind of barbarism" .They went on to point to a paradox, namely that 'The Enlightenment had always aimed at liberating men from fear, and establishing their sovereignty. Yet the fully Enlightened Earth radiates disaster triumphant. The programme of the Enlightenment was the disenchantment of the world: the dissociation of myths and the substitution of knowledge for fancy." They detected a fundamental flaw, that of the drive towards a cold reason, all other considerations aside, which created a general characteristic of a 20th century specifically leading to organizations and management styles based on a rational technological system with stark expressions: by "the administered life" and a "rational organization of men, nature and knowledge itself for the achievement of the objectives of this world."

Knowledge was being turned into a commodity as a result of its intense rationality, rationality very much conditioned by the dominant politico-economic system. Thus the needed connections among the 'production' of knowledge, truth and wisdom broke down. These critics said that "Once viewed as a commodity to be bought and sold, knowledge itself became merely a means to an end and culture became wholly a commodity disseminated as information without permeating the individuals who acquired it." Technology, a particular form of knowledge, was a specific culprit: "technology does not work by concepts and images, by the insight of fortune, but refers to method, the exploitation of others' work and capital. What men want to learn from nature is how to use it in order to wholly dominate it and other men...on the road to modern science, men renounce any claim to meaning." This divorce with ultimate purpose, this mechanistic extrapolation from the humanistic ethos of the Enlightenment was questioned to devastating effect, by Horkheimer and Adorno's argument that knowledge now started to function as a specific form in the marketplace which ceased to be internalized by individuals but instead became externalities for manipulation for the ultimate purposes of greed.

Understandably an underlying contemporary emotion seems to prevail pushing people to turn to religions, not so much to a belief in god but because of a fear of modern science. The worry is that scientists and their employers are becoming arrogant, too powerful, playing with things we barely understand, such as the Earth's climate and our genetic code. The concern is partly about scientific ethics and a horror over anything that looks like genetic manipulation and eugenics. This view is hardly sustained by the profound ethical concerns that so marked the best writings of the Enlightenment. Science is a child of the Enlightenment, but it grew and developed in societies with State or market capitalism and the big State. This marriage is a marriage of Dracula and Vampira.

What happened? The liberality towards religion and the gradual growth of the benevolent State are two conspicuous examples of what occurred. A loss of ethical rigour overtook the Enlightenment's intellectual discipline. The building of the State was accompanied by a widely desired need for efficiency and for 'the even distribution of wealth.' On the one hand the thirst for security/stability in what seemed a chaotic world, was often accompanied by a deep ignorance of Nature on the other. We looked at the turbulent flow of ecosystems with little understanding that the ecological dynamics observed were more horizontal than hierarchical. Humans projected their hierarchical social structures onto Nature. The poorly understood 'chaos' of Nature contributed to an overwhelming need for order and security.

During this period another German theorist in disagreement with Horkheimer and Adorno, Jurgen Habermas offered another analysis. In 1962 he published '*The Structural Transformation of the Public Sphere*' in which he argued that building on the potential of the Enlightenment was still possible and useful, and that starting from Kant, the process needed to be completed. He contended that the potential for human emancipation from particularism was very present and was the basis of making us human, thus linking humans together by common values such as freedom, justice and a thirst for objectivity. Habermas assumed that there is universality in these values. However we know that there is a series of cultural distinctions born of differences of religion, language and ethnicity that stand in the way of these universalities.

What is striking about the Habermas contribution to this mid-20th century debate is his insistence that the Enlightenment created a 'public realm' as no other, where opinions are discussed and transformed partly because of the presence of books, newspapers, periodicals and currently the Internet , in what eventually becomes 'public opinion.' This in turn creates a means of freedom wherein individuals escape their prescribed roles as subjects and thus can become social actors articulating their own opinions and ideas. This Habermas interprets as a new culture, one which is conducive to historical analysis and which can have a positive moral role.

Habermas twins with Michel Foucault who also saw Kant's essay as an important point of evolution for the Enlightenment from which critical reason becomes an agent of change. Both thinkers agreed that the Enlightenment needed to be re-evaluated for the present.

Curious Contradictions

During the period ending with the Second World War, and following the Cold War and its aftermath, the political Left was seriously crippled by Marxist-Leninism and its different political parties, large or small, as well as its "fronts." During this period the so-called atheists of this school sought accommodations with one religion or another: recall the Marxist-Christian dialogue. When Roger Garaudy, a former theoretician of the Stalinist French Communist Party turned Christian, (and before he became a Muslim) came to Montreal, he met Canada's Marxist historian and one time Stalinist disciplinarian, Stanley Ryerson (who left the Canadian Communist Party only after the invasion of Czechoslovak in 1968). Ryerson invited me to his home to meet his Parisian visitor. I was both puzzled and reluctant to accept the invitation, but good manners prevailed and I came to a session of empty chatting. Is this what happens when men leave one orthodoxy to search for something else, I mused?

The social democrats are also well-known for their accommodations. Live and let live is their motto to the point of embracing eclecticism. It matters little where the source of our moral values comes from, the vote has to be brought out during elections, the ultimate objective being to strengthen the parliamentary wing of the party with the hope of eventually better managing the State.

The post-sixties Left has largely been individualized and organizationally fragmented. The career minded have been absorbed by the Academy, a cradle to grave welfare mini-state. To be sure, some are intellectuals and do honest labour and some stimulate public interest in this or that critical issue while helping young people think critically. Others have become professionals of one sort or another very much taken in by convention and the dominant consumerist drives of market capitalism.

Under the skin however a new set of protest movements has not only maintained its space, some have grown considerably; the ecology movement is clearly one of these. There is, in the last decade a convergence of the diversity of causes through the anti-globalization world-wide movement.

Open Letter to the Left: Come Out of the Closet

Within this mass movement the non-religious and religious often work together. Such coalition building among liberal religionists and non-believers, if it is to be politically useful, needs to address honestly two questions:

First, when and how are the fundamentalists to be confronted and returned to the box of the past? And how is this to be done? The struggle is not unimportant and we cannot pretend that it is marginal and will simply go away. It is after all, and to recap, the religionists who bang on our doors promoting their beliefs, seeking to convert the innocent and lonely; it is they who seek to promote their belief system in the schools, who rival each other to the point of condemning their fellows to death and damnation, and who promote the belief that without their book and its preaching, the streets would be overrun with endless sexual orgies, while the capitalist marketplace and private property would cease. The fundamentalists go so far as to insist that we must bow to their god, and that my sister should be killed if she is seen in public with a man who is not her brother. The poet Shelley called for the necessity of atheism and with good cause. We cannot and should not avoid taking a position, just as we must and can overcome our fear of death and the dark. It is bad enough to believe in a supreme god, it is even worse to wallow in the cult that the "Truth" has been made known to some and is to be interpreted by some select group to the rest.

Second, when are the atheists among the non-religious going to come out of the closet and say who they are and what they believe in, root and branch? We are here, working for fundamental social change in the here and now, and yes, we are prepared to work with some others who are different from ourselves, but this work should be based on honesty. The novelist Salman Rushdie, put it thus on U.S. television, ABC's "Nightline" February 13, 1989 with regard to his book *The Satanic Verses*:

> [My book says] that there is an old, old conflict between the secular view of the world and the religious view of the world, and particularly between texts which claim to be divinely inspired and texts which are imaginatively inspired…I distrust people who claim to know the whole truth and who seek to orchestrate the world in line with that one truth. I think that's a very dangerous position in the world. It needs to be challenged constantly in all sorts of ways, and that's what I tried to do.

In openly taking this direction we should be modest in that it has a long and distinguished pedigree.[1] Everywhere religion is legitimized, theology is taught freely, and the fundamentalisms swirl around the monotheist religions with homes, institutions, and media access. The point of this book and this open letter is to add legitimacy to atheism, and to argue that it also has a rightful place that should be recognized, openly and frankly. We wish to defend the Western intellectual tradition of the right to dissent, even radical dissent.

What Are the Basic Tenets of the New Enlightenment?
The Second Wave of the Enlightenment

This book is both a tocsin and a call for a second wave Enlightenment. In doing so we outline below some intellectual and philosophical parameters to consider as we engage in a public debate in a public place.

The new atheists have served us well. However is not religion the effect of much human suffering rather than the cause? The cause is insecurity, fear and ignorance. Religion *becomes the justification*, an ideology, proclaiming of the "Truth" that confidently justifies barbarism of all sorts. Thus the challenge should be that both the effect *and* the cause must be put in their places. What are the causes that lead to a tumor which in turn spreads like a cancer?

Atheism anchored in a humanist philosophy can be a basis of thought and action guiding those who have overthrown for themselves the supernatural, god, superstition, and religion. Human beings are accorded a primary place in the affairs of society always in balance with the natural environment. Gone is the notion of dominating and exploiting Nature for our selfish needs. The term atheism specifically reflects a naturalistic philosophy that rejects supernaturalism and relies upon critical reason and science, democracy and empathy.

As important as atheism is however, it is in itself a limited perspective. It should be the core around which humanism rotates. Humanism has many additional enriching tenets which are outward-looking, which are an integral part of a new politics. Some of the new atheists for instance have taken some very questionable political positions, and these inconsistencies with the larger humanist tableau have to be confronted, although this is not the place to do so.

The world view of humanism includes some of the following values:

- Ethics—a pursuit of individual and social conduct which incorporates an ethics based on the common good, on the need to sustain and develop community, enhancing human well-being and individual moral and political responsibility , and a promotion of a strong and participatory democracy in its most authentic forms. This ethical sensibility is based on an ecological understanding of the natural environment which requires that we profoundly need a fundamentally new understanding of society's relationship to Nature, one that is balanced and not predatory.

- Building a better society—with a conviction that with reason, an open exchange of ideas and debate, in a climate of individual and collective understanding, progress can be made in different areas of daily life which enhance a better world for us and future generations.

- A concern for Life—a commitment to making life meaningful and purposeful, creating the conditions wherein every human being can maximize her/his potential through educating oneself and one another about our history, and its intellectual and cultural achievements, coupling this with a desire to understand the same of others. Thus life will be one of fulfillment, growth and creativity. Humanism is a philosophy of imagination, intuitive feelings, hunches, speculation, flashes of inspiration, emotions which, while not valid sources of knowledge can remain useful sources for some notions that can lead us to new ways of looking at the world. What is rejected in these sources and those of arbitrary faith, authority, revelations, and altered states of consciousness are that they are substitutes for critical reason and scientific inquiry.

- The method in the search for truth is one with a commitment to the use of critical reason, factual evidence, and scientific methods of inquiry, instead of mysticism and faith, in seeking alternative values and solutions to those the dominant society promotes. Humanism is a philosophy for people who think for themselves. It makes no claims to possess or have access to supposed transcendental knowledge. It is a philosophy in constant evolution, and therefore more of a rushing river toward the sea than an enclosed lake. As such humanists take responsibility for their own lives and relish the adventure of taking risks and the adventure of being part of new discoveries, seeking new knowledge, new sensations and pleasures, exploring new options. Instead of finding comfort in prefabricated answers to the great questions of life, there is an openness to quest and the freedom of discovery.

- Atheism is at the core of this philosophy as it is a direct challenge to all forms of mystification and authority. By its very nature it states defiantly "Neither God nor Master." Politically the defiance of religious and secular authority has led to more democracy, human rights and the protection of the environment.

Perhaps if humanity is to survive we will need to live in a world without the State and Capital, without classes, without sexism and patriarchy, and consequently at peace with each other, and with Nature.

But someone will say, religion has been with us from the start. Depending on your definition this is not quite true. There are many religions, for example those of the Far East, which have no need for a personal god. Apart from this, modern science has revealed that the naturalness of religion may be in the end a genetic predisposition for many. Prof. Michael A. Goldman, a biologist at San Francisco State University, says in reviewing the work of molecular biologist Dean Hamer:

> Geneticists are the first to admit that genes don't explain everything, and that most important features of human behavior represent a complex interplay among many genes and the environment. Although we have now learned the most fundamental secrets of the human genome, and understand hundreds of Mendelian genetic traits in molecular detail, we have been far less successful in our studies of the traits and genes that are vastly more important from the medical, economic, social and intellectual perspectives. We have been gun-shy when it comes to dealing with questions about how genetics interprets cognitive ability, race, personality and behavior. Once again, National Institute of Health molecular biologist Dean Hamer fills the gap with a radical treatment of no less than the genetic basis for spirituality.

He draws a sharp distinction between spirituality, which is a personality trait that some of us have to a greater or lesser extent than others, and religion or belief in a particular god, which is a culturally transmitted expression of spirituality. It might be that some of that variation in spirituality is explained by genetics, although spirituality is probably a complex trait influenced by many genes as well as the environment. If there are genetic influences, ever-more sophisticated techniques in molecular genetics should be able to tease them out.

Religion down through the ages probably helped individual self-interest and collective survival by codifying its requirements and rules as morality. When inequalities of wealth and power developed, however, religion also extended moral codes to include obligations of dominance and submission. Today, facing ecological disaster, exhaustion of essential natural resources, and the proliferations of nuclear, chemical and biological weapons of mass destruction, religion no longer provides a collective defense mechanism for the human species. Instead, the solutions religion provides have now become central to the problem of human survival.

On all these matters we have to speak out. The Left should take the lead.

Note

1. Recall that the ancient Greeks began to lay their Olympian myths to rest several hundred years before Christ, as their democracy strengthened. Epicurus of Samos [432-370 BCE] believed that the root of evil, which most religionists dwell on, was fear, above all the fear of death and the beyond. Death it was supposed was merely a long, untroubled sleep. Take away the fear of death by suggesting that there was no immortal soul to survive, and what prevents the enjoyment of happiness? This meant to Epicurus, friendship, and just dealing with 'Life quietly.' Pain could be endured. Ultimately chance ruled everything. The universe was composed of atoms whose random encounters produced life. It is much like a machine, neutral between right and wrong, without caprice or malevolence. As late as circa 200 CE, one of the longest and most elaborate funerary inscriptions, that of Diogenes of Oenoanda in Asia Minor included the creed 'There is nothing to fear in God. There is nothing to feel in death. Evil can be endured, Good can be achieved.'

   There is a link from Greek mythology to us today. Such a link rarely, if every, is manifested in other cultures, and does not exist in the religions of today. Consider the character of Prometheus. He stands out because he was idolized by the Greeks because he defied Zeus. He stole the fire of the gods and gave it to humans. For this he was severely punished throughout continuing his defiance amidst his torments. Thus was born the fundamental challenge to authority. The next time we encounter a Promethean character is Lucifer in John Milton's *Paradise Lost*. But now the rebel becomes the Devil, and is evil incarnate. Whoever defies god must be the personification of wickedness. This illustrates all the difference at the core of religion. The Greeks did not agree; Zeus, for all his power, could be mistaken and even irrelevant.

I grew tired of religion some time not long after birth.
—*John Malkovich, actor*

I'm dyslexic, so I hear dog when you say God.
—*Robert Altman, director*

I can't even call myself an 'atheist' because it is not at all clear what I'm being asked to deny.
—*Noam Chomsky, linguist, philosopher, political activist*

There is no direct evidence, so how could you ask me to believe in God when there's absolutely no evidence that I can see?
—*Jodie Foster, actor*

I'm not somebody who goes to church on a regular basis. The specific elements of Christianity are not something I'm a huge believer in.
—*Bill Gates, entrepreneur, software executive, philanthropist*

For some people. I hope so, for them. For the people who believe in it, I hope so. There doesn't need to be a God for me.
—*Angelina Jolie, actor*

I don't believe in God now, but I can still work up an envy for someone who has a faith. I can see how that could be a deeply soothing experience.
—*Jack Nicholson, actor*

I don't have the evidence to prove that God doesn't exist, but I so strongly suspect he doesn't that I don't want to waste my time.
—*Isaac Asimov, author*

I myself do not believe in a god who has or had a human form and to whom I owe an existence. I believe it is man who created God in his image and not the other way around; also I see no reason to believe in life after death.
—*Richard Leakey, paleontologist, author, Kenyan politician*

I don't think we're for anything, we're just products of evolution. You can say "Gee, your life must be pretty bleak if you don't think there's a purpose," but I'm anticipating a good lunch.
—*James Watson, co-discoverer of the DNA molecule and Nobel Prize winner*

We must question the story logic of having an all-knowing all-powerful God, who creates faulty Humans, and then blames them for his own mistakes.
—*Gene Roddenberry, writer and producer*

It's an incredible con job when you think about it, to believe something now in exchange for something after death. Even corporations with their reward systems don't try to make it posthumous.
—*Gloria Steinem, journalist and women's rights advocate*

Notes On The Contributors

Benedict de Spinoza (1632–1677) was a 17th century Dutch philosopher whose major work, the *Ethics*, is one of the most important—and disparaged—philosophic texts of the Western tradition. Its doctrine of immanent parallelism has impacted not only the field of ethics, but equally metaphysics, ontology, and political theory. Spinoza held that God coincides with all being, or Substance; thus he abolishes the transcendent distinction between Nature and God central to monotheistic religions. Whether Spinozism proffers a pantheistic or atheistic worldview is an ongoing debate, but for succeeding philosophers and theologians alike, the term 'Spinozist' was wholly synonymous with 'heathen.' In this vein, in 1656, Spinoza was given a severe excommunication from the Jewish community, which considered his view of God apostasy. Inured to the rejection of his theory, cynical of the vicissitudes of his contemporary intellectual scene, Spinoza rejected numerous prestigious positions and accolades, instead living humbly, working until his death in 1677 as a lens grinder.

Denis Diderot (1713–1784) was an 18th century French philosopher and writer, as well as editor-in-chief of the famous *L'Encyclopédie*. This tome, a watershed for modern scholasticism, sought to collect in one place all the work of what was then a fertile, but disparate 'Republic of Letters'—a term which reflects the surge of intellectual efforts in pursuit at the time. *L'Encyclopédie* bore a plague of controversy for its editor. Particularly, ecclesiastics and aristocrats were threatened by its vanguard doctrines of democracy, reason, and freedom, precepts which Diderot's own writings extol.

Paul-Henri Thiry, Baron D'Holbach (1723–1789) was a French author, philosopher, and contributor to Diderot's *L'Encyclopédie*. He is noted as one of the first self-described atheists. D'Holbach developed a radically materialist theory of morality, denying any deistic code of ethics, and wrote fiercely against organized religions.

Although **David Hume**'s (1711–1776) philosophic contributions have yet to be fully unpacked, his writings on philosophy were initially discarded by the British intellectual society of his time. Today, however, Hume is considered a seminal thinker, central to the history of Western philosophy and the Scottish Enlightenment in particular. His theoretical innovations stemmed from a desire to reconceive metaphysics and human rationality within a naturalist framework. One principal offshoot of Hume's naturalism consists in a rejection of then-dominant notions of the human mind as an analogous, but less potent and expansive version of the divine intellect. With this, Hume places faith in the capacity of humans to employ logic and deliberate to the best of their abilities, not in a god whose absolute knowledge renders him far more intelligent than we.

Thomas Paine (1737-1809) often credited as the father of the American Revolution, gave amplitude to the nationalist movement through his strident, vastly disseminated writings. His promulgation of independence in *Common Sense,* a series of pamphlets Paine initially funded himself and whose copyright he donated to the State, garnered a readership of over a hundred thousand, a sum which placed it, at that time, second in popularity only to the Bible. His immense influence in denouncing monarchic rule, which, with his *Rights of Man*, extended to the French Revolution, is paralleled by his excoriation of organized religion, in particular the doctrines of Christianity and the corrupt, power-hungry Church that they founded. Though, as a deist, Paine cannot be categorized as an atheist proper, he remains an edifying revolutionary figure and a favoured source for admirers such as Thomas Edison and Christopher Hitchens.

Percy Bysshe Shelley (1792-1822), English born, was as denigrated in his lifetime as his legacy has been honoured since his death. Admired by generations of poets for his rich, lyrical style, and by socialists for his unwaveringly rebellious views, Shelley's staunch atheism and opposition to the monarchy garnered him an undeserved opprobrium from his contemporaries. Although chiefly noted for his poetry, Shelley also wrote a number of essays on a host of subjects, from anarchism to vegetarianism, which give voice to his anachronistically progressive views, and which have secured his eminence in the history of radical thought. Today, Oxford University, which once expelled Shelley for refusing to refute his atheism, memorializes one of its most illustrious alumni with a statue portraying the poet's drowned corpse.

John Stuart Mill (1806-1873), student and exponent of Jeremy Bentham's utilitarianism, advocated free speech, environmental consciousness, and human rights, while publicly denouncing slavery. His work has been instrumental to the development of philosophy and economic theory alike, and liberalism owes no small debt to his scholarly, rigorous treatises. Mill served as Lord Rector of the University of St. Andrews and represented Westminster in the British Parliament, where he was closely associated with the Liberal Party. There, he championed the right for women to vote, and submitted several parliamentary reforms in line with his democratic principles. Mill's insistence on individual liberties situates his thought in opposition to the dogmatic authoritarianism ubiquitous in religious institutions.

George Eliot, nee Mary Ann (Marian) Evans (1819 –1880) was one of the most significant and popular writers of the English Victorian era. Her novel *Middlemarch* is exemplary of realist fiction, and eminently displays the political criticism which Eliot laced into her ornate, character-driven storylines. Eliot's humble, pastoral provenance resurfaced in the settings of her prose, and her sympathy with the underclass was not undermined by her experience of success, which was not minor—Princess Louise, daughter of Queen Victoria, was an avid reader of her works.

Eliot's youth was steeped in Anglican values, but a fomentation of religious dissent in the Midlands spurred her doubt. This potential was realized upon her travel to Coventry, where she met such notable figures as Ralph Waldo Emerson and Herbert Spencer. Here, Eliot's introduction to a society of progressive thinkers galvanized her rejection of religious faith.

William Edward Hartpole Lecky (1838-1903) is arguably the foremost historian of the British Empire. Sadly, however, his work as a disinterested, masterful researcher and documentarian often overshadows his compelling philosophic and political texts. His interest in ethics produced controversial works such as *Democracy and Liberty*, whose critical appraisal of Britain, France, and America were at times hotly resented. Lecky produced a prolific, enduring oeuvre, served as a member of Parliament, and was appointed a Privy Councillor.

Elizabeth Cady Stanton (1815–1902), for all intents and purposes, led the organized struggle for women's rights in the United States: her Declaration of Sentiments, orated at an inaugural women's rights convention held in 1848 in Seneca Falls, New York, is often traced as the starting point of the American feminist suffrage movement. Stanton's political scope had, before narrowing on feminism, included emphases on abolition of slavery and civil rights. She was also a vocal proponent of the 19th-century temperance movement. Stanton's radical views, among which an anti-religious thread prevailed, often ostracized her from other feminist suffragists. Recent scholarship, however, has revisited Stanton's writing and the documentation of her actions with an eye to her rigorous, unwavering devotion to the emancipation and liberation of women and the oppressed.

Charles Bradlaugh (1833 –1891), although more than a century of atheists have succeeded him, remains unmatched in his fearless, public denunciation of and political mobilization against Christian doctrine. English born, in his lifetime, he founded the National Secular Society, was President of the London Secular Society, figured prominently in the Reform League and the Land Law Reformers, all the while writing and publishing countless pamphlets, essays, and treatises contesting the religious establishment. Bradlaugh, who began his career as a Sunday school teacher, was suspended from his post, estranged from his family, and later charged with obscenity for his views. His invariable support of trade unionism, republicanism, and women's suffrage garnered him respect from leftists as much as his resistance to socialism alienated him from their circles.

Anatole France (1844–1924), born François-Anatole Thibault, embodied, with his edified wit and cultured cynicism, the man of letters that was the ideal of his time and society. France was elected to the Académie française in 1896, and was awarded the Nobel Prize for Literature in 1921. His satirizations of human nature, which often alluded to the role of religious doctrine in suppressing reason, helped place his writings on the index of *Libri prohibiti*, books censured by the Vatican.

Charles Darwin's (1809–1882) 1859 book *On the Origin of Species*, which presented evolution by common descent as the chief scientific explanation for biological diversity, situated him, along with Freud and Marx, at the vanguard of modern thought. Public interest in Darwin's book, though initially underwhelming, soon built to a massive controversy which challenged the very roots of the religious establishment. In due time Darwin's propositions were the substrate of virulent debates, often staged by the likes of writer Thomas Huxley, who asserted himself "Darwin's bulldog" and took to task the theological rebuttals of evolutionary theory.

As he aged, Darwin's religious views exhibited their own evolution. Although initially a religious man, his faith destabilized as scientific research confronted him with biological forms that creationism could but feign explain. Doubt mounted with the death of his daughter Annie in 1851 grieving, his belief waned and he grew skeptical of organized religion and a monotheistic god. Darwin, timid and often experiencing long bouts of illness, generally shied from the confrontations which discussion of his work inevitably produced. Nevertheless, Darwin once commented on his faithlessness, naming his beliefs as Agnostic.

The philosophy of German born **Friedrich Wilhelm Nietzsche** (1844–1900) continues to astound in its anachronism: many of his century-old texts anticipate postmodern themes and concerns. His critiques of religion, reason, morality, and contemporary culture are in line with, and often basic to, much of today's work in continental philosophy. His aphoristic style and elusive argumentation lend his writing to multifarious interpretations. Although he began his career prodigiously, taking on the Chair of Classical Philology at the University of Basel at the age of 24, Nietzsche soon fell prone to physical and mental illnesses which would plague him until his death. His infamous utterance that "God is dead" illustrates the irreverence with which he condemned religion as a synthetic emancipation which actually enslaves.

Although **Colonel Robert Green Ingersoll's** (1833 –1899) radical views on religion, slavery, woman's suffrage, and other issues of the day in the USA, curtailed his rise in the political ranks, his commanding oral presence and resilience to public libel secured his popular clout. The son of an abolitionist Presbyterian preacher, Ingersoll continued his father's work, and fought for the Union in the Civil War. Delving into politics after the war, Illinois Republicans tried to pressure Ingersoll to conceal his agnosticism, but he refused on the grounds that it would constitute an immoral public perjury. He consistently and stridently advocated freethought and humanism, while denouncing religious belief and the church as impediments to human freedom and flourishing.

Ludwig Andreas von Feuerbach, (1804 –1872) a pivotal figure in German Idealist philosophy, remains a necessary entry on the reading list of any student of continental philosophy. His placement between Hegel and Marx—as a student of the former, and an object of criticism for the latter—makes his work a hinge point for the trajectory of that intellectual movement. Many of Feuerbach's ideas indeed served as a bridge between the two thinkers, and his critique of Christianity is central to Marx's elaboration of his own rebuttal of religion.

Mikhail Alexandrovich Bakunin (1814–1876) is a revolutionary figure whose political philosophy is canonical to radical anarchist thought. His doctrine of collectivist anarchism continues to shape the theory and praxis of students and activist organizers seeking to contest imperialist and authoritarian regimes. Born into a family of Russian nobility, Bakunin's travels led him to the fertile intellectual scene of Paris, where he commingled with Karl Marx, among others. There his radicalism attracted the concern of the Emperor Nicholas of Russia, who subsequently stripped him of his noble privileges, civil rights and land. His mettlesome support for revolutionary movements would render him further disenfranchised; he was eventually exiled to Siberia for his participation in the Czech rebellion of 1848. Bakunin played a leading role in the planning and execution of the many uprisings and insurgencies that characterized the tumultuous political scene of mid-19th century Eastern Europe. Not averse to spiritual practices, Bakunin's early thought explored an extra-ecclesiastical immanentism, defined by divine reason and love. Later, however, he recognized the necessity of abolishing the religious establishment as an authoritarian structure endemic to the State.

Karl Heinrich Marx (1818–1883) left an indelible mark on philosophy and political theory, producing an expansive corpus of works with which academics and activists alike continue to grapple. Marx addressed a gamut of political, social, historical, and economic issues, and displayed a scholarly grasp of the nefarious theories developed by his contemporaries. Consequently, his own theory is often conflated with an adoption of these strains. Marx's work, however, is better characterized as an unremittingly deracinating criticism of established ideas and ideologies. Unlike anarchist theorists, who often proffer alternative socio-political models, Marx simply held that capitalism is fundamentally premised on its own self-destruction.

Emma Goldman (1869–1940) was a pivotal anarchist theorist, born in Russia and active in the United States and Europe throughout the first half of the twentieth century. Her work has gained much import for feminist theory, although her relationship to feminist movements was often marked by disputes and theoretical divergences. Goldman, like many anarchists, saw religion to be a grounding tenet of authoritarianism, and an instrument of the capitalist state. Consequently, a rebuttal of religious belief must occur on the microcosmic plane of individual emancipation, and across a wider terrain of grassroots struggle against all established systems of domination.

Henry Louis (H. L.) Mencken's (1880–1956) parents inculcated, from a young age, an emphasis on the practicality of knowledge, a trait which would grow to define Mencken's grounded, accessible writing. This value translated into his career as a journalist and shaped Mencken's cultural criticism, whose popular renditions were shaped by a desire to foster public, compelling debates on contemporary political issues. Mencken is perhaps best known for his work on the Scopes trial, reprinted here in part. Loyal to his Baltimore hometown, he lived, wrote, and published there till his retirement and death.

Clarence Darrow (1857–1938) American born, was an exemplar civil libertarian, a lawyer who used his legal skill to defend such vehemently contested cases as the Scopes Trial in Tennessee. His compassion for those ostracized from society was in line with his work with labour unions, which he began after abandoning a more profitable and less arduous path in corporate law. Darrow's struggles against the institutional control of personal rights and liberties were equally informed by his firm agnosticism.

Carl Clinton Van Doren (1885–1950) was a well-known American literary critic, historian, and Pulitzer Prize-winning biographer, holding his post as professor of English at Columbia University for several decades. Doren has authored such works as *The American Novel* and *Benjamin Franklin*. Doren was a world federalist, holding the importance of international cooperation to merit the instantiation of global policies and bodies of governance. His views on religion, correlatively, saw secularism to be key and held human's ability to reason as the only tenable measure of justice.

The philosophy of British born **Bertrand Arthur William Russell** (1872–1970) has had immeasurable import on the fields of metaphysics, epistemology, and the philosophy of language. Yet his highly analytic method, informed by his studies in mathematics and a propensity for scientific inquiry, sometimes occludes his vibrant humanism. His clear, lucid style and efforts to popularize his philosophy have, however, ensured his place as a public intellectual, and his thought has been instrumental to countless public debates. Notably, Russell was a vigorous proponent of nuclear disarmament and highly critical of cold war ideologues. His vocal criticism of the Vietnam War and Communist totalitarianism helped attribute to him a pacifist reputation. Russell held that religion is little more than superstition: faith ought to be invested in scientific method and logical reasoning—otherwise, arrogant intellects overstep their bounds, wreaking misery and impeding human progress.

Sir Alfred Jules Ayer (1910-1989), staunch proponent of logical positivism, is a canonical figure in British analytic philosophy. Akin to Bertrand Russell in his linkage of humanist ideals to the principles of empirical analysis, Ayer acted as president of the British Humanist Association and wrote extensively on the topic of humanism. His criticism of religious irrationality was very public, and the BBC often sought his commentary on the matter; yet his relationship to religion has been wrought with rumours of conversions and lapses into prayer. Regardless, his writing remains a forceful defence of human freedom and reason. Ayer was knighted in 1970.

Albert Camus (1913–1960), by displaying ceaseless invention in his fictional works, and unwavering independence in his political views, embodied the values of the existentialist school of philosophy with which he was so often associated, and to which he characteristically refused to ascribe. His perspective as an Algerian displaced to France, in a revolutionary moment in which intellectuals played no small part, situated him at the crest of the resistance movement. Indeed, rebellion defined his thought and proliferated his writing—his insistent bucking of any institutionalized or established powers manifested in explicit breaks with Jean-Paul Sartre and Communism, as well as affiliating him with the freedom fighters leading an array of struggles. Unsurprisingly, his views directly contravene religious orthodoxy, and he denounced it throughout his career.

Albert Einstein (1879–1955), German born and naturalized American, is, perhaps, the scientific theorist whose work is most often—and arguably, most aptly—attributed as "revolutionary." Einstein's legacy accrued over a long and prolific career, but in 1905, his 'Annus Mirabilis,' he produced four papers which have come to occupy the core of his repute. These papers detailed conceptual re-evaluations of particle and wave theories of light, atomic theory, electrodynamics, and of course, theories of special and general relativity. Displaying early on what would prove to be an unparalleled aptitude for conceptual, abstract thinking, Einstein had by the tender age of ten years already absorbed Kantian philosophy and, by the age of twelve, mastered Euclidean geometry. This formative encounter with theory shaped Einstein's approach to science, which superseded positivism and regularly expanded the borders of the scientific concepts he examined. Indeed, his affinity to philosophy, particularly philosophers of science such as Poincare and Mach, as well as more canonical figures such as Hume and Spinoza, was often explicit: for example, in his twenties, he formed a weekly discussion club on science and philosophy. Indeed, Einstein's often-quoted endorsement of Spinoza's God points to the scientific determinism which opposed his work to Niels Bohr's. Einstein's elegant contrast of science and religion, articulated in a Spinozist vein, endows the atheist tradition with one of its most pregnant theoretical challenges.

Eugene Luther Gore Vidal (1925–) has given a contemporary redefinition to the renaissance ideal: an American man of letters whose prose, political essays, and works for the stage all bear the mark of prodigy. Irreverent, imaginative, and unrelentingly incisive in his critiques of American politics and social mores, Vidal consistently imbricated themes of gender, sexuality, and popular culture into baroquely researched historical narratives. His powerful argumentation won him the National Book Award for *United States (1952-1992)* a collection of essays from which our excerpt has been extracted.

Kai Nielsen's (1926–) philosophic defense of atheism is an eminent contribution to the contemporary debate on religious faith and freedom. A Canadian, he is currently an adjunct professor of philosophy at Montreal's Concordia University; Nielsen has also taught at New York University and the University of Calgary, as well as served as the president of the Canadian Philosophical Association. Nielsen has authored numerous philosophic texts on subjects ranging from globalization to skepticism.

Christine Overall (1949–), a Canadian, is a Professor of Philosophy and holds a Research Chair at Queen's University, Kingston, Ontario. Her teaching and publications are in the areas of feminist philosophy, social philosophy, applied philosophy, and the philosophy of religion. She is the editor or co-editor of three books and the author of five. The most recent is *Aging, Death, and Human Longevity: A Philosophical Inquiry,* which won both the Canadian Philosophical Association's 2005 Book Prize and the Royal Society of Canada's Abbyann Lynch Medal in Bioethics in 2006.

Sam Harris (1967–) a neuroscientist, has written provocatively on the perils of religious dogmatism. His first book, *The End of Faith*, was as highly acclaimed as it was hotly contested, fueling a debate which Harris himself responded to in his subsequent *Letter to a Christian Nation*, addressed to his American compatriots. Chiefly, Harris' aim is to dislodge the barricades which impede honest and open dialogue about religious belief. Although his atheist views are clear, Harris sees a contestation of religious faith to form neither a theoretical nor political viewpoint, but to be a simple "deconstruction of bad ideas." Rigorous and responsible use of reason, then, is the proper antidote that Harris submits in opposition to religious belief.

Clinton Richard Dawkins, (1941–) ethologist, and evolutionary biologist, has contributed immeasurably to the scientific defense of atheism through his writing, which, by presenting lucidly complex scientific systems, has made evolutionary theory accessible and relevant to a widespread audience. He holds the Charles Simonyi Chair for the Public Understanding of Science at Oxford.

Dawkins has given vehement opposition to Creationism, ardently opposing the practice of teaching intelligent design, which he denounces to be pseudoscientific religiosity posturing as rational thought. Dawkins insists that his objection to religion is not solely that it is construed to justify wars and violence, but also that it lends itself as an excuse for some to hold beliefs not based on evidence.

Christopher Eric Hitchens (1949–) is a widely read author, journalist, literary critic and columnist, and a bona fide polemicist. Noted for his raucous break with the Anglo-American political left, Hitchens' views have evolved. His *God is Not Great: How Religion Poisons Everything* is a necessary read for any student of what commentators have named the 'new atheism' movement. Indeed, Hitchens' atheism has been a guiding concept throughout his decades of critiquing everything from global foreign policy to Mother Theresa. In place of religion, Hitchens maintains an avid devotion to the Enlightenment values of secularism, humanism, and rational progress.

Philosopher Michel Onfray (1959–) is one of the select academics who realize the circumscriptions of reason which accompany the institutionalization of knowledge. His subversion of the University is manifested in his Université populaire de Caen, a free-of-charge, non-degree-granting school established by Onfray in 2002. Onfray's engagement with philosophy is not relegated to the scholastic explication or exegesis of well-trod intellectual avenues; rather, he often steps outside the frame of philosophy and examines it from askew. For example, he insists on the interdependence of philosophy and other fields, such as psychoanalysis. He is an exponent of hedonism, reason, and atheism, Onfray's three chief interests, are under his auspices rendered not as distinct, but complementary fields.

Daniel Dennett (1942–) has characterized his intellectual project to have remained unchanged since his doctorate, completed at Oxford in 1963: to bring to bear the scientific principles of empirical research upon the subtlety of philosophy of mind. This pursuit has drawn him to evolutionary theory, and his adaptationist views, as well as advocacy of memetics, align him with Richard Dawkins. Dennett's work has been recognized by a host of lecture posts and fellowships, from the John Locke lectures at Oxford, to a Fulbright Fellowship; he is currently the Austin B. Fletcher Professor of Philosophy, University Professor, and Co-Director of the Center for Cognitive Studies at Tufts University.

Louise M. Antony (unknown) is Professor of Philosophy at the University of Massachusetts, Amherst. She is the author of *A Mind of One's Own* and *Chomsky and His Critics*. Antony specializes in the philosophy of language, philosophical issues in cognitive science, the philosophy of mind and feminist theory. She is also the editor of *Philosophers without Gods*, a collection the introduction of which is reprinted here.

Elizabeth Anderson (1959–) is the Arthur F. Thurnau Professor and John Rawls Collegiate Professor of Philosophy and Women's Studies at the University of Michigan. Her research focuses on democratic theory, equality in political philosophy and American law, racial integration, the ethical limits of markets, as well as theories of value and rational choice. Anderson has written widely on ethics, social and political philosophy, and feminist theory—as well as feminist epistemology, in particular.

Tariq Ali (1943–), born in Pakistan and living in Britian, is one of an elite born which manage to preserve both the radicalism of their politics and the relevance of their views into maturity. Ali has furnished the Left with a critical review of American foreign policy, religious and capitalist fundamentalism, and the media-industrial complex. Historian, novelist, filmmaker, political campaigner, and commentator, Ali is a member of the editorial committee of the *New Left Review* and *Sin Permiso*, and regularly contributes to *The Guardian*, *Counterpunch*, and the *London Review of Books*. He is the author of numerous books, including the roiling *Clash of Fundamentalisms: Crusades, Jihads and Modernity*.

Salman Rushdie (1947–), British-Indian author, first achieved fame with his second, Booker prize-winning novel, *Midnight's Children*. Since, his lyrical style—often classified as magical realism— and his irreverent, bold interrogation of religion, race, migration and oppression have garnered him a privileged, if notorious status in the field of contemporary literature. Rushdie's fourth novel, *The Satanic Verses*, provoked a surge of protest and censure from conservative Islam. Issued several death threats and a *fatwa* by Ayatollah Ruhollah Khomeini, then Supreme Leader of Iran, Rushdie was forced into secret exile, reducing public appearances to a few, sporadic events. Rushdie was appointed in 2007 a Knight Bachelor for "services to literature," an announcement condemned by certain Muslim officials and factions. In this same year, he began a five-year term as Distinguished Writer in Residence at Emory University.

Kurt Vonnegut, Jr. (1922–2007) has written some of the most profoundly loved novels of his generation, works which offset their political and philosophic subtexts with playful satire and absurdist science fiction. These subtexts often pointed to the nonsense of capitalist consumerism, xenophobic McCarthyism, and cartoonish homogeneity of suburbia. His admiration of early socialist labour leaders like Powers Hapgood and Eugene V. Debs, figures oft quoted in his works, fed into the Leftist politics that infiltrated his books. Vonnegut has served in what he termed a "totally functionless capacity," Honorary President of the American Humanist Association. He was a lifetime member of the American Civil Liberties Union.

Resource Guide

The Richard Dawkins Foundation for Reason and Science (www.richarddawkins.net) is an excellent resources guide for those seeking to escape superstition.

African Americans for Humanism

P.O. Box 664

Amherst, NY 14226-0664 USA

Weblink: http://www.secularhumanism.org/index.php?section=aah&page=index

Email: nallen@centerforinquiry.net

Phone: (716) 636-7571 Fax: (716) 636-1733

About: The need for critical thinking skills and a humanistic outlook in our world is great. This is no less true in the Black community than in others. Many African Americans have been engulfed by religious irrationality, conned by self-serving "faith healers," and swayed by dogmatic revisionist historians. Many others, however, have escaped the oppression of such delusions, and live happy and upstanding lives free of superstition. African Americans for Humanism (AAH) exists to bring these secular humanists together, to provide a forum for communication, and to facilitate coordinated action. In an irrational world, those who stand for reason must stand together.

American Atheists

PO Box 5733

Parsippany, NJ 07054-6733 USA

Weblink: http://www.atheists.org

Email: info@atheists.org

Phone: 1-908-276-7300 (Voicemail) Fax: 1-908-276-7402

About: It is the goal of American Atheists to provide you with new avenues for learning about the Atheist philosophy. At this site, we will work to inform you about state-church separation issues, and give you the Atheist perspective on them. This information is thought-provoking, intellectually challenging and pure hard-core Atheist. It's something that you won't find anywhere else. We encourage you to make visits to our web site a part of your Atheist lifestyle. We also urge you to share Atheism with friends and family. We need to be activists for Atheism! By making your Atheism known to others, you will be surprised how easy it becomes for others to admit that perhaps they, too, are Atheists! The world will become a less-lonely place in an otherwise unrelentingly religious society. We hope that you find the American Atheist web pages to be challenging and informative. Remember that this site is under "permanent construction." We will be adding new features and offerings in the future. Enjoy! —Ellen Johnson, President, American Atheists

American Humanist Association
1777 T Street, NW
Washington, DC 20009-7125 USA
Weblink: http://www.americanhumanist.org
Email: kfrantz@americanhumanist.org
Phone: (202) 238-9088 | Toll Free: 1-800-837-3792 Fax: (202) 238-9003

About: Strategically located in Washington, DC, the AHA actively educates the public about Humanism, brings Humanists together for mutual support and action, defends the civil liberties and constitutional freedoms of Humanists—indeed of all peoples—and leads both local and national Humanist organizations toward progressive societal change. Through a strong network of over 100 grassroots organizations, appearances in national media, an advanced Internet presence, regular public appearances, and a broad spectrum of publications, the AHA is the Voice of Humanism.

Over the years, many women and men who embrace Humanism and who have worked closely with the AHA have contributed greatly toward the betterment of our world. Among them are: novelists Margaret Atwood, Kurt Vonnegut, and Alice Walker; environmentalist Lester R. Brown; women's rights proponents Betty Friedan and Gloria Steinem; elder citizens advocate Maggie Kuhn; economist John Kenneth Galbraith; entrepreneur Ted Turner; evolutionary scientist Edward O. Wilson; abortion rights champions Faye Wattleton and Bill Baird; director Oliver Stone; Nobel laureate Steven Weinberg. Earlier Humanists included Carl Sagan, Isaac Asimov, Andrei Sakharov, Erich Fromm, A. Philip Randolph, Margaret Sanger, Gene Roddenberry, Julian Huxley, Brock Chisholm, John Dewey, Bertrand and Dora Russell, and Albert Einstein. The American Humanist Association has honored these individuals as well as many others to recognize their contributions on behalf of humanity. Join this list of prominent Humanists! For their newsletter, go to: http://www.thehumanist.org/.

Apostates of Islam
Weblink: http://www.apostatesofislam.com/index.htm

About: Who we are: We are ex-Muslims. Some of us were born and raised in Islam and some of us had converted to Islam at some moment in our lives. We were taught never to question the truth of Islam and to believe in Allah and his messenger with blind faith. We were told that Allah would forgive all sins but the sin of disbelief (Quran 4:48 and 4:116). But we committed the ultimate sin of thinking and questioned the belief that was imposed on us and we came to realize that far from being a religion of truth, Islam is a hoax, it is hallucination of a sick mind and nothing but lies and deceits.

Atheist Alliance International
PO Box 242
Pocopson, PA 19366 USA
Weblink: http://www.atheistalliance.org
Email: info@atheistalliance.org
Phone: 1-866-HERETIC

About: Atheist Alliance International (AAI) is an organization of independent religion-free groups and individuals in the United States and around the world. Our primary goals are to help democratic, atheistic societies become established and grow and to work in coalition with like-minded groups to advance rational thinking through educational processes. Virtually all income goes to these causes. We have little paid staff. Our members make all the decisions and do almost all of the work. The Alliance sponsors annual conventions publishes *Secular Nation* magazine, a quarterly magazine of interest to atheists, and *The Freethought Directory*, an attempt to list all freethought organizations in the world, and the *Journal of Higher Criticism,* a respected scholarly publication of Biblical study. We sponsor Objectivity, Accuracy, and Balance in Teaching About Religion (OABITAR), a resource for teachers. We maintain a web site that hosts member societies' web sites free of charge.

Applications for Alliance membership from democratic local, regional, or international atheist organizations are always welcome. Member societies pay no dues but contribute to the grassroots organizing work of Atheist Alliance. Each member society has its own representative on the AAI board. Individual members are also welcome. They do pay dues (see http://www.atheistalliance.org/aai/membership.html, under the Individual Memberships section) and receive *Secular Nation* as a benefit of membership. They also have a representative on the AAI board, with the representative being selected at an individual members' group meeting during the annual AAI convention. The Individual Members Group maintains contact through an online chat group and *Secular Nation* magazine. An entirely internet-based connection to AAI for individuals is also available through the Atheist Internet Outreach member society. Its role is to use online services to connect isolated atheists with atheist and freethought issues, and to support the programs, policies and activities of the Alliance.

Atheist Foundation of Australia Inc
Private Mail Bag 6
Maitland
South Australia 5573 Australia
Weblink: http://www.atheistfoundation.org.au/
Email: info@atheistfoundation.org.au

Phone: +61 8 8835 2269

About: The Atheist Foundation of Australia recognises scientific method as the only rational means toward understanding reality. To question and critically examine all ideas, testing them in the light of facts, leads to the discovery of truth. As there is no scientific evidence for supernatural phenomena, atheists reject belief in 'God,' gods and other supernatural beings. The universe, the world in which we live, and the evolution of life, are entirely natural occurrences. No personality or mind can exist without the process of living matter to sustain it. We have only one life—here and now. All that remains after a person dies is the memory of their life and deeds in the minds of those who live. Atheists reject superstition and prejudice along with the irrational fears they cause. We recognise the complexity and interdependence of life on this planet. As rational and ethical beings we accept the challenge of making a creative and responsible contribution to life.

Atheists For Human Rights
5146 Newton Ave. N.
Minneapolis, MN 55430 USA
Weblink: atheistsforhumanrights.org
Email: mac@mtn.org
Phone: 612-529-1200 (Minneapolis / St. Paul) or 1-866-ATHEIST

About: Atheists For Human Rights was founded in February of 2002 by atheists with a 15-year history of activism and leadership in the freethought community, locally and nationally. Although we are located in Minneapolis/St. Paul, we are a semi-national organization with a third of our membership from distant parts of the state and from other states. Our goal is to make atheism publicly visible. Our innovative Moral High Ground fund remains the free thought community's most positive response to the religious right's inhumane agenda. We provide real help—financial help—to members of those groups most fiercely attacked by the religious right: gays and lesbians, poor women in need of abortions, the terminally ill who desperately want help to die peacefully, and stem cell research programs. We have our own Hub of Atheism that ensures a reliable, available and free meeting space.

Australian Skeptics
PO Box 268
Roseville, NSW 2069 Australia
Weblink: http://www.skeptics.com.au
Email: skeptics@bdsn.com.au
Phone: 02 9417 2071

About: The Australian Skeptics Inc. is a group that investigates the paranormal and pseudo-science from a responsible scientific viewpoint. Most people are familiar with the more popular subjects that we investigate such as astrology, fortune telling, UFOs and crop circles. Did you know that we also investigate topics like fundamentalism, Feng Shui, subluxations and vitamin supplements? A list of all the major topics that we investigate can be found at the end of this page where we list What we are sceptical of. Test your sceptical knowledge and see how many of the topics on the list are unfamiliar to you. If you've never heard of the Australian Skeptics before then you should also take time to read The Aims of The Australian Skeptics.

Brights, The
PO Box 163418
Sacramento, CA 95816 USA
Weblink: http://www.the-brights.net
Email: the-brights@the-brights.net

About: Currently the naturalistic worldview is insufficiently expressed within most cultures, even politically/socially repressed. To be a Bright (someone who fits the definition and registers on this Web site) is to participate in a movement to address the situation. There is a great diversity of persons who have a naturalistic worldview. Some are members of existing organizations that foster a supernatural-free perspective. Far more individuals are not associated with any formal group or label. Under the broad umbrella of the naturalistic worldview, the constituency of Brights can undertake social and civic actions designed to influence a society otherwise permeated with supernaturalism. The movement's three major aims are: a) Promote the civic understanding and acknowledgment of the naturalistic worldview, which is free of supernatural and mystical elements. b) Gain public recognition that persons who hold such a worldview can bring principled actions to bear on matters of civic importance. c) Educate society toward accepting the full and equitable civic participation of all such individuals.

British Humanist Association
1 Gower Street
London, WC1E 6HD UK
Weblink: http://www.humanism.org.uk
Email: info@humanism.org.uk
Phone: 020 7079 3580 Fax: 020 7079 3588

About: The BHA is the largest organisation in the UK supporting and representing the non-religious and campaigning for a secular society.We help humanists and other non-religious people to gain confidence in their beliefs and build a foundation from which to live their lives with integrity, supporting networks for families, teachers and others to share ideas and experience and provide mutual support. We work for an open and inclusive society with freedom of belief and speech, and for an end to the privileged position of religion—and Christianity in particular—in law, education, broadcasting and wherever else it occurs. We campaign for the inclusion of humanism within the school curriculum, for inclusive schools where children with parents of all faiths and none learn to understand and respect each other, instead of being segregated in the growing number of faith and sectarian schools, and for the abolition of school worship. We are also renowned for the provision of humanist funerals, weddings, baby-namings and other non-religious ceremonies which meet a very real need in the community.

Center For Inquiry/Campus Freethought Alliance
PO Box 741
Amherst, NY 14228 USA
Weblink: http://www.campusfreethought.org
Phone: 716.636.7571 ext. 422

About: The Center for Inquiry/On Campus is dedicated to promoting and defending reason, science and freedom of inquiry in education, and to the enhancement of freethought, skepticism, secularism, humanism, philosophical naturalism, rationalism, and atheism on college and high school campuses throughout North America and around the world. CFI/On Campus consolidates international resources toward this end.

Center For Inquiry Transnational
3965 Rensch Road
Amherst, NY 14228 USA
Weblink: http://www.centerforinquiry.net
Email: web@inquiringminds.org
Phone: (716) 636-4869 Fax: (716) 636-1733

About: The purpose of the Center for Inquiry is to promote and defend reason, science, and freedom of inquiry in all areas of human endeavor. The Center for Inquiry is a transnational nonprofit 501(c)(3) organization that encourages evidence-based inquiry into science, pseudoscience, medicine and health, religion, ethics, secularism, and society. Through education, research, publishing, and social services, it seeks to present affirmative alternatives based on scientific naturalism. The Center is also interested in providing rational ethical alternatives to the reigning paranormal and religious systems of belief, and in developing communities where like-minded individuals can meet and share experiences. The Center for Inquiry is a Global Federation committed to science, reason, free inquiry, secularism, and planetary ethics

Council for Secular Humanism
P.O. Box 664
Amherst, NY 14226-0664 USA
Weblink: http://www.secularhumanism.org
Email: info@SecularHumanism.org

Phone: (716) 636-7571 Fax: (716) 636-1733

About: The Council for Secular Humanism cultivates rational inquiry, ethical values, and human development through the advancement of secular humanism. To carry out its mission the Council for Secular Humanism sponsors publications, programs, and organizes meetings and other group activities. The Council's specific objectives are: To promote secular humanist principles to the public, media, and policy-makers; to provide secular humanist activities and communities; to serve the needs of nonreligious people and foster human enrichment; to demonstrate the viability of the secular humanist eupraxophy as an alternative naturalistic life-stance; to engage in research relating to the critical examination of religious and supernatural claims and the humanist outlook; to conduct educational programs for all age levels

Council of Australian Humanist Societies
GPO Box 1555
Melbourne, Victoria 3001 Australia
Weblink: http://home.vicnet.net.au/~humanist/resources/cahs.html
Email: AMcPhate@bigpond.net.au
Phone: 613 5974 4096

About: The Role of the Council of Australian Humanist Societies (CAHS) includes: Acting as the umbrella organisation for the Member Societies; organising an annual Convention; publishing a quarterly journal, the *Australian Humanist*; monitoring legislation, especially to ensure the protection of human rights; promoting ethical standards in the community without reliance on blind faith; making submissions to governments on social and ethical issues; awards the Australian Humanist of the Year and Outstanding Humanist Achiever; liaising with other Humanist organisations around the world; participating as a member of the International Humanist and Ethical Union.

Dr Homa Darabi Foundation
PO Box 11049
Truckee, CA 96162 USA
Weblink: http://www.homa.org/
Email: homa@homa.org
Phone: (530) 582 4197 Fax: (530) 582 0156

About: To promote the rights of women and children under Islam. Dr. Homa Darabi's Foundation is a non-profit organization, independent from all present political, social and religious factions with goal and objective to promote the Rights of women and children as defined by the Universal Declaration of the United Nations 1948 General Assembly. To Separate Church and State To Establish Democracy To Abolish Gender Apartheid and to Establish the Equality of the Sexes.

Federación Internacional de Ateos

Spain

Weblink: http://www.federacionatea.org/

About: Dear friends: The FIdA (Federación Internacional de Ateos/Atheists International Federation) is integrated by atheists of many countries, and our objective is to be able of taking part in global actions, demasking the fundamentalisms of the churches anywhere in the world. We have compiled the directions of other associations that you can see in: http://www.federacionatea.org/index.php?id=18 and, as a federation, we are trying to create an interactive network regarding possible international campaigns. In Spain the 'Ateus de Catalunya' (http://www.ateus.org/), the 'Union de Ateos y Librepensadores' (http://ateos.org/) are the other atheistic association constituted, as far as we know. There are no other atheistic local groups, or we have not been able to locate them. As FIdA organization, we have participated actively in the citizen platform opposition to the visit of Ratzinger to Spain.

Atheistic International Federation: Religion affirmations cannot be the object of theoretical knowledge. The feeling of man of the awareness of his constant blame and his aspiration of happiness produces in him the faith in a god that punishes and loves; but there are no evidences of this faith truthfulness. All religions dogmas result, under this concept, as subjective and arbitrary.

The reason and historical experience demonstrate that religious prejudice become into a serious obstacle for the full freedom development and individuals' happiness. Spokesmen of irrationality demand faith and submission fearing of a future eschatological catastrophe, working with threats of hellish tortures and promises of paradisiacal enjoyments.

Conditioned by its hypnotic power, a big part of human kind remain chained to this fiction, being at the same time accomplice and victim of a massive fraud represented by religions. The liberation of this spiritual chains has a decisive meaning in society development and in the liberation process of the human being. Therefore, the combat against religion cannot be limited only to the political or economical scope. It must include, inevitably, as a base of a new view of the world and a new ethical attitude, guided against the religious totalitarian ideology. In front of the barbarism represented by dogmatisms, we propose a return to reason, a new vision of reality and a will to release individuals of fables derived from magical thought. Atheistic thought development has been historically tortuous and contradictory. But the manifestations of this development have been links towards a consequent atheism. In front of reason judgment, religion in whole results definitely condemned. Nevertheless, the organized religious superstition still has narrow alliances with political and economical power, with moral and culture. Such superstition allows and supports the influence that irrationality exercises over our age, with a form of fundamentalisms.

Some opposition forms against the established conditions are not effective but through a collectivization of efforts. We intend to integrate a global atheistic movement endowed with concrete objectives and with planned public activities. We think that atheism never has been awarded with the importance that it has as ground of scientific, politic and philosophical bases of Occident.

We think that it is necessary to go deep into the historical, sociological, psychological and philosophical grounds of atheism, to section the roots of our inherited Judeo &#65533; Christian moral and to critically analyze the role that religions has exercised and exercise over social behavior. We are convinced about the atheism role as catalyst of transformer forces. The Atheistic International Federation is integrated by men and women that are sure of the necessity to disregard of a god idea, to combat the fatal mistake of this believe and to progressively delimit the influence of religions and their kindred ideologies in our respective societies. Through it will be possible to canalize in a positive manner our analysis and response abilities before the threat represented by religiosity and by the idealist prejudice for the full development of civil rights and liberties in the political system where we live. It is a necessary step in the formation of a more critical, aware, free and autonomous society, able to confront collective and coherently the pressure exercised by religious obscurantism. Free thought is never stopped before the fetishism. This is the moment to converge in an international atheistic association, concreted in a clear and effective conspiracy against all kind of irrationalism.

Freedom From Religion Foundation
PO Box 750
Madison, WI 53701 USA
Weblink: http://www.ffrf.org
Email: info@ffrf.org
Phone: (608) 256-5800 Fax: (608) 256-1116

About: The Freedom From Religion Foundation, Inc., is an educational group working for the separation of state and church. Its purposes, as stated in its bylaws, are to promote the constitutional principle of separation of state and church, and to educate the public on matters relating to nontheism. Incorporated in 1978 in Wisconsin, the Foundation is a national membership association of freethinkers: atheists, agnostics and skeptics of any pedigree. The Foundation is a non-profit, tax-exempt organization under Internal Revenue Code 501(c)(3). All dues and contributions are deductible for income tax purposes.

Gay and Lesbian Humanist Association
UK
Weblink: http://www.galha.org/
Email: info@galha.org
Phone: United Kingdom: 01926 858 450 / International: +44 1926 858 450
About: GALHA provides a voice for the many non-religious in the lesbian and gay community in the United Kingdom and elsewhere and promotes a rational humanist approach to homosexuality and to lesbian, gay and bisexual rights as human rights.

Giordano Bruno Stiftung
Johann Steffen Straße 1
56869 Mastershausen, Germany
Weblink: http://www.giordano-bruno-stiftung.de/
Telefon: 06545/910 285 Fax: 06545/910 287
About: The Giordano Bruno Foundation, to which numerous renowned scientists, artists and philosophers belong, collects most recent research in the humanities and in social and natural sciences to work out their significance for the humanist goal of a "peaceful and equal co-existence of people in the here and now." As a "think tank of Enlightenment" the foundation has set its aim at developing the foundations of a naturalistic world-view as well as a secular, evolutionary-humanistic ethics and politics, and sustainably bringing them into social debates. The reactions to the foundation from the populace have been promising. Apparently more and more people recognised today that we cannot continue living as we have done, that there have to be satisfying answers beyond fundamentalism and arbitrariness to the existential problems of being human in general and to the social dissonances in global society in particular.

Godless Americans Political Action Committee (GAMPAC)
GAMPAC
PO Box 5674,
Parsippany, NJ 07054 USA
Weblink: http://www.godlessamericans.org/
About: Godless Americans PAC Chooses Winners In 2006. The Democrats have taken the House of Representatives and the majority of Godless Americans Political Action Committee endorsements won election. We endorsed Jim McDermott (WA-7), Pete Stark (CA-13), and Rush Holt (NJ-12) all won their elections, as well as Sen. Feinstein in California. The best news of course is the loss of Sen. Rick Santorum, but I am even more enthralled over the loss of John Hostettler (IN-8). He is the Congressman who introduced H.R. 2679, Public Expression of Religion Act that passed the House. A very good night all around. Now the bad news: The successful passage of anti-gay-mar-

riage laws in seven out of eights states yesterday. The bans passed in Idaho, South Carolina, Tennessee, Virginia, Wisconsin, Colorado and South Dakota. It narrowly lost in Arizona. Today we have 27 states, or just over half the nation that decided bronze-age laws are still valid for today's world. Even though 280 clergy in Virginia publicly came out opposed to the state's constitutional amendment, it was, by and large, the Catholics and Evangelicals who successfully passed this measure. So, those 27 states can now proclaim that Christianity is the officially established religion in those states and that religion stands firmly committed to the principles of bigotry, hatred, and intolerance. "[Tolerance is a] kind of watchword of those who reject the concept of right and wrong. It's a kind of desensitization to evil of all varieties. Everything has become acceptable to those who are tolerant." —James Dobson, Focus On The Family radio broadcast, Nov. 4, 1996

Humanist Association of Canada
PO Box 8752, Station T
Ottawa, Ontario K1G 3J1 Canada
Weblink: http://humanists.ca
Email: HAC@Humanists.ca
Phone: 877-HUMANS-1 Fax: (613) 739-4801

About: The Humanist Association of Canada is a not-for-profit organization seeking to provide guidance to individuals who do not feel the need for religious beliefs in their life.

Humanist Institute, The
NACH/The Humanist Institute
c/o Kristin Wintermute, Business Manager 
PMB #220, 8014 Olson Memorial Hwy
Golden Valley, MN 55427-4712 USA
Weblink: http://www.humanistinstitute.org/
Email: manager@humanistinstitute.org

About: Founded in 1982 as the North American Committee for Humanism, the Humanist Institute exists to equip humanists to become effective leaders in a variety of organizational settings, including within the humanist movement itself. In order to give reality to humanist ideals and practices, we are dedicated to fostering leadership that is: ethically grounded; wise and well informed; skillfully strategic in addressing institutional dynamics; committed to meeting the real needs of real people; Globally responsible and personally sustainable. We strive to prepare humanist leaders to be: self-differentiated individuals who are models of the humanist perspective; activists in their communities who know how to get things done; advocates who are persuasive articulators of the humanist world view in the public sphere; innovative thinkers who keep our movement alive with their provocative insights and writings; experts who have the skills to help organizations function and help people achieve important goals. The Institute is an independent graduate level program that works in cooperation with existing humanist organizations. It provides a unique opportunity to bring together a diverse faculty and student body of those who take a nontheistic and naturalistic approach to humanism, whether interpreted in secular, religious, or life-stance terms. The Institute works with individuals who are in or aspiring to roles of: community/congregation/chapter-based leadership; regional and national organizational leadership; specialized leadership roles as spokespersons, educators, and counselors; leadership within the various serving professions. Research and publications are an essential element of the Institute's program, including the annual Faculty Colloquium, the journal *Humanism Today*, and periodic weekend conferences and workshops.

Humanist Society of New Zealand
PO Box 3372
Wellington, New Zealand
Weblink: http://www.humanist.org.nz/
Email: jeffhunt90@yahoo.co.nz

About: The Humanist Society of New Zealand (Inc) is an organisation that promotes Humanist philosophy and ideals. It meets in Wellington with members throughout New Zealand, and is affiliated internationally to the IHEU and the United Nations Association of NZ. The Society is incorporated in New Zealand.

Humanist Society of Scotland
272 Bath Street
Glasgow, G2 4JR UK
Weblink: http://www.humanism-scotland.org.uk/
Email: secretary@humanism-scotland.org.uk
Phone: 0870 874 9002

About: The Humanist Society of Scotland (HSS) exists to promote Secular Humanism—an ethical life stance which asserts that we can lead good lives without religion or superstition—and to represent those who adopt this progressive philosophy. The Society is a registered charity run by a National Executive Committee elected from among its membership.

Humanists of Florida Association, The
PO Box 1227
Bradenton, FL 34206 USA
Weblink: http://www.floridahumanist.org
Email: info@floridahumanist.org

Phone: 915-745-7181

About: The Humanists of Florida Association (HFA) is an association of Florida individuals and groups that affirm the Humanist worldview, a progressive philosophy of life that, without supernaturalism, affirms our ability and responsibility to lead ethical lives of personal fulfillment that aspire to the greater good of humanity. We work to promote Humanism and to promote the use of reason and compassion in the solving of human problems. We also work to build a more humane society. We achieve our goals, through education, example, and progressive social action.

Institute for Humanist Studies
48 Howard St
Albany, NY 12207 USA
Weblink: http://www.humaniststudies.org
Phone: (518) 432-7820 Fax: (518) 432-7821

About: The Institute for Humanist Studies (IHS) is a think tank whose mission is to promote greater public awareness, understanding, and support for humanism. The Institute specializes in pioneering new technology and methods for the advancement of humanism.

Institute for the Secularization of Islamic Society
Weblink: http://www.secularislam.org/Default.htm; email: info@SecularIslam.org

About: We believe that Islamic society has been held back by an unwillingness to subject its beliefs, laws and practices to critical examination, by a lack of respect for the rights of the individual, and by an unwillingness to tolerate alternative viewpoints or to engage in constructive dialogue. The Institute for the Secularisation of Islamic Society (ISIS) has been formed to promote the ideas of rationalism, secularism, democracy and human rights within Islamic society. ISIS promotes freedom of expression, freedom of thought and belief, freedom of intellectual and scientific inquiry, freedom of conscience and religion, including the freedom to change one's religion or belief, and freedom from religion: the freedom not to believe in any deity.

International Humanist and Ethical Union, UK
1 Gower Street
London, WC1E 6HD UK
Weblink: http://www.iheu.org/
Phone: 020 7631 3170 Fax: 020 7631 3171

About: IHEU is the world union of Humanist, rationalist, secular, laïque, ethical culture, atheist and freethought organizations. Our mission is to represent and support the global Humanist movement. Our goal is a Humanist world in which human rights are respected and all can live a life of dignity.

International Humanist and Ethical Union: Appignani Center for Bioethics
P.O. Box 4104, Grand Central Station
New York, NY 10162-4104 USA
Weblink: http://www.humanistbioethics.org/
Email: analita@iheu.org
Phone: 212.687.3324 Fax: 212.661.4188

About: The IHEU/Appignani Center for Bioethics is a non-partisan, non-governmental organization (NGO) providing thoughtful, timely research and analyses of bioethical challenges facing the global community. The Center helps inform local, state, national and international policy debates about global issues in medical and biotechnological sciences through collaboration with NGOs and UN departments, bodies and agencies. The Center also sponsors scholarly endeavors dedicated to preventive medicine and seeks partnerships with health care professionals and other NGOs to provide educational venues and opportunities for confronting various medical issues facing developing world countries.

The Center's mission is carried out by providing a forum for convening scholars, government and international organization officials, health care professionals, and community leaders to develop innovative solutions to global problems, including: organ and human trafficking; end-of-life care and decision-making; reproductive and sexual rights; stem cell research and therapeutic applications; neuroscience; infectious diseases and human epidemics. The Center leverages the knowledge and experience of experts and other professionals in government, academia, and private industry as well as its own Advisory Board. With offices at 777 UN Plaza, overlooking the United Nations headquarters in New York, the Center is a branch of the International Humanist and Ethical Union (IHEU). IHEU is a union of more than 100 organizations from 40 nations, with special consultative status with the United Nations in New York, Geneva and Vienna, and a general consultative status at UNICEF in New York and the Council of Europe in Strasbourg. IHEU also maintains operational relations with UNESCO in Paris.

Internet Infidels
PO Box 142
Colorado Springs, CO 80901-0142 USA
Weblink: http://www.infidels.org
Fax: (877) 501-5113

About: The Secular Web is a website operated by the Internet Infidels, a nonprofit educational organization dedicated to defending and promoting a naturalistic worldview on the Internet. In the words of Paul Draper, naturalism is "the hypothesis that the physical universe is a 'closed system' in the sense that nothing that is neither part nor product of it can affect it. So naturalism entrails the nonexistence of all su-pernatural beings, including the theistic God."

James Randi Educational Foundation
201 S.E. 12th St (E. Davie Blvd)
Fort Lauderdale, FL 33316-1815 USA
Weblink: http://www.randi.org
Email: jref@randi.org
Phone: (954) 467-1112 Fax: (954) 467-1660

About: The James Randi Educational Foundation is a not-for-profit organization founded in 1996. Its aim is to promote critical thinking by reaching out to the public and media with reliable information about paranormal and supernatural ideas so widespread in our society today.

The Foundation's goals include: Creating a new generation of critical think-ers through lively classroom demonstrations and by reaching out to the next genera-tion in the form of scholarships and awards; Demonstrating to the public and the media, through educational seminars, the consequences of accepting paranormal and supernatural claims without questioning; Supporting and conducting research into paranormal claims through well-designed experiments utilizing "the scientific method" and by publishing the findings in the JREF official newsletter, *Swift*, and other periodicals; Providing reliable information on paranormal and pseudoscientific claims by maintaining a comprehensive library of books, videos, journals, and archi-val resources open to the public; Assisting those who are being attacked as a result of their investigations and criticism of people who make paranormal claims, by main-taining a legal defense fund available to assist these individuals. To raise public awareness of these issues, the Foundation offers a $1,000,000 prize to any person or persons who can demonstrate any psychic, supernatural or paranormal ability of any kind under mutually agreed upon scientific conditions. This prize money is held in a special account which cannot be accessed for any purpose other than the awarding of the prize. Located in Fort Lauderdale, Florida, the Foundation is funded through member contributions, grants, sales of books and videos, seminars, and conferences.

Minnesota Atheists
PO Box 6261
Minneapolis, Minnesota 55406 USA
Weblink: http://www.MinnesotaAtheists.org
Email: info@mnatheists.org
Phone: (612) 588-7031

About: Minnesota Atheists provides a community for atheists, educates the public about atheism, and promotes separation of state and church. They have monthly meetings and social events, as well as summer picnics and a winter solstice party. They have a website, newsletter (free sample issue; free pdf back issues), and cable TV program "Atheists Talk" (free podcasts). They offer free Atheists Weekly E-mail (AWE) listings of events. They provide speakers to public high schools, Christian colleges, and other venues. They lobby at the Minnesota State Capitol on separation of state and church issues. They help sponsor Camp Quest of Minnesota (campquest.org). They are a 501(c)(3) nonprofit, educational organization. They are affiliated with Atheist Alliance International (AAI), American Atheists, Center for Inquiry (CFI), American Humanist Association (AHA), and the International Humanist and Ethical Union (IHEU), and have excellent relations with the Freedom From Religion Foundation (FFRF).

Moscow Atheistic Association
Moscow, Russia
Weblink: http://www.atheism.ru/library/?div=8

Mukto-Mona, South Asia
Weblink: http://www.mukto-mona.com
About: Bengla translation of the first chapter of www.mukto-mona.com Since its appearance on the net back in the mid 2001, Mukto-mona has been able to draw the attention of many like-minded thinkers including many distinguished authors, scientists, philosophers and human rights activists from all around the world. We are against all kinds of social injustices, religious and oppressive dogmas, doctrines, and discrimination. We critique everything that hinders people's access to civil liberty, freedom, democracy and secularism. We take a strong stand against all kinds of human rights violations such as oppression of ethnic/religious minority community and gender-based discrimination against women, homosexuals and others.

Many of our writers and activists include figures that are quite prominent for their talent, integrity and the firm commitments to the causes of liberty, democracy, secularism and rationalism. Examples include, to name a few, Late Prof. Humayun Azad (writer, social thinker and educator; Dhaka, Bangladesh), Prof. Sirajul Islam Chowdhury (writer, social thinker and educator; Dhaka), Prof. Ajoy Roy (scientist, rationalist, educator, and writer; Dhaka), Dr. Jaffor Ullah (scientist, writer, and columnist; USA), Prabir Gosh (rationalist, writer, and investigator of unusual claims; Calcutta), Dr. Ghulam Murshid (author, researcher, and journalist of BBC; Calcutta), James Randi (professional magician, author, lecturer, and renowned investigator of paranormal phenomenon; USA), Prof. Paul Kurtz (secular humanist, philosopher, and writer; USA), Prof. Pervez Hoodbhoy (scientist, educator, columnist; Pakistan), Dr. Mark Perakh, Dr.Victor Stenger (scientist, philosopher, and author; USA), Dr. Austin Dacey, Dr. Mozammel H. Khan (Professor and writer) and many more budding writers and socio-political activists. Mukto-Mona is politically a non-partisan and non-profit organization and as a whole, we are not affiliated with any political party anywhere in the world. However, we strongly endorse Universal Declaration of Human Rights and want to work for implementations of the same in Bangladesh and other South Asian countries.

National Secular Society
25 Red Lion Square
London, WC1R 4RL UK
Weblink: http://www.secularism.org.uk/
Email: enquiries@secularism.org.uk
Phone: 020 7404 3126 Fax: 0870 762 8971

About: We want a society in which all are free to practise their faith, change it or not have one, according to their conscience. Our belief or lack of it should neither advantage or disadvantage. Religion should be a matter of private conscience, for the home and place of worship; it must not have privileged input into the political arena where history shows it to bring conflict and injustice. The National Secular Society is the leading pressure group defending the rights of non-believers from the demands of religious power-seekers. We campaign on a wide range of issues, including religious influence in the government, the disestablishment of the Church of England, the removal of the Bench of Bishops from the House of Lords and for conversion of religious schools (paid for by the taxpayer) to community schools, open to all.

New Humanist
1 Gower Street
London, WC1E 6HD UK
Weblink: http://www.newhumanist.org.uk
Email: info@newhumanist.org.uk
Phone: 020 7436 1151 Fax: 020 7079 3588

About: *New Humanist* magazine is one of the world's oldest continuously published magazines (starting life as *The Literary Review* in 1885). During that time *New Humanist* has distinguished itself as a world leader in supporting and promoting humanism and rational inquiry and opposing religious dogma, irrationalism and bunkum wherever it is found. A list of contributors includes great figures from past and present from H.G. Wells to Richard Dawkins, Eric Hobsbawm to Phillip Pullman, Polly Toynbee to Christopher Hitchens, Eileen Barker to Amartya Sen. The current editorial board includes broadcaster Laurie Taylor, and Dean of Arts and Media at Westminster University, Sally Feldman. In addition the New Humanist website features daily updates and a lively weblog. *New Humanist* is published bi-monthly by the Rationalist Press Association, which also publishes books, the two most recent are: *Humanism Today* by Jim Herrick and *A History of the RPA* by Bill Cooke.

New Zealand Skeptics
NZCSICOP Inc., PO Box 29-492
Christchurch, New Zealand
Weblink: http://skeptics.org.nz
Email: skeptics@spis.co.nz

About: The New Zealand Skeptics form a network of New Zealanders including magicians, teachers, scientists, health professionals and many others from all walks of life. Members have a variety of religious faiths, economic beliefs and political leanings, but are all interested in examining what objective scientific support there is for claims of such things as psychic abilities, alternative health practices, creationism and other areas where science, pseudo-science and shonky science interact.

NO GOD/Ateismo è Libertà
Via Sisto IV, 113
00167 Rome, Italy
Weblink: http://www.nogod.it/
Email: nogod@email.it
Phone: 06.6280646 347.9901611

Rationalist Association
1 Gower Street
London, WC1E 6HD UK
Weblink: http://www.rationalist.org.uk/
Email: info@rationalist.org.uk
Phone: 020 7436 1151 Fax: 020 7079 3588

About: In 2002 the Rationalist Press Association—a radical freethinking publisher for over 100 years—changed it's name to the Rationalist Association. The Rationalist Association continue to own the RPA. While we are updating this site you will see reference to both the RPA and the RA—they are in effect the same organisation. Nothing has changed other then the name—we still aim to publish the best in rationalist, secularist and humanist thought. While we still publish books our main activity is the production and distribution of *New Humanist* magazine. Published six times a year *New Humanist* is not only the best rationalist publication in the world, it is one of the livliest and best written magazines anywhere.

Rationalist International
PO Box 9110
New Delhi, 110091 India

Weblink: http://www.rationalistinternational.net/
Email: info@rationalistinternational.net
Phone: + 91-11-556 990 12

About: Rationalist International is a forum for rationalist ideas and positions of world-wide concern. It aims at representing the rationalist view where public opinion is formed and making the voice of reason heard and considered, where decisions are taken which will shape our future.

Secular Coalition for America
PO Box 53330
Washington, DC 20009-9997 USA
Weblink: http://www.secular.org
Phone: (202) 299-1091

About: The Secular Coalition for America is the new Washington-based lobbying organization for atheists, humanists, freethinkers, and other nontheistic Americans. Our mission is to increase the visibility and respectability of nontheistic viewpoints in the United States and to protect and strengthen the secular character of our government as the best guarantee of freedom for all.

Secular Student Alliance
PO Box 3246
Columbus, OH 43210 USA
Weblink: http://www.secularstudents.org
Email: ssa@secularstudents.org
Phone: Toll-free Voicemail: 1-877-842-9474 Fax: 1-877-842-9474

About: The mission of the Secular Student Alliance is to organize, unite, educate, and serve students and student communities that promote the ideals of scientific and critical inquiry, secularism, and human based ethics.

Settimanale di cultura e informazione laica
Dr. Paolo Perticone
Istituto di Biologia e Patologia Molecolari del CNR
Sezione di Genetica (ex Centro di Genetica Evoluzionistica del CNR)
c/o Dipartimento di Genetica e Biologia Molecolare
Città Universitaria Universi
Roma, Italy
Weblink: http://www.italialaica.it/
Email: info@italialaica.it
Phone: 0039/06/49917516 or 49917518 or 4457527 Fax: 0039/06/4457529

Skeptics Society, The
PO Box 338
Altadena, CA 91001 USA
Weblink: http://www.skeptic.com
Email: editorial@skeptic.com
Phone: (626) 794-3119   Fax: (626) 794-1301

About: The Skeptics Society is a scientific and educational organization of scholars, scientists, historians, magicians, professors and teachers, and anyone curious about controversial ideas, extraordinary claims, revolutionary ideas, and the promotion of science. Our mission is to serve as an educational tool for those seeking clarification and viewpoints on those controversial ideas and claims. Under the direction of Dr. Michael Shermer, the Society engages in scientific investigation and journalistic research to investigate claims made by scientists, historians, and controversial figures on a wide range of subjects. The Society also engages in discussions with leading experts in our areas of exploration. It is our hope that our efforts go a long way in promoting critical thinking and lifelong inquisitiveness in all individuals.

Society for Humanistic Judaism
28611 W. 12 Mile Rd
Farmington Hills, MI 48334 USA
Weblink: http://www.shj.org/
Email: info@shj.org
Phone: (248) 478-7610   Fax: (248) 478-3159

About: Humanistic Judaism embraces a human-centered philosophy that combines the celebration of Jewish culture and identity with an adherence to humanistic values and ideas. Humanistic Judaism offers a nontheistic alternative in contemporary Jewish life. It was established by Rabbi Sherwin T. Wine in 1963 in Detroit, Michigan, and has grown into a worldwide movement. Humanistic Jews value their Jewish identity and the aspects of Jewish culture that offer a genuine expression of their contemporary way of life. Humanistic Jewish communities celebrate Jewish holidays and life cycle events (such as weddings and bar and bat mitzvah) with inspirational ceremonies that draw upon but go beyond traditional literature.

Solidarity for Freedom of Conscience
Octavian Goga st., nr. 12 bl. M23, et. V, ap. 67 - sector 3,
Bucharest, Romania
Weblink: http://www.humanism.ro
Email: remuscernea@gmail.com
Phone: (004)-0727-583-594

About: The association Solidarity for Freedom of Conscience has been established in order to draw attention to discrimination based on faith and religion and to fight this very resilient phenomenon in today's Romania. Over time, Romanian society and authorities have acknowledged discrimination targeting other types of groups and have taken steps to eliminate it. Nevertheless, religious discrimination has reached alarming proportions, while remaining a largely unacknowledged occurrence, frequently misunderstood by the public opinion.

The association's main priorities include the adoption of an adequate legal framework guaranteeing religious freedom and the clarification of the current state of confusion, enhanced by the long tradition of state authoritarianism in this country. The Solidarity for Freedom of Conscience believes that the violation of the secular character of the state is instrumental in the perpetuation of the current crisis of freedom of conscience. Although implicit in constitutional provisions and in the values of the international system of which Romania aims to be a part, the secular character of the state is in practice violated on a regular basis. The interference of religious institutions in the affairs of the state has become an established fact of public life, substantial assets are transferred to religious institutions, clerics are involved in the activities of public authorities, religious symbols are associated to the symbols of the state, while cultural policies and the existing practices in religious education undermine the principles of secularism.

The Solidarity for Freedom of Conscience militates for the affirmation of the secular character of the state as a fundamental value of modernity and a foundational principle of European culture. The association will encourage legislative and political measures furthering the goal of a secular society. The Solidarity for Freedom of Conscience promotes the values of rationality, openness, and free inquiry, which we consider to be indispensable ingredients in the individuals' ability to achieve their full humanity.

The association emphasizes that freedom of conscience means liberty to hold and enjoy together with others a religious faith, as well as the freedom not to share in any religion or religious association. The extraordinary pressures put by leaders of religious groups on public life in Romania, as well as the increasingly manifest religious attitudes expressed within public institutions, constitute in our opinion a formidable obstacle to the country's modernization. While fully respecting religious conscience and encouraging its free manifestation, the Solidarity for Freedom of Conscience will, in view of the current social context, promote the values of secular humanism.

South Place Ethical Society (UK)
Conway Hall, Red Lion Square
London, WC1R 4RL UK
Weblink: http://www.ethicalsoc.org.uk
Email: library@ethicalsoc.org.uk
Phone: 020 7242 8037/4 Fax: 020 7242 8036

About: Based at Conway Hall, London, the South Place Ethical Society is, we think the oldest freethought community in the world. It was founded in 1793 as a dissenting congregation and for more than two centuries has been a focus for serious discussion of basic ethical principles. By 1888 SPES had rejected the existence of God and become an Ethical Society, the only one which now survives in the UK. It is now an educational charity and maintains a proud tradition of free enquiry in all areas of thought and action. It arranges many talks, courses and seminars for members and interested non-members as well as the famous seasons of Sunday chamber music concerts.

The Finnish Freethinkers' Society
Neljäs linja 1
00530 Helsinki, Finland
Weblink: http://www.vapaa-ajattelijat.fi/
Email: val@vapaa-ajattelijat.fi
Phone: (09) 715 601 (in Finland) Fax: (09) 715 602 (in Finland)

The Finnish Humanist Union
Finland
Weblink: http://www.humanistiliitto.fi/english.htm

About: Finnish Humanist Union speaks for rationalistic thinking, unquestionable human value and tolerance between people and nations. It supports a free discussion about ideological issues in society. Union presents the point of view of people who aren't committed to any religious community or church.

The Finnish Skeptics
PL 483, 00101
Helsinki, Finland
Weblink: http://www.skepsis.fi/
Email: info@skepsis.fi
Phone: 0208-355 455 (in Finland)/+358-208-355 455 (from abroad)

About: The Finnish Skeptics. Visit http://www.skepsis.fi/ for more information.

Italian Union of Rationalist Atheists and Agnostics
Casella Postale 749 35122 Padova
Padova, Italy
Weblink: http://www.uaar.it/Unione degli Atei e degli Agnostici Razionalisti/
Email: segretario@uaar.it
Phone: +39 049 876 2305 Fax: +39 049 876 2305

About: General purposes: civil rights to atheists; no religion in public schools; organization each year of a "Darwin's Day"; elimination of the "Concordato" (a sort of agreement between Italy and Vatican to gave numerous advantages to them).

Vantru
Pósthólf 24, 121 Reykjavík
Reykjavík, Iceland
Weblink: http://www.vantru.is
Email: ritstjorn.vantruar@gmail.com

About: Vantru promotes skepticism and fights the spread of faith and pseudo science in society at large. For this purpose Vantru runs an active web site, on which new material is published every day, focusing on atheism and current events, as well as addressing more classical issues of faith and non-belief. Vantru was founded in August 2003, when a group of non-believers started the web site vantru.net. Having in common the passion for debating matters of religion and superstition, they set out to create a web based community for Icelandic atheists, which could serve as a dedicated venue for candid discussions on faith and related issues. The presence of Vantru has become substantial in Icelandic society, both in and out of cyberspace. Members meet regularly, often over dinner or brunch, and take part in various activism, such as debating, holding lectures and staging protests.

Credits And Permissions

HEART OF A HEARTLESS WORLD: Religion as Ideology

Scott Mann

Charles Darwin, Karl Marx and Sigmund Freud each started out in a field of study that would lay foundations for a range of new scientific disciplines, and through so doing, they radically changed ideas of what it is to be human. This book provides an accessible introduction to these ideas and shows how Marxism and psychoanalysis can cast light upon major currents of religious thinking from stone age times through to the modern world. Topics covered include the religious beliefs of hunter-gathers, shamanism, goddess worship in Neolithic times, religion and ecology, religion and the origin of the state, Jesus as magician or social revolutionary, the psychology and politics of celibacy, and mythico- religious dimensions of modern physics.

Scott Mann has taught philosophy and social theory at the universities of Sussex, Sydney and Western Sydney. He is the author of *Psychoanalysis and Society: An Introduction.*

400 pages, paper 1-55164-126-7 $24.99 ◈ cloth 1-55164-127-5 $53.99

ONE GOD: The Political and Moral Philosophy of Western Civilization

Ernesto Lorca

One God evaluates the political and moral theory contained within the sacred books of three great religions: that of the Jews, the Christians, and the Muslims. It focuses on monotheism and its observable social consequences, particularly in pluralistic societies, and argues that religious texts supply not only the ideology but also the motivation and organizational structure for the perpetrators of violent acts. A major contribution to the sociology of religion that makes a forceful argument regarding the consequences of religious beliefs.

Dr. Ernesto Lorca (1923-2002) taught Ethics and Society and was a regularly invited lecturer to various American, Canadian, and British universities.

416 pages, paper 1-55164-210-7 $31.99 ◈ cloth 1-55164-211-5 $60.99

WOMEN AND RELIGION

Fatmagül Berktay

While taking women's subjectivities and their reasons for their taking to religion into account, this book focuses mainly on the *functions* of religion: the way it relates to women; its contribution to gender differences; and the status of women within it, particularly the relationship between gender on the one hand, and power and social control on the other. Undertaken as well, is an exposition of contemporary Fundamentalism (in both its Protestant and Islamic variants, in America and Iran).

Fatmagül Berktay is an associate professor with the Department of Philosophy at the University of Istanbul, Turkey.

240 pages, paper 1-55164-102-X $24.99 ◈ cloth 1-55164-103-8 $53.99

Also by DIMITRIOS ROUSSOPOULOS

THE NEW LEFT: Legacy and Continuity

As the contributors to this anthology revisit the sixties to identify its ongoing impact on North American politics and culture, it becomes evident how this legacy has blended with, and has influenced today's world-wide social movements. Apart from evoking memories of past peace and freedom struggles from those who worked on the social movements of the 1960s, this work also includes a number of essays from a rising generation of intellectual and activists, too young to have experienced the 1960s firsthand, whose perspective enables them to offer fresh insights and analyses.

> An eclectic mix of memoir and commentary that accents the legacies of the 60s rebellious youth, and the continuities of the political dissent and oppositional challenges of that decade. —*Canadian Dimension*

Contributors include: Dimitrios Roussopoulos, Andrea Levy, Anthony Hyde, Jacques Martin, Mark Rudd, Katherina Haris, Gregory Nevala Calvert, Natasha Kapoor, and Tom Hayden.

224 pages, paper 978-1-55164-298-7 $19.99 ◈ cloth 978-1-55164-299-4 $48.99

---

send for a free catalogue of all our titles

C.P. 1258, Succ. Place du Parc
Montréal, Québec
H2X 4A7 Canada

or visit our website at http://www.blackrosebooks.net

to order books

In Canada: (phone) 1-800-565-9523 (fax) 1-800-221-9985
email: utpbooks@utpress.utoronto.ca

In United States: (phone) 1-800-283-3572 (fax) 1-800-351-5073

In UK & Europe: (phone) London 44 (0)20 8986-4854
(fax) 44 (0)20 8533-5821
email: order@centralbooks.com

Printed by the workers of

for Black Rose Books